MW00677748

Rave Reviews for Seven

"Very exciting . . . a treme
—Joe Crews, *Amazi*

"Challenging . . . just what the world needs today."
—LaVerne Tucker, *Search* Telecast Speaker

"Up-to-date . . . refreshing . . . earned my approval."
—Roland Hegstad, *Liberty* Magazine Editor

"An old message in modern dress . . . splendid job."
—George Vandeman, *It Is Written* Speaker

"Excellent treatment of creation *versus* evolution
. . . two outstanding books."—Dr. Duane T. Gish,
Vice President, Institute of Creation Research

Prophecy
Opal Epperly
Mindy

"A man will turn over
half a library
to make **one book.**"
—Dr. Samuel Johnson

Seven
Mysteries
. . . Solved!

Volume One

by

Howard A. Peth

Lessons from Heaven Library
A Division of Lessons from Heaven, Inc.
1988

SEVEN MYSTERIES ... *SOLVED!*

Volume One

ISBN 0-9618580-0-1

Additional copies of this book
may be obtained by sending $9.95 to
Lessons from Heaven, Inc.
P. O. Box 700
La Puente, CA 91747

This book is dedicated to
my mother
Margaret Kinsella Peth
whose unswerving faith and courage
were my most inspiring example.

"Rather than love, than money, than fame, give me **TRUTH.**"

—Henry David Thoreau

Table of Contents

Volume One

List of Illustrations

Volume One

Page

Foreword to the Reader

We're creatures of curiosity, with minds that seek for answers. Like insatiably inquisitive children, we're intrigued by riddles, fascinated by puzzles, entertained by quiz shows. But "inquiring minds want to know" **more** than the latest gossip of sensational tabloids like the *National Enquirer*. We like to apply our minds to some of the more worthwhile questions of life which perplex us all in our more thoughtful moments.

You hold in your hands a rare book—one that addresses the **great, ultimate, eternal** questions. Volume 1 opens with the basic question of God's existence and closes with the final mystery of death, stopping by the way to examine the claims of evolutionary theory and the deity of Christ.

Volume 2 investigates the issue of Christian days of worship to determine their Biblical validity. Then the panorama of prophecy is scrutinized to find what the future holds. Finally the Beast power is revealed as we unmask Antichrist in **"a theological thriller."**

You'll find *real-life mysteries like these will prove more fascinating than fiction* as you examine point after point of evidence and track down every clue. Once you "connect all the dots," you'll see the whole picture emerge very clearly.

This book does not take the conventional, "party line" approach to its subject for fear of being different. For instance, it differs from most religious books in that it does not assume the reader begins by believing in God, in Christ, in divine Creation, *etc.* It meets the reader where he is and leads him to logical solutions for seven of the most puzzling mysteries ever to confront mankind.

Provocative? Yes. Controversial? Perhaps. But the answers uncovered by this book are unquestionably sound and satisfying, based as they are on solid research and documentation.

SEVEN MYSTERIES . . . *SOLVED!* is as suspenseful as a good thriller, culminating in the most vitally important **manhunt** of all time—that of the Antichrist/Beast. Fictional detective stories are popular in books and other media, but no imagination could concoct mysteries more challenging —or more worthy of our best efforts to solve—than the seven presented here.

+ + +

References to the Bible are from the King James Version unless otherwise noted.

Titles and **pronouns** referring to deity are capitalized, even in quotations where they were not so printed.

Emphasis is supplied, even in quotations, to *telegraph* meaning for instant intelligibility. Subtle nuances are thus made so clear that one can almost hear the author's voice.

Contractions are freely used to achieve a lighter, more conversational tone in what might otherwise be heavy and bookish. Popular nonfiction presents scholarly facts to the masses, but a serious subject needn't be a *solemn* one!

Los Angeles, California
January, 1988

1

? ? ? ? ? ? ? ? ? ? ? ? ? ? ?

?   MYSTERY #1 ✓   ?

?   GOD'S EXISTENCE   ?

?   Does God **exist**? How can we **know**   ?

?   there **really is** a Divine Being?   ?

? ? ? ? ? ? ? ? ? ? ? ? ? ? ?

"Acquaint thyself now with Him,
and be at peace:
thereby **good** shall come unto thee."
—Job 22:21

Chapter 1

The Folly of Atheism

What can we believe about the realm of religion? Is prayer mere mumbo-jumbo? Is faith simply superstition? Did God create man, as the Bible says, or did man create God as a figment of his own imagination? We've all asked ourselves questions like these:

> **Does God exist?**
> **Where did I come from?**
> **Why am I here?**
> **Where am I going?**
> **Is there any meaning or purpose in life?**

These questions are not unanswerable—though I didn't always feel this way. In college I took some courses that made me doubt God's existence, but I was willing to investigate these basic questions of life, and God supplied answers that gave a deep and satisfying personal faith.

I don't pretend to have all the answers. But I write with the firm conviction that **answers ARE available** and that truth is revealed to all who earnestly seek it. The words of Jesus apply here: "**Ask**, and it shall be given you; **seek**, and ye shall find. . . ."[1]

---

1. Matthew 7:7 and Luke 11:9.

4

- 4 *Seven Mysteries . . . Solved!*

WHAT to DO with DOUBT

Did you know the Bible approves a certain kind of doubt? It encourages questions and invites investigation. God is willing to run the risk of honest inquiry. The Apostle John advised, "Beloved, believe not every spirit, but **try** [test] the spirits whether they be of God: because many false prophets are gone out into the world."[2] And Paul wrote, "**Prove** all things; **hold fast** that which is **good.**"[3]

You see, sincere doubt seeks not to reject truth but to find it. Even the best thinkers have been subjected to the agony of mental struggle in order to reach certainty in the realm of truth. So we need not suppress doubt on the basis that it's wrong in itself, and we mustn't construe a reasonable doubt as a denial of faith.

As Alfred, Lord Tennyson wrote:

"There lives more faith in honest doubt,
Believe me, than in half the creeds."[4]

And poet P. J. Bailey echoed, "He who never doubted, never half believed." In fact, honest doubt may well be an important step toward faith, for it can spur us on to **study** these important questions. And we must be willing to study. Simply to raise a doubt or question and then neglect to **search** diligently for the answer is unfair and unwise. A tragic sight is someone whose mind has gone out of business as far as spiritual values are concerned. Our minds must be actively aroused on these matters, and God may use uneasy feelings of doubt to accomplish this.

But we must also understand that God **condemns** doubt of another kind. Preoccupation with doubt is a form

---

2. 1 John 4:1.
3. 1 Thessalonians 5:21.
4. Alfred, Lord Tennyson, *In Memoriam*, Part XCVI, Stanza 3.

of spiritual sickness. Some even use their doubts as an excuse for shedding personal responsibility to the claims of God in their lives.[5] When doubt represses a genuine conviction, our spiritual nature is undermined, for stifling the truth destroys our capacity for it. A confirmed **habit** of doubt is spiritual suicide.

The DEVIL'S TARGET: YOUR MIND

This deadly habit of doubt is what Satan seeks to plant in your mind. There's nothing he wants more than to destroy confidence in God and His Word—and to a large extent he's been successful. It's become fashionable to doubt. Many distrust the Word of God for the same reason they reject its Author—because it condemns sin. "This is the condemnation, that light is come into the world, and **men loved darkness** rather than light, **because** their deeds were evil," said Jesus.[6] This class of doubter raises questions as a substitute for commitment. He claims the reason for his doubt is lack of evidence, when the real reason is an obstinate will.

Another class of doubter feels he can gain intellectual distinction simply by stating that he doesn't believe. He thinks it a virtue, a mark of intelligence, to question and quibble. But those who in their pride of mind **choose**

---

[5] Denying God's existence is an ESCAPE MECHANISM often resorted to by those who want to deny **moral accountability** for their actions. They don't like to be told that certain things are RIGHT or WRONG, so they "ERASE" God from their philosophy—and they think that takes care of the whole matter. John Bunyan, author of the classic *Pilgrim's Progress*, explained it this way: "When wicked persons have gone on in a course of sin, and find they have reason to fear the just judgment of God for their sins, they begin at first to wish that there were no God to punish them; then by degrees they persuade themselves that there is none; and then they set themselves to study for arguments to back their opinion."

6. John 3:19.

to remain in doubt rather than make a firm commitment
for belief in God have, by their very attitude, condemned
themselves. We are **responsible** for the use of our minds
when confronted with the truth of God.

Yet some are reluctant to give up this habit of doubt.
Per-haps this is because, having openly expressed unbelief,
they feel they must maintain their position. But why should
they resign themselves to being assailed by dismal doubts?
How frustrating, how utterly unsatisfying it must be to go
through life and never encounter the ultimate Answer!

CAN WE LOVE GOD with the MIND?

Can a man be both religiously devout and intellectually
honest? Or must he abdicate his sense of reason in order to
believe in a Supreme Being? Is the believer a gullible, naive
person playing a solemn game of "Let's Pretend"? Religion
has been labeled a crutch, a delusion, a hang-up, an escape
from reality. But it certainly wasn't an "escape" for the early
Christians—when following the Lord might have meant
being thrown to the emperor's lions! God isn't an escape:
He's a direct encounter with Reality.

Christ doesn't ask us to leave our mind on the doorstep
when we enter into a Christian experience. Since the mind is
our supreme possession, it's reasonable that we **use** it in our
worship of God. In fact, the mind gives us our capacity to
worship—it distinguishes us from the lower animals.

Can we love God with the mind? God Himself actually
commands us to do so when He says: "Thou shalt love the
Lord thy God . . . with all thy mind."[7]

But some may say, "I can't love something or someone
I've never even seen, and I can't believe in anything I can't
see, either." Can't you, really? Think about this:

_____

[7]. Matthew 22:37, Mark 12:30, & Luke 10:27. Cited from Deuteronomy 6:5.

The UNSEEN PRESENCE

We're surrounded this moment—and have been since we were born—by the substance most vital to our very existence. It's not only around us but within us and part of us. If separated from it, we'd lose consciousness in five minutes, experience brain damage in eight minutes, and be dead in fifteen minutes.

This substance is the most abundant element on earth. It's nearly equal in quantity to all the other elements put together. But in spite of its abundance and importance, it was unknown to man till just two hundred years ago, when Joseph Priestley, an English scientist, demonstrated the existence of oxygen.

Since the beginning of time oxygen had surrounded man; yet he'd been unaware of it. This isn't too surprising, for oxygen cannot be directly perceived through the senses. We can't **see** it or **smell** it or **taste** it.

Thus the man who accepts nothing but what his own feeble senses can verify is severely limited even in the scientific world. (For instance, no one has ever seen the atomic particle called an electron, yet scientists have no doubt of its existence.) And this type of shortsighted skeptic is even more limited in the spiritual realm, for as Shakespeare's Hamlet said to his friend:

"There are **more things** in heaven and earth, Horatio,
Than are **dreamt of** in your philosophy." [8]

Yes, there's much more to life than meets the eye! For it's in the **mind's eye** that the heavenly vision is seen. This doesn't mean we should go around imagining things. It simply means we should keep our spiritual eyes open. American philosopher Ralph Waldo Emerson said, "All I have **seen** teaches me to trust the Creator for all I have **NOT** seen."

---

8. William Shakespeare, *Hamlet, Prince of Denmark*, Act I, Scene v, lines 166-167.

And Jesus told His doubting disciple, "Thomas, because thou has seen Me, thou hast believed: blessed are they that have **not** seen, and yet have believed."[9]

As the great Apostle Paul put it: "We look not at the things which are seen, but at the things which are not seen: for the things which are **seen** are temporal; but the things which are **not** seen are eternal."[10] How true! Material things which are seen, like buildings and monuments of the past, soon crumble into dust and are quite temporary compared to spiritual things that endure through time, like faith and hope and love.

No, my friend, our belief must not be limited only to those things we perceive through our senses or those things we fully comprehend. Blaise Pascal, the famous French mathematician, jotted some thoughts in his *Pensees* that are pertinent here: "The last step of a reasoning mind is the recognition that there are an infinite number of things which are beyond it. . . . If **natural** things are beyond it, what are we to say about **supernatural** things?"[11]   Remember also the truth expressed in these words of Pascal: "Everything that is incomprehensible does **not** cease to exist."[12]

THREE VARIETIES of RELIGIOUS EXPERIENCE

Yet apparently it's not easy for everyone to have the same measure of faith—or even to believe at all. Many who inherently *want* to believe confess they have serious reservations. Because of this, it's possible to delineate at least three categories of religious experience: the **atheist**, the **agnostic**, and the **believer**. Let's examine each of these.

9. John 20:29.

10. 2 Corinthians 4:18.

11. Blaise Pascal, *Pensees*, translated by A. J. Krailsheimer (Harmondsworth, England: Penguin Books, Ltd., c. 1966), p. 85, #188.

12. Pascal, *Pensees*, translated by Krailsheimer, p. 101, #230.

1. THE ATHEIST

Strictly speaking, atheism is the **absence** of a "religious experience," for it's the belief that there is no God. An atheist rejects all religious beliefs and absolutely denies God's existence. But one clergyman, Bishop Fulton J. Sheen, observed that atheists "talk an awful lot about God. They find it hard to **stop** talking about Him; they seem to meet Him at every turn and around every corner." One man who found fault with today's religion exclaimed: "**Thank God** I'm an atheist!" And one of my college students gave a talk in which she set out to prove that God is indeed in the life of even an atheist. Among other points made was that she would ask the atheist, "Do you **swear**? Do you ever say, 'God damn it!'? Many atheists do, but why? Why does a man who claims he doesn't believe in God call on this **supposedly non-existent** God to damn something for him? God **IS** in the life of even the atheist, you see—or there's a strange inconsistency here."

Both this student speaker and Bishop Sheen touched upon something Sir Francis Bacon commented on four hundred years ago in his essay "Of Atheism" when he declared:

> The Scripture saith, "**The fool hath said in his heart, There is no God**";[13] it is not said, "The fool hath **thought** in his heart"; [it's] as if he rather said it by rote to himself than that he can thoroughly believe it, or be persuaded of it. . . . Atheism is rather in the **lip** than in the **heart** of man.

In other words, *though man may deny God at the top of his voice, he still believes in Him at the bottom of his heart.*

---

13. Psalms 14:1 and 53:1.

Atheistic thoughts are really a psychological "set" of mind, a mind closed to the possibilities and ignoring the probabilities of God. The atheist is like a blind man refusing to believe in the sun and claiming its warmth comes from some other source.

Louis Nizer, the brilliant trial lawyer, states: "The best reply to an atheist is to give him a good dinner and ask him if he believes there's a cook." Yet the chances are that such a question will merely bring an amused smile to the lips of the unbeliever and a comment that the question is "irrelevant."

But the remarkable fact is that man—and I mean all mankind, including the atheist—is inescapably religious. This fact is amply demonstrated by the late Dr. Harry Emerson Fosdick, renowned minister at New York City's Riverside Church. In his sermon on "The Impossibility of Being Irreligious," Dr. Fosdick builds a convincing case to support his contention that religion is inescapable and inevitable in the life of everyone. He begins by observing an obvious fact in the ancient world—the universality of religion. Then he goes on to say:

> In our modern world many suppose that situation to be outgrown. . . . Yet look at our world today! Were the Nazis irreligious? On the contrary, they saw that they could never do what they were determined to do on the basis of the Jewish-Christian faith, so they set themselves to find a substitute religion. They said they wanted "no God but Germany"; they put the Fuehrer in the place of Christ; they glorified this religion in impressive ritual, confirmed it in a fanatical fellowship, and gave it a devotion that makes us Christians wish we could match it in our loyalty to Him whom

we call Lord. Hitler never could have done what he did had he not made of his cause a religion. [14]

Fosdick goes on, exploring the fact that:

A man's real religion is what he **puts his faith in** and **gives his devotion to.** The consequence of that, however, at once confronts us. Faith is a capacity in human nature that we cannot get rid of; we exercise it all the time on something or other. One man in our New York community we would naturally call irreligious. He certainly doesn't believe in God. "I am," he writes contemptuously, "for all religions equally, as all impress me as being equally hollow." But just at the point where we begin to think, Here is really an irreligious man, he says this: "To me, pleasure and my own personal happiness . . . are all I deem worth a hoot." So **that** is what he has faith in! He does have an inner shrine where he worships —himself. He does have an altar—not to an unknown god but to his own ego, put first in this whole universe as all he deems worth a hoot. That is his religion.

All through this congregation are folk, I suspect, who habitually think of religion as a matter of their free election; they can be religious or not, as they choose. But that is a delusion. Every last man and woman of us puts faith in something, gives devotion to something, is coerced by a psychological necessity to make a religion of something. Isn't the conclusion

---

14. Dr. Harry Emerson Fosdick, "The Impossibility of Being Irreligious," in his *On Being Fit to Live With,* (New York: Harper & Brothers, 1946), pp. 79-80.

urgent? Thus **compelled** to be religious—with momentous consequence to ourselves and to our influence in the world—let's get the best religion we can find, the very best![15]

In this way Dr. Fosdick drives home his point that **all** men—atheist or believer, conformist or "hippy"—put their faith in **something** (though not all have their confidence equally well placed!). Therefore, if we cannot give up religion any more than we can give up eating, if by our deepest nature we're **made** for religion, then we're faced with this unavoidable choice:

> not, Will we **HAVE** any religion at all?
> but, What **KIND** of religion will we have?

When you make your own choice, ask yourself quite candidly: What does atheism have to offer? Some famous (or infamous!) examples of men who **didn't** believe in God were Adolf Hitler and Karl Marx. (It was Marx who said, "Religion . . . is the opium of the people."[16]) Pertinent here are Jesus' words, "By their fruits ye shall know them."[17] How many leper colonies have been founded by atheists? Is this the kind of work they're known for? On the contrary, no one is amazed when an **infidel** indulges in wickedness and debauchery. Instead, the usual reaction is, What else could we expect?

As Don Herold put it: "Atheists may be pretty smart fellows, but you don't find them doing any great organized good in the world. You never hear of an Atheists' Hospital

---

15. *Ibid.*, pp. 80-81.
16. Karl Marx, *Introduction to A Critique of the Hegelian Philosophy of Right* (1844). To show what kind of person Karl Marx was, he also said: "There are **no morals** in politics; there is only expediency." Furthermore, he said: "PROMISES are like PIE-CRUST—**made to be broken.**"
17. Matthew 7:20.

or an Atheists' Committee for the Relief of Starving Whoosis Tribes. Atheists don't even have their own glee clubs, picnics or bowling teams. It seems to take some kind of faith to get people together to do some good or even to have some fun."

Yes, atheists may be pretty smart fellows—but rather shortsighted ones. The skeptic's dilemma is the PARADOX that, though he doubts all religion and is skeptical about philosophy and may even take pleasure in doubting **everything** right down to the ground, there's **one** thing he doesn't doubt: **He doesn't doubt DOUBTING**—he fails to doubt the wisdom of being a skeptic. Perhaps Samuel McCrea Cavert was right when he said, "The worst moment for an atheist is when he feels grateful and has no one to thank."

2. THE AGNOSTIC

The agnostic is not so bold as the atheist. He doesn't come right out and say, "There is no God," as the atheist does. No, the agnostic simply says, "I **don't know** if God exists; He may or He may not."

The word *agnostic* comes from the Greek language and literally means "not known." So an agnostic thinks it's impossible to know whether or not there is a God, or a future life, or anything beyond physical phenomena.

At first glance, agnosticism seems different from atheism, and agnostics may feel offended if told there is *no essential difference* between their position and that of the atheist. Agnostics see themselves as being simply uncommitted—and that's vastly different from the outright skepticism of atheists, isn't it? After all, agnostics have taken a comfortable middle-of-the-road position: They're neither fish nor fowl, neither atheist nor believer. (Perhaps that's why poet Robert Frost said, "Don't be an agnostic. Be **something**."[18])

---

18. Robert Frost, in "A Walk with Robert Frost," *Reader's Digest* (April 1960), p. 79.

But there's no refuge, no safety in agnosticism. God is patient, yet He cannot permit us to waver in indecision forever—we **MUST decide** one way or the other. As free moral agents, we have freedom OF choice but not freedom FROM choice. The need to choose, the responsibility to decide, "comes with the territory"—it's a part of life we can't escape. "And Elijah came unto all the people, and said, **How long halt ye between two opinions?** If the Lord be God, follow Him: but if Baal, then follow Him."[19] You see, there's no neutrality in this war—God expects us to stand up and be counted.

So, as Harvard theologian Harvey Cox points out, "**Not to decide is to decide.**" No fence-sitting is allowed. Jesus decisively declared: "He that is not **with** Me is **against** Me."[20] Therefore Joshua urges us, "**Choose you this day whom ye will serve.** . . . As for me and my house, we will serve the Lord."[21]

I like the way Dr. Fosdick shows that there's an ISSUE to be faced here:

> Consider, in the first place, that we indeed **must** choose. I know all about agnosticism, and how it seems a place of neutral retreat. We neither **believe** in God, **nor disbelieve**, men say; **we do not know.** But that is a DECEPTIVE NEUTRALITY. Real faith in God is a positive matter—you either **have** it or you **don't.** . . . If a man is an atheist, he hasn't got it, but if a man is an agnostic he hasn't got it either. Positive faith in God is something we either have, or have not. . . .
>
> Like it or not, life is full of forced decisions. A man can love and trust his wife, and deepening with the years such love and trust can be a glorious ex-

19. 1 Kings 18:21.
20. Matthew 12:30 and Luke 11:23.
21. Joshua 24:15.

perience. A man either has that experience or he hasn't. If, as the alternative, he distrusts his wife, he has missed it. And if he tries to be agnostic about his wife, saying, "I neither trust her nor distrust her; I suspend judgment as to whether she is trustworthy or not," he has missed it too. In all such vital matters **there is no escape into neutrality.** Life presents us with forced decisions.[22]

But if the choice is a forced one, it need not be a painful one. The classic words of Pascal still ring true in his analogy of "The Wager":

This much is certain, either God is, or He is not; there is no middle ground. But to which view shall we be inclined? Think of **a COIN being spun** which will come down either heads or tails. How will you wager? Reason can't make you choose either, reason can't prove either wrong in advance. ... But you *must* wager, for you are already committed to life, and not to wager that God is, is to wager that He is not. Which side, then, do you take?

Let's weigh the gain or loss involved in calling heads that God exists: **If you WIN you win everything, if you LOSE you lose nothing.** Don't hesitate then; wager that He **does** exist. For there is an infinity of infinitely happy life to be won, and what you're staking is finite. That leaves no choice. Since you are obliged to play, you must be renouncing reason if you hoard your life rather than risk it for an infinite gain which is just as likely to occur as a loss amounting to nothing.[23]

---

22. Harry Emerson Fosdick, "Why We Believe in God," in his *On Being a Real Person,* (New York: Harper & Brothers, 1943), pp. 29-90.
23. Pascal, *Pensees,* #418.

English poet Lord Byron agrees: "The Christian has greatly the advantage over the unbeliever, having everything to gain and nothing to lose."

If you find it hard to believe in God, remember that no mere mortal can ever comprehend ALL of the great God of the universe. A god *small enough for our minds* wouldn't be *big enough for our needs*. Believe in as much of God as you can—that's the way to start.

3. THE BELIEVER

The believer, we say, has "faith." But what does that term mean? A small boy once defined faith as "believin' whatcha know ain't so." That's a good definition of what faith is **not**, for no one—in either sacred or secular affairs—has ever been so credulous as to believe something he **knew** wasn't true.

Furthermore, we've already learned from Fosdick's sermon on "The Impossibility of Being Irreligious" that even atheists put their "faith" in something. If both the atheist and the believer exercise some kind of faith, then where does the difference lie? What's the virtue in being a "believer"? Hannah W. Smith supplies the answer in her book *The Christian's Secret of a Happy Life:*

> The virtue does not lie in your believing, but in the thing you believe. If you believe **the truth**, you are saved; if you believe **a lie**, you are lost. **The act of believing** in both cases is the same: the **things believed** are exactly opposite, and it is this which makes the mighty difference. Your salvation comes, not because your faith saves you, but because it LINKS you to the Saviour who saves; and your believing is really nothing but the link.[24]

---

24. Hannah W. Smith, *The Christian's Secret of a Happy Life* (New York: Fleming H. Revell Company, c. 1883), p. 70.

Implicit in those words is the thought that study is important, **study that helps us know the difference** between "the truth" and "a lie." Bible study will help us here, for the Good Book says, "Faith cometh . . . by the Word of God."[25] And this same Word of God defines faith with these inspired words: "Faith is the **substance** of things hoped for, the **evidence** of things NOT seen."[26]

Let's keep this Biblical definition in mind as we think about the question "Does God exist?" For faith, by its very nature, cannot deduce proof—if it could, it would be something other than faith. Faith is always "the evidence of things NOT [yet] seen." And that brings us to our next point.

God's Existence Cannot Be PROVED
or DISPROVED

The candid admission that man cannot prove God exists may come as a surprise to some, but why should it seem surprising? After all, to say that we can't use science or logic to prove the existence of the supernatural is simply to recognize the limitations of science and logic: these have their proper sphere within which they function quite effectively —but the world of the spirit transcends them both.

As world-famous physician Sir William Osler wrote: "Nothing in life is more wonderful than FAITH—the one great moving force we can neither weigh in the balance nor test in the crucible."[27]

These thoughts have been echoed by many, such as W. T. Stace, philosophy professor at Princeton. We may summarize a portion of his book *Time and Eternity* [28] as follows:

---

25. Romans 10:17.
26. Hebrews 11:1.
27. Sir William Osler, *Life of Sir William Osler*, Volume I, Chapter 30.
28. Walter Terence Stace, *Time and Eternity* (Princeton, New Jersey: Princeton University Press, 1952), pp. 136-144.

Religious consciousness lies in a region forever
beyond all proof or disproof. If God does not lie at the
end of any telescope, neither does He lie at the end of
any line of logic. We can never, starting from the
natural order, prove the divine order. Proof of the
divine must somehow lie within itself and be its own
witness. But if, for these reasons, God can never be
proved by arguments that take natural facts for their
premises, for the very same reason He can never be
disproved by such arguments.

Nevertheless God is not without witness. Nor is
His existence any less certain. God is "in the heart."
It's in the heart, then, that the witness of Him, the proof
of Him, must lie, and not in any external circumstance
of the natural order. God is known only by intuition,
not by the logical intellect. Exactly the same situation
exists in regard to the **aesthetic** consciousness by
which we perceive art. For **artistic values** are incapa-
ble of being proved except by aesthetic intuitions.

Stace draws a striking analogy between **art** and **religion**
when he says that asking for proof of the existence of God
is on a par with asking for proof of the existence of beauty.
It's exactly as absurd, and for identical reasons. Either you
directly perceive beauty, or you do not. And either you directly perceive God in intuition, or you do not. Both the
beautiful and the divine are matters of direct experience.
No LOGIC will bring you a sense of the beauty of a poem
or symphony, if you don't feel it. A skillful critic may tell
you where to look, what other people have found beautiful,
what elements in the work of art are those in which the artistic may be found. Such a process may lead you to see beauty
where you did not see it before. But in the end you must
SEE it for yourself; that is, you must recognize it intuitively.
Just as it would be absurd to accuse artistic judgments of

being "irrational," so it is unfair for unbelievers to level
the same charge against religious truths.

Along this same line, you may remember *A Man Called
Peter*, the best-selling biography by Catherine Marshall about
her late husband, who became an extraordinary minister and
served as Chaplain of the United States Senate. She wrote:

> Peter's favorite thought was that "spiritual reality
> is a matter of perception, not of proof. ... There are
> some things that never can be proved. Can you
> prove—by logic—that something is lovely? Could
> you prove that a sunset is beautiful?. ... Either we see
> beauty—or we do not."[29]

Both Stace's book and Marshall's book were published in
the 1950's, but what they said was expressed long ago by
an ancient prophet: "Can you fathom the mysteries of God?
Can you probe the limits of the Almighty? They are higher
than the heavens—what can you do? They are deeper than
the depths of the grave—what can you know? Their measure
is longer than the earth and wider than the sea."[30]

In other words, God can't be searched out scientifically
or proved logically. But faith is not concerned with proofs—
it dares to plunge beyond sight. Centuries ago Augustine, a
great thinker and theologian, said: "Faith is to **believe** what
we do not see, and the REWARD of faith is to **see** what
we believe."

This is not to say that Christian faith is irrational, illogical,
or unscientific! Our next chapter, for instance, will present
strong arguments, composed of logical reasons and persuasive evidence, answering the question "Does God exist?"

---

29. Catherine Marshall, *A Man Called Peter* (New York: McGraw-
Hill Book Company, 1951), pp. 43-44.

30. Job 11:7-9, New International Version.

20

You'll find that **God has given sufficient evidence which to base an intelligent faith if you WISH to believe.**

WHAT DO YOU STAND TO LOSE?

Many years ago this story came out of Russia, long before the Communist regime began.

It seems that a certain atheist was parading up and down the countryside, pouring out his verbiage against the very thought of God, and ridiculing all those who believed in God.

On one occasion he addressed a group gathered in a large hall. He stirred them to a high pitch and then hurled a challenge to God, that **IF** there **BE** a God, He reveal it by striking him dead. Of course, God did not, so the atheist turned to his audience and sneered: "See, there is no God."

Whereupon a little Russian peasant woman with a shawl about her head arose to speak. She addressed her remarks to the speaker and said: "Sir, I cannot answer your arguments. Your wisdom is beyond me. You are an educated man—I'm just a peasant woman. With your superior intelligence will you answer me one question?

"I've been a believer in Christ for many years. I've rejoiced in His salvation, and I've enjoyed my Bible. His comfort has been a tremendous joy. If when I die I learn that there is no God, that Jesus is not His Son, that the Bible is not true, and that there is no salvation and no heaven —pray, sir, what have I lost by believing in Christ during this life?"

The room was very still. The audience grasped the woman's logic, and then they turned to the atheist, who by that time was swayed by the woman's simplicity.

In quiet tones he replied: "Madam, you haven't lost a thing."

The peasant woman smiled, "You've been kind and answered my question. Permit me to ask another. If, when it comes **your** time to die, you discover that the Bible **IS** true, that there **IS** a God, that Jesus **IS** His Son, and that there **IS** a heaven **AND** a hell—pray, sir, **what will YOU stand to lose?**"

The atheist had no answer.

The <u>WILL</u> to BELIEVE [31]

People who **do** not believe in God are usually those who **will** not believe in Him. Unbelievers **choose** NOT to believe in God. The problem lies not in the **MIND** but in the **WILL**. Those **willing** to know God will **find** Him—and will find the **evidence** for His existence satisfying and abundant. The atheist or agnostic, by closing his eyes to the very real evidence of God's existence, is playing a game he cannot win.

The trouble is, man's **head** has overshadowed his **heart**: He has knowledge without wisdom, facts without faith, logic without love. But while the agnostic is adrift on a sea of uncertainty, the believer has anchored his faith in the pages of God's Word. While some people want an affidavit from God certifying that He really exists, Faith sees the invisible, believes the incredible, and receives the impossible.

You need not succumb to atheism. You need not submit to the agony of religious doubt. You can free your mind from the shackles of unbelief. Your faith in God will grow as you continue to seek Him. For God Himself said:

---

31. William James of Harvard, the American pioneer in psychology, gave an important lecture in 1896 called "The **Will** to Believe" which he described as "an essay in justification of faith, a defence of our right to adopt a believing attitude in religious matters."

"Ye shall **seek** Me, and **FIND Me**,
when ye shall **search** for Me
with all your heart."[32]

*** *** ***

No God—no peace. **Know** God—know peace.

---

32. Jeremiah 29:13.

Chapter 2

=====================

Does God Exist?

When Napoleon Bonaparte was sailing down the Mediterranean toward Egypt with his great military force, the officers, most of whom were skeptics, were standing under the glittering stars on the ship's deck expressing their atheistic theories. After a while Napoleon grew tired of it all and said: "Your arguments are all very clever, sirs, but who made all these stars?" A heavy silence followed as Napoleon walked away to his sleeping quarters and left the men gazing up at the dazzling majesty of the heavens.

Yes, that's the question: How do we explain the *existence* of the *universe*? We live in a world of unfailing cause-and-effect relationships. Nothing happens in and of itself—it invariably results from one or more causes. In science, causality is always a basic assumption. In fact, this assumption is so obviously true that it's called **the Law of Cause and Effect**. Now this law, as we'll see in a moment, provides potent evidence of

God's existence.[1] In fact, the evidence for the existence of
God is overwhelming. But we may still be unimpressed by it
unless we're willing to believe.

THE PRIMARY REQUIREMENT:
A WILLING MIND

When we embark on an inquiry like this, we must be
willing to re-educate our minds and re-groove our thinking
out of the ruts of worldly skepticism, to seek what James
calls "the WISDOM that is from **above.**"[2]

Our chapter on "The Folly of Atheism" stated that it's
impossible to prove the existence of God. Now, don't mis-
understand—there's plenty of **evidence** that God exists, but
no **absolute proof.** The evidence is reasonable and ample,
but those who reject God do so, not because the evidence is
weak, but because they've **already chosen** not to believe in
God, for other reasons. Belief in God rests on abundant, logical evidence, but the possibility of doubt always remains.

Some may wonder, Why doesn't God send proof? Well,
the time is coming when God WILL prove to everyone that
He exists. Proof will then make unbelievers non-existent.
But for the present, God has **left room** for DOUBT in order
to **make room** for FAITH.

The reality of God's existence can be sustained by exceedingly strong arguments, but **God never FORCES the will.**
No argument will ever convince someone who doesn't **want**
to submit to God. Even if he's completely overpowered
and silenced by the arguments, he'll still be of an unbelieving
heart, and that's what really counts. As the poet said:

---

1. English poet William Cowper said, "*Nature* is but a name for
an **EFFECT** whose **CAUSE** is God."
2. James 3:17.

"A man convinced against his will
Is of the same opinion still."

To experience the illumination God is eager to give us, we need a certain frame of mind. We need a receptive attitude toward truth. We need to be open-minded. One man said, "Minds are like parachutes: They function only when open." But some minds are like concrete—all mixed up and permanently set! The person who's **willing** to believe has already taken the first step toward a satisfying faith. The importance of this willingness, this open-mindedness, cannot be overemphasized. For all who **desire** to believe, all who are open and willing to believe, the evidence is persuasive.

CLUES TO UNRAVEL THE MYSTERY

The Bible says, "No man hath seen God at any time."[3] But the fact that God is hidden or invisible is not the whole story, for God provides **signs** of His presence and activity. However, God discloses Himself when and where **He** chooses and not as man might want. So although God is a mystery, He gives clues to help us unravel a part of that mystery. These clues to reality are **pointers, indicators, evidences** of the existence of God. They provide **REASONS** for rational belief in the invisible God.

Now we come to the crux of our investigation: **What specific REASONS are there for believing in God?** Man's inquiring mind has long sought such reasons—as long ago as the 13th century Thomas Aquinas systematized some of the reasons for believing in God's existence. You'll find there's not just one but several compelling reasons for belief.

---

3. John 1:18.

> # CLUE #1:
> # PHYSICAL MATTER

The inexorable Law of Cause and Effect teaches that things don't just "happen"—they must be brought about by a cause that **precedes** the effect and that's **sufficient** to produce it. We can explain a puddle in the road by talking of a summer shower, but it's impossible to explain the *ocean* that way, for great effects call for great causes.

The existence of **physical matter** is a reality beyond all dispute. Yet where did it **come** from? You see, in a universe governed by the Law of Cause and Effect, it's impossible to account for the origin of matter by natural means. *Ex nihilo nihil fit* is a Latin phrase meaning "out of nothing comes nothing" or "nothing is made from nothing."

Some scientists reject the Bible account: "In the beginning God created the heaven and the earth."[4] But they have nothing to put in its place. Evolutionary theories sometimes speculate about this, but they're hardly worthy of being called theories of **origin**, for they don't account for beginnings. They always **assume the pre-existence** of matter in some state, speaking of "primeval dust" or "gaseous matter" solidifying to form our little planet—but no man-made theory even pretends to explain how this whole **universe** with its **unnumbered worlds** and **stars** first came into existence! If we cannot explain the origin of the universe by NATURAL causes, then we must look to the existence and action of a SUPERNATURAL Cause for its origin.

---

4. Genesis 1:1.

"The heavens declare the glory of God," said the Psalmist.[5] God challenges us to "Lift up your eyes on high, and behold who hath created these things."[6] The fact that matter exists is a clue, a pointer to the existence of the God who made it. The existence of **even one single ATOM** is a mighty argument for God as Creator.[7] The evidence of God's existence is all around us, from the tiny grain of sand to the majestic mountain looming on the horizon.

Matter—whether solid, liquid, or gas—**had** to have a beginning. It makes no difference what we consider the first step in creation, or how far back into prehistoric time we push the event. There must have been a Creator to bring the universe into being. The believer maintains that without God there is no answer; to him God is the glorious First Cause.

CLUE #2:
MOTION & KINETIC ENERGY

An Arab camel driver, when asked how he knew there's a God, replied by asking another question: "How do I know whether a camel or a man passed by my tent last night? By their footprints in the sand." So, from the most minute molecule to the most remote galaxy, all the universe reveals the **footprints** of its Maker.

5. Psalm 19:1.
6. Isaiah 40:26.
7. Often such evidence is taken for granted and passed by without notice. But Ralph Waldo Emerson said, "If the STARS should appear **just one night in a thousand years,** how men would believe and adore!"

We've just seen that one of the footprints of God is the existence of matter, but another is the presence of **motion** in the universe. In order to have motion (of the earth and other heavenly bodies) there must be **a moving force**. The laws of physics teach that things don't set **themselves** in motion—they stay at rest until **moved** by some other moving object. If we set a book on the table, it will stay there **forever** unless and until it's acted upon by some outside force. If we see a ball suddenly roll across the floor, we naturally turn to see who or what started it rolling. Instinctively we realize that motion is not natural to inanimate objects.

Yet we see great masses of matter hurtling through space at tremendous speeds![8] Countless worlds ceaselessly circle the boundless realms of space. Think of planets in their orbits and the march of constellations—what started them moving? What great force provided the initial impetus? Whence came such colossal energy? Motion without a mover is as impossible as creation without a Creator. Here again the only explanation that meets the demands of fact is that God not only **created** the world, but He also **set it in motion**. The believer sees God as the great Prime Mover.

---

8. A renowned astronomer asks us to "Reflect on how many ways you are now moving through space. In England you have a speed of about 700 miles an hour round the Solar axis of the Earth. You are rushing with the Earth at about 70,000 miles an hour along its pathway round the Sun. ... On top of all this, you have the huge speed of about 500,000 miles per hour due to your motion around the Galaxy."—Fred Hoyle, *The Nature of the Universe* (New York: Harper & Row, Publishers, 1960), pp. 67-68.

CLUE #3:
LIFE

The unbeliever, leaving God out of the picture, finds it hard enough to account for the existence of **matter** and **motion** in our universe, but he also faces the insurmountable task of **explaining the origin of LIFE** itself. And there's a tremendous difference—a vast gulf—between the **living** and the non-living, between **organic** and inorganic matter. A small seed looks tiny beside a boulder, but the seed has within it a promise and potency that the inert boulder entirely lacks. The marvelous nerves and tissues of pulsing, living creatures —both plants **and** animals—must be accounted for.

How did this vital force originate? **Where** did that first spark of life come from? Men may speculate and propose theories, but no one really knows. Some believe nature is self-activating; they think nature possesses in itself some "vital principle." But this is not true—nature is **not** self-activating.

No less a scientist than Louis Pasteur himself, the father of microbiology, exploded the theory of spontaneous generation by proving it false in a series of classic experiments in the mid-1800's. Pasteur showed that microbes, like other forms of life, arise only from pre-existing, similar living things. Only life begets life. More will be said on this point in Chapter 4 in our study on evolution.

Perhaps you can see the magnitude of the problem confronting the atheist, for there's not one chance in billions that life on our planet is an accident. Professor Edwin Conklin, biologist at Princeton University, has often said, "The probability of life originating from accident is comparable to the probability of **the Unabridged Dictionary** resulting from an **explosion in a printing shop!**"[9]

The existence of even simple forms of **life demands a Lifegiver**, the living God.

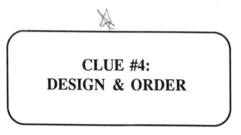

```
CLUE #4:
DESIGN & ORDER
```

So far we've seen that God is a MUST: any rational explanation of the *matter* and *motion* and *life* we see all around us presupposes the **necessary** existence of God. As a matter of fact, even Voltaire, the famous French skeptic, had to admit: "If there were no God, it would be necessary to invent Him." Believers, of course, have no more "invented" God than they've invented or imagined the physical evidence we've just examined as manifestations of His creative power, but they see the logical necessity of His existence.

A fourth clue pointing to the reality of God is the presence of order, purpose, and DESIGN. All through nature there's variety, yet order and beauty. Every leaf on a tree is different from every other leaf, yet they all serve the same purpose—of producing food from the air and sunshine, and of providing beauty and shade for man. Fish are designed to live in the sea, as animals are designed for the dry land.

---

9.   Edwin Conklin, quoted in *The Evidence of God in an Expanding Universe*, edited by John Clover Monsma (New York, G. P. Putnam's Sons, 1958), p. 174. This excellent book contains the affirmative religious views of forty American scientists.

If the world came into existence as a result of blind chance, without a divine Intelligence, it could have been a chaos with no law or order. The fact that earth is not in a chaotic state calls for explanation. Albert Einstein, seeing a sense of order in the universal laws of nature, said: "The most incomprehensible thing about the world is that it IS comprehensible." Astrophysicists recognize an **amazing** precision in the **mathematical order** of the universe!

So many exacting conditions are necessary for life on earth that they couldn't possibly exist in proper relationship by chance. The earth rotates on its axis 1000 miles an hour at the equator; if it turned at 100 miles an hour, our days and nights would be ten times as long as now, and the hot sun would likely scorch our vegetation each day, while in the long night any surviving sprout might well freeze.

Furthermore, the sun has a surface temperature of 10,000 degrees Fahrenheit, and our earth is just far enough away so this ball of fire warms us **just enough and not too much!** If the sun gave off only one-half its present radiation, we'd **freeze**, and if it gave half as much more, we'd **roast**.

Our ATMOSPHERE of life-supporting gases is sufficiently **high** and **dense** to blanket the earth against the deadly impact of twenty million meteors that daily enter it at speeds of about thirty miles-per-second. Among its many other functions, the atmosphere also maintains the temperature within safe limits for life, and carries the vital supply of fresh water-vapor far inland from the oceans to irrigate the land, which otherwise would become a barren desert.

If the earth were as small as the moon (one-fourth its present diameter), the force of gravity would be only one-sixth as strong and would fail to hold both atmosphere and water, so temperatures would be fatally extreme. If the moon were only 50,000 miles away instead of its actual distance, our tides would be so enormous that twice a day all continents would be submerged, and even the mountains could soon be eroded away.[10]

You may have heard the oft-told account of how Sir Isaac Newton had a skilled craftsman build him a scale model of our solar system which was then displayed on a large table in Newton's home. Not only did the excellent workmanship simulate the various sizes of the planets and their relative proximities, but it was a working model in which everything rotated and orbited when a crank was turned.

One day while Newton was reading in his study, a friend came by who happened to be an atheistic scientist. Examining the model with enthusiastic admiration, he exclaimed: "My! What an exquisite thing this is! Who made it?" Without looking up from his book, Sir Isaac answered, "Nobody."

Stopping his inspection, the visitor turned and said: "Evidently you misunderstood my question. I asked who made this."

Newton, no doubt enjoying the chance to teach his friend a lesson, replied in a serious tone, "Nobody. What you see here just happened to assume the form it now has."

"You must think I'm a fool!" retorted the visitor. "Of course somebody made it, and he's a genius. I want to know who he is."

Laying his book aside, Newton arose and laid a hand on his friend's shoulder, saying:

> This thing is but a puny imitation of a much grander system whose laws you know, and I am not able to convince you that this mere toy is without a designer and maker; yet you profess to believe that the great original from which the design is taken has come into being without either designer or maker! Now tell me by what

10. A. Cressy Morrison, "Seven Reasons Why a Scientist Believes in God." *Reader's Digest*, October 1960, pp. 71-72, and *The Evidence of God in an Expanding Universe,* pp. 21-22.

sort of reasoning do you reach such an incongruous conclusion?[11]

Many other examples could be cited showing the critical adjustments of design we take for granted. The late Dr. Wernher von Braun, former German rocket expert who headed the American space effort that took man to the moon, had a bad word for scientists who believe in unseen electrons but reject an unseen Deity. He said: "One cannot be exposed to the **order** and **beauty** of the universe without conceding there must be a divine intent behind it."

Observe the delicate design of a **flower**. Take a microscopic look at the **human eye**—hardly bigger than a marble, yet with complete photographic equipment and marvelous features man cannot duplicate. Consider the **ear**,[12] with its minute bones and sensitive nerves—all these point to an intelligent Designer. The **human brain**—seat of perception, memory, imagination—is another amazing example of intelligent design. It can do all and more than a computer weighing several thousand pounds can do, yet it weights only a few ounces. Who hasn't marvelled at the wonders of the human body—or even at the unique designs of **snowflakes**?

From the minutest atom to the greatest world, all things, animate and inanimate, declare that the Hand that made them is divine. To propose that the intricately designed organs mentioned above arose spontaneously from nothing, or perhaps from chaos by pure chance or accident, is somewhat uncomplimentary to a man's reason. That would be a greater miracle

---

11. "Who Made It?" *Minnesota Technolog* XXXVIII (October 1957), p. 11.

12. "**The hearing ear** and **the seeing eye**, the Lord has made them both." Proverbs 20:12, Revised Standard Version. The study of **anatomy** could convert many an atheist.

by far than the work of Creation by divine decree, and requires much more faith—or gullibility—than to believe in God.

The existence of a *watch* demands a *watchmaker*. Dozens of additional examples could be cited, but suffice it to say that **DESIGN DEMANDS A DESIGNER.** For the believer, the undeniable fact of ever-present order and design leads to God as Intelligent Designer.

CLUE #5:
MAN'S RELIGIOUS IMPULSE

The evidence we've already considered lies in the objective, physical world that's largely **outside** of man. Yet there are still other reasons for believing in God as the only credible explanation for the universe. Some of these clues the Creator has placed **within** man himself—in man's very nature—and these we must consider now.

A fifth clue to God's existence is **the universality of man's religious impulse.** We are not gods, nor have we ever seen God. Then how did we get the idea that there is a God? Why did even the pagan Greeks erect an altar "To the Unknown God"?[13] Men everywhere seem to have come to the conclusion that there is a supreme God, though they know little about Him.

---

13. Acts 17:22-23.

Religion is one of man's oldest institutions. One authority states: "History is unable to show us any age in which man lived without religion; even in the earliest periods of which we have any record man was a religious being, and the question concerning the **origin** of religion, history is unable to answer."[14]

What we may call "the Idea of God" has been tenaciously persistent throughout man's history. Thousands of years of idolatry dimmed man's knowledge of the one true God, yet never submerged it. Cultural anthropologists are kept busy studying the religions of all peoples in all ages, for there seems to be an undying need to worship something, a restless conviction that some Power of Mind lies beyond ourselves.

Distinguished Oxford professor Max Müller observed, "Man is an incurably religious animal." Müller was right: man IS by nature religious. To deny religion is to deny our very humanity, for man is **more** than an animal, **more** than a chance organism of space and time. Man, the seeker, is a child of God. He can come to terms with himself only when he realizes what he is and what he might be. As Augustine put it,

"Bless Thee, Lord, that we are restless
Till our souls find rest in Thee!"

The basic stuff of our HUMANITY simply demands something to worship. Human beings have a compelling need to worship a god. But though this seems universally true, like a common denominator among the races of MAN, there's no evidence that this restless religious impulse is exhibited among the lower animals. An animal sees the same earth and sky as we do but never discerns the invisible God. All the researches of science haven't uncovered a single instance

14. Herman Bavinck, *The Doctrine of God*, (Grand Rapids, Michigan: Wm. B. Eerdmans Publishing Company, 1951), p. 76.

of any ANIMAL erecting an altar for worship. Man's need
to worship could not possibly have evolved from **animals**—
it's a unique characteristic appearing only in human beings.

The great psychoanalyst Dr. Carl Jung declared that "There
is in every man **a God-shaped vacuum** which can be filled
only by the divine." The INNER LIFE of man, with the deep
issues of life's purpose and destiny, evokes in man a sense of
the holy and leads him to worship. These facts aren't private
fancies of the individual but experiences shared among vast
numbers of men and women. This consciousness is too universal and constant to be accounted for by imagination and
self-delusion. Even Socrates, who knew not the God of the
Bible, regarded the knowledge of God as **natural** to man.[15]

For man lives not by calories alone: There's a **soul hunger** only God can satisfy. If we could glimpse what lies within
the human heart, we'd see some sordidness and selfishness—
but we'd also see a hunger after divine things: what theologian Karl Barth called "the Godsickness of the human heart,"
for God is a LONGING that LODGES in the heart.

This **eternal attraction to the eternal God** arises because men and women are created **BY** God **FOR** God. So
people need God. They need His Word. They need His assurance. Though not all are church-goers, all feel this *spiritual
hunger* to some degree. And many discover the satisfying
solution to their *heart craving* by reading the Bible or literature on vital Biblical themes. After all, where else can they
turn? For the Lord says: "I am God, and there is none else;
I am God, and there is none like Me."[16]

Religion, meeting a deeply-felt human need, provides
an INNER EXPERIENCE missing from many lives today. A

---

15. Socrates, see *Plato, The Republic*, trans. by W. H. Gillespie,
p. 273, and *Works of Plato*, Volume IV, translated by George Burges,
pp. 375 ff.
16. Isaiah 46:9.

survey reported in the November 1974 issue of *Pyschology Today* Magazine testifies to this fact. Forty thousand replies to the *Psychology Today* religion questionnaire reveal that Americans "still **ache** to believe . . . there is something beyond our personal and collective reach." Editors were surprised at both the number of responses and the pervasive religious sentiment among readers of this sophisticated, secular magazine.

Today many young people seek ultimate answers to the profound questions of life. The young exhibit this universal need to worship, for the young person wants, needs, is in fact **desperate** to believe in **something.** He's in constant search of it—in astrology, in love, in radicalism, in mind-bending drugs, in Zen Buddhism—in anything he feels might satisfy his spiritual hunger.

The *seed of faith* God plants in every man's soul[17] may be dwarfed, may have feeble roots, but it comes to fruition somehow, even in the parched lives of apparent unbelievers. The fact that all people have a universal concept of a Supreme Being, and have some form of worship, is a strong argument for God's existence. It certainly harmonizes with the Biblical record of Creation, which declares God created man in His own image. Those who deny God's personal existence have no argument to equal it in support of their theory.

Why does man alone have this "God consciousness"? Is this innate, instinctive urge in man a **mere accident?** Far from it: The believer is convinced that here we see another evidence of God implanted by the Creator in man's very nature.

---

17. The Bible says, "God hath dealt to EVERY MAN the measure of faith." Romans 12:3.

> # CLUE #6:
> # THE MORAL ARGUMENT

In 1781 German philosopher Immanuel Kant published his *Critique of Pure Reason* and initiated this line of moral argument, holding that reflection upon man as a moral being can lead us to the idea of God. In his conclusion Kant wrote: "Two things fill me with constantly increasing admiration and awe the longer and more earnestly I reflect upon them— the **starry heavens** without and the **moral law** within."

Many besides Kant have recognized man's moral sense as another pointer to the reality of God. Among those was the late C. S. Lewis of Cambridge University who wrote *The Case for Christianity* in which he considers the moral experience of men. His Book One, called "Right and Wrong as a Clue to the Meaning of the Universe," begins as follows:

> Everyone has heard people quarrelling. Sometimes it sounds funny and sometimes it sounds merely unpleasant; but however it sounds, we can learn something very important from listening to the things they say. They say things like this: "That's my seat, I was there first"—"Give me a bit of your orange, I gave you a bit of mine"—"Come on, you promised." People say things like that every day, educated people as well as uneducated, and children as well as grown-ups.[18]

---

18. C. S. Lewis, *The Case for Christianity*, in *Mere Christianity* (New York: The Macmillan Company, 1960), p. 17.

What interests Lewis about these remarks is that the man who makes them isn't just saying that the other man's behavior doesn't happen to please him. He's appealing to some standard of behavior he expects the other man to know about. And the other man very seldom replies, "To hell with your standard." Nearly always he tries to prove that what he's been doing doesn't really go against the standard, or that if it does, there's some special excuse, some special reason in this particular case why the person who took the seat first should not keep it, or that things were quite different when he was given the bit of orange, or that something has turned up which lets him off keeping his promise. In fact, it looks as if both parties had in mind some Law or Rule of fair play or decent behavior or morality or whatever you like to call it, about which they really agreed. And they have. If they hadn't, they might fight like animals, but they couldn't quarrel in the human sense of the word. Quarrelling means trying to show that the other man's in the wrong. And there'd be no sense in trying to do that unless you and he had some agreement as to what Right and Wrong are.[19]

So the Moral Law God put into our minds is another bit of evidence pointing to His existence. Believers and unbelievers alike recognize **obligation** and **guilt** as facts of experience. All know the sense of "ought," but not all recognize its profound significance. For the atheist, it's "just one of those things," a mysterious power that creates feelings of guilt if resisted. For the believer, the duty to do what's right and the obligation to pursue what's good are neither a mystery nor simple human policy for the sake of society. If the moral law were mere policy, guilt would lack its power to shame us.

You see, if God doesn't exist, neither does an objective standard of Good and Evil. For if it's not God who condemns murder, then we have no way of declaring murder evil. All we

---

19. Lewis, *op. cit.*, pp. 17-18.

can say is that we don't happen to like it. If moral standards
don't come from a Higher Source, then each of us is his own
source of morality. Each becomes "a law unto himself," and
Right and Wrong become matters of purely personal taste:
"What **you** think is good is good for you, and what **I** think is
good is good for me." If ethics are not based on God but become "a do-it-yourself project," then the morality of Attila
the Hun is as valid as that of St. Paul.

Man's moral sense, our innate recognition of "goodness,"
means that no matter how far we personally fall short, we
automatically respect such things as honesty, sincerity, kind-
ness, fairness, and other things we consider good while we
denounce deceit, corruption, brutality, treachery and other
things we consider evil. This universal recognition of "good"
is another significant pointer to the reality of God. For the
believer, man's inherent sense of Moral Law demands a
Lawgiver.

> # CLUE #7:
> # FULFILLMENT OF PROPHECY

The remarkable **fulfillment** of Bible prophecies gives yet
another convincing clue to the existence of God—but this must
be dealt with in a future chapter, Chapter 14, to do justice to this
important subject. Only a divine all-intelligent Being can
know the future. Man may make "educated guesses," but it's
only by chance if he occasionally succeeds in being correct.

When we study fascinating prophecies of the Bible and
trace their unmistakable fulfillment, we'll see God's hand on
the helm of history—we'll see, too, that the validity of the Bible
and the reality of God go hand in hand.

CLUE #8:
GOD'S SELF-PORTRAIT

No discussion of the evidence of God's existence would be complete without mention of Jesus Christ, who has been called "God's Self-portrait." The prophet Isaiah spoke truth when he said, "Thou art a God that hidest Thyself."[20] But God has seen fit to **reveal Himself** in three important ways:

- In the beauty and majesty of **NATURE,** through His creative power;
- In the pages of His written Word, the **BIBLE**; and
- In the Person of His Son, the Lord **JESUS CHRIST**, who veiled His divinity in humanity.

The evidence for Christ's deity and resurrection is presented in Chapters 7, 8 and 9, but Christian believers know that the supreme Proof of God's existence occurred when the Emperor of the Universe walked the dusty roads of Galilee, living among men and revealing His love by dying for them. Every kind word He said, every loving act He did was another BRUSH STROKE on Jesus' *portrait* of His Father, giving us a perfect picture of God.[21]

---

20. Isaiah 45:15.
21. See John 14:8-9.

WHO MADE GOD?
DID GOD HAVE A BEGINNING?

Some may ask, "But where did **God** come from? How did He begin?" The fact is that God is ETERNAL—**without beginning** of days **or end** of years. He stands **beyond** the dimensions of TIME. Time, measured by the movement of the planets and the rotation of the earth, is ever-present in our earth-bound existence. But time as we know it may not exist at all in the heavenly New Earth—we're told that "there shall be **no night** there."[22] The simple truth is:

> Just as God **will have** an infinite existence
>   in the FUTURE, **without END,**
> He **has had** an infinite existence
>   in the PAST, **without BEGINNING.**

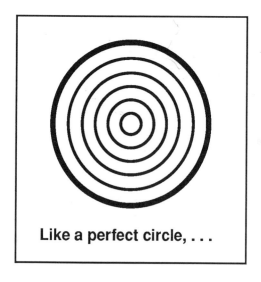

Like a perfect circle, . . .

---

22. Revelation 21:25.

Time-oriented humans may find this concept new and strange. It IS rather difficult to comprehend. But that's just another proof of the fact that **FINITE minds cannot comprehend the INFINITE.** In a world where nations rise and fall, where mountains crumble and governments collapse, we need to stretch our minds to comprehend the Psalmist's sublime thought: "FROM everlasting TO everlasting, Thou art God."[23] We mortals think in terms of beginnings and endings, but God is eternal: "The same yesterday, and to day, and for ever."[24] The unchanging Father, "with whom is no variableness, neither shadow of turning," declares: "I am the Lord, **I change not.**"[25] Like a **perfect circle,** there's **no BEGINNING** and **no ENDING** to "The mighty God, the *EVERLASTING* Father."[26]

CONCLUSION: GOD *DOES* EXIST!

As we survey the landscape of IDEAS, we see peaks and valleys, plains and mountains. But towering above all trivial facts and mundane concepts is the MOST REMARKABLE FACT of all time—the timeless thought that **GOD EXISTS!** The reality of a loving, personal God who's interested in all details of our lives is a tall, majestic peak that intrigues us and beckons us on to explore the heights of Truth.

We've seen many evidences of God's existence. Some are **external** clues that lie in the objective world of reality beyond man (such as the existence of physical matter, motion and energy, life itself, and orderly design). Some are **internal** clues that lie within man himself (such as man's religious impulse and his moral sense).

---

23. Psalms 90:2.
24. Hebrews 13:8.
25. James 1:17 and Malachi 3:6.
26. Isaiah 9:6.

As I said at the beginning, I don't insist that these clues are absolute proofs—but they ARE pointers whose **cumulative testimony** is impressive. The atheist must explain the origin or **existence** of EACH of the clues discussed above. To explain even **one** of these apart from God is something that science and worldly philosophy have never been able to do—but they ALL must be explained before God, the Creator, can be taken out of the picture!

Paul tells us that spiritual things "are spiritually discerned."[27] If we open our minds—if we lay aside our pride and prejudice—we'll understand and admit that the EXISTENCE of God is a basic REALITY of life. The universe is not a cosmic accident but a masterpiece **designed** by a Master Architect and **built** by a Master Craftsman. Faith in God is not "a leap in the dark" but a conviction and commitment based upon **more than adequate evidence** of the living, loving God who made us all.

---

27. 1 Corinthians 2:14.

? ? ? ? ? ? ? ? ? ? ? ? ? ? ?
?   **MYSTERY #2**   ?
?   **EVOLUTION**   ?
?   Is the evolutionary theory   ?
?   **a valid explanation**   ?
?   for the nature of things?   ?
? ? ? ? ? ? ? ? ? ? ? ? ? ? ?

"Professing themselves to be **wise,**
they became **fools.**"—Romans 1:22

Chapter 3

THE THEORY of EVOLUTION:
Weighed and Found Wanting
Part I.

"The first point to make about Darwin's theory is that **it is no longer a theory, but a fact**. No serious scientist would deny the fact that evolution has occurred, just as he would not deny the fact that the earth goes around the sun."[1]

This bold declaration was made on a television panel celebrating the centennial of Charles Darwin's book *Origin of Species* by famous British biologist Sir Julian Huxley, who has exerted a profound influence on 20th century thought even as his grandfather, Thomas Henry Huxley, did in the 19th century.

Of course, Huxley is a rather rash advocate for evolution, and his assertions are often pervaded by a spirit of missionary fervor. Even so, the quotation found above is not an isolated statement, but typical of evolutionary pronouncements. For years we've been bombarded by assertions geared to gain our acceptance of evolution as one of "the facts of life." Militant evolutionists make dogmatic declarations that sometimes go far

---

1. Sir Julian Huxley, "At Random: A Television Preview," in Sol Tax, editor, *Issues in Evolution*, Volume 3 of *Evolution After Darwin* (Chicago: The University of Chicago Press, 1960), p. 41.

beyond the FACTS of science. Let's look at a few of these statements:

Richard B. Goldschmidt, Professor at the University of California at Berkeley, emphatically stated that "Evolution of the animal and plant world is considered by all those entitled to judgment to be **a fact for which no further proof is needed.**"[2]

Theodosius Dobzhansky, geneticist and well-known evolutionist, Professor at Columbia University, has said that "Among the present generation **no informed person** entertains any doubt of the validity of the evolutionary theory in the sense that evolution has occurred."[3]

And H. H. Newman, Professor Emeritus at the University of Chicago, minced no words in declaring, "There is no rival hypothesis [to evolution] except **the outworn and completely refuted one of special creation,** now retained only by the **ignorant,** the **dogmatic,** and the **prejudiced.**"[4]

To quote just one more biologist, Dr. R. S. Lull, Professor of Paleontology at Yale: "Since Darwin's day, Evolution has been more and more generally accepted, until now in the minds of informed, thinking men there is no doubt that it is the only **logical** way whereby the creation can be interpreted and understood. We are not so sure, however, as to the *modus operandi,* but we may **rest assured** that the great process has been in accordance with great natural laws, some of which are as yet **unknown,** perhaps **unknowable.**"[5]

Commenting on this statement, chemist Anthony Standen says, "And so biologists continue to 'rest assured.' But one

2. Richard B. Goldschmidt, *American Scientist,* Volume 40 (1952), p. 84.

3. Theodosius Dobzhansky, *Genetics and the Origin of Species,* Second Edition (New York: Columbia University Press, 1941), p. 8.

4. Horatio H. Newman, *Outlines of General Zoology,* (New York: The Macmillan Company, 1924), p. 407.

5. Richard Swann Lull, *Organic Evolution* (New York: The Macmillan Company, 1948), p. 15.

may be tempted to ask, IF some of the great natural laws
are as yet **unknown**, how do we know that they are there?
And if some are perhaps **unknowable**, how do we know that
they are 'logical'?"[6]

In the light of these strong statements by such eminent
scientists, anyone trying to refute the teachings of evolutionists must feel like David approaching Goliath! But remember that young David didn't win the battle in his own
strength, and in this case truth will be determined not by me
or any other man but by the facts themselves.

The assertions of the evolutions quoted above, if in fact
true, would definitely tip the scales of Truth in favor of the
evolutionary theory. But let's weigh in the balance some
other statements, equally forceful and made by equally eminent men of science.

ADMISSIONS Made by Evolutionary Scientists

We've already seen that Horatio H. Newman feels
that any alternative to evolution can be held "only by the
ignorant, the dogmatic, and the prejudiced." But in another
book Newman is candid enough to write: "**Reluctant** as he
may be to admit it, **honesty compels** the evolutionist to admit
that **there is NO absolute proof** of organic evolution."[7]

Professor Ernst Mayr of Harvard, a heavyweight among
evolutionists, confesses: "The fact that the synthetic [evolu-
tionary] theory is now so universally accepted is not in itself
proof of its correctness. . . . The basic theory is in many
instances **hardly more than a postulate.**"[8] (A postulate, by

6. Anthony Standen, *Science Is a Sacred Cow* (New York: E. P.
Dutton & Company, 1950), p. 106.

7. Horatio H. Newman, *Evolution, Genetics, and Eugenics*, Third
Edition (Chicago: University of Chicago Press, 1932), p. 57.

8. Ernst Mayr, *Animal Species and Evolution* (Cambridge, Massachusetts: Harvard University Press, 1963), pp. 7-8.

the way, is defined by Webster as "a position or supposition assumed without proof.")

Some time ago Oxford University Press published a book entitled *A Short History of Science*, by Charles Singer. The author frankly confesses to his faith in the evolutionary theory. Despite this, he declares: "Evolution is perhaps **unique** among major scientific theories in that the appeal for its acceptance is **NOT that there is EVIDENCE for it**, but that any **other** proposed interpretation is wholly incredible."[9] Statements like this betray *a non-scientific bias* which is devastating to any search for truth.

And Thomas Hunt Morgan, founder of the Morganian school of genetics and esteemed Professor at both Columbia and Caltech, frankly declared: "Within the period of human history **we do not know of a single instance** of the trans mutation of one species into another one. . . . Therefore it may be claimed that the theory of descent is **lacking** in the most essential feature that it needs to place the theory on a scientific basis. **This must be admitted.**"[10]

Paul Ehrlich and Richard Holm, biologists at Stanford University, criticize the dogmatic assumptions of those like Huxley in saying: "Perpetuation of today's theory as **dogma** will not encourage progress toward **more satisfactory explanations** of observed phenomena."[11]

Wistar Institute in Philadelphia published a Symposium Monograph in 1967 entitled, *Mathematical Challenges to*

9. Charles Singer, *A Short History of Science* (New York: Oxford University Press, 1946), p. 387.

10. Thomas Hunt Morgan, *Evolution and Adaptation* (New York: The Macmillan Company, 1903), p. 43.

11. Paul R. Ehrlich and Richard W. Holm, "Patterns and Populations," *Science*, Volume 137 (August 31, 1962), p. 656.

the Neo-Darwinian Interpretation of Evolution.[12] And in a company publication, *Scientific Research*, McGraw-Hill, Inc., published two such articles: **"Heresy in the Halls of Biology:** Mathematicians **Question** Darwinism"[13] and "Thinking the Unthinkable: Are Evolutionists **Wrong?"**[14]

W. R. Thompson, for many years Director of the Commonwealth Institute of Biological Control at Ottawa, Canada, is a world-renowned entomologist. Dr. Thompson was chosen to write the Foreword to the new edition of Darwin's *Origin of Species* published in the Darwinian Centennial Year as part of the *Everyman's Library Series.* His entire Foreword is **a devastating indictment** and refutation of Darwinian evolution and perhaps even more so of the scientific morality of evolutionists! Note the follow excerpts:

> As we know, there is a great divergence of opinion among biologists, not only about the causes of evolution but even about the actual process. This divergence exists because **the evidence is unsatisfactory** and does NOT permit any certain conclusion. **It is therefore right and proper to draw the attention of the non-scientific public to the disagreements about evolution.** But some recent remarks of evolutionists show that they think this unreasonable. This situation, where men rally to

---

12. Paul S. Moorhead and Martin M. Kaplan, editors, *Mathematical Challenges to the Neo-Darwinian Interpretation of Evolution*, Symposium Monograph No. 5 (Philadelphia: The Wistar Institute Press, 1967).

13. Robert Bernhard, "Heresy in the Halls of Biology: Mathematicians Question Darwinism," *Scientific Research*, Volume 2, No. 11 (November, 1967).

14. Robert Bernhard, "Thinking the Unthinkable: Are Evolutionists Wrong?" *Scientific Research*, Volume 4, No. 18 (September, 1969).

the defense of **a doctrine they are unable to define
scientifically, much less demonstrate with scientific
rigor,** attempting to maintain its credit with the public
by the **suppression** of criticism and the elimination
of difficulties, is abnormal and undesirable in science.[15]

G. A. Kerkut, Professor of Physiology and Biochemistry
at the University of Southampton, England, is an evolutionist but is critical enough and honest enough as a scientist to
admit: "The evidence that supports it [the theory of evolution]
is **not sufficiently strong** to allow us to consider it as
anything more than a working hypothesis."[16]

Thus Kerkut concluded his book written to expose the
weaknesses and fallacies in the evidence used to support
evolutionary theory.   But the REVIEW of Kerkut's book,
written by John T. Bonner, one of the nation's leading biologists and Professor at Princeton, was as startling as the book
itself—note Dr. Bonner's words:

This is a book with a disturbing message; it
points to some unseemly **cracks** in the **foundations.**
One is disturbed because what is said gives us the uneasy feeling that **we knew it for a long time deep down
but were never willing to admit it even to ourselves.**
It is another of those cold and uncompromising situa-
tions where the naked truth and human nature travel in

---

15.   W. R. Thompson, "Introduction" to *The Origin of Species* by
Charles Darwin (New York: E. P. Dutton & Company, Everyman's Library,
1956). Thompson's Introduction has also been reprinted in the *Journal of
the American Scientific Affiliation*, Volume 12 (March, 1960), pp. 2-9.
16.   G. A. Kerkut, *Implications of Evolution* (New York: Pergamon
Press, 1960), p. 157.

different directions. The particular truth is simply that we have **NO reliable evidence** as to the evolutionary sequence of invertebrate phyla. . . . We have all been telling our students for years **not** to accept any statement on its face value but to **examine the evidence**, and, therefore, it is rather a shock to discover that **we have failed to follow our own sound advice.** [17]

IS EVOLUTION SCIENTIFIC?

What criteria must be met for a theory to be considered scientific? George Gaylord Simpson, Professor at Harvard and perhaps the foremost writer on evolution, has stated that "It is inherent in any definition of science that **statements that cannot be checked by OBSERVATION are not . . . science.**"[18]

A definition of science given by the *Oxford English Dictionary* is: "A branch of study which is concerned either with a connected body of **DEMONSTRATED truths** or with **OBSERVED facts** systematically classified."

Note that science deals with "**demonstrated . . . observed**" data arrived at by experimenting in a laboratory or observing in the real world of nature. But evolution cannot be studied in a laboratory or seen in nature, since its assumed mechanisms operate so slowly as to require millions of years for demonstrable results. This fact is admitted by David Kitts in a recent issue of *Evolution* Magazine: "Evolution, at least in the sense that Darwin speaks of it, **cannot be detected** within the lifetime of a single observer."[19]

---

17. John T. Bonner, Review of Kerkut's book, *American Scientist*, Volume 49, No. 2 (June, 1961), p. 240.

18. George Gaylord Simpson, *Science*, Volume 143 (1964), p. 769.

19. David G. Kitts, "Paleontology and Evolutionary Theory," *Evolution*, Volume 28 (September, 1974), p. 466.

As a matter of fact, the whole question of ORIGINS
(whether by creation OR evolution) is really **outside** the limits
of science, not being subject to scientific experimentation
and analysis. Both creationists and evolutionists alike agree
that **no human observer witnessed** the origin of our earth
and its life, so the observational aspect of scientific investigation is automatically ruled out in any consideration of origins.
    Another limitation of a scientific theory is that it must
be capable of falsification. That is, it must be possible to
conceive some experiment the **failure** of which would disprove
the theory, for in order to be sure a theory is **right**, there
must be some way of proving it **wrong**. Francisco Ayala,
of Rockefeller University, recently wrote: "A hypothesis or
theory which cannot be, at least in principle, falsified by
empirical observations and experiments **does not belong
in the realm of science.**"[20] Yet evolutionists consider
everything in the world a VERIFICATION of their theory!
    Nobel Prize-winner Peter Medawar, a leading biologist
at Oxford University, admits: "It is too difficult to imagine
or envisage an evolutionary episode which could NOT be
explained by the formulae of neo-Darwinism."[21] This is true
because even when evolutionists are forced to admit that
evolution is impossible **NOW**, they invoke long ages of time
during which, they say, **anything** can happen—and who is
to prove them wrong?
    But Sir Karl Popper, Professor of Logic and Scientific
Method at the London School of Economics, is a connoisseur
of the scientific method who says: "A theory which is not

    20. Francisco J. Ayala, "Biological Evolution: Natural Selection or
Random Walk?" *American Scientist*, Volume 62 (November-December,
1974), p. 700.
    21. Peter Medawar, in Moorhead and Kaplan, eds., *Mathematical
Challenges to the Neo-Darwinian Interpretation of Evolution*, Symposium
Monograph No. 5 (Philadelphia: The Wistar Institute Press, 1967), p. xi.

refutable by any conceivable event is **non**-scientific. Irrefutability is not a **virtue** (as people often think) but a **vice**."[22] This is why Paul Ehrlich and L. C. Birch, Professors of Biology at Stanford University, say quite candidly: "Our theory of evolution . . . is thus 'outside of empirical science.' . . . No one can think of ways in which to **TEST** it. Ideas, either without basis or based on a few laboratory experiments carried out in extremely simplified systems have attained currency far beyond their validity. They have become part of an **evolutionary DOGMA** accepted by most of us as part of our training."[23]   But *dogma* is a religious term, not a scientific one!

Actually, much of evolutionistic thinking lies more in the realm of religion or philosophy than science. Belief in evolution obviously requires a tremendous exercise of faith, faith in an assumption. (Assumptions are proper working tools, but never forget that they **are** assumptions!)   Some evolutionists freely acknowledge this need for faith to bridge the gap between evidence and proof. For instance, Dr. Louis T. More, Dean of the Graduate School at the University of Cincinnati and a staunch evolutionist, delivered a series of lectures at Princeton University which were then published in his book *The Dogma of Evolution,* in which he says: "The more one studies paleontology, the more certain one becomes that **evolution is based on FAITH alone,** exactly the same sort of faith which it is necessary to have when one encounters the great mysteries of religion."[24]

---

22. Sir Karl R. Popper, *Conjectures and Refutations* (London: Routledge and Kegan Paul, 1963), pp. 33-37.

23. Paul R. Ehrlich and L. C. Birch, "Evolutionary History and Population Biology," *Nature,* Volume 214 (April 22, 1967), p. 352.

24. Louis Trenchard More, *The Dogma of Evolution* (Princeton, New Jersey: Princeton University Press, 1925).

Dr. More's conclusion had been reached earlier by none other than Thomas Henry Huxley, who frankly declared: "To say, therefore, **in the admitted absence of evidence,** that I have any belief as to the mode in which the existing forms of life have originated would be using words in a wrong sense. . . . **I have no right to call my opinion anything but an act of philosophical faith.**"[25]

Remember that T. H. Huxley was the one man more responsible for the acceptance of evolution than Darwin himself. Darwin was a rather retiring person who had no heart to be at the forefront of the controversy. But Huxley, as the foremost champion of evolution, became "Darwin's bulldog." Thomas Henry Huxley became a brilliant press agent and enthusiastic salesman for the theory—debating, defending, promoting it with untiring voice and pen.

How strange, then, that in 1896 (many decades after *Origin of Species* was published in 1859, after Darwinism had triumphantly risen to full flower, after Darwin lay buried in Westminster Abbey among the honored of England for fourteen years) Huxley **admits** the "absence of evidence" for the evolution of living protoplasm from nonliving matter and says, "I have no right to call my opinion anything but **an act of philosophical FAITH**"!

Evolutionary theory is no less religious and no more scientific than special creation. Throughout the rest of this study we'll see that the evidence for evolution is circumstantial at best and contradictory at worst. Now let's turn to a candid examination of the facts—for after all, **one FACT is worth a thousand THEORIES.**

---

25. Thomas Henry Huxley, *Discourses Biological and Geological* (1896 edition), pp. 256-257.

I. VARIATION ONLY WITHIN KINDS

Variation among living things is a most obvious fact. Unless born an identical twin, each human being is unique, different from all others. The same seems true of all plants and animals. There can be no argument about the fact that CHANGE takes place in all nature. Some things have changed a great deal since creation. The difference between the theory of evolution and the doctrine of creation is NOT that one **accepts** the fact of change and the other doesn't, for change is obvious to and admitted by all. The difference lies in the **AMPLITUDE** of change, the **DEGREE** of change produced by natural processes. The evolutionist claims that these processes **know no bounds** in producing change. The creationist maintains that all variation lies within clearly defined limits.

Darwin mistakenly thought change was without limit, that the lid was off, as it were: "Slow though the process of selection may be . . . I can see NO LIMIT to the amount of change."[26] So Darwin gave free rein to his imagination. He cherished the idea that variation could proceed endlessly. Thus his closing sentence in *Origin of Species* declared: "From so simple a beginning ENDLESS FORMS most beautiful and most wonderful have been, and are being, evolved."[27] And the majority of scientists today, like Darwin, speak unjustifiably of **unlimited variation.**

It's understandable that evolutionists take this attitude, for they realize that unless change can proceed to the point of producing NEW KINDS of living things, evolution is impossible. **Limited change** of life already created does not fulfill the requirements of the theory of evolution. So there's a difference between **mere variation** and **actual evolution.**

---

26. Charles Darwin, *On the Origin of Species: A Facsimile of the First Edition* (Cambridge, Massachusetts: Harvard University Press, 1964), p. 109.
27. *Ibid.*, p. 490.

The term "evolution," when used as the theory demands, means **the ultimate changing of one kind of plant or animal into another basic type.**

Let me underscore the fact that **evolution does NOT simply mean CHANGE.** This is important, for the evidence cited by most writers in favor of their claim that evolution is a "fact" is simply evidence of change. But true evolution in the Darwinian sense would be a certain KIND of change, a high DEGREE of change not seen in the world of reality.

To describe degrees of variation, let's use the terms "micro" for small changes and "macro" for large ones. Members of the dog family have undergone many **micro** changes of color, size, etc., so that there are many varieties of dogs in the world today —but they're all unmistakably DOGS! The same may be said of cats, horses, and all other animals as well as plants. They may vary **within their basic kinds** but horses remain horses, cows remain cows, and wheat remains wheat.

Creationists recognize that **"micro-evolution"**—change **within** basic kinds—**has** occurred. But evolutionists are eagerly searching for mechanisms that will provide for **macro**-evolution of organisms from one basic type into another basic kind. *No one has ever seen* a **macro** change take place, either in the living world or among the fossils.

At no time has a laboratory experimenter or field investigator shown that any plant or animal has changed into another basic kind. Changes always take place **within a charmed circle, within the circumscribed limits of the basic kinds.** This is a FUNDAMENTAL LAW of all living things, both plants and animals.

Read this devastating admission by Richard Goldschmidt, evolutionary biologist from UC Berkeley: "Microevolution does **not** lead beyond the confines of the species, and the typical products of microevolution, the geographic races, are not incipient species. There is **no such category** as incipient species."[28] *Incipient*, of course, refers to "the early, initial stages of something new." Goldschmidt also says: "Microevolution by accumulation of micro-mutations . . . leads to diversification strictly WITHIN the species. . . . Subspecies are actually, therefore, neither incipient species nor models for the origin of species. They are more or less diversified blind alleys within the species. The decisive step in evolution, the first step toward macroevolution, the step from one species to another, requires another evolutionary method than that of sheer accumulation of micro-mutations."[29]

And evolutionist Loren Eiseley is forced to the same conclusion: "It would appear that careful domestic breeding, whatever it may do to improve the quality of race horses or cabbages, is NOT actually in itself the road to the endless biological deviation which is evolution. There is great irony in this situation, for more than almost any other single factor, domestic breeding has been used as an argument for the reality of evolution."[30]

Unfortunately, not all evolutionists are this frank. They know that what Goldschmidt and Eiseley say is true, but their allegiance to the theory leads them to say, "Maybe evolution doesn't create new living things today, but just give it time, and you'll get a new kind"—but this is philosophy, not science. Their faith in the theory also leads them to extrapolate. Extrapolating (estimating beyond the known range) is a dangerous procedure, warns Dr. Norman Macbeth: "If you have a broad base of sound observations, you can extend a little at the ends without too much risk; but if the base is short or insecure, extension can lead to

---

28. Richard B. Goldschmidt, *The Material Basis of Evolution* (Paterson, New Jersey: Pageant Books, Inc., 1960), p. 396.
29. *Ibid.*, p. 183.
30. Loren Eiseley, *The Immense Journey* (New York: Vintage Books, 1958), p. 223.

grotesque errors. Thus if you observe the growth of a baby during its first months, extrapolation into the future will show that the child will be **eight feet tall** when **six years old.** Therefore all statisticians recommend caution in extrapolating. Darwin, however, plunged in with no caution at all." [31]

Note Mark Twain's views on extrapolation: "In the space of 176 years the Lower Mississippi has shortened itself 242 miles. That is an average of a trifle over a mile and a third per year. Therefore any calm person who is not blind or idiotic can see that . . . 742 years from now the Lower Mississippi will be only a mile and three-quarters long, and Cairo [Illinois] and New Orleans will have joined their streets together and be plodding along comfortably under a single mayor and a mutual board of aldermen. There is something fascinating about science. One gets such **wholesale returns of conjecture** out of such a **trifling investment of fact.**" [32]

Discontinuity Among Kinds

The fact of discontinuity is as obvious as the fact of variation. We find the different kinds of living things standing distinctly separated—cats, dogs, and elephants; palm trees, clover, and tumbleweed. The same clear-cut discontinuity occurs among the fossils (which we'll consider in the next chapter).

So even though there are many varieties or breeds of horses, and the same is true of cows, there exists between horses and cows a clear-cut gap. There are **unbridgeable gaps** between all the different kinds, and no amount of variation has even made a start at crossing these gaps. But if evolution were true, **THE GAPS SHOULDN'T BE THERE**

31. Norman Macbeth, *Darwin Retried* (New York: Dell Publishing Company, 1971), p. 31.
32. Mark Twain, quoted in Macbeth, *op. cit.*, pp. 37-38.

AT ALL. For if all organisms really descended from a common ancestor, they'd be all **interconnected** by imperceptible gradations.

This crucial fact is admitted by no less an evolutionist than Professor Dobzhansky of Columbia University when he says: "If we assemble as many individuals living at a given time as we can, we notice at once that the observed variation does **NOT** form any kind of **continuous** distribution. Instead, a multitude of **separate**, discrete distributions are found. The living world is **NOT** a single array in which any two variants are connected by an **unbroken** series of intergrades, but an array of more or less **distinctly separate** arrays, intermediates between which are absent or at least rare."[33]

So everywhere we look in the world of nature, we see **clusters, families, or distinct groups** of living things which make up the basic kinds. And these families cannot be cross-bred. Dogs may cross-breed with dogs but can never successfully mate with cats or other animals to produce offspring. **Only like kinds can reproduce.**

George Gaylord Simpson, an evolutionist with impressive credentials, freely admits: "Cross breeding . . . is almost never satisfactorily possible at the level of the genera, and absolutely never above that level."[34]

And evolutionist Gavin De Beer notes in his book on Darwin: ". . . one species **does not grow** from the seed of another species."[35]

33. Theodosius Dobzhansky, *Genetics and the Origin of Species*, Third Edition, Revised (New York: Columbia University Press, 1951), p. 4.

34. George Gaylord Simpson, *The Major Features of Evolution* (New York: Columbia University Press, 1953), p. 340. *Genera* is the plural of *genus*, the biological class one step above a basic species.

35. Sir Gavin De Beer, *Charles Darwin: Evolution by Natural Selection* (Garden City, New York: Doubleday and Company, 1964), p. 1.

Hybrids, of course, may be produced. Hybridization is simply the crossing of two organisms diverse enough to constitute at least different varieties of a single kind, such as red sunflowers and yellow sunflowers or wolf and coyote. But the variability is still limited within a basic kind. For instance, farmers have succeeded in raising high-yield hybrid corn. Yet no matter what was done to that corn, **it always stayed corn.** It did not, and can not, change into some other kind of plant.

Furthermore, the offspring of hybrids are often **sterile** and require constant hybridizing. A **horse**, for example, may mate with a **donkey** and produce the hybrid we call a mule. But mules have reached the limits of variability and cannot reproduce themselves as a permanent species. Note this illuminating statement from Professor Goldschmidt: "**Nowhere** have the limits of the species been transgressed, and these limits are separated from the limits of the next good species by the **unbridged gap,** which also includes **sterility.**"[36]

Darwin's Tragedy

While working on his yet-unpublished book, Darwin wrote a significant letter to his friend and confidant the botanist Joseph Hooker, in which he said: **"I am almost convinced (quite contrary to the opinion I started with) that species are not (it is like confessing a murder) immutable."**[37] **WHY** should Darwin feel that saying species are not unchangeable "is like confessing a murder"?

---

36. Richard B. Goldschmidt, *The Material Basis of Evolution* (Paterson, New Jersey: Pageant Books, Inc., 1960), p. 168.

37. Letter from Darwin to Joseph Hooker, January 11, 1844, in *The Life and Letters of Charles Darwin*, edited by his son Francis Darwin, (New York: D. Appleton and Company, 1896 [Reprinted 1972]), Volume I, p. 384.

Darwin's tragedy was his misunderstanding of the teaching of Genesis in the Bible. He permitted men who were poor scholars of the Bible to tell him what the Bible taught. You see, the church in Darwin's day held a narrow view on origins, especially on the **fixity of species**. The great church universities taught (and young Charles Darwin had studied theology at Cambridge) that the offspring of any plant or animal were **as alike as coins from the mint**—that there could be NO change whatever. Apparently without studying Genesis for himself, Darwin believed that it said "no variation." Yet he looked on the earth and saw variation, and his theory attempted to account for it. Darwin undoubtedly believed he had proved the Bible wrong, but he proved only the **misinterpretation** of it wrong.

Actually, the erroneous assumption that the Bible required rigid fixity led many to reject the Bible entirely. But the old idea of "fixity of species" is NOT part of the Biblical concept of special creation. That would be an impossibly narrow and inaccurate conception of special creation. For the Bible speaks of mankind having originated from a single pair, yet recognizes the difference between a Jew and an Ethiopian[38] and between normal men and giants.[39]

Other texts suggest that **change was to be expected**: The fact that the serpent was cursed "above" all cattle and wild animals suggests a general curse that would change those living things, and the fact that "thorns . . . and thistles" were to spring up suggests that the cursed plant world would also change.[40]

Thus the old argument that any change in living things refutes the Bible is without support. Many evolutionists today think that if a Christian opposes the theory of evolution

---

38. See Numbers 12:1 and Jeremiah 13:23.
39. Genesis 6:4.
40. See Genesis 3:14-19.

it's because he supports the idea of "fixity of species." But the Bible doesn't even use the word "species." It simply says God created living things "after their kind." For example, the Bible mentions "the owl . . . after his kind."[41] But the owl is NOT just a species—the owl is an entire "order" (Strigiformes), so the term "kind" can obviously include **several species.**

Kind is an old word with roots in the word **kin.** TEN TIMES in the first chapter of Genesis we're told that the created forms, both plant and animal, were to bring forth "after their kind"—not after some other kinds.[42] The Biblical idea of "kind" is not to be confused with the modern term "species," for **no one knows** what a species is. The *Encyclopedia Britannica* informs us that "The nature of species is a question of considerable importance in general biology . . . but despite its wide use **its definition remains elusive. . . . An exact definition of the species concept has given zoologists much trouble.**"[43]

So creationists do believe in "fixity"—but not in the fixity of so-called "species." Exactly what constitutes a species is largely a matter of opinion of the authority who classifies and names it. Large groups are often split into smaller "species," varying from each other in minor points such as color. Many of the modern supposed "species" have developed right before our eyes, not taking millions of years but only a few generations. But these variations are merely strains of a common stock. We start with pigeons and end with pigeons. No evolution of new **kinds** is occurring.

Creationists don't shut their eyes or close their ears to the evidence. Variation **within** permanently fixed basic kinds

---

41. Leviticus 11:16.
42. See Genesis 1, verses 11, 12, 21, 24, 25.
43. *Encyclopedia Britannica* (1967 edition), Volume 20, p. 1149, Article "Species" and Volume 23, p. 1006, Article "Zoology."

is a fact open to the observation of all, scientist and layman alike. That is, living things DO vary, but they vary only within certain fixed limits. And variation **within the kind** is NOT THE TYPE of evolution that could possibly build our modern organic world from a few one-celled forms, as Darwin theorized.

LIKE always begets LIKE: a cow always gives birth to a calf, not an ostrich; and if you plant an acorn, only an oak will grow. One basic kind may produce many **varieties**, but it never changes into another basic kind. This is always true in the REAL world—as opposed to the hypothetical world of evolutionary speculation and the imaginary world of children's fairy tales, where pumpkins turn into coaches and mice into men.

We've seen that the fact of **change** and variation in living things is certainly no proof that Darwin's theory is right and the Bible is wrong. We've also seen that the **discontinuity** evident everywhere, with gaps among different kinds, is much more in harmony with the doctrine of creation than with the assumptions of evolution. In other words, defenders of the theory are wrong when they say evolution HAS taken place. Now let's consider what they say about HOW it supposedly takes place.

II. LAMARCKISM WAS NOT THE ANSWER

In the early 1800's those who believed in evolution accepted the idea that characteristics **acquired** by an organism during its lifetime could be transmitted to its offspring. The doctrine of the inheritance of acquired characteristics came to be known as "Lamarckism," after a French zoologist named Jean Baptiste Lamarck. But Lamarck himself was by no means the only evolutionist who taught this idea.

Darwin, for instance, "believed that any variation **acquired by the body** can, sooner or later, impress itself in the germ cells [sex cells of reproduction] and become an

inherent variation (inheritance of acquired characteristics). Therefore, he did not mind accepting the idea that certain variations of the Lamarckian type—variations determined by **use**, by **activity**—might play an evolutionary role."[44] A book called *The Evidence of Evolution* quotes Darwin as admitting his agreement with Lamarck: "The conclusions I am led to are not widely different from his."[45]

Darwin, Lamarck, and others reasoned that use and disuse, exercise and activity could affect one's body **and those effects could be *passed on* to one's offspring.** Thus giraffes got long necks because they ran out of vegetation and had to stretch their necks to reach higher leaves. In this way, each generation passed on to its offspring a slightly longer neck. (No one has ever seen evidence, either living or fossilized, of giraffes with **short** necks, but no matter!) By the same logic, birds probably developed wings by flying so much.

If Lamarck's theory were correct, cats would be able to operate a can opener by now, and all mothers would have twelve hands! But Lamarckism is simply not true and has been utterly disproved both by experiments and by our growing knowledge of genetics. Characteristics acquired by the individual during his life may affect his **body** but cannot bring about a corresponding change in his **reproductive cells,** which carry all hereditary information. If you lose a finger in an accident, your children will still be born with a full set. Though Chinese women kept their feet small by tight binding for many centuries, modern Chinese women still have feet of normal size.

---

44. Jean Rostand, *The Orion Book of Evolution* (New York: The Orion Press, 1960), p. 61.
45. Charles Darwin, quoted in Nicholas Hotton III, *The Evidence of Evolution* (Garden City, New York: Doubleday and Company, 1962), p. 138.

Herbert Spencer, an influential evolutionist contemporary with Darwin, was so convinced about Lamarckism that he wrote, "Close contemplation of the facts impresses me more strongly than ever with **two alternatives**—either there HAS BEEN inheritance of acquired characters or there has been NO EVOLUTION." [46]

But others, like August Weismann, could not accept Lamarckism. Weismann was one of the first German scientists to support Darwin's theory but also one of the first to demonstrate the **falsity** of the inheritance of acquired characteristics. In one experiment he cut off the tails of mice for many generations, but the young mice were always born with tails as long as ever. "His critique on this point is authoritative and has never been refuted." [47]   But doesn't evolution **NEED** Lamarck's idea? "To this, Weismann answered that it is unworthy of the scientific mind to make a case for an unlikely and unproved phenomenon because a theory needs bolstering." [48]

Still, pet theories die hard, and Ernst Haeckel, a notorious evolutionist born in Germany the same year as Weismann, wrote: "Belief in the inheritance of acquired characters is **a NECESSARY axiom**. . . . Rather than agree with Weismann in denying the inheritance of acquired characters, **it would be better** to accept a mysterious creation of all the species as described in the Mosaic account [of the Bible]." [49]

Today we know that inheritance is controlled by the genes found only in the sex cells. Only alternations **in the genes**

------

46. Herbert Spencer, *Contemporary Review*, February and March, 1893.

47. Jean Rostand, *The Orion Book of Evolution* (New York: The Orion Press, 1960), p. 62.

48. *Ibid.*, p. 64.

49. Ernst Haeckel, quoted in J. A. Thompson, *Heredity*, Fifth Edition (New York: Coleman, 1926), p. 190.

of the reproductive cells are inheritable. Acquired traits play no part in evolution, and Lamarckism today exists only on the "lunatic fringe" of biology, now and then catching the fancy of some speculative thinker.

III. MUTATIONS ARE NOT THE ANSWER

The new science of genetics (of which Darwin knew nothing, since it emerged after his time) has found four causes of variation in living things: (1) recombinations, (2) hybridization, (3) chromosome changes, and (4) gene mutations. The first of these, **RECOMBINATIONS** of genes, is the ordinary cause of change. It's always present when sexual reproduction takes place and accounts for virtually all the variation seen in nature today. It simply combines, in one individual, traits of two parents—as we say, "He's got his mother's eyes and his father's chin."

Recombination works like this: Inside the nucleus of **every** plant or animal cell are tiny rod-shaped bodies called chromosomes. The chromosomes always come in pairs— one member of each pair has come from one parent and one from the other. When reproduction takes place, it's by means of sex cells: sperm in the male and eggs in the female. But these sex cells differ from ordinary cells in that their chromosomes are **not** in pairs, but are single. (This is because a **reduction** division occurred when the sex cells were formed, and the pairs of chromosomes split. In the male, one member of a chromosome pair goes into one sperm and the other goes into another. In the female, when the egg cell is formed, it receives one chromosome member and discards the other.)

Thus, because the sperm and egg each carry only half of each pair of chromosomes, when fertilization occurs and the sperm joins the egg, the full chromosome number is restored. This process is known as "recombination," and in every generation there is a **reduction** and a **recombination** of chromosomes.

Since the chromosomes contain **genes** that determine such characteristics as color, size, shape, etc., and since we never know exactly how the parents' genetic factors will recombine in new offspring, recombination is a potent force for change. Obviously, **God PLANNED for variety**, for the number of possible gene combinations is astronomical, since virtually everyone except identical twins has a gene combination different from any other individual that ever lived!

However, as the term itself implies, recombination of genes does not introduce anything **new** but only rearranges factors already present. Recombination cannot produce new basic types, because it consists merely of a new grouping, a different assortment, a reshuffling of genes already on hand.

As Dr. Burns explains in his book *The Science of Genetics: An Introduction to Heredity,* "Recombination . . . merely **redistributes** existing genetic material among different individuals; it **makes no CHANGE** in it."[50] It's clear, then, that this process has little to do with evolution.

HYBRIDIZATION, too, offers little hope to the evolutionist in his search for a mechanism of evolutionary change. For hybrids, as we know, are nearly always sterile. More importantly, it's obvious that hybridization is merely another form of recombination, with nothing present in the hybrid form that wasn't already present in one or both of the parents.

CHROMOSOME CHANGES, called **ploidy** (heteroploidy, polyploidy), result when the number of chromosomes is sometimes doubled or tripled, etc. But polyploidy, in the first place, hardly ever **exists** among *animals* and is quite rare even among plants. In the second place, it often produces feeble offspring with lowered viability and consequent loss of competitive power. Polyploids, therefore, when they

---

50. George W. Burns, *The Science of Genetics: An Introduction to Heredity* (New York: The Macmillan Company, 1969), p. 291.

do occur among plants, offer no promising material for progressive evolution. And finally, polyploidy does not add new kinds of genes to the plants, for the doubled chromosomes contain the same variety of genes as appeared in the race before the doubling or tripling. So this method has been rejected as a mechanism of evolution, because nothing new is added.

This brings us to **MUTATIONS**, a term coming from a Latin word meaning "to change." Mutations are due to actual changes in the genes themselves. It was Dutch botanist Hugo De Vries who, around 1901, first theorized that the evolutionary formation of species was due not to gradual changes but to sudden mutations. It's true that mutations offer more promise than Lamarckism (which is powerless to change the genes in the sex cells) and recombination (which cannot add anything new). Mutations are a very real occurrence in nature and are responsible for hornless cattle, seedless grapes, and navel oranges.

But some evolutionists think of mutation as an Aladdin's lamp that will create the changes needed to bridge the evolutionary gaps. Both Sir Julian Huxley and Dobzhansky of Columbia University say that mutation provides "the **raw material** of evolution."[51] And Ernst Mayr, Professor of Zoology at Harvard and a leading authority on the subject, agrees: "It must not be forgotten that mutation is the ultimate source of **ALL** genetic variation found in natural populations and the **ONLY** raw material available for natural selection to work on."[52]

The desperation of the evolutionists' search for a mechanism to produce evolution is shown by the fact that they've

51. Sir Julian Huxley, *Evolution in Action* (New York: Harper & Brothers, 1953), p. 38, and Theodosius Dobzhansky, *The Biological Basis of Human Freedom* (New York: Columbia University Press, 1956), p. 56.
52. Ernst Mayr, *Animal Species and Evolution* (Cambridge, Massachusetts: Harvard University Press, 1963), p. 176.

been forced to select mutation. They selected mutation **not** because it offered a **good** logical possibility but because those means which had seemed to offer really good possibilities had all been eliminated. One by one, it was shown that these could NOT have operated to produce evolution, because they added nothing new but just reshuffled those characteristics already present in the mechanism of heredity. Mutations may constitute the last best hope on earth for an evolutionary mechanism—but, unfortunately for evolutionists, **mutations pose more *problems* than possibilities.**

Most Mutations Are Very SMALL

The effect of any one mutation is now believed too small to have any significant evolutionary value. To quote Professor Mayr again (in a statement which practically contradicts his words quoted two paragraphs above): "We now believe that mutations do not guide evolution; the effect of a mutation is very often **far too small** to be visible."[53]

Evolutionists know that mutations with slight effects are much more common than those with marked effects, and they contend that mutations with NO visible effects are the most common of all (though there is some nonsense in this, for if we can't see a mutation or in some way detect it—how can anyone say it exists at all?!).

"After observing mutations in fruit flies for many years, Professor Goldschmidt fell into despair. The changes, he lamented, were **so hopelessly MICRO** that if a **thousand** mutations were **combined** in *one specimen*, there would still be no new species."[54] But Goldschmidt, the respected geneticist from the University of California, perhaps found the only way out for evolutionists. His unique solution? A *BIG*

---

53. *Ibid.*, p. 7.
54. Norman Macbeth, *Darwin Retried* (New York: Dell Publishing Company, 1971), p. 33.

mutation; one that didn't accumulate gradually; one that violated all the gene theories; one that would be fatal under normal circumstances. He named it "The Hopeful Monster." It would simply happen that something laid an egg—and something **else** got born![55]

But many even among evolutionists believe Goldschmidt is the one who laid the egg, since there's not a shred of evidence to support his "hopeful monster" hypothesis. As Dobzhansky puts it: "Systemic mutations [large mutations which transform one species **at once** into another] have \NEVER been observed, and it is **extremely improbable** that species are formed in **so abrupt** a manner."[56]

Mutations Are Very, Very RARE

Mutations are not only small but also exceedingly rare. The lucky combination of favorable mutations required to produce even a **fruit fly**, let alone a **man**, is so much rarer still that the odds against it would be expressed by a number containing as many *zeros* as there are *letters* in an average novel, "a number greater than that of **all the electrons and protons in the visible universe**," to quote Sir Julian Huxley.[57]

Huxley's statement is true because mutations are so rare that they simply **don't accumulate** in any organism. Even *single* mutations are rare. In *Science Today* evolutionist C. H. Waddington, Professor of Animal Genetics at Edinburgh University, says a mutation "happens RARELY, perhaps

---

55. Richard Goldschmidt, *The Material Basis of Evolution* (Paterson, New Jersey: Pageant Book, Inc., 1960), p. 390ff.

56. Theodosius Dobzhansky, *Genetics and the Origin of Species,* Second Edition (New York: Columbia University Press, 1941), p. 80.

57. Sir Julian Huxley, in Huxley, Hardy, and Ford, eds., *Evolution As a Process* (London: 1954), p. 5.

once in a million animals or once in a million lifetimes."[58] To say that mutations are few and far between is classic understatement!

Because mutations are so rare, scientists have used as a laboratory subject the common fruit fly. Thomas Hunt Morgan and his colleagues at Columbia University subjected the fruit fly *Drosophila melanogaster* ("black-bellied lover of dew") to genetic experiments for **more than one thousand generations**, since fruit flies can go through at least 26 generations in a year. Also, Professor Hermann J. Muller found that bombarding *Drosophila* with x-rays would increase the mutation rate one hundred and fifty times.

So they x-rayed the daylights out of those fruit flies— and did succeed in causing mutations. The eyes changed color, the wings changed this way and that, and the number of body bristles changed within certain limits. But the mutant flies that survived were *still* fruit flies. They never changed into a mosquito or anything else.

Since single mutations are so rare, multiple, simultaneous mutations are impossible. Professor George Gaylord Simpson, an ardent evolutionist, faces this fact: "Obviously," he concludes, "such a process [of multiple mutations] has played **no part whatever** in evolution." He explains that even under the most favorable circumstances, "The chances of multiple, simultaneous mutation seem to be . . . indeed negligible." He estimates that the probability of even five mutations in the same nucleus would be:

$$.000000000000000000001$$

(that's a decimal point with **21** zeros between it and the number **ONE**)! Simpson explains: "With an average effective breed-

---

58. *Science Today*, chapter entitled "EVOLUTION: The Appearance of Design in Living Things," by C. H. Waddington (New York: Criterion Books, First American edition, 1961), p. 36.

ing population of **100 million individuals** and an average length of generation of **one day**, again extremely favorable postulates, such an event [of five mutations in one organism] would be expected only *once* in about **274 BILLION YEARS**, or about a hundred times the probable age of the earth. Obviously, . . . such a process has played *no part whatever* in evolution." [59]

Mutations Are Usually HARMFUL and Sometimes LETHAL

It's a good thing that mutations are as rare as they are, for they're nearly always harmful. In the experiments with fruit flies, most of the mutations were lethal. Lethal changes may cause death at any stage of development from fertilized egg to adult.

Even Sir Julian Huxley admits: ". . . the great majority of mutant genes are *harmful* in their effects on the organism." [60] Dr. Ernst Mayr echoes his words: "It can hardly be questioned that most visible mutations are **deleterious**." [61] And Professor Hermann J. Müller, the geneticist who received the Nobel Prize in 1946 for his work with fruit flies, declared flatly: "In **MORE than 99 per cent** of cases the mutation of a gene produces some kind of *harmful* effect, some *disturbance* of function." [62]

----

59. George Gaylord Simpson, *The Major Features of Evolution* (New York: Columbia University Press, 1953), p. 96.

60. Sir Julian Huxley, *Evolution in Action* (New York: Harper & Brothers, 1953), p. 39.

61. Ernst Mayr, *Animal Species and Evolution* (Cambridge, Massachusetts: Harvard University Press, 1953), p. 174.

62. Hermann J. Müller, "Radiation and Human Mutation," *Scientific American* (November, 1955), p. 58.

Again, Müller stated: "Most mutations are **bad.** In fact, good ones are so rare that we can consider them **ALL** as bad."[63]

Gene mutations are most often caused by bombardment with *radiation* or by *chemical* agents. The atomic bombs that exploded over Japan in 1945 caused many mutations, resulting in damage, deformity, or death. That's why research workers take great precautions to protect themselves from radiation. Chemicals like the tranquilizer drug thalidomide also caused harmful mutations, producing horribly deformed babies, some without arms or legs. Chance mutations have also produced albino men and other albino animals, mental disorders, blood-clotting problems (hemophilia), and other harmful effects. Most mutants are simply considered monstrosities or freaks of nature: **two-headed** fish, **one-eyed** fish, and Siamese twins.

So a change in a gene is usually **a change for the worse.** Practically all mutations—like ACCIDENTS in the genetic machinery of living things—are **degenerative,** and when they're extensive, the organism is usually destroyed.

John J. Fried, in his book *The Mystery of Heredity*, speaks of the true character of mutations: "We have to face one particular FACT, one so peculiar that in the opinion of some people it **makes *nonsense* of the whole theory of evolution:** Although the biological theory calls for incorporating BENE-FICIAL variants in the living populations, a vast majority of mutants observed in any organism are DETRIMENTAL to its welfare."[64]

This paradox forces Dobzhansky to admit: "A majority of mutations, both those arising in laboratories and those stored in natural populations, produce DETERIORATIONS

---

63. Hermann J. Müller, in "Gloomy Nobelman," *Time* (November 11, 1946), p. 96.
64. John J. Fried, *The Mystery of Heredity* (New York: The John Day Company, 1971, p. 135.

of the viability, hereditary DISEASES, and MON-
STROSITIES. **Such changes, it would seem, can hardly
serve as evolutionary building blocks.**"[65]

And in his 1963 book *Progress and Decline* Professor
Hugh Miller speaks of "The relative RARITY of these . . .
mutant changes" and says their effect upon development
is *"more often than not LETHAL.* . . . The great importance currently attached to gene-mutations as a factor in
evolutionary history is in part the result of **erroneous
expectations** initially aroused by their discovery."[66] Thus
we can understand Professor Hooton of Harvard when he
confesses: "Now I am afraid that many anthropologists
(including myself) have **sinned against genetic science**
and are leaning upon **a broken reed** when they depend
upon mutations."[67]

Finally, it's well to remember that in all the thousands
of mutations studied, mutational change has **never** accomplished more than to produce a new **variety** of an organism
already in existence. No new basic types arose among the
mutants. Dr. Maurice Caullery was an honorary professor at
the Sorbonne in Paris when he observed that mutation, as a
mechanism of evolutionary change, fails miserably and totally, for: "Out of the 400 mutations that have been provided
by *Drosophila melanogaster*, there is NOT ONE that can be
called a new species. **It does *not* seem, therefore, that
the central problem of evolution can be solved by
mutations.**"[68]

-----

65. Theodosius Dobzhansky, *Genetics and the Origin of Species*, Third
Edition, Revised (New York: Columbia University Press, 1951), p. 73.

66. Hugh Miller, *Progress and Decline* (New York: 1963), p. 38.

67. Earnest Albert Hooton, *Apes, Men, and Morons* (Freeport, New
York: Books for Libraries Press, 1970), p. 118.

68. Maurice Caullery, *Genetics and Heredity* (New York: Walker
and Company, 1964), p. 119.

IV. NATURAL SELECTION, or
THE SURVIVAL OF THE FITTEST

Now we come to the heart of Darwin's theory. Natural selection was his *modus operandi*, his answer to **how** and **why** evolution takes place. Darwin even went so far as to entitle his book *On the Origin of Species BY MEANS OF Natural Selection.* "Without natural selection, Darwin declared, the theory of descent was unintelligible and unprovable." [69]

Darwin's idea here is based on the simple fact that living things produce more offspring than survive the struggle for life and that any favorable advantage individuals have over others will give them the best chance to survive and reproduce their kind. But this idea was not really original with Darwin. George Gaylord Simpson, a convinced evolutionist and perhaps the leading writer on the theory, admits that ". . . there is *practically nothing* in Darwin's theories that had not been expressed by others long before him." [70]

For example, Darwin titled his chapter on this subject: "Natural Selection; or **the Survival of the Fittest.**"   The second part of that title was borrowed from Herbert Spencer, who coined this phrase and published his ideas on biological evolution before the views of Darwin were known. And the title of another key chapter, "Struggle for Existence," Darwin borrowed from Thomas Malthus, after having read his *Essay on the Principle of Population.*

Malthus was an economist, not a biologist, who stated that life tends to increase faster than food, resulting in overpopulation and a struggle for existence.   Though Darwin

---

69. Gertrude Himmelfarb, *Darwin and the Darwinian Revolution* (Garden City, New York: Doubleday and Company, 1962), p. 312.

70. George Gaylord Simpson, *Life of the Past: An Introduction to Paleontology* (New Haven: Yale University Press, 1953), p. 142.

praised Malthus extravagantly, he should have recognized that there can be no distinction between life and food since *food IS living things* (or substances provided by living things) and that plants and small animals, serving as food for larger animals, reproduce faster than the large animals. Himmelfarb speaks of "the **basic fallacy** of Malthus . . . the **internal contradiction** in Malthus' theory which Darwin, like so many others, failed to recognize. . . . For if human beings tended to increase geometrically, so did animals and plants—and perhaps even more than geometrically, their natural rate of reproduction being, if anything, *higher* than that of man."[71]

The fact that this central idea in Darwin's theory was not original is not important **IF** natural selection still holds some **value** in helping science unlock the secrets of nature. Obviously Darwin thought it was a valuable idea, or he would not have made it basic to his theory. And some modern evolutionists like Julian Huxley still argue that natural selection is **the sole factor** in evolution: "The discovery of the principle of natural selection . . . has rendered all other explanations of evolution untenable. So far as we now know, not only is natural selection inevitable, not only is it **AN** effective agency of evolution, but it is **THE ONLY** effective agency of evolution."[72] Sir Gavin De Beer, eminent British zoologist, sides with Huxley: ". . . so **only** natural selection is left, and it is selection, **not** mutation, that controls evolution."[73]

---

71. Gertrude Himmelfarb, *Darwin and the Darwinian Revolution* (Garden City, New York: Doubleday and Company, 1962), p. 164. This is not the place to enter into an extended discussion of Malthus, but for a good critique, see Himmelfarb's article on Malthus in *Encounter*, V (1955), pp. 53-60.

72. Sir Julian Huxley, *Evolution in Action* (New York: Harper & Brothers, 1953), p. 36. The bold-faced words are emphasized by Huxley in the original.

73. Sir Gavin De Beer, *Charles Darwin: Evolution by Natural Selection* (Garden City, New York: Doubleday and Company, 1964), p. 192.

But their enthusiasm for natural selection is rare among evolutionists today. As confirmed evolutionist Sir James Gray, Professor of Zoology at Cambridge University, put it: "All biologists are not equally satisfied. . . . We have either to accept natural selection as the only available guide to the mechanism of evolution, and be prepared to admit that it involves a considerable element of **speculation**, or feel it in our bones that natural selection, operating on the random mutations, *leaves too much to chance.* . . . But, **your guess** is as good as mine."[74]

And Ernst Mayr, an eminent evolutionist, states: "Natural selection is **no longer** regarded as an all-or-none process but rather as a purely statistical concept."[75] Does evolutionary biologist Jean Rostand feel natural selection is an adequate explanation? "No, decidedly, I cannot make myself think that these 'slips' of heredity [mutations] have been able, **even with the cooperation of natural selection**, even with the advantage of the immense periods of time in which evolution works on life, to build the entire world. . . . I cannot persuade myself that the eye, the ear, the human brain have been formed in this way. . . . Should a person say he is convinced when he is not? For whatever my denial is worth, I cannot change it to assent."[76] And no less an evolutionist than George Gaylord Simpson says of natural selection that ". . . the theory is *quite unsubstantiated* and has status only as a *speculation.*"[77]

---

74. *Science Today*, chapter entitled "The Science of Life," by Sir James Gray (New York: Criterion Books, First American edition, 1961), pp. 29-30.

75. Ernst Mayr, *Animal Species and Evolution* (Cambridge, Massachusetts: Harvard University Press, 1963), p. 7.

76. Jean Rostand, *The Orion Book of Evolution* (New York: The Orion Press 1960), p. 79.

77. George Gaylord Simpson, *The Major Features of Evolution* (New York: Columbia University Press, 1953), pp. 118-119.

Finally, even Darwin himself, in a remarkable confession found in his second major book, *The Descent of Man*, explained that he formerly erred in giving too much prominence to natural selection: "*I now admit* . . . that in the earlier editions of my *Origin of Species* I probably **attributed TOO MUCH** to the action of natural selection or the survival of the fittest."[78]

WHY this startling reappraisal of the value of this crucial point? It's because *natural selection falls short in two ways.* As we shall now see, natural selection is both

(1) **powerless** as a **mechanism** for evolutionary change and (2) **meaningless** as a **statement** for scientific explanation.

What Natural Selection CANNOT Do

Himmelfarb reports that "A growing number of scientists . . . have come to question the **truth** and **adequacy** of natural selection. And these are neither religious nor philosophical malcontents. So unexceptional a devotee of science and scientific method as Bertrand Russell has said that 'the particular mechanism of "natural selection" is *no longer* regarded by biologists as *adequate.*'"[79]

The old war cry of "natural selection" has lost most of its popularity because all who have thought carefully on the subject know that mere selection cannot possibly **originate** anything. Selection—either by man OR nature—cannot create anything *new* but only make *more* of a certain type already existing. Natural selection **fails** as a causative agent because the mere sifting out of the fit by exterminating unfavored

---

78. Charles Darwin, *The Descent of Man*, First Edition (London: 1871), Volume I, p. 152.

79. Gertrude Himmelfarb, *Darwin and the Darwinian Revolution* (Garden City, New York: Doubleday and Company, 1962), p. 445. Her Bertrand Russell quotation is taken from Russell's *The Scientific Outlook* (London, 1931), pp. 43-44.

forms cannot initiate *new* variations. So as an originator of favorable variations, natural selection is **completely impotent** and never explains the **real origin** of anything at all. Someone has said that natural selection may explain the *survival* of the fittest, but it can never explain the *arrival* of the fittest!

"A Rose Is a Rose Is a Rose . . ."

Gertrude Stein's thought quoted above may be adequate as a poetic comment, but it's hardly illuminating as a scientific statement—and neither is the evolutionary idea of natural selection. The reason is that natural selection or the survival of the fittest is a *tautology* (needless repetition of a single idea, as if more than one idea were being expressed). For example, it doesn't explain much to say, "Your deafness is caused by the impairment of your hearing." The statement is a meaningless tautology.

Dr. Norman Macbeth, a Harvard-trained lawyer who wrote a devastating indictment of evolution and evolutionistic thinking in his penetrating book, *Darwin Retried*, focuses on this inherent weakness, this inability of the theory to explain the HOW of evolution. He points out that some species have multiplied while others have remained stable and still others have dwindled or died out. This obvious fact is conceded by all and needs no further demonstration. The problem is *to explain* **why** and **how** this happens. "Thus we have as **Question:** *Why* do some multiply, while others remain stable, dwindle, or die out? To which is offered as **Answer:** *Because* some multiply, while others remain stable, dwindle, or die out. The two sides of the equation are the same. We have a tautology. The definition is meaningless." [80]

---

80. Norman Macbeth, *Darwin Retried* (New York: Dell Publishing Company, 1971), p. 47.

For instance, Professor Simpson says, "I . . . define *selection*, a technical term in evolutionary studies, as **anything tending to produce systematic, heritable CHANGE in population between one generation and the next.**"[81] And Macbeth asks, "But is such a broad definition of any use? We are trying to explain what produces change. Simpson's explanation is natural selection, which he **defines** as what produces change. Both sides of the equation are again the same; again we have a tautology. . . . If selection is anything tending to produce change, he is merely saying that **change is caused by what causes change.** . . . The net explanation is nil."[82]

When evolutionists are asked how we determine who are the fittest, they inform us that we determine this by *the test of survival*—there is no other criterion. But this means that a species **survives** because it is the **fittest** and is the **fittest** because it **survives**, which is CIRCULAR REASONING and is equivalent to saying that whatever IS, is FIT. Nothing has been explained; it's a meaningless tautology.

Surprisingly enough, some leading evolutionists like C. H. Waddington *recognize* this shortcoming and **still do not object to it!** He said: "Natural selection, which was at first considered as though it were a hypothesis in need of experimental or observational confirmation, turns out on closer inspection to be a tautology. . . . It states that the fittest individuals in a population (**defined** as those which leave most offspring) **will** leave most offspring. . . . This fact in no way reduces the magnitude of Darwin's achievement . . . biologists realize the enormous power of the principle as a weapon of EXPLANATION"!![83]

---

81. George Gaylord Simpson, *The Major Features of Evolution* (New York: Columbia University Press, 1953, p. 138.

82. Norman Macbeth, *Darwin Retried* (New York: Dell Publishing Company 1971), p. 49.

Others like J. B. S. Haldane minimize the problem by saying, ". . . the phrase, 'survival of the fittest,' IS something of a tautology. . . . There is no harm in stating the same truth in two different ways."[84]   But Macbeth says, "This is extremely misleading. There is no harm in stating the same truth in two different ways, if one shows what one is doing by connecting the two statements with a phrase such as *in other words*. But if one connects them with *because*, which is the earmark of the tautology, one deceives either the reader or oneself or both; and there **is** ample harm in this. The simplest case, where one is informed that a cat is black because it is black, may be harmless, though irritating and useless; but the actual cases are always harder to detect than this, and may darken counsel for a long time."[85]

Decades ago Professor E. W. MacBride, in the leading English scientific journal *Nature*, declared: "Of one thing, however, I am certain, and that is that 'natural selection' affords **no explanation** of mimicry or of any other form of evolution. It means nothing more than 'the survivors survive.' *Why* do certain individuals survive? Because they are the fittest. *How do we know* they are the fittest? Because they survive."[86]

It's noteworthy that many of the world's leading scientific minds can find only this amount of real thought in that slogan which for so long was hailed by millions as the very essence of scientific wisdom!

---

83. C. H. Waddington, "Evolutionary Adaptation," in Sol Tax, editor, *The Evolution of Life*, Volume 1 of *Evolution After Darwin* (Chicago: The University of Chicago Press, 1960), p. 385.

84. J. B. S. Haldane, "Darwinism Under Revision," *Rationalist Annual* (1935), p. 24.

85. Norman Macbeth, *Darwin Retried* (New York: Dell Publishing Company, 1971), p. 63.

86. E. W. MacBride, *Nature* (May 11, 1929), p. 713.

V. CLASSIFICATION & COMPARATIVE ANATOMY

The arguments for organic evolution from classification and comparative anatomy are so intimately connected that they can best be considered together. The argument from classification is short and easily stated. It's that the modern system of naming and classifying plants and animals, besides being a convenient system, also shows their true blood relationship to one another.

But today's system of classification has largely been **made by** evolutionists for the purpose of illustrating the supposed evolutionary heritage of living things (that's like cutting the *pattern* to fit the *cloth!*). This is admitted by Sir Julian Huxley himself.[87] Thus classification is **not an independent witness** for evolution. It has been **in collusion** with the defendant and has been **coached** to testify. Even so, its evidence can still be interpreted much more reasonably **in favor of** creation and **against** evolution, as we'll see.

The field of classification is also called "taxonomy" or "systematics." Notice what Earnest Albert Hooton, evolutionary anthropologist at Harvard for more than forty years, says about it: "The business of taxonomy, or zoological classification (pigeon-holing), works well enough for coarse categories, such as classes . . . orders . . . and families. Like big business in the commercial world, it **masquerades** under a guise of efficiency and accuracy which proves to be illusive under closer examination. Formerly I was under the impression that **taxonomic indiscretions** were peculiar to anthropologists, but now I am convinced that **a zoological classificationist may be as dissolute and irresponsible as a lightning-rod salesman.** Further, the more I inspect *the family trees* of man, so facilely constructed by students

---

87. Sir Julian Huxley, *Evolution: The Modern Synthesis* (New York: Harper & Brothers, 1943), p. 391.

of human paleontology, including myself, the more I am inclined to agree with the poet that 'only God can make a tree.'" [88]

Professor Hooton is justified in his indictment of taxonomists because classification is so highly subjective. It's often true that **subjective opinion**, not **objective fact**, is what chiefly decides the degree of supposed evolutionary relationship. The pigeon-holes used by classifiers are often a matter of opinion. E. W. MacBride, of London University, deplores "**to what an enormous extent** the PERSONAL EQUATION enters in the determination of these questions."[89]

And Paul Weatherwax, Professor of Botany at Indiana University, says: "Botanists still **disagree widely** on the **proper grouping** of many plants, but this is because **they do not agree** in their theories as to the ORIGIN of the differences which separate the groups."[90]

We've already seen how taxonomists have found great difficulty in defining a basic, crucial term like "species." This difficulty is by no means imaginary. As Dr. Ernst Mayr says: "It may not be exaggeration if I say that there are probably as many species concepts as there are thinking systematists and students of speciation."[91] Sir Julian Huxley concurs: "Even competent systematists do not always agree as to the delimitation of species."[92] In other words, by no means do all biologists speak the same language when they use the word *species.*

88.   Earnest Albert Hooton, *Apes, Men, and Morons* (Freeport, New York: Books for Libraries Press, 1970), pp. 115-116.

89.   E. W. MacBride, *Cambridge Natural History*, Volume 1, p. 460.

90.   Paul Weatherwax, *Plant Biology* (Philadelphia: W. B. Saunders, Second Edition, 1947), p. 257.

91.   Ernst Mayr, *Systematics and the Origin of Species* (New York: Columbia University Press, 1942), p. 115.

92.   Sir Julian Huxley, *Evolution: The Modern Synthesis* (New York: Harper & Brothers, 1943), p. 157.

Another dispute in the ranks of taxonomists is between the "splitters" and the "lumpers." The "splitters" like to elevate mere varieties into new, full-fledged species and therefore **divide** one species into several. The "lumpers," on the other hand, prefer large species and tend to **combine** several old species into a larger one. This may seem like a joke to the uninitiated, but Sir Julian solemnly informs us that "the battle of the 'splitters' and the 'lumpers' still continues."[93] Thus we see that classification (which sounds grandly awesome with its Latin names and seems quite "scientific" to the average person) is simply man-made and often rests at bottom on *mere opinion.*

Speaking of the **chaos** that exists in primate taxonomy, Harvard paleontologist and taxonomist George Gaylord Simpson declares: "A major reason for this **confusion** is that much of the work on primates [the highest order of animals, including man, apes, monkeys, etc.] has been done by students who had *no experience* in taxonomy and who were *completely incompetent* to enter this field, however competent they may have been in other respects."[94] No wonder, then, that specimens which one investigator groups as a "family" may, in the opinion of another, deserve no more than "genus" rank!

So at best, the system of classification is man-made and may or may not have any real meaning in itself. Assuming that it does show some real relationship, the relationship may well be that of a **common Designer** instead of a **common ancestor.** Does resemblance among CARS like Mustang II, Thunderbird, and Lincoln show that they "evolved" from the Galaxie—or simply that they were all designed and built by Ford Motor Company? Likewise, a **fish** and a **submarine**

---

93. *Ibid.,* p. 402.

94. George Gaylord Simpson, "The Principles of Classification and a Classification of Mammals," *Bulletin of the American Museum of Natural History,* Volume 85 (1945), p. 181.

have roughly similar shapes, but no one says they must be blood brothers. Similarity may imply not common **relationship** but only a common **design.**

Professor W. R. Thompson, in his Foreward to the Centennial Edition of Darwin's *Origin of Species,* warned fellow evolutionists against assuming an evolutionary relationship in the classification of living things. He makes plain that **not all** things that can be classified have a parent-child relationship: "The arrangement of the **chemical elements** . . . is a true classification and so is the arrangement of **geometric forms;** yet no genealogical considerations are involved. . . . If we wish to erect a *genealogical* classification . . . we must discover through what forms the existing organisms have *actually descended.* IF these historical facts **cannot** be ascertained, then **it is useless to seek for substitutes,** and from the fact that a *classification IS possible* we certainly cannot infer that it is genealogical and is in any sense a proof of evolution."[95]

As a matter of fact, the very **possibility** of a classification is *strong evidence AGAINST evolution.* For example, organisms are neatly categorized in terms of species, genus, family, order, class, phylum, and kingdom. But the ease with which we can "pigeon-hole" basic kinds—with clear-cut gaps between—does NOT indicate an evolutionary relationship. Just the OPPOSITE is indicated, for if all organisms arose by slow descent from a common ancestor, there should be a **continuous blending** from one kind into another. It should be **impossible** to tell where one species stops and another begins, so that any system of classification would be quite impossible.

---

95. W. R. Thompson, "Introduction" to *The Origin of Species* by Charles Darwin (New York: E. P. Dutton & Company, Everyman's Library, 1956). This quote is from the reprint of Thompson's Introduction in the *Journal of the American Scientific Affiliation,* Volume 12 (March, 1960), p. 146.

Yet Dr. Goldschmidt says: "It is not difficult to show that between them [species] exist the '**bridgeless gaps**' which we are discussing."[96] Because this is true, very little experience is needed to distinguish a birch from a beech tree, a flying squirrel from a bat, or humans from chimpanzees. Scientists should use our classification system merely as a convenient device to avoid confusion in naming plants and animals and should cease to maintain that it provides a picture of evolutionary heritage.

Now let's look at *COMPARATIVE ANATOMY*, also called **morphology.** Here's what evolutionists say about it: "Morphology deals with the FORM and STRUCTURE of organisms, and **it affords some of the strongest evidence of organic evolution.**"[97] If *this* evidence constitutes "some of the strongest" that evolutionists can find, it's unfortunate for the theory because here again the so-called "evidence" rests on subjective opinion, not objective fact.

Of course, anyone who compares anatomical structures is impressed with certain similarities among various creatures. For instance, the forelimbs of all limbed vertebrates have the same three bones—humerus, radius, and ulna. Many also have what are called pentadactyl limbs—that is, limbs with **five** fingers and toes. Those are the FACTS, but what do they MEAN? Well, **here the evidence ends and speculation begins.** Evolutionists begin at this point and speculate that such agreement in bones can mean only descent from a common ancestor. The creationist believes that such similarities actually result from the fact that **creation is based on the master plan of the Master Planner.** Where *similar functions* were required, God used *similar structures*, merely

96. Richard Goldschmidt, *The Material Basis of Evolution* (Paterson, New Jersey: Pageant Books, Inc., 1960), p. 145.
97. Nathan Fasten, *Introduction to General Zoology* (Boston: Ginn and Company, 1941), p. 640.

modifying these structures to meet the individual requirements of each organism.

Always remember that *the FACTS of SCIENCE* are one
thing, but *the CONCLUSIONS of SCIENTISTS* may be quite
another. There's a difference between **observing** certain facts
and **drawing conclusions** from those facts. Darwin saw the
similarities and jumped to the conclusion of evolution.
But similarity of form cannot in any way prove **ORIGIN**.
One can show similarities of form all day long and not even
approach the question of origin. Such similarities by themselves prove **nothing** about origins—yet the question of origin
is what it's all about, isn't it? You see, the fact that certain
plants and animals resemble each other does not supply the
information that evolutionists so earnestly seek, which is
where the plants and animals **came from.** By arranging his
books on a shelf in a graded system (depending on their size
or complexity), a student could just as well prove their "evolution." You can see the absurdity of such an argument, for
it **assumes** the very thing which needs to be **proved.**

This "evidence" is largely **circumstantial** and therefore
quite unsatisfactory. None of us would wish to be sentenced
to life imprisonment or the gas chamber on nothing but circumstantial evidence. The fact that we were in a house at the
time a murder was committed in it would not prove we had
any part in the murder. And the argument for evolution in
this case rests on the same kind of unsatisfactory evidence.
Far from providing "clear proof" of evolution, the common
patterns of design point just as well to common origin from
the one Architect or Designer.

Genesis informs us that God created **all** the original types
of life, from the simple forms to those more complex. But
in making more complex forms, WHY shouldn't He employ certain rules of structure for all of them—for example,
a **backbone** for a whole category of animals? If the backbone is good for one, why is it not good for another? It's

nonsense to suppose that because the Creator had **once** used a good plan, He must **never again** utilize it in creating other animals with this plan only slightly modified. Must every kind of creature be *so completely different* from all others that we can detect *no* resemblance between any two? Inevitably, then, as we survey the wonderful variety of living things, we'll find similarities.

But it's amazing that evolutionists seem unable to give proper weight to the **dissimilarities** between man and animals. We read that "The comparative anatomist finds that physically man is bone for bone, muscle for muscle, nerve for nerve, in striking agreement with the higher apes."[98] But what about the **differences**? Though evolutionists may try to minimize the fact, there are vast differences between man and even the "highest" animal forms.

For instance, man differs from the apes in his efficiency as *a ground-dwelling* **biped** whereas the ape is basically *a tree-dwelling* **quadruped.** Only man walks upright on two feet. Apes are called "knuckle-walkers" because, contrary to popular belief, they seldom walk on their hind legs and usually move about on all fours. Except for a few birds like the ostrich, man is the only creature that moves exclusively on two feet.

Man has a *nose* with a prominent bridge and elongated tip, while the apes' nose lacks both of these. Man has *red lips* formed by an extension of the mucous membrane from inside his mouth, whereas apes don't have lips of this nature. The skull in man is *perfectly balanced* on the upper end of the spinal column, but the curvature of the spinal column in apes is convex (humped) toward the back. The *arms* of man are shorter than his legs, yet all apes have elongated forelimbs. The human *foot* is constructed for walking and running, having

---

98. M. F. Guyer, *Animal Biology*, Third Edition (New York: Harper & Brothers, 1941), p. 517.

a well-formed arch and the big toe in line with the others. All four feet in apes are hand-like with an opposable "thumb" which may grasp objects. Other differences along this line could be mentioned, such as features of man's *skin* and the sparsity and distribution of his *hair*. But perhaps we should turn to man's great power of *intellect*. It's this tremendous difference between animal brain and human mind that lifts man above any classification with the beasts. *Only man is teachable*; you can *train* an animal such as an ape, but you cannot teach him to exercise independent judgment as human beings can. At times animals may draw simple inferences, but even apes and monkeys possess little or no capacity for abstract thought or conceptual reasoning. A monkey can look at the starry heavens, but only man can ponder their meaning.

The proportional size of the *brain* compared to the body is unquestionably an indicator of intelligence. When comparable body weight is considered, the **gulf** between man's brain size and that of the anthropoid apes is **enormous**. Think of man's capacity for *articulate speech*—far beyond the whines and growls of the brute creation. And man alone can also use *written language,* as you now prove by perusing these black marks on white paper! Man designs, constructs, and uses complex *tools and machines* of which animals know nothing. Only man can appreciate truth, beauty, and moral values. Only man is *self-conscious* and possessed of the ability to understand the *difference* between right and wrong. Human beings are the only creatures who *weep* as an emotional response.

Many other characteristics might be considered, such as man's *spiritual* nature and elements of man's *culture*, which are never exhibited in the animal world. But we can't explain man's mental machinery simply in terms of physics and chemistry. The science of biology misses the point if it feels anatomy alone constitutes the creature. It becomes a science of dead remains if it feels man can be explained on the basis of his dissected body.

No, man did not evolve by slow degrees from lower forms of animal or vegetable life but came into being as a son of God, formed by the Creator in His own image. To some extent Darwin acknowledged man's noble qualities, but his closing words in *The Descent of Man* are: "Man still bears in his bodily frame the indelible stamp of **his lowly origin**." We may with greater truth reply: Man's inner being, his **mind**, gives unmistakable proof that his origin was a high and noble one.

VI. VESTIGIAL ORGANS

Thus the arguments offered for evolution by classification and comparative anatomy are greatly weakened by subjective whim and wishful thinking. Closely related to comparative anatomy is the subject of VESTIGIAL ORGANS, which evolutionists say are the last vestiges of organs that once had a use but are no longer needed because of man's advance up the evolutionary ladder. Believers in evolution often cite these as "sufficient to show that the human body cannot be considered as a perfect final work of **creation** but rather the ultimate product of eons of evolutionary change, resulting in a very imperfect being from the physical point of view—a veritable **museum** of antiquities!"[99]

But the supposed presence of so-called "vestigial" organs in man gives less and less proof for evolution as time goes by, for our list of "useless" organs **decreases** as our knowledge of anatomy and physiology **increases**. Evolutionists at one time listed about 180 organs in the human body considered "useless relics of the past" that were useful in *man's animal*

---

99. Richard Swann Lull, *Organic Evolution*, Revised Edition (New York: The Macmillan Company, 1945), p. 669.

ancestors. With increasing knowledge, however, this list has steadily **shrunk** till the number has been reduced to practically zero.

For instance, this list once included such organs or structures as the appendix, the adrenal glands, the tonsils, the coccyx (the lower end of man's spinal column), the thymus gland, and others all said to be vestigial—so much "excess baggage" we carry around. But note what a report in the November 1966 *Reader's Digest,* entitled "The 'Useless' Gland That Guards Our Health," states:

> For at least 2000 years, doctors have puzzled over the function of . . . the thymus gland. . . . Modern physicians came to regard it, like the appendix, as a useless, vestigial organ which had lost its original purpose, if indeed it ever had one. In the last few years, however, . . . men have proved that, **far from being useless,** the thymus is really the master gland that regulates the intricate immunity system which protects us against infectious diseases. . . . Recent experiments have led researchers to believe that the appendix, tonsils and adenoids may also figure in the antibody responses.[100]

The *Encyclopedia Britannica* also declared: "Many of the **so-called** vestigial organs are **now known** to fulfill important functions."[101]

The coccyx (composed of several terminal vertebrae) is often cited as a functionless remnant of a tail in man, but it serves as the **anchor** for important muscles of elimination

---

100. "The 'Useless' Gland That Guards Our Health," *Reader's Digest* (November, 1966), pp. 229, 235.
101. *Encyclopedia Britannica* (1946 edition), Volume 8, p. 926.

(its removal would interfere with defecation). It also helps support the pelvic cavity, furnishes a surface for attachment of a portion of the large gluteal muscle which extends and rotates the thigh, and encloses the terminal portion of the spinal cord. Furthermore, one cannot **sit** comfortably following removal of the coccyx.

The appendix is possibly the only organ still on the vesti gial list, but scientists are no longer so sure. Professor William Straus states that "there is **no longer any justification** for regarding the vermiform appendix as a vestigial structure."[102] It should be noted that the **higher** apes (gorilla, chimpanzee, etc.) possess an appendix, whereas their immediate relatives, the **lower** apes, do not; but it appears again among the still lower mammals such as the opossum. How does the evolutionist account for this?

Furthermore, the absurdity of calling the appendix "vestigial" in man is apparent from this fact: that its function is unknown **not only** in man but also in **every other** species of animal that possess it. **Tonsils** were once almost routinely removed, but removal of the tonsils and appendix is now believed to increase susceptibility to Hodgkin's disease.[103] Finally, these so-called vestigial organs prove nothing in favor of evolution, for EVEN IF man's appendix had a clear and obvious function, even if he possessed fully functional wisdom teeth, etc., he would **still** be a **MAN** and would **not** thereby become a new basic type of animal.

The atrophied optic stalk of blind cave fish may be considered by some to be vestigial, but it certainly offers no help to Darwin's theory, because **a fish is a fish whether blind or sighted**. And the whole suggestion of vestigial structures possessing **any** evolutionary significance is open to serious question when we realize that they're **entirely absent** from

---

102. William Straus, *Quarterly Review of Biology*, 1947, p. 149.
103. See *Science News*, March 20, 1971.

PLANTS. *IF* plants evolved from simpler forms, why don't they display the same sort of *vestigial FORGET-ME-NOTS* that animals are supposed to show?

Remember that even if an organ could be identified as a useless vestige of a once-useful organ, this would constitute evidence **not** of evolution, but of deterioration, and would thus prove the wrong thing. Truly vestigial organs fit better into a pattern of *regressive* change and DEGENERATION than of *progressive* change and IMPROVEMENT. What evolution needs is rudimentary or nascent organs in various stages of *development,* on their way toward the fully-formed state. But the entire **lack** of such hopeful structures pointing toward new organs must be disappointing to even the most avid evolutionists.

The absence of developing, rudimentary organs poses such a problem for evolutionists that they seldom mention it. Darwin admitted: "If it could be demonstrated that any **complex** organ existed, which could **not possibly** have been formed by numerous, successive, slight modifications, **my theory would absolutely break down.**"[104] And he was right, of course; Darwin's theory does break down on this very point. Take as an example some organ such as **the EYE.** The eye is an enormously complex mechanism and poses a tremendous challenge to evolutionary theory. Darwin himself said: "To suppose that the **eye,** with all its inimitable contrivances for adjusting the focus to different distances, for admitting different amounts of light, and for the correction of spherical and chromatic aberration, could have been formed by natural selection, seems, I freely confess, **absurd** in the highest degree."[105]

104. Charles Darwin, *On the Origin of Species: A Facsimile of the First Edition* (Cambridge, Massachusetts: Harvard University Press, 1964), p. 189.

105. *Ibid.,* p. 186.

And other evolutionary scientists agree with him. Professor Ernst Mayr says: "It must be admitted, however, that it is **a considerable strain on one's credulity** to assume that finely balanced systems such as certain sense organs (the **eye** of vertebrates . . .) could be improved by random mutations."[106] George Gaylord Simpson of Harvard is forced to the same conclusion: "Evolution in the mutationist world is **not merely AIMLESS but DIRECTIONLESS.** The origin of such an organ as an eye, for example, entirely at random seems almost *infinitely improbable.*"[107]

That's the reason why, in a letter to American botanist Asa Gray dated April 3, 1860, Darwin said: "I remember well the time when the thought of the **eye** made me cold all over."[108] But obviously he wasn't the only evolutionist who shudders at the thought. Dr. Garrett Hardin, Professor of Biology at the University of California at Berkeley, asks: "How then are we to account for the evolution of such a **complicated** organ as the eye? . . . If even the slightest thing is wrong—if the *retina* is missing, or the *lens* opaque, or the *dimensions* in error— the eye fails to form a recognizable image and is consequently useless. **Since it must be either perfect, or perfectly useless,** HOW could it have evolved by **small,** successive, Darwinian steps?"[109]

Hardin must have been burdened by the magnitude of the problem, for he returns to it later in his book, saying: ". . . **That damned eye**—the human eye . . . which Darwin

106. Ernst Mayr, *Systematics and the Origin of Species* (New York: Columbia University Press, 1942), p. 296.

107. George Gaylord Simpson, *This View of Life* (New York: Harcourt, Brace & World, 1964), p. 18.

108. Letter from Darwin to Asa Gray, April 3, 1860, in *The Life and Letters of Charles Darwin,* edited by his son Francis Darwin (New York: D. Appleton and Company, 1896 [Reprinted 1972]), Volume II, p. 90.

109. Garrett Hardin, *Nature and Man's Fate* (New York: Mentor Books, 1961), p. 71.

freely conceded to constitute a severe strain on his theory of evolution. Is so simple a principle as natural selection equal to explaining so complex a structure as the image-producing eye? Can *the step-by-step process* of Darwinian evolution carry adaptation so far? **Competent opinion has wavered on this point.**"[110]

These evolutionary scientists are so candid because they have no choice. How could an eyeless creature begin a million-year project of forming an eye that would be *of no use until* the million years were over? Why would this rudimentary organ be **retained** before it would work? (For it must be complete or it won't function, and partially-formed, *non*-functioning organs would be a disadvantage and be eliminated by natural selection.) Could an organ **on-its-way-to-becoming-an-eye** give any advantage in the struggle for survival? And if it *would* give some advantage, **why are there not now MANY of these developing organs?**

So the old argument of vestigial organs has no demonstrative value. On the contrary, that argument **itself** requires demonstration.

*** *** ***

---

110. *Ibid.*, p. 224.

Our discussion of evolution will be concluded in **PART II**,
which follows. There we'll consider such matters as
the origin of LIFE,
the origin of SEX,
ENTROPY,
the FOSSIL record,
EARLY MAN,
and other vital issues.

Chapter 4

The THEORY of EVOLUTION: Weighed and Found Wanting Part II.

VII. THE ORIGIN OF LIFE

Another important fact challenges the evolutionist: his failure to offer any satisfactory explanation for the origin of LIFE. People wonder, **Where did we come from?** The birth process cannot account for us. For all the human body does is **transmit** life it did **not produce!** To say that life comes only from existing life is to state a fact of science as firmly established as the Law of Gravitation.

Until the 1860's, many men believed the theory of "spontaneous generation"—that is, that life (particularly lower forms of life) can arise or be generated spontaneously (from characteristics within the substance itself, as in spontaneous combustion). Perhaps no view has ever seemed more self-evident, more safely beyond debate. After all, didn't worms spring from mud, and maggots from spoiled meat? If one left rags in the corner, mice would appear. Frogs were created spontaneously in pond water. And wheat would generate rats. Even Sir Francis Bacon (1561-1626) believed that insects were "creatures bred from putrefaction," lice were "bred by sweat close kept," and fleas "principally of straw and mats, where there hath been little moisture."[1]

Then came the great scientist Louis Pasteur, who with a series of brilliant experiments concluded in 1864 disproved once and for all the idea of spontaneous generation. Pasteur's experiments, which involved a procedure of sterilization, showed that any substance kept free from infection or contamination would never allow the anticipated creatures (such as maggots from decaying meat) to develop. Pasteur was a convinced creationist, and from his day to the present moment virtually no educated person has given credence to the idea of spontaneous generation.

But the spontaneous generation of life is **the first LINK in the CHAIN** of evolution. Obviously, if that link cannot be forged, the whole evolutionary theory is hopelessly weakened. *There must be LIFE before there can be DIVERSITY of life.* So it's quite necessary for the evolutionist to insist on some form of spontaneous generation, as that's the only way life can be accounted for apart from a Creator.

Note the way Dr. George Wald, Professor of Biology at Harvard, puts it in an article in the *Scientific American.* He first traces the history of the collapse of the old idea of spontaneous generation as a result of Pasteur's experiments, then adds immediately: "We tell this story [of Pasteur's work] to beginning students of biology as though it represents a triumph of reason over mysticism. In fact it is very nearly the opposite. The reasonable view was to believe in spontaneous generation; the only alternative, to believe in a single, primary act of supernatural creation. **There is no third position.** For this reason many scientists a century ago chose to regard the belief in spontaneous generation as a 'philosophical necessity.' It is a symptom of the philosophical poverty of our time that

1. Sir Francis Bacon, quoted in Ernest E. Stanford, *Man and the Living World*, Second Edition (New York: The Macmillan Company, 1940), p. 34.

this necessity is no longer appreciated. Most modern biologists, having reviewed with satisfaction the **downfall** of the spontaneous generation hypothesis, yet unwilling to accept the alternative belief in special creation, are left with nothing."[2]

An Exhibit in Blind Faith

Dr. Wald goes on to show how infinitely impossible would be the chance combination of proper elements to produce life, but draws this remarkable conclusion: "One has only to contemplate the **magnitude** of this task to concede that *the spontaneous generation of a living organism is IMPOSSIBLE. Yet here we are—as a result, I believe, of spontaneous generation.*"[3]

Professor Wald may be admired for his refreshing frankness but pitied for his slavish adherence to a theory. How much "science" is involved in believing something totally disproved by all scientific experiments? Wald and those who agree with him hold this position *not* because of any scientific evidence for spontaneous generation, but because of their preconceived ideas, personal prejudice, or disbelief in God.

Some evolutionists try to dodge the issue by saying that life must have originated on earth by coming from another world, perhaps via a meteorite or similar object. But this answer is neither scientific nor satisfactory. It's not *scientific* because we know of no natural way in which protoplasm could bridge the deadly celestial gap. If the **cold** temperatures and **absence of oxygen** in interstellar space did not destroy it, the **heat** generated by the vehicle (meteors become **incandescent** through friction as they strike our atmosphere) would most certainly kill it. And it's not a *satisfactory* answer, for even if we grant that life could have been brought here from another

2. George Wald, "The Origin of Life," *Scientific American*, Volume 191, No. 2 (August, 1954), p. 46.
3. *Ibid.*

planet, we haven't solved the problem of the origin of life; we've simply **transferred** the problem to another world. Though the problem is **moved** a great distance away, it nevertheless is still **entirely unsolved!**

It's also certain that IF one little speck of protoplasm **were** started alone in the world—from *whatever* source—**it would live only long enough to STARVE to death.** For there must be a *balance of life*, a *web* of life, to enable any living things to maintain their existence. That's why God created ALL living things, plants and animals as well as man, during a few days of creation week. (See Chapter 6, "How Long Were the Days of Creation?" for more information on this point.)

You can see that the problem is not an easy one to solve within the framework of atheistic evolution. I appreciate the honesty of evolutionist John Tyler Bonner, Professor of Biology at Princeton University, when he admits in his book *The Ideas of Biology*: "The study of early evolution really amounts to **EDUCATED GUESSWORK.**"[4]

Of course, cherished ideas and pet theories die hard, so scientists sometimes try to create life in the laboratory. You may have read some press release purporting to announce the "creation of life in a test tube." Careful reading reveals that such claims are exaggerated and misleading. Most reports the average person encounters are mere rumors or hearsay. The next time an evolution enthusiast tells you he's "sure that science has produced life in the laboratory," ask him the **name** of the wonder-worker. He won't be able to tell you, despite the fact that the man who creates LIFE would automatically become much more famous than Thomas Edison or Jonas Salk.

It's interesting that A. R. Moore found that if the plasmodium of slime mold is allowed to **flow** through a sieve, even a very fine one, it will accomplish the feat **unharmed.** How-

4. John Tyler Bonner, *The Ideas of Biology* (New York: Harper & Brothers, 1962), p. 18.

ever, if **forced** through even a moderately fine sieve, it will be found on the other side apparently unchanged physically and chemically, but **dead**.[5] The individual who can explain the results of this simple experiment will be able to explain the difference between living and nonliving systems.

But until man is able to take the dead slime mold, which was alive only a moment before and which seemingly has all its chemical elements and substances present, and make it alive again, he stands no chance whatever of synthesizing living protoplasm by mingling substances from the bottles in his laboratory.

Where Is the "Simple" Cell?

Discovery of the world of *viruses* has led some evolutionists to speculate that perhaps here are entities resembling primitive life or pre-life—a link, a step between lifeless chemicals and the simplest cells. Viruses are extremely small, much smaller than true cells. It's been calculated that a **single** average-sized human cell could hold **more than 60 MILLION** polio viruses![6]

But our knowledge of the virus eliminates it as a candidate for the first life. Though it's simpler than the simplest cell, the virus presents too many problems. In the first place, its only "food" is living cells. This fact alone is sufficient to disqualify it from being the first life. Also, because viruses cannot function and reproduce apart from living cells or cell substance, may virologists feel that they are **not actually living bodies**, but only agents that modify the activities of living cells which they infect or parasitize. Viruses don't have the basic components to carry on life processes independently.

----

5. A. R. Moore, "On the Cytoplasmic Framework of the Plasmodium," *Science Reports*, Tohoku Imperial University, Japan, 4th series, Volume 8 (December, 1933), pp. 189-191.

6. John Pfeiffer and the Editors of Time-Life Books, *The Cell* (New York: Time-Life Books, 1972), p. 171.

Most believers in evolution now agree that the **single cell** rather than the virus must have been the first life from which other forms evolved. But the time is long gone when scientists viewed the living cell as a mere "blob" of jellylike protoplasm. Scientists are just beginning to understand how fantastically complex the so-called "simple" cell is. Each year produces newly-discovered complications of which Darwin knew nothing. Even George Wald, whose credulous faith in spontaneous generation we noted above, admits: "The most complex machine man has devised—say an electronic brain—is **child's play** compared with the simplest of living organisms. The especially trying thing is that complexity here involves such small dimensions. It is on the *molecular* level; it consists of a detailed fitting of molecule to molecule such as no chemist can attempt."[7]

Consider this evaluation made in 1971 by Garret Vanderkooi, Professor at the University of Wisconsin. Vanderkooi is a scientist who studies **enzymes**, the chemical "workmen" in body cells so vital for life. He says: "In the past, evolutionists were confident that the problem of the origin of life would be solved by the new science of biochemistry. To their dismay, the **converse** has occurred. The more that is learned about the chemical structure and organization of living matter, the more difficult it becomes **even to speculate** on how it could have developed from lower forms by natural processes." In fact, "from the scientific point of view, evolution may have been a plausible hypothesis in Darwin's day, but it has now become untenable, as a result of fairly recent developments in molecular biology," Vanderkooi states.[8]

---

7. George Wald, "The Origin of Life," *Scientific American*, Volume 191, No. 2 (August, 1954), p. 46.

8. Garret Vanderkooi, "Evolution as a Scientific Theory," *Christianity Today* (May 7, 1971), p. 13.

This area of scientific investigation has developed largely in the last few decades. In recent years there have been important advances in the study of cell contents and structure, made possible by the development of the *electron microscope* and other methods of study. Formerly it was thought that a cell was composed of a nucleus and a few other parts in a "sea" of cytoplasm, with large spaces in the cell unoccupied. Now it's known that a cell literally "swarms," that is, is *packed full* of important, functioning units necessary to the life of the cell and the body containing it. The theory of evolution **assumes** life developed from a "simple" cell—but science today demonstrates that there's NO SUCH THING as a simple cell.

Emphasizing the enormous gap between molecules and cells, Vanderkooi quotes from a recent book by two prominent biochemists, Dr. D. E. Green and Dr. R. F. Goldberger, entitled *Molecular Insights into the Living Process*: "There is one step [in evolution] that far outweighs the others in enormity: the step from macro-molecules to cells. All the other steps can be accounted for on theoretical grounds—if not correctly, at least elegantly. However, the macro-molecule to cell transition is *a jump of fantastic dimensions*, which lies beyond the range of testable hypothesis. **In this area, all is conjecture.**"[9]

In other words, the REAL "missing link" in the evolutionary chain is not a half-monkey, half-man. Neither is it a half-fish, half-animal. It's an intermediate stage (or a **thousand intermediate stages**) between a molecule and a cell—"a jump of **fantastic** dimensions. . . . In this area, all is **conjecture.**"

LOOK Magazine was understating the enormous complexity when it declared: "The cell is as complicated as New York City."[10] And evolutionist Loren Eiseley quotes German

---

9. D. E. Green and R. F. Goldberger, *Molecular Insights into the Living Process*, quoted in Vanderkooi, *op.cit.*, p. 14.

10. *Look* (January 16, 1962), p. 46.

biologist Von Bertalanffy as stating: "To grasp in detail the physico-chemical organization of the *simplest* cell is FAR beyond our capacity."[11]

Still, much has been learned since the early 1950's when James Watson and Francis Crick discovered the structure of the DNA (deoxyribonucleic acid) molecule, for which work they won the 1962 Nobel Prize. DNA is incredibly tiny, residing **within** the chromosomes which are found **within** the nucleus which is found **within** each and every living cell. But DNA is the marvelous molecule that contains the secret of heredity. It "spells out" an incredibly complex coded message that transmits to the offspring all instructions needed for every genetic trait.

The LIFE Science Library volume on *The Cell* says that it's the particular make-up of "DNA molecules that make a horse give birth to a horse instead of a giraffe, an oyster or a fern—that determine color of eyes, texture of hair, shape of fingers."[12] (And as shown in the preceding chapter, it's DNA which guarantees that **all variations remain WITHIN the basic kind.**)

The amount of information coded in the DNA of an organism is amazing. The information in a **single** cell of human DNA is estimated as equivalent to 1,000 printed volumes, with 600 pages per volume and 500 words per page. The staggering complexity of the supposedly "simple" cell is absolutely mind-boggling! Instead of evolution's search being a **converging** one where we're finding all the answers, biochemistry and molecular biology have made it a **diverging** one where we're raising more questions. For instead of simplicity emerging from investigation, we find increasing *complexity.*

---

11. Von Bertalanffy, quoted in Loren Eiseley, *The Immense Journey* (New York: Random House Modern Library Paperback, 1957), p. 206.

12. John Pfeiffer and the Editors of Time-Life Books, *The Cell* (New York: Time-Life Books, 1972), p. 68.

That's why Sir James Gray, Professor of Zoology at Cambridge University, says: "A bacterium is FAR MORE COMPLEX than ANY inanimate system known to man. There is not a laboratory in the world which can compete with the biochemical activity of the **smallest** living organism."[13] Within a **single** bacterial cell *(Escherichia coli)* are an estimated 1,000,000 to 3,000,000 protein molecules, including 2,000 to 10,000 different *kinds* of enzymes—all in a space 1/25,000 of an inch in diameter and 3/25,000 of an inch long. A **single** liver cell contains an estimated 53,000,000 protein molecules, which would probably include tens of thousands of different kinds of enzymes, all organized into a smoothly-running cellular "machine."

So next time you hear an evolutionist theorizing about how "Life originated in a simple cell," tell him that the idea of a "simple" cell went out with World War II.

The Statistical Impossibility of Evolution

From all this and much more besides, it's increasingly clear that it would be easier for science to show that evolution is **impossible** than to explain **how** it happened. One branch of mathematics deals with statistical probability—the chance that undirected, accidental events will occur. For instance, since a coin has two faces, the probability of tossing a head is therefore 1 in 2. One of a pair of dice has six faces; therefore the probability of throwing a four would be 1 in 6. To figure the chance of throwing **two** fours in a row we'd multiply the probability of the first event, which is 1/6, by the probability of the second event, also 1/6, and find the answer to be 1 in 36.

Obviously, the probability is much less when the number of possibilities is increased. Mathematicians found that a

---

13. *Science Today*, chapter entitled "The Science of Life" by Sir James Gray (New York: Criterion Books, First American edition, 1961), p. 21.

person wishing to throw the same number ten times in succession would have only one chance in about *sixty million* tosses of the lone dice. And if the dice—like a living cell—were made of a fragile material that lasts for only a few hundred tosses, the chances of getting the same number ten times in a row would be greatly reduced, so much that it would be *virtually impossible.*

Scientists and mathematicians have spent much time computing the possibility that LIFE could have started by chance. Lecomte du Nouy, a French scientist, has done a great deal of work on this. His book, *Human Destiny*, tells of these investigations.[14] Lecomte du Nouy consulted Professor Charles Eugene Guye, a Swiss mathematician, as to the possibilities of a *single* protein molecule being formed by chance. The protein molecule contains the elements carbon, hydrogen, nitrogen, and oxygen—plus a trace of one of the metallic elements such as iron, copper, or sulphur. Most scientists agree that **this molecule represents the** *simplest, most basic* **form of living matter**. But even so, note the complexity of a molecule of insulin, one of the *smallest* and *simplest* of the proteins: Like all proteins, insulin consists of **complicated chains** of amino acids. The insulin molecule has 51 amino acid units, in two chains, one having 21 units, the other 30. EACH UNIT (of the fifty-one) has 254 carbon atoms, 377 hydrogen atoms, 65 of nitrogen, 75 of oxygen, and 6 of sulphur—*a total of 777 atoms* in **exact** combination!

To simplify the problem as much as possible, Professor Guye considers a molecule containing *only TWO* elements instead of the usual *five*. The first conclusion was that **there was not enough matter in existence** to provide an opportunity for such a molecule to form by chance combination. According to Professor Guye, it would take a mass of material

---

14. Pierre Lecomte du Nouy, *Human Destiny* (New York: Longmans, Green & Co., Inc., 1947), p. 30.

millions of times *greater* than all the known universe, including the farthest galaxies.[15]

To form even a simplified protein molecule, it would be necessary for a great number of atoms to combine, under exactly the right conditions. Taking into consideration the great complexity of the atoms concerned, the chance that such a protein molecule could have formed is almost nothing. Not only is there not enough matter in the universe for such a complex combination to take place, there is also not enough TIME. Even if the material of this huge mass were shaken together at many times per second, it would still require billions and billions of years to provide **one** opportunity for this protein molecule to be formed by chance. So even supposing the earth has existed for the evolutionary estimate of 4.5 billion years, not nearly enough **time** has elapsed for this one chance to appear.

Of course, these figures concern the formation of only a SINGLE MOLECULE of protein matter, very much simplified at that. The same mathematician states that if we tried to express the chance formation of a CELL, "the preceding figures would seem negligible."[16] In other words, the time necessary for the formation of a cell is **so fantastically greater** than the **earth's age** that it may be considered **mathematically impossible**. With these facts in mind we can well understand the statement of Lecomte du Nouy: "It was impossible to explain, or to account for, not only the birth of *life* but even the appearance of the SUBSTANCES which seem to be required to *build* life, namely, highly dissymmetrical molecules."[17]

Thus we see that Darwin was right about one thing: The apostle of evolution himself admitted, "The birth both of the

---

15. Charles Eugene Guye, cited in Lecomte du Nouy, *op. cit.*, p. 35.

16. *Ibid.*, p. 36.

17. Pierre Lecomte du Nouy, *Human Destiny* (New York: Longmans, Green & Co., Inc., 1947), p. 39.

species and of the individual are equally parts of that grand sequence of **events which our minds REFUSE to accept as the result of blind chance. The understanding REVOLTS at such a conclusion."** [18]

For a frog to turn into a handsome prince in an *instant* is an act of MAGIC found only in children's fairy tales. Evolutionists pretend that for the same thing to happen over a *billion years* is SCIENCE. Time becomes the fairy's magic wand. Strippping us of both our *divine origin* and *heavenly destiny,* evolution is a **GRIM** fairy tale indeed! Evolutionists pay lip service to science but postulate the creation of life spontaneously, magically. Creationists are accused of resorting to magic when they accept God's supernatural act of creation. But creationists, unlike evolutionists, don't disguise magic behind high-sounding words intended to sound scientific. Faith in evolutionary theory is faith, not in a scientific fact, but in a mathematical impossibility.

VIII. THE ORIGIN OF SEX

When it comes to an "explanation" for the origin of life, evolution is a blind alley leading nowhere. But aside from the origin of life, another question evolution cannot answer is: Where did not only Adam but EVE come from? How did the **two sexes** originate?

Evolutionists teach that life evolved from the simple, lower forms of life to the complex, higher forms. But what do we see when we look at the lower forms of life? There are NO *male* or *female* protozoa, no masculine or feminine amoebas! One-celled organisms like the amoeba reproduce asexually by cell division, simply dividing in two to form a duplicate. IF asexual reproduction was satisfactory—and it *was*, for such organisms survive today, multiplying in exactly the same way—then WHY should sexual reproduction arise?

18. Charles Darwin, *The Descent of Man,* Second Edition in One Volume (Philadelphia: David McKay, 1901), Chapter XXI, p. 637.

Evolutionists like J. William Schopf, Paleontologist and Geologist at UCLA, contend that sex apparently did not exist on earth for the first two thirds of biological history (this would be for the first 3 billion of the estimated 4.7 billion years of the earth's age). But scientists are baffled by the question of how sex got started. There's no need for breeding or mating among the simple forms of life, for they are asexual. Then, **why sex? Where** did it originate? **How** did it develop?

Males and females are so very different that we even give them different names within the same species: man and woman, rooster and hen, stallion and mare, etc. These differences must be accounted for if things "just happened" by chance.

But males and females are not only very different, they're also obviously *inter-dependent*: a group of males or a group of females by themselves spell doom for any species. But HOW could male and female sex organs that **perfectly complement each other** arise gradually, paralleling each other, yet remaining **useless** until completed?

If the female mammary glands came about by slow evolution, HOW did females feed their young **in the meantime?** If they **already HAD another way** to feed them, why develop breasts? And if breasts developed because they were a superior way of feeding, then why do we still have animals that feed otherwise and survive just as well?

The February 1984 issue of science magazine *Discover* carried a provocative article entitled "WHY SEX?" The authors quote Dr. Graham Bell, a geneticist at Montreal's McGill University, as saying: "Nobody's got very far with the problem of how sex began."[19]

They explain that "Asexual reproduction (without sex) seems a likelier choice for nature to make. It is faster and

---

19. Graham Bell, quoted in Gina Maranto and Shannon Brownlee, "Why Sex?" *Discover*, Volume 5, Number 2 (Februrary 1984), p. 28.

more efficient. . . . Says George Williams, a population biologist of the State University of New York at Stony Brook, 'At first glance, and second, and third, it appears that sex shouldn't have evolved.'"[20]

The authors sum up the question "Why Sex?" by admitting: "It is evolution's single most important and **most perplexing riddle.**"[21]

In contrast to extremely speculative theories about the origin of sex, the Bible tells plainly where Adam and Eve came from. The very first chapter of Genesis tells about the creation of mankind: "**male and female** created He them."[22] Yes, God Himself gave Adam a companion, creating woman from a rib of man. She was made not from his **head** to top him or control him, nor from his **feet** to be trampled upon as an inferior, but from a rib of his **side** to stand by his side as an equal, under his arm to be protected, and near his heart to be loved. A part of man, bone of his bone and flesh of his flesh, she was his second self, showing the close union and affection that should exist in this relationship.[23] So in addition to all His other wonders of creation, God invented sex.

IX. ENTROPY *versus* EVOLUTION

There's an important law in science known as the Second Law of Thermodynamics which is **diametrically opposed** to the basic idea of evolution. This law, sometimes called the principle of ENTROPY, did not arise from speculation. It's firmly founded on countless thousands of experiments on systems ranging in size from the nuclear to the astronomic, and there's never been an exception to it observed.

20. George Williams, quoted in Maranto and Brownlee, "Why Sex?" *Discover*, Volume 5, Number 2 (February 1984), p. 24.

21. Gina Maranto and Shannon Brownlee, "Why Sex?" *Discover*, Volume 5, Number 2 (February 1984), p. 24.

22. Genesis 1:27.

23. Genesis 2:20-23.

Sir Arthur Eddington showed insight when he called this law *'time's arrow,'* for it helps illustrate nature's time sense —the one-wayness of events. When events take place, they do so in a way that serves to distinguish between **backwards** and **forwards**. The ancients even made lists of events which never take place in reverse: Rivers do not flow uphill, plants and men do not grow backwards, forest fires do not turn ashes into fully grown trees.

Only in world of magic or dreams can we imagine a different, backward trend of events; a world where food, already eaten, emerges whole, or Niagara Falls tumbles up the mountainside in reverse, or an atomic bomb explodes and turns gigantic piles of rubble into houses, streets, and crowds of people. In the world of reality, the world of science, events go in only one direction—a direction in which *dis*order increases and order is destroyed.

Entropy is a measure of this loss of order, this loss of available energy. It's based on the observation that **there's a continuous flow of heat from warmer to colder bodies** and never spontaneously in the reverse direction. Place a hot object, such as an electric iron, in a room and unplug it. After a time the iron has cooled, the air has warmed, and all objects in the room approach the same uniform temperature—the heat energy tends to be evenly distributed but less available.

The iron in the room is like the sun in the sky. Energy from the sun tends to dissipate and be distributed throughout the universe. The Second Law of Thermodynamics or entropy indicates that the universe is "running down" to a condition when all bodies will be at the same extremely low temperature and no energy will be available. This burning out or running down has been called **heat death** and will certainly occur if present processes continue indefinitely (that is, if God doesn't intervene as Christians believe He will).

The words of Sir James H. Jeans, eminent English astronomer and physicist, are still as true as when written some years ago: "The universe is like a clock which is running down, a clock which, so far as science knows, no one ever winds up, which cannot wind itself up, and so must stop in time. It is at present a partially wound-up clock, which must, at some time in the past, have been wound up in some manner unknown to us."[24] This sober man of science goes on to say: "Everything points with overwhelming force to a definite event, or series of events, of creation at some time or times **not infinitely remote.** The universe can not have originated by chance out of its present ingredients, and neither can it have been always the same as now."[25]

You see, the existence of matter, physical matter throughout the universe, has always been an embarrassing problem for evolutionists because they cannot explain its origin. Realizing the truth of the dictum *ex nihilo nihil fit* (out of nothing, nothing is made) they're left with only two alternatives to account for the reality of matter: Either it was created or it has always existed. Not willing to accept the former possibility, atheistic evolutionists lean toward the latter explanation, saying: "Matter is not so difficult to account for, because it's possible that matter is eternal. For all we know, the universe has **always** existed."

This explanation may have sounded plausible or at least possible before scientists understood the principle of entropy. But the fact of entropy is absolutely *devastating* to this argument AND to the theory of evolution in general! Matter cannot possibly be eternal—the universe cannot possibly have always existed—IF the available energy is decreasing, as we know it is.

---

24. Sir James Jeans, *Eos, or the Wider Aspects of Cosmogony* (London: 1928), p. 52.
25. *Ibid.*, p. 55.

Nature, you see, points definitely to a **beginning** of things. Science clearly shows that the universe could NOT have existed from all eternity, or it would have run out of useful energy and ground to a halt long ago. For instance, radium, uranium, and other radioactive elements are constantly emitting radiation and are constantly losing weight as they slowly change to other elements until at last the element we call *lead* remains. In a universe that had no beginning but had always existed, **no** radioactive elements would remain.

In any system, some energy is lost for future use. When we burn wood, chemical energy is converted into heat; this can be used in a engine to do work, but a certain amount of energy is never available again, being degraded into non-usable heat energy by friction. This principle of entropy makes it obvious that ultimately ALL energy in the universe will be unavailable energy. If the universe were infinitely old, if it had **always** existed, this state of absolute entropy would already have happened. The fact that the universe has **not yet** "died" in this fashion proves, as certainly as science can prove anything, that the universe had a beginning. A supposedly **eternal** universe can therefore be eliminated from consideration.

Disintegration a Fixed Law

But the principle of entropy does more than demolish atheistic theories on the eternity of matter. The Second Law of Thermodynamics says that time causes decay. This is easy to understand, as every material thing within our experience verifies the Second Law: Houses decay, trees decay, people decay. Even pyramids decay. Of course, this innate tendency toward decay may be **temporarily** offset in the growth of a child, the formation of a crystal, or the raising of a building. But that child or crystal or building or anything else will eventually start to grow old or wear out or decay. Everywhere there's an innate, universal tendency toward disorder and disintegration, not growth and development.

Popular scientific writer Isaac Asimov, in an article in the *Smithsonian Institute Journal*, interestingly expresses the idea of entropy as follows: "Another way of stating the Second Law then is: 'The universe is getting more disorderly!' Viewed that way, we can see the Second Law all about us. We have to work hard to straighten up a room, but left to itself it becomes a mess again very quickly and very easily. Even if we never enter it, it becomes dusty and musty. **How difficult** to maintain houses, and machinery, and our own bodies in perfect working order; **how easy** to let them deteriorate. In fact, all we have to do is nothing, and **EVERYTHING collapses, breaks down, wears out, all by itself**, and that is what the Second Law is all about."[26]

But this is the REVERSE of evolution. Actually, as Dr. Henry M. Morris puts it, "It would hardly be possible to conceive of two more **completely OPPOSITE principles** than this principle of entropy increase and the principle of evolution. Each is precisely the converse of the other. As Huxley defined it, evolution involves a continual INCREASE of order, of organization, of size, of complexity. The entropy principle involves a continual DECREASE of order, of organization, of size, of complexity. It seems axiomatic that both cannot possibly be true. But there is no question whatever that the Second Law of Thermodynamics is true!"[27]

So entropy and evolution are "two diametrically opposed systems. They are alike in only one respect, in that both involve a continual *change*. But one is a change UP, the other is a change DOWN. One is development, the other deterioration; one growth, the other decay."[28]

---

26. Isaac Asimov, "In the Game of Energy and Thermodynamics You Can't Break Even," *Smithsonian Institute Journal* (June, 1970), p. 10.

27. Henry M. Morris, *The Twilight of Evolution* (Ann Arbor, Michigan: Baker Book House Company, 1963), p. 35. (Note: The author has found this book and others by Dr. Morris to be particularly valuable.)

28. *Ibid.*, p. 41.

Evolutionists, seeing the insurmountable problem this poses for their theory, sometimes say that the principle of entropy applies only in the physical realm, not in the biological realm of living things. But entropy seems to be everywhere: Physical systems, left to themselves, run down and stop; biological systems grow old and die. And evolutionist Harold F. Blum, in his book *Time's Arrow and Evolution*, admits the parallel between living and non-living systems: "Like any other machine, the living system must have a supply of energy for its operation. If it does external work as, for example, in bodily movement or in the expulsion of waste products, free energy must be expended."[29]

But just for the sake of argument, let's assume that entropy does apply only to inanimate matter. **The Second Law of Thermodynamics would STILL work against the build-up of amino acids and proteins needed** before that original spark of life could develop on the earth. How could *complex* molecules **organize themselves BY themselves** when the universal trend is not toward organization but toward disorder and disintegration? Even Dr. Wald of Harvard, noted before as perhaps the world's lone believer in spontaneous generation, admits that forces of "spontaneous dissolution" make "the spontaneous generation of a living organism . . . impossible." For, he explains, "In the vast majority of the processes in which we are interested the point of equilibrium lies far over toward the side of dissolution. That is to say, spontaneous dissolution is much more probable, and hence proceeds much more rapidly, than spontaneous synthesis. For example, the spontaneous union, step by step, of amino acid units to form a protein has a certain small probability, and hence might occur over a long stretch of time. **But the dissolution . . . is much more probable**, and hence

---

29. Harold F. Blum, *Time's Arrow and Evolution* (Princeton, New Jersey: Princeton University Press, 1951), p. 87.

will go ever so much more rapidly. The situation we must
face is that of patient Penelope waiting for Odysseus, yet
much worse: each night she undid the weaving of the preceding day, but here a night could readily undo the work of
a **year** or a **century.**"[30]

Wald states immediately that *living organisms* in our
present-day world are able to synthesize or put together these
complex organic compounds in spite of the forces of dissolution. Thus they're able to live and grow. He observes
that "a living organism is an **intricate** MACHINE for performing exactly this function" of combining, synthesizing,
building organic compounds. A cow, for instance, can build
amino acids and proteins into the milk it gives—but a cow
is a living milk factory. *Lifeless* elements of matter *cannot*
so combine to create the building blocks of life. This leads
Wald to confess: "What we ask here is to synthesize organic
molecules without such a machine. I believe this to be **the
most stubborn problem** that confronts us—**the weakest link**
in our argument."[31]

How devoted to a theory can a man become? But that's
not a *scientist* speaking—it's *a special pleader for a cause*
displaying a **will** to **believe.**

One last point that might be made here is that *mutations*
offer a perfect illustration of the Second Law of Thermodynamics among living things. For the Second Law says that
the natural tendency of all change is toward a greater degree
of disorder. Thus the overall direction of change is deteri-
orative rather than developmental. And that's exactly what
mutations are—degenerative changes which are harmful and
often deadly to the organism that suffers them. Even those
rare mutations which may seem rather desirable as a con-

30. George Wald, "The Origin of Life," *Scientific American,* Volume
191, No. 2 (August, 1954), p. 49.
31. *Ibid.,* p. 50.

venience to man, such as the seedless navel orange, offer no real benefit to the plant itself.

The universe was to maintain itself in perfect running order—until man fell into sin and ruined God's creation. At that point man began to die, animals began to die, and the universe started to run down. I believe the curse that fell upon man as a result of sin included the degenerative effect of the Second Law of Thermodynamics—one of the best-proved and most universal laws known to science. There's no such thing as the evolution of **nothing** into matter and of **matter** into life—the trend is all in the other direction. The FACT of entropy and the THEORY of evolution are contradictory principles which are forever incompatible and irreconcilable.

X. FOSSILS—THE RECORD OF THE ROCKS

In many ways the crust of the earth is like a giant layer cake. Over vast areas layer upon layer of sedimentary rocks are found to contain fossils. This special study lies in the fields of **geology**—the study of the earth itself—and **paleontology**—the study of ancient things, especially the study of ancient life as preserved in fossils.

It's no mere play on words to say that the **rocks** are viewed by evolutionists as the real **foundation** of their theory. W. E. Le Gros Clark, the well-known British evolutionist, has said: "The really *crucial* evidence for evolution must be provided by the paleontologist whose business it is to study the evidence of the fossil record."[32]   Thomas Hunt Morgan also declares that this evidence from the earth's strata is "by all odds the *strongest* evidence of the theory of evolution."[33] And Yale geologist Carl O. Dunbar says: "Although

---

32. W. E. Le Gros Clark, *Discovery* (January, 1955), p. 7.
33. Thomas Hunt Morgan, *A Critique of the Theory of Evolution* (Princeton, New Jersey: Princeton University Press, 1916), p. 24.

the comparative study of living animals and plants may give very convincing *circumstantial* evidence, **fossils** provide the ONLY historical, documentary evidence that life has evolved from simpler to more and more complex forms."[34] So fossils supposedly furnish the **only real proof** for evolution.

It's true that the only evidence (apart from divine revelation, which evolutionists refuse to accept) concerning prehistoric life on earth is that which can be deduced from the fossil remains of creatures buried in rocks of the earth's crust. As W. R. Thompson puts it, "Evolution, if it has occurred, can in a rather loose sense be called a **historical** process; and therefore, to show that it has occurred, historical evidence is required. . . . The only evidence available is that provided by the fossils."[35]

But contrary to common evolutionary claims, the fossil record constitutes one of the most telling arguments AGAINST evolutionary assumptions possible! As a matter of fact, geology strongly **contradicts** evolution, providing compelling evidence against the theory. Historian Himmelfarb, in her landmark [36] book, states: "Geology, however,

---

34. Carl O. Dunbar, *Historical Geology*, Second Edition (New York: John Wiley and Sons, Inc., 1961), p. 47.

35. W. R. Thompson, "Introduction" to *The Origin of Species* by Charles Darwin (New York: E. P. Dutton & Company, Everyman's Library, 1956). This quote is from the reprint of Thompson's Introduction in the *Journal of the American Scientific Affiliation,* Volume 12 (March, 1960), p. 6.

36. Historian Gertrude Himmelfarb (Mrs. Irving Kristol) worked under grants from the American Philosophical Society and the John Simon Guggenheim Memorial Foundation to produce this well-documented book that was studied and commended by scholars even before its publication. As Ronald Good puts it in *The Listener*: "The reason why her study is so valuable is, paradoxically, that she is not a biologist but a historian, and so she has the inestimable advantage of being able to view her subject free from professional partisanship."

has been notably UNforthcoming, and *instead* of being the *chief support* of Darwin's theory, it is one of its **most serious weaknesses.**"[37] Interestingly enough, Darwin himself didn't think fossils gave much support for his theory of evolution. The weaknesses inherent in the record of the rocks were of such concern to him that he wrote an entire chapter in *The Origin of Species* entitled, "On the Imperfection of the Geological Record."

We cannot take time here to explore **all** the geological and fossil evidence that allegedly supports evolution. Your attention is called simply to **three main points** regarding this fossil evidence in an attempt to determine how valid it really is.

1. The SUDDEN Appearance of Life

Geologists have given names to the various layers, or strata, of rock in the earth's crust. One of the lower layers is called the Cambrian layer. Though it is by no means the lowest layer or "basement level" of rock, it is the first that contains fossils of living things, or the lowest "fossiliferous" strata. This fact directly contradicts the evolutionary theory, which says that life originated during the Pre-Cambrian era. Noteworthy is the fact that EVERY major invertebrate form of life is found in Cambrian strata—in fact, billions and billions of fossils are found in Cambrian strata. Yet not a single fossil (other than alleged fossil micro-organisms) has ever been found in Pre-Cambrian rock!

Even Darwin recognized this problem. He wrote:

There is another and allied difficulty, which is much more serious. I allude to the manner in which species belonging to several of the main divisions of the animal kingdom **suddenly** appear in the lowest known fossil-

_____
37. Gertrude Himmelfarb, *Darwin and the Darwinian Revolution* (Garden City, New York: Doubleday and Company, 1962), p. 330.

iferous rocks. . . . If the theory be true, it is indisputable that before the lowest Cambrian stratum was
deposited long periods elapsed, as long as, or probably
far longer than, the whole interval from the Cambrian
age to the present, day; and that during these vast
periods the world swarmed with living creatures. Here
we encounter a formidable objection. . . . To the
question why we do not find rich fossiliferous deposits
belonging to these assumed earliest periods prior to the
Cambrian system, I can give no satisfactory answer.
. . . The difficulty of assigning any good reason for the
absence of vast piles of strata rich in fossils beneath
the Cambrian system is very great. . . . The case at
present must remain inexplicable; and may be truly
urged as **a valid argument AGAINST the views
here entertained.**[38]

Darwin wrote those words well over a century ago.
TREMENDOUS amounts of sedimentary rock were laid
down before the Cambrian, yet they contain NO fossils. So
the SUDDEN OUTBURST of life in the Cambrian period
is a real puzzle, when there should be *billions* of years of
evolution shown before this. In recent years George Gaylord
Simpson conceded that the absence of Pre-Cambrian fossils
is the **"major mystery** of the history of life."[39] Bear in mind
that Dr. Simpson, a paleontologist at Harvard University, was
formerly Professor of Vertebrate Paleontology at Columbia
University. Before that he was long associated with the
American Museum of Natural History in New York City
where he was Curator of Fossil Mammals and Birds. He's a
world-renowned paleontologist and ardent evolutionist.

38.   Charles Darwin, *The Origin of Species*, Sixth Edition (New York:
P. F. Collier & Son, 1909), Chapter X, pp. 359-361.
39.   George Gaylord Simpson, *The Meaning of Evolution*, Revised
Edition (New Haven, Connecticut: Yale University Press, 1967), p. 20.

Simpson honestly admits: "Fossils are abundant only from the Cambrian onward, which is probably not more than one-fourth of the whole history of life. . . . Then, with the beginning of the Cambrian, unquestionable, abundant, and quite varied fossil animals appear . . . the change is great and abrupt. This is not only the **most puzzling** feature of the whole fossil record but also its **greatest inadequacy.**"[40]

Note this illuminating statement from the geology textbook by Kay and Colbert: "The introduction of a variety of organisms in the early Cambrian, including such **complex** forms of the arthropods as the trilobites, is **surprising.** . . . The introduction of abundant organisms in the record would **not be** so surprising IF they were simple. Why should such **complex** organic forms be in rocks about six hundred million years old and be **absent** or unrecognized in the records of the preceding **two billion years?** . . . IF there **has** been evolution of life, the absence of the requisite fossils in the rocks older than the Cambrian is PUZZLING."[41]

The World We Live In, one of the attractively illustrated books by the editorial staff of *LIFE,* puts it this way: "For at least three-quarters of the book of ages engraved in the earth's crust, the **pages are blank.**"[42] Note also what the *Scientific American* of August 1964 says: "Both the sudden appearance and the remarkable composition of the animal life characteristic of Cambrian times are sometimes explained away or overlooked by biologists. Yet recent paleontological research has made the puzzle of this sudden proliferation of

40. Geoge Gaylord Simpson, "The History of Life," in Sol Tax, editor, *The Evolution of Life,* Volume 1 of *Evolution After Darwin* (Chicago: University of Chicago Press, 1960), pp. 143-144.

41. Marshall Kay and Edwin H. Colbert, *Stratigraphy and Life History* (New York: John Wiley and Sons, 1965), pp. 102-103.

42. Lincoln Barnett and the Editors of Time-Life Books, *The World We Live In* (New York: Time-Life Books, 1955), p. 93.

living organisms **increasingly difficult for anyone to evade.**
. . . Neither can the general failure to find Pre-Cambrian
animal fossils be charged to any **lack of trying.**"[43]

Evolutionists attempting explanation usually say:

(1) "Wait. This apparent lack of Pre-Cambrian fossils
is due to insufficient collecting—give us time to
do more searching."

(2) "Perhaps the earlier fossils were destroyed by
metamorphism—heat and pressure in the rock."

(3) "The earlier forms of life must have been soft-
bodied types not likely to be preserved as fossils."

But none of these supposed explanations holds up well
under careful scrutiny. Let's let Dr. Norman D. Newell,
Paleontologist from Columbia University, deal with these
three attempts at explanation:

(1) A **CENTURY of intensive search** for fossils in the
Pre-Cambrian rocks has thrown **very little light**
on this problem.

(2) Early theories that these rocks were dominantly
non-marine or that once-contained-fossils have
been destroyed by heat and pressure have been
abandoned because the Pre-Cambrian rocks of
many districts are **very similar** to younger rocks
in all respects **except** that **they rarely contain
any records whatsoever** of past life. . . .

(3) Unequivocal fossils of *soft*-bodied invertebrates,
although by no means common, **are known in
many places** and **should** have turned up in Pre-

43. *Scientific American* (August, 1964), pp. 34-36.

Cambrian rocks by now.[44]   Although such localities are rare, in a single Cambrian locality in the Canadian Rockies, C. D. Walcott collected **thousands** of specimens of more than 130 species of delicately preserved *soft*-bodied animals.[45]

Finally, Dr. Daniel I. Axelrod, Professor of Geology at the University of California at Los Angeles, sums up the problem facing evolutionists:

> **One of the major unsolved problems** of geology and evolution is the occurrence of diversified, multicellular, marine invertebrates in Lower Cambrian rocks on all the continents. . . . However, when we turn to examine the *Pre*-Cambrian rocks for the **forerunners** of these Early Cambrian fossils, they are **nowhere to be found.** Many THICK (over 5,000 feet) sections of sedimentary rock are now known to lie in unbroken succession **below** strata containing the earliest Cambrian fossils. These sediments apparently were suitable for the preservation of fossils, because they often are **identical** with overlying rocks which are fossiliferous, yet NO FOSSILS ARE FOUND IN THEM. Clearly, a significant but unrecorded chapter in the history of life is **missing** from the rocks of Pre-Cambrian time.[46]

---

44. Norman D. Newell, "The Nature of the Fossil Record," *Proceedings of the American Philosophical Society*, Volume 103, No. 2 (April, 1959), p. 269.

45. See Richard M. Ritland, *A Search for Meaning in Nature* (Boise, Idaho: Pacific Press Publishing Association, 1970), p. 141.

46. Danile I. Axelrod, "Early Cambrian Marine Fauna," *Science*, Volume 128 (3314) (1958), pp. 7-9.

2. The "Missing Link" Is STILL Missing!

So the fossil record does not support the evolutionary assumption in at least one major respect—if the evolutionary **ancestors** of the Cambrian fossils ever existed, they've certainly never been found. But a much worse, almost insurmountable, problem exists in the fossil record—the problem of **missing links**.

You see, the very essence of evolutionary thinking is **slow change**. So according to the theory there should be a continuous array of living forms, an unbroken chain of gradations, with all groups imperceptibly merging. There **should be NO missing links or gaps** between phyla, classes, orders, etc. Therefore, if evolutionary theory is ever to have any scientific basis, **gradual transitions** of fossils must be found.

But such is not the case. If we look closely at the fantastic idea of evolution as reflected in the fossil record, we note SO MANY "missing links" it's impossible to enumerate them. **Countless** numbers of connecting links are needed to bridge the gaps that separate EVERY major group and its supposed neighbors. The study of fossils reveals the **complete lack** of intermediate stages of evolution which would link one stage of life with another.

Here's how Darwin himself described the difficulty:

> Why, if species have descended from other species by **fine gradations**, do we not everywhere see innumerable **transitional forms**? . . . As by this theory innumerable transitional forms **must** have existed, **WHY do we not FIND them** embedded in countless numbers in the crust of the earth? . . . Why then is not every geological formation and every stratum **full** of such intermediate links? Geology assuredly does NOT reveal any such finely-graduated organic chain; and this, perhaps, is the **most obvious and serious objection** which can be urged against the theory. . . . What

geological research has **not** revealed, is the former
existence of infinitely numerous gradations, as fine as
existing varieties, connecting together nearly ALL existing and extinct species. . . . The **absence** of innumerable transitional links between the species which
lived at the commencement and close of each formation, pressed so hardly on my theory. The **abrupt**
manner in which **whole groups** of species **suddenly**
appear in certain formations, has been urged by several
paleontologists . . . as **a FATAL objection** to the belief
in the trans-mutation [evolution] of species. If numerous species, belonging to the same genera or families,
have **really STARTED INTO LIFE AT ONCE**, the fact
would be FATAL to the theory of evolution through
natural selection. For the development by this means
of a group of forms, all of which are descended from
some one progenitor, MUST have been an extremely
slow process; and the progenitors must have lived long
before their modified descendants. . . . Geological
research . . . does *not* yield the infinitely many fine
gradations between past and present species *required*
by the theory; and **this is the most OBVIOUS of the
MANY objections which may be urged against it.** [47]

Of course, Darwin tried to take refuge in what he called
"the extreme imperfection of the geological record" and "the
poorness of paleontological collections." [48] He and his enthusiastic *early* followers were optimistic that the prominent
gaps would soon be filled in. They argued that much of the
earth was still unexplored and that such transitional forms
would yet be found. But they were doomed to bitter disap-

47. Charles Darwin, *The Origin of Species*, Sixth Edition (New York:
P. F. Collier & Son, 1909), pp. 178, 179, 334, 352, 354-355, 503.
48. *Ibid.*, pp. 334 and 340.

pointment. After **more than a century of intensive search,** such links between diverse groups have yet to be unearthed. Scientific historian Charles Singer states: "It has now LONG been apparent that such 'links' are, in fact, **conspicuous** by their **absence.**"[49] And Professor Newell of Columbia University notes "the systematic discontinuity" (missing links) in the fossil record and admits: "Many of the discontinuities tend to be **more and more EMPHASIZED with increased collecting**" over the years.[50]

Thus Darwin recognized the seriousness of this difficulty —**and more than one hundred years of research has in no way lessened** the validity of this objection. But he's by no means the only one who's noticed this *fatal flaw* in the evolutionary theory. Many scientists have expressed wonder over the fact that no connecting links are found between the supposed stages of evolution.

For example, Dr. Alfred S. Romer, Professor of Zoology and Curator of Vertebrate Paleontology at the Museum of Comparative Zoology of Harvard University, makes this startling admission: "'Links' are **missing** just where we most fervently **desire** them, and it is all too probable that many 'links' will **continue** to be missing."[51]

Professor G. G. Simpson, also of Harvard, confesses that "transitional sequences are **not merely RARE,** but are **virtually ABSENT.** . . . Their absence is so nearly UNIVERSAL

49. Charles Singer, *A History of Biology*, Third Revised Edition (London and New York: Abelard-Schuman, 1959), p. 277.

50. Norman D. Newell, "The Nature of the Fossil Record," *Proceedings of the American Philosophical Society*, Volume 103, No. 2 (April, 1959), p. 267.

51. Alfred S. Romer, "Time Series and Trends in Animal Evolution," in Glenn L. Jepson, Ernst Mayr, and George Gaylord Simpson, editors, *Genetics, Paleontology and Evolution* (Princeton, New Jersey: Princeton Univeristy Press, 1963), p. 114.

that it cannot, offhand, be imputed entirely to chance. . . ."[52] In another book Simpson says: "It remains true, as every paleontologist knows, that most new species . . . appear in the record **suddenly** and are **NOT led up to by known, gradual, completely continuous transitional sequences.**"[53]

If Dr. Simpson were not the world's foremost evolutionary paleontologist, his words might not carry so much weight—though facts are facts no matter who states them. In a book written to commemorate the centennial anniversary of the publication of Darwin's *Origin of Species*, Simpson tells us: "It is a feature of the known fossil record that most taxa [kinds of plants and animals] appear **abruptly**. They are NOT, as a rule, **led up to** by a sequence of almost imperceptibly changing forerunners such as Darwin believed should be usual in evolution. . . . GAPS among known orders, classes, and phyla are **systematic** and almost always **large**."[54] Here is a very important statement by this specialist. Simpson says the gaps are systematic! But this is precisely what cannot be allowed if the theory is to be supported scientifically.

IF evolution were a universal law of nature, as evolutionists claim, then there should be **abundant** evidence of CONTINUITY and TRANSITION between all the kinds of organisms—both in the present world **and** in the fossil record. Instead, we find GREAT GAPS between all the basic kinds—and essentially the **same clear-cut discontinuity** seen in the LIVING world today between dog and cat, horse and cow, etc., is found in the FOSSIL record of the past.

52. George Gaylord Simpson, *Tempo and Mode in Evolution* (New York: Columbia University Press, 1944), pp. 105-106.

53. George Gaylord Simpson, *The Major Features of Evolution* (New York: Columiba University Press, 1953), p. 360.

54. George Gaylord Simpson, "The History of Life," in Sol Tax, editor, *The Evolution of Life*, Volume 1 of *Evolution After Darwin* (Chicago: The University of Chicago Press, 1960), p. 149.

Even if the intermediates once lived but are now extinct, at least a few of them should be preserved as fossils. But except for a few extinct species such as dinosaurs (which I believe did not enter Noah's Ark and thus perished in the Genesis Flood), we're left without a solution. Is it plausible that "blind fate" or "chance" would *always* miss recording such transitions between groups and yet preserve abundant remains of the stable basic types? The more natural explanation is that the missing links never existed.

And that's exactly what was stated some years ago by Austin H. Clark, in his book *The New Evolution.* Clark, a famous biologist on the staff of the Smithsonian Institution and himself an evolutionist, states: "Since we have **not the slightest evidence**, either among the living or the fossil animals, of any intergrading types following the major groups, it is a fair supposition that **there NEVER HAVE BEEN any such intergrading types.**"[55]

Elsewhere in the same book Dr. Clark asserts that "from the very earliest times, **from the very first beginnings** of the fossil record, the broader aspects of animal life upon the earth **have remained unchanged.** When we examine a series of fossils of any age we may pick one out and say with confidence, 'This is a crustacean'—or a starfish, or a brachiopod, or an annelid, or any other type of creature as the case may be. . . . If they are sufficiently well preserved we have no difficulty in recognizing at once the group to which each and every fossil animal belongs. . . . Since all the fossils are determinable as members of their respective groups . . . it follows that **throughout the fossil record** these major groups have remained essentially unchanged. This means that the interrelationships between them likewise have remained unchanged."[56]

---

55. Austin H. Clark, *The New Evolution: Zoogenesis* (Baltimore: Williams and Wilkins, 1930), p. 196.
56. *Ibid.*, pp. 100-101.

All these statements, honestly made by evolutionists themselves, are diametrically opposed to the theory of slow evolutionary change. Sir Julian Huxley was quite right when he made the following assertion in a superbly illustrated children's book, *The Wonderful World of Life*: *"IF* evolution is true, fossil history will reveal a branching plan for the advance of life, with each branch showing **gradual improvement** for its particular mode of existence."[57] At the top of the page is a diagram showing various land animals branching off from a common ancestor. Each branch illustrated has broad connections with the trunk. The amoeba-to-man theory demands such connections. But they **do not**, in fact, exist!

The first sponges are complex sponges; the first starfish are unquestionably starfish; the first whales, plainly whales; the first turtles, clearly turtles; and so on through the animal kingdom. If fish evolved into amphibia, **where** are the transitional forms? How did **gills** change to become **lungs**? How did **fins** change into **feet** and **legs**? And if reptiles gave rise to birds, where are those transitional forms? How did **scales** change into **feathers**? How did **heavy** reptilian bones become **hollow** bones for birds? W. E. Swinton, an evolutionist expert on birds at London's British Museum of Natural History, states: "The origin of birds is largely a matter of deduction. There is **NO fossil evidence** of the stages through which the remarkable change from reptile to bird was achieved."[58]

WHY is it always the same story—that the transitions, the links between major groups of plants and animals, are MISSING? And plants, incidentally, do present the same picture. Evolutionist E. J. H. Corner, Professor of Botany at England's

---

57. Sir Julian Huxley, *The Wonderful World of Life* (New York: Garden City Books, 1958), p. 12.
58. W. E. Swinton, in A. J. Marshall, editor, *The Biology and Comparative Physiology of Birds* (New York: Academic Press, 1960), Volume 1, p. 1.

Cambridge University, frankly admits that the fossil record of plants gives no support for evolution, but "to the unprejudiced, **the fossil record of plants** is in favor of **special creation**."[59]

In the light of these statements and many others which may be brought to bear on this question, we see that W. R. Thompson was correct in stating "that Darwin in the *Origin* was NOT able to produce paleontological evidence sufficient to prove his views but that the evidence he did produce was **adverse** to them; and I may note that **the position is not notably different today**."[60]

Therefore, if there's no real evidence, PAST or PRESENT, that there ever was a continuous series of forms from the most simple to the most complex, then HOW can any scientist **justify** the assumption that all organisms have evolved from simpler forms? Such an assumption is not in keeping with the facts—and, as stated above, one fact is worth a thousand theories.

Both of these problems, (1) the absence of fossils in **Pre-**Cambrian strata, and (2) the absence of connecting **links** between kinds of organisms, are enormous difficulties for evolutionists. If **either** or **both** of these problems cannot be solved—and they've remained unsolved for over a hundred years —then the theory of progressive evolution must be considered inadequate.

3. Reasoning in a Circle

So not only is the **first three-quarters** of the evolutionary record entirely missing, but the fossils fail to supply connecting links even in the **last** quarter of the evolutionary chain!

---

59.   E. J. H. Corner, in A. M. MacLeod and L. S. Cobley, editors, *Contemporary Botanical Thought* (Chicago: Quadrangle Books, 1961), p. 97.

60.   W. R. Thompson, "Introduction" to *The Origin of Species* by Charles Darwin (New York: E. P. Dutton & Co., Everyman's Library, 1956). This quote is from the reprint of Thompson's Introduction in the *Journal of the American Scientific Affiliation*, Volume 12 (March, 1960), p. 7.

The weight of evidence the fossils give against evolution is already crushing, but let's briefly consider a third point. *Circular logic* is used in dating the rocks and the fossils: The assumed age of each is used to prove the age of the other. The **fossil** is dated by the **rock** in which it is found, and the **rock** is dated by the **fossil** it contains. If a paleontologist finds a dinosaur bone, he'll announce that it is 70 million years old because of the rock strata in which it's found. Obviously anything found buried in rock laid down 70 million years ago had to be buried when that rock was formed and would have to be 70 million years old also. But how do we KNOW that certain rock strata are really 70 million years old? Simply because dinosaurs are found in it!

This is a glaring example of **reasoning in a circle.** Each element is used to "prove" the other. But after a scientist has used the **fossils** to tell the ages of the **rocks,** why should he be allowed to turn around and use such rock formations to tell the age of the fossils? AROUND AND AROUND WE GO! One can prove ANYTHING if he starts with his conclusion and then reasons in a circle.

When I first learned this fact, the revelation came as quite a shock to me. I had assumed that rocks were usually dated by their mineral or lithographic nature, but such is not the case. Professor Henry Shaler Williams, whom Dana picked to succeed himself at Yale, tells us: "The **character** of the **rocks themselves,** their composition, or their mineral contents have **NOTHING to do** with settling the question as to the particular system [or age-level] to which the new rocks belong. The **fossils ALONE** are the means of correlation."[61] Other recognized authorities in geology say the same thing, as for instance Grabau in *Principles of Stratigraphy:* "The

---

61. Henry Shaler Williams, *Geological Biology* (New York: Henry Holt and Company, 1895), p. 38.

primary divisions of the geological timescale are, as we
have just seen, based on changes in life, with the result
that **fossils ALONE** determine whether a formation belongs
to one or the other of these great divisions."[62]

E. M. Spieker, Professor of Geology at Ohio State University, emphasizes that the geologic time-scale is based pre
dominantly on paleontological evidence (fossil sequences)
rather than on any physical evidence such as the **nature** of
the rocks themselves or their relative **position** in terms of
vertical layers, etc.: "And what is this actual time-scale?
On what criteria does it rest? When all is winnowed out
and the grain reclaimed from the chaff, it is certain that
the **grain** in the product is mainly the paleontological record
[the *fossils*] and highly likely that the *physical* evidence is
the **chaff**."[63]

And one of the most prominent European paleontologists
declares: "The ONLY chronometric scale applicable . . . for
dating geologic events exactly is furnished by the fossils."[64]

You see, "the geologic ages are **identified and dated
BY the fossils** contained in the sedimentary rocks. The fossil record also provides the chief evidence for the theory
of evolution, which in turn is the basic philosophy upon
which the sequence of geologic ages has been erected. The
evolution-fossil-geologic age system is thus a CLOSED
CIRCLE which comprises **one interlocking package.**
Each goes with the other two."[65]

---

62. Amadeus William Grabau, *Principles of Stratigraphy*, Second
Edition (New York: A. G. Seiler, 1924), p. 1103.

63. E. M. Spieker, "Mountain-Building Chronology and the Nature
of the Geologic Time-Scale," *Bulletin, American Association of Petro-
leum Geologists*, Volume 40 (August, 1956), p. 1806.

64. O. H. Schindewolf, "Comments on Some Stratigraphic Terms,"
American Journal of Science, Volume 255 (June, 1957), p. 394.

65. Henry M. Morris, *The Remarkable Birth of Planet Earth*
(San Diego: Institute for Creation Research, 1972), pp. 76-77.

Evolution assumes that **older** rocks contain fossils of animals that are more simple whereas **younger** rocks contain fossils of animals that are more complex. Then it determines the age of rocks by the fossils found in them, so rocks containing fossils of **simpler** animals are considered older, and those containing fossils of more **complex** animals are considered younger. With a system like this, it would seem that evolutionists couldn't miss!

Resorting to this MERRY-GO-ROUND type of reasoning embarrasses evolutionists, so they don't talk about it much. But R. H. Rastall, of Cambridge University, admits it in the *Encyclopedia Britannica*: "It cannot be denied that from a strictly philosophical standpoint geologists are here **arguing in a circle.** The succession of organisms has been determined by a study of their remains buried in the rocks, and the relative ages of the rocks are determined by the remains of organisms that they contain." [66]

To me, this is a fatal admission, for I have my doubts about theories that involve the fallacy of reasoning in a circle. But perhaps even this circular logic wouldn't be so bad IF it were fully consistent—that is, if the fossils and the rock layers containing them were always found in the assumed order. But **countless contradictions and inconsistencies are found everywhere!** In many places—in *every* mountainous region on *every* continent—are many examples of strata with fossils which are LESS complex *on top of* MORE complex fossils. We'd naturally think that strata on top are more recent than those underneath, but since they contain "less evolved" fossils, they're called older. It's as if some *giant* took a huge pancake turner, scooped up thousands of square miles, and flipped them over **upside down** so that the layers are reversed.

---

66. Robert H. Rastall, *Encyclopedia Britannica*, Fourteenth Edition (1956), Volume 10, p. 168, article "Geology."

The problem of how rocks laid down earlier could **climb on top** of rocks laid down later is so serious for evolutionists that, to resolve it, they say that the rocks on top did not **form there** by sedimentation but **came** from **other places.** This might be plausible if it were limited to small amounts of rock, but as it is, countless MILLIONS of TONS of rock would have to be moved, sometimes for **hundreds of miles,** to find themselves on top of "more recent" strata. Even this might occasionally be possible if we were dealing with gravel or boulders, but it's often *layers* which are even and smooth—in many cases thousands of square miles in area.

This problem has necessitated building theory upon theory upon theory. We hear of "displaced geological beds" and "overthrust" theories, but they can account for only small shifts at the most. Yet some of these "displaced" beds cover an immense expanse. For instance, the Lewis Overthrust in the area of Montana is 6 miles thick and 135 to 350 miles long, weighing approximately 800,000 **BILLION TONS!** Its rock layers are in **reverse order** to that demanded by the theory of evolution, but there's no real physical evidence of a thrust fault —no evidence of sliding, grinding, or abrasive action between the layers, not to mention the problem of the source of the tremendous **energy** required to move such gigantic blocks of rock.

But these out-of-order strata are quite common. In the strange world of geologic dating, *any* combination of geologic ages can occur in ANY vertical order. Any age may be present or absent, in normal chronological order or inverted, with supposedly "ancient" rock formations resting on supposedly "young" formations. This is **exactly contrary** to the requirements of both evolution and common sense, which would require the oldest rocks at the bottom.

Thus the record of the rocks, as interpreted by evolutionary geologists, provides a **very SHAKY foundation** for the theory of evolution. In fact, Robin S. Allen, a geologist of some importance, made this startling statement: "Because of the sterility of its concepts, historical geology, which includes paleontology and stratigraphy, has become static and unproductive. **Current methods . . . of establishing chronology are of *dubious* validity.** Worse than that, the criteria of correlation—the attempt to equate in time, or synchronize the geological history of one area with that of another—are *logically vulnerable.* **The findings of historical geology are SUSPECT** because the PRINCIPLES upon which they are based are either *inadequate,* in which case they should be reformulated, or *false,* in which case they should be discarded. Most of us REFUSE to discard or reformulate, and the result is **the present deplorable state of our discipline.**"[67]

Exhibit A: The Horse

The classic example which convinces many people of the supposed truth of evolution, is the fossil record of ancient horses. The development of the horse is allegedly one of the most **concrete** examples of evolution. But how valid, really, is this example?

1. Textbook illustrations and museum displays impress the casual observer with the apparent stages in the so-called horse "series" of development. But the fact is that this succession is entirely man-made and has been assembled from several localities. The bones of fossil horses were gathered from different parts of the world and deliberately arranged in evolutionary sequence. In not even one place can this order be found in the actual rocks. The only reason for arranging the fossils in this order (from the most "primitive" to the modern horse) is the ASSUMPTION that evolution

---

67. Robin S. Allen, "Geological Correlation and Paleoecology," *Bulletin of the Geological Society of America*, Vol. 59 (January, 1948), p. 2.

has taken place. Thus after *artificially* arranging the fossils to tell the story of evolution, evolutionists turn around and offer the same as **proof** of evolution! Scientist Theodosius Dobzhansky frankly states: "Many textbooks and popular accounts of biology represent the evolution of the horse family as starting with *eohippus* [the primitive "dawn horse"] and progressing in a direct line towards the modern horse, *Equus*. This evolutionary progress involved, allegedly, the animals getting steadily larger and larger, while their feet were losing toe after toe, until just a single hoof was left. According to Simpson, **this OVERSIMPLIFICATION really amounts to a FALSIFICATION.**" [68]

Here one eminent evolutionist quotes another to tell us that what is commonly taught about the supposed evolution of the horse is an **"oversimplification . . . a falsification"**! And anthropologist Ashley Montagu, a leader in his field, deplores the misleading charts shown in evolutionary textbooks to illustrate the assumed development of the horse. Such a diagram, he says, "puts the *chart* before the *horse"!* [69]

2. Even in this famous horse "series," transitional links between the major stages are missing. Evolutionist Lecomte du Nouy, speaking of the horse family, admits: "The known forms remain separated like the piers of a ruined bridge. . . . The continuity we **surmise** may **never** be established by FACTS." [70]

---

68. Theodosius Dobzhansky, *Evolution, Genetics, and Man* (New York: John Wiley & Sons, Inc., 1955), p. 302.

69. M. F. Ashley Montagu, *An Introduction to Physical Anthropology*, Third Edition (Springfield, Illinois: Charles C. Thomas, Publisher, 1960), p. 267.

70. Lecomte du Nouy, *Human Destiny* (New York: Longmans, Green & Co., Inc., 1947), p. 95.

Professor Goldschmidt echoes du Nouy's statement: "Within the slowly evolving series, like the famous horse series, the decisive steps are **abrupt WITHOUT transition**."[71] So here again the "links" are missing!

3. As for the assumed increase in *size*, that, too, "is **subjective** and NOT supported by the data," says evolutionist George Gaylord Simpson. He adds, "The diagrams of steady increase in size [of fossil horses] are made by **selecting** species that FIT this PRECONCEIVED idea."[72] Furthermore, many fossil horses have been found in many regions, **fully as large** and sometimes **larger** than the modern horse. Besides, there's a great range in size among *living* horses today: On the one hand we see huge draft horses like the Clydesdale or Percheron, and yet "A miniature type of pony bred in England often grows no taller than 28 inches."[73] So differences in size are certainly no proof of evolution.

4. There's an interesting **discrepancy** in the skeletal development of this series—the anatomy of the various models does not compare. For example, the RIB COUNT VARIES back and forth from 15 to 19: *Eohippus* had 18 pairs of ribs; *Orohippus* had only 15 pairs; then *Pliohippus* jumped to 19; and *Equus scotti* is back to 18. Also, the lumbars of the backbone vary back and forth from 6 to 8. Therefore, many eminent scientists disagree on the theoretical chain of fossil horses.

5. Finally, consider the CHANGE in the **number of toes**. The evidence for a gradual change from **four** toes on the

---

71. R. B. Goldschmidt, *American Scientist*, Volume 40 (1952), p. 97.
72. George Gaylord Simpson, *Tempo and Mode in Evolution* (New York: Columbia University Press, 1944), p. 160.
73. *World Book Encyclopedia* (1964 edition), Volume 13, p. 311.

front legs and **three** on the back to just **one** toe on each
is presented as a proof of evolution. But it really proves
the wrong thing, because it moves from the COMPLEX to
the SIMPLE—from **more** toes to **less**! Evolution demands
an *increase* in complexity which proponents of the theory
say has brought us from the simple cell to life as we know
it today. **Losing** toes makes an animal more simple, not
more complex. The process carried to an absolute extreme
could reduce the horse to a one-celled organism, but it could
never evolve a one-celled creature into a horse. At the most,
the horse "series" demonstrates **degeneration** rather than
progressive evolution.

How much credence can we place in a theory based on
this kind of evidence as its strongest "proof"?

XI. MAN—FROM THE APES, OR NOT?

Over the years, I've had occasion to discuss Darwin's
brainchild with many evolutionists. In these discussions I've
encountered an extremely interesting, though inexplicable,
reaction. Whenever I voice my disbelief in the idea that
human beings descended from apes, the evolutionist smiles
indulgently and replies in a very predictable way: He patiently explains that the evolutionary development of **man**
from **apes** is a popular misconception—he asserts that
Darwin never taught such a thing, that evolutionists today
do not teach it, and he suggests in a kindly way that I should
get my facts straight.

Often he'll go on to say that evolution merely states that
both apes and men have evolved from some unknown ancestor. So he concludes that I'm guilty of **slander** against
evolution when I erroneously impute ideas to the theory
which it never taught.

Naturally, after encountering this reaction I began to wonder where people ever got the idea that, according to evolution, man came from the apes. Here's a little of what I found: Darwin really DID say man evolved from monkeys. In the conclusion of Chapter VI in his book *The Descent of Man*, the apostle of evolution declared: "The Simiadae then branched off into two great stems, the New World and Old World *MONKEYS;* and **from the latter,** at a remote period, **Man,** the wonder and glory of the Universe, **proceeded.**"[74] Modern evolutionists perpetuate this idea almost as a ceaseless refrain. Professor Earnest Albert Hooton, Harvard anthropologist, puts it this way: *"Fossil man* invented the first tools and discovered the use of fire; he was probably the originator of articulate speech. **He made himself from an APE** and created human culture."[75]

Let's look at a few key chapters among the beautifully illustrated (and, unfortunately, widely influential) books in the Life Nature Library put out by TIME-LIFE Books. One volume is called *Early Man* and contains a chapter entitled **"Back Beyond the APES"** and another significantly called **"Forward from the APES."** A volume on *The Primates* has a concluding chapter entitled **"From APE Toward Man."** *Early Man* contains a five-page foldout chart showing apes in a straight line of development leading to modern man. This full-color chart has been reproduced in countless magazine advertisements for the books. Under one of the **APES** pictured (*Ramapithecus*), we're told that some experts believe that beast to be "the oldest of **man's ancestors in a direct line.**"[76]

74. Charles Darwin, *The Descent of Man*, Second Edition in One Volume (Philadelphia: David McKay, 1901), Chapter VI, p. 181.
75. Earnest Albert Hooton, *Apes, Men, and Morons* (Freeport, New York: Books for Libraries Press, 1970), p. 105.
76. F. Clark Howell and the Editors of Time-Life Books, *Early Man* (New York: Time-Life Books, 1970), p. 42.

The public is further misled by deliberately depicting the apes **walking upright** on two feet like a man, though apes always are "knuckle-walkers," shuffling about on all fours. This misrepresentation of posture supposedly is done "for purposes of comparison," but the average reader is left with the erroneous impression that the evolution of **man from ape** is very plausible.

Those books, thoroughly steeped in evolutionary philosophy, represent one of the greatest publishing ventures ever undertaken. And Desmond Morris wrote a popular book about man called *The Naked APE*. Subtitled *A Zoologist's Study of the Human Animal,* Dr. Morris's book was given wide circulation as a BOOK-OF-THE-MONTH CLUB SELECTION. There he calmly declares that "There are one hundred and ninety-*three* living species of monkeys and apes. One hundred and ninety-*two* of them are covered with hair. The exception is a naked APE self-named *Homo sapiens. . . .* He is proud that he has the biggest brain of all the primates, but . . . in becoming so erudite, *Homo sapiens* has remained a naked **APE** nonetheless." [77]

Perhaps the popular idea connecting man's supposed evolution with apes is **not** so much of a misconception after all! For it's not just **popular** books put out for public consumption like those mentioned above which teach the *ape / man* connection—it's **scholarly textbooks** used by the college students of our nation which make one wonder: Is there a **MONKEY** in your family tree? Is man a miracle?—or a mutation? Did man come from *GOD*—or *GORILLA?*

An example of such a textbook (used at the college where I teach and at countless others across the country) is one edited by famed evolutionary anthropologist Louis Leakey entitled *Adam, or Ape: A Sourcebook of Discoveries About*

---

77. Desmond Morris, *The Naked Ape: A Zoologist's Study of the Human Animal* (New York: McGraw-Hill Book Company, 1967), p. 9.

Early Man. When impressionable college freshmen are presented with the "**Adam or APE**" alternative by instructors who themselves have been brain-washed by evolutionary dogma, you can guess to which side they will lean.

Before we can accept the contention that evolution *does not teach* that "Man came from apes," the evolutionists are going to have to get their stories straight!

Bones of Contention: "Early Man" Fossils

For years, evolutionists have tried to link man to lower forms of life. Their efforts are doomed to failure, since man did not originate that way. But millions of young boys and girls in school have been exposed to pictures and stories of "cave men" which promote evolutionary concepts. No doubt men **did** live in caves many years ago—in some parts of the world they still do. Some isolated tribes can be found living under extremely primitive conditions today, and future generations could dig up **their** remains and judge them to be thousands of years **older** than other societies also living today.

The discovery of "primitive" human remains, evolutionists say, proves that man has evolved from ape-like creatures. To clinch their argument, they show a series of effigies of the more notorious human fossils—a regular "rogues' gallery" of fossil men, such as Neanderthal Man, Cro-Magnon Man, Java Man, Peking Man, Nebraska Man, Piltdown Man, etc., ending with a representation of modern man.

Schools often have students visit museums displaying such evolutionary exhibits. But Thomas Hunt Morgan, himself an evolutionist, deplores this practice and says: "I have never known such a course to fail of its intention. In fact I know that the student often becomes **so thoroughly convinced** that he RESENTS any such attempt as that which I am about to make to point out that **the evidence for his conviction is not above criticism.**"[78]

---

78. Thomas Hunt Morgan, *A Critique of the Theory of Evolution* (Princeton, New Jersey: Princeton University Press, 1916), p. 9.

In the first place, the evidence provided by fossils to anthropology (the study of man) is extremely limited. Discussing the recent discovery of a bone fragment purportedly human, *Newsweek* Magazine reports: "The EVIDENCE for man's evolution **could hardly be more tenuous**: a collection of a few hundred fossilized skulls, teeth, jawbones and other fragments. Physical anthropologists, however, have been ingenious at reading this record—perhaps **too ingenious**, for there are almost as many versions of man's early history as there are anthropologists to propose them. There are only a few facts on which all the scientists have agreed."[79]

Though the evidence for human evolution is scarce and sketchy, **fossil man** is still a **live issue** among evolutionists. Let's examine this evidence briefly.

NEANDERTHAL MAN: In 1856 portions of a skeleton were dug out of a cave in the Neander Valley near Dusseldorf, Germany. Fourteen pieces of bone were found, but only the skull-cap was of much diagnostic value. Darwin's followers claimed this find was a "link" between man and ape, and in 1856 it was classified as *Homo* (man) *neanderthalensis*. Partial remains of three similar skeletons were discovered in 1886 in Belgium, and a few other finds have also been made.

Evolution-minded scientists of the day depicted Neanderthal Man as a squat, stooping, ape-like creature. In an article called "Upgrading Neanderthal Man," *Time* Magazine explained: "Neanderthal's apish image was further enforced by the writings early in this century of the respected French paleontologist Pierre Marcellin Boule. His portrait of Neanderthal as a stunted, beetle-browed creature who walked with bent knees and arms dangling in front of him served as the model for several generations of artists and cartoonists."[80]

---

79. "Bones of Contention," *Newsweek* (February 13, 1967), p. 101.
80. "Upgrading Neanderthal Man," *Time* (May 17, 1971), p. 76.

Boule's prestige as Director of the French Institute of Human Paleontology was great, and his work on Neanderthal Man was considered the final authority. The only trouble was, Boule was mistaken—and many other evolutionary scientists perpetuated his error over the years before the truth was discovered. It's now known that Boule based his con clusions on a **poor specimen:** because the skeleton he studied had curvature of the spine, he felt this was good evidence that man did not always walk upright.

But later Neanderthal discoveries brought forth skeletons that stood perfectly upright. Subsequently the Boule specimen with curvature of the spine was re-examined and found to have suffered from a form of arthritis. Two anatomists, Dr. W. L. Straus of Johns Hopkins and Dr. A. J. E. Cave of St. Bartholomew's Hospital Medical College in London, have published a thorough study on the **posture** of Neanderthal Man that shows the supposed ape-like features are mistaken interpretations without foundation in fact. Concerning the fossil remains they write:

> We were somewhat unprepared for the fragmentary nature of the skeleton itself and for the consequent extent of restoration required. Nor were we prepared for the severity of the *osteoarthritis deformans* affecting the vertebral column. . . . There is thus no valid reason for the assumption that the posture of Neanderthal Man . . . differed significantly from that of present-day men. . . . There is nothing in this total morphological pattern to justify the common assumption that Neanderthal Man was other than a fully erect biped when standing and walking. It may be that the arthritic [specimen used by Boule] . . . of Neanderthal Man did actually stand and walk with something of a pathological kyphosis; but, if so, he has his counterparts in modern men similarly afflicted with spinal

osteoarthritis. He cannot, in view of his manifest pathology, be used to provide us with a reliable picture of a healthy, **normal** Neanderthalian. Notwithstanding, if he could be reincarnated and **placed in a New York subway**—provided that he were bathed, shaved, and dressed in modern clothing—it is doubtful whether he would attract any more attention than some of its other denizens. [81]

It's true that Neanderthal fossils do possess certain characteristics, particularly in the shape of the skull and face, which differ from the average modern man. But scientists believe this was due to the pituitary disorder known as *acromegaly*. In his book *Up from the Ape*, Harvard evolutionist Earnest Albert Hooton informs us that "acromegaly, a disease . . . of the pituitary gland, produces in its victims an elongation of the **face** and **jaws** and an enlargement of the **brow-ridges** and increase in the forehead slope. . . . It is possible that the great brow-ridges, deep jaws, and other features common to . . . the Neanderthal type have been developed through some hyperfunctioning of the pituitary. . . ." [82]

While much is made of the fact that some fossil men had brains somewhat smaller than those of modern man (a fact which could easily be explained by their being degenerate strains), it's remarkable that Neanderthal's brain chamber was LARGER than the average for men today. Modern man has a brain capacity somewhere between 1200 and 1500 cc., but in *Up from the Ape* evolutionary anthropologist Hooton tells us that Boule's specimen of Neanderthal Man "had a

81. William L. Straus, Jr., and A. J. E. Cave,"Pathology and the Posture of Neanderthal Man," *Quarterly Review of Biology*, Volume 32, No. 4 (December, 1957), pp. 348-363.

82. Earnest Albert Hooton, *Up from the Ape*, Revised Edition (New York: The Macmillan Company, 1946), p. 346.

cranial capacity of about 1600 cc., which is *far above the average* of male Europeans today. In the gross size of the brain, the Neanderthal ancients were quite up to the level of modern man." [83]

And, far from being the barbaric brutes that fictionized science paints them to be, Neanderthal Man made cave paintings, cultivated flowers, and buried his dead. A recent book calls the Neanderthals "the first flower people" and reports that an archeological expedition found that at least one of the nine Neanderthal skeletons uncovered in the Shanidar cave was buried with flowers. Comments Dr. Carleton S. Coon, anthropologist at the University of Pennsylvania and past president of the American Association of Physical Anthropologists: "On the ground of **behavior** alone, the Shanidar folk merit the title of *Homo sapiens* [that is, fully human, "thinking" man]." [84]

Finally, referring to the "Many misconceptions . . . found in popular books, even textbooks," particularly concerning the "brutish Neanderthals," French prehistorian Francois Bordes declares: "Reconstructions show him as only a little better off than the big apes, and his tools are described as 'crude'by people who would not, to save their lives, be able to make them. The TRUTH is, indeed, **quite different.**" [85]

CRO-MAGNON MAN: Named for a cave in southwestern France where the remains of these men were found in 1868, Cro-Magnon Man was skilled in working with both bone and stone. Dr. William C. Putnam, Professor of Geology at UCLA, reports that the Cro-Magnons "developed the

---

83. *Ibid.*, p. 329.

84. Carleton S. Coon, quoted in "Upgrading Neanderthal Man," *Time* (May 17, 1971), p. 75. See also Ralph S. Solecki, *Shanidar: The First Flower People* (New York: Alfred A. Knopf, 1971).

85. Francois Bordes, "Mousterian Cultures in France," *Science*, Volume 134 (September 22, 1961), p. 803.

technique of fashioning stone tools and weapons to a degree
of **perfection never equalled since.**[86] Also, these people
were a highly artistic race. Objects of art include a variety
of ivory carvings, and on the walls of their caves are drawings and colored paintings of many of the animals they hunted.
Portraits or caricatures include human faces, some of which
are bearded and others clean-shaven. These drawings, of
superb artistic quality, are "vibrantly life-like."[87]

Cro-Magnon Man, like his Neanderthal brother, had
learned to make and use fire. He also buried his dead. Professor Hooton reports the discovery of one Cro-Magnon family
"buried with **tombstones** at their heads and at their feet."[88]

And the Cro-Magnon race was known to have been superior to modern man, in both physical size and brain capacity.
They were tall and well-proportioned, the men often reaching
more than six feet in height. As to cranial capacity, it aver-
aged larger than that of either Neanderthal or modern man.
Note how Dr. Hooton speaks of "the skull of the Cro-Magnon
man that is supposed to define the type. It is a *massive* skull,
large in every dimension. . . . The brain-case of this old man
is estimated to have contained 1660 cc., which is roughly
150 cc. above the modern European average [and the modern
European average is larger than the average for other living
races of the world]."[89] As the *Science Digest* puts it: "Since
the Cro-Magnon man . . . the human brain has been **decreasing** in size."[90] This indicates **degeneration**, not evolution.
In fact, modern man himself may be a somewhat deterio-
rated descendant of these ancestors.

---

86. William C. Putnam, *Geology* (New York: Oxford University
Press, 1964), p. 463.

87. *Ibid.*

88. Earnest Albert Hooton, *Up from the Ape*, Revised Edition
(New York: The Macmillan Company, 1946), p. 371.

89. *Ibid.*, pp. 367-368.

90. *Science Digest* (April 1951), p. 33.

JAVA MAN: The discovery called Java Man fills an important niche in the evolutionary Hall of Fame. It was made in 1891 by Eugene Dubois, a Dutch army doctor. Dubois had gone to the island of Java with the announced purpose of discovering primitive man, and there, on the bank of the Solo River, he unearthed two teeth and a piece of a skull-cap. The teeth were found separated from the skull-cap, lying several feet away. A year later, and at a distance more than fifteen yards from the place where he had found the skull-cap, Dubois uncovered a thigh bone. [91] Despite the fact that the thigh bone and skull-cap were so widely scattered, Dubois asserted that "both of them, and the teeth as well, belonged to **one skeleton**"! [92]

Pictures and reconstructions in museums of Java Man (complete even to the hair) give the unsuspecting public the impression that the specimen must have been quite intact. But as you can see, the scattered remains were very meager. In 1894 Dubois returned from Java and published his scientific report on the famous "missing link." *Evolution*, a volume in the *Life Nature Library*, says, "Deliberately and almost provocatively, Dubois named this creature he had materialized from the past *Pithecanthropus erectus*" [93]—"erect ape-man," from the Greek *pithekos* for **ape**, and *anthropos* for **man**. Dubois unhesitatingly declared that his find "represents a so-called transition form between man and apes . . . the immediate progenitor of the human race."[94]

---

91. Eugene Dubois, *"Pithecanthropus erectus*—a Form from the Ancestral Stock of Mankind," in Louis S. B. Leakey, editor, *Adam, or Ape: A Sourcebook of Discoveries About Early Man* (Cambridge, Massachusetts: Schenkman Publishing Company, 1971), p. 167.

92. *Ibid.*, p. 175.

93. Ruth Moore and the Editors of LIFE, *Evolution* (New York: Time Incorporated, 1962), p. 131.

94. Eugene Dubois, in Louis S. B. Leakey, *op. cit.,* p. 175.

Naturally, his assertions caused quite a controversy in society, even among the scientists of his day. Then Dubois, annoyed at the skepticism and criticism that greeted his discovery, "became increasingly suspicious and eccentric."[95] "In 1895 he locked the fossils in a strongbox . . . and permitted no one to see them for the next 28 years."[96] It was not until 1923, after Dr. Henry Fairfield Osborn, head of the American Museum of Natural History, appealed to the president of the Dutch Academy of Sciences, that Dubois opened his strongbox and again allowed scientists to see the original bones. So there is some basis for questioning the integrity and judgment of Dubois. He considered anyone who opposed his ideas a personal enemy. For thirty years he refused to allow his finds to be studied by other scientists. "If anyone came to his door in whom he scented a colleague, he was simply not at home." On other occasions, "he was stated to be ill."[97]

Dubois estimated the cranial capacity of Java Man to be about 900 cc., about two thirds of that for modern man—but it's impossible to determine cranial capacity from a skull-cap alone. Furthermore, Dubois concealed the fact that he had also discovered at nearby Wadjak, and at approximately the same level, two human skulls (known as the Wadjak skulls) with a cranial capacity of about 1550-1650 cc., somewhat **above** the present human average. To have revealed this fact at that time (1890's) would have made it difficult, if not impossible, for his Java Man to have been accepted as a "missing link." It wasn't until 1920, when a similar discovery was about to be announced, that Dubois revealed the fact that

---

95. F. Clark Howell and the Editors of Time-Life Books, *Early Man* (New York: Time-Life Books, 1970), p. 13.

96. Ruth Moore and the Editors of LIFE, *Evolution* (New York: Time Incorporated, 1962), p. 132.

97. Richard M. Ritland, *A Search for Meaning in Nature* (Boise, Idaho: Pacific Press Publishing Association, 1970), footnote on p. 250.

he had possessed the Wadjak skulls for thirty years. (Apparently such concealment of evidence that did not conform to the theory was not a rare or isolated practice. Evolutionary anthropologist Hooton, for instance, brings this candid indictment: "Heretical and non-conforming fossil men were **banished** to the limbo of dark museum cupboards, **forgotten** or even **destroyed**."[98])

Puzzlingly enough, evolutionists report that "Dubois became, as it were, **his own opponent**. Having discovered the earliest man, he fought doggedly throughout the rest of his life to maintain that *Pithecanthropus* was NOT an early man but a giant man-like ape."[99] The work of Dubois on Java was continued by German paleontologist G. H. R. von Koenigswald, who also informs us that Dubois finally decided that his *Pithecanthropus* bones belonged to a larger gibbonlike ape.[100] Von Koenigswald concludes: "It therefore becomes manifest on what **shaky ground** Dubois erected his hypothetical building, and we can only wonder at the *boldness* and *t enacity* with which he defended his *Pithecanthropus*."[101]

PEKING MAN: Near Peking, China, in 1927, Davidson Black found a lower molar tooth. From this **single tooth** he created a new genus and named it *Sinanthropus pekinensis* ("Chinese man of Peking"). Two years later, further digging at this site led to the discovery of some fourteen

---

98. Earnest Albert Hooton, *Apes, Men, and Morons* (Freeport, New York: Books for Libraries Press, 1970), p. 107.

99. Marcellin Boule and Henry V. Vallois, *Fossil Men* (New York: The Dryden Press, 1957), p. 3.

100. G. H. R. von Koenigswald, *Meeting Prehistoric Man* (New York: Harper & Brothers, 1956), p. 55. Also, on page 147 of *Man's Evolution*, by C. L. Brace and M. F. Ashley Montagu (Toronto, Ontario: The Macmillan Company), we read that "Strangest of all, however, was the view of Dubois himself when he once again began to publish on his discoveries. His revised opinion was that *Pithecanthropus* had been **a giant gibbon and quite unrelated to the human** line of development."

101. Von Koenigswald, *op. cit.*, p. 34.

skull-caps, portions of facial bones, many teeth, and a few limb bones. By comparing pieces and combining information from all fourteen skull-caps or parts, it still was not possible to restore one complete skull. Professor Hooton explains: "It appears that these skulls were trophies of head hunters, and, furthermore, that said hunters usually bashed in the bases of the skulls when fresh, presumably to eat the brains therein contained. Many crania show that their owners met their deaths as a result of skull fractures induced by heavy blows."[102]

Thus the evidence given by Peking Man was always sparse—but **now** it's non-existent, for it was lost when the Japanese advanced on Peking in December, 1941. All that existed of Peking Man has disappeared, never to be seen again.[103] To this day no record has come to light of the unhappy fate of Peking Man.

"Put Not Your Faith In RECONSTRUCTIONS"

Fossil evidence of man's evolution is, therefore, extremely scarce. As recently as 1956, the paleontologist G. H. R. von Koenigswald, who spent much of his earlier life searching for human fossils, calculated that if ALL the then-known fragments of *Homo erectus* were gathered together they could be comfortably displayed on a medium-sized table.[104]

But this scarcity has not hindered evolutionists from "reconstructing" fragmentary fossils into full-fledged individuals. How precarious a business this restoration of a fossil specimen can be is seen from Dr. Hooton's statement: "No

---

102. Earnest Albert Hooton, *Up from the Ape* (New York: The Macmillan Company, 1946), Revised Edition, p. 304.

103. Ruth Moore and the Editors of LIFE, *Evolution* (New York: Time Incorporated, 1962), p. 136. See also James Stewart-Gordon, "The Mystery of the Missing Bones," *Reader's Digest* (September, 1976), pp. 177-186.

104. G. H. R. von Koenigswald, *Meeting Prehistoric Man* (New York: Harper & Brothers, 1956), p. 18.

anthropologist is justified in reconstructing the entire skeleton of an unfamiliar type of fossil man from parts of the skull-cap, one or two teeth, and perhaps a few oddments of mandible [jaw] and long bones. . . . Inferences concerning the **missing** parts are very precarious, unless more complete skeletons of other individuals of the same type are available to support the reconstruction." [105]

A reconstruction is nothing more than an interpretation by the scientist making it, and entering into such an inter pretation will inevitably be his subjective opinion and personal prejudice. "When a scientist finds a single bone or tooth which supposedly dates back a few hundred thousand years, on what basis of measurement can he draw a picture of the whole creature? When the first fossil bones were discovered many years ago, there were no other bones with which to compare them, no other measurements by which to judge them, so the first drawings of ancient men were the products of **imagination**. The men who drew the first pictures **imagined** man as rather ape-like in appearance, so they drew him with the facial features of a creature sort of half-way between a man and an ape. They gave him a slightly crouching stance, a long face with huge jaws, and a look of doubtful intelligence. This picture has *stayed with us* down through the years."[106]

Harvard anthropologist Earnest Albert Hooton warns us, "Put *not* your faith in reconstructions," for scientists can't tell what the eyes, ears, nose, and lips looked like. They don't know what the skin color was or the hair color or texture, or whether there was a light or heavy beard or no beard at all. In fact, a Neanderthal skull can be made to look very modern or very primitive.

---

105. Earnest Albert Hooton, *Apes, Man and Morons* (Freeport, New York: Books for Libraries Press, 1970), p. 115.

106. David D. Riegle, *Creation or Evolution?* (Grand Rapids, Michigan: Zondervan Publishing House, 1971), pp. 47-48.

Professor Hooton concludes with this penetrating statement: "Some anatomists model reconstructions of fossil skulls by building up the **soft parts** of the head and **face** upon a skull cast and thus produce a bust purporting to represent the appearance of the fossil man in life. When, however, we recall the **fragmentary** condition of most of the skulls, the faces usually being missing, we can readily see that even the reconstruction of the facial **skeleton**, leaves room for a good deal of DOUBT as to details. To attempt to restore the **soft parts** is an *even more hazardous undertaking.* The lips, the eyes, the ears, and the nasal tip leave *no clues* on the underlying bony parts. You can, with equal facility, model on a Neanderthaloid skull **the features of a CHIMPANZEE or the lineaments of a PHILOSOPHER.** These *alleged* restorations of ancient types of man have very little, if any, scientific value and are likely only to *mislead* the public."[107]

Skull Duggery

Evolutionists, proceeding as they do on the basis of such flimsy evidence, are bound to make some embarrassing mistakes. One such fiasco was the case of **NEBRASKA MAN.**

Nebraska Man was actually nothing more than a tooth, a single rather worn molar tooth found in Nebraska by an individual named Harold Cook in 1922. Cook mailed the tooth to the famous paleontologist Henry Fairfield Osborn, director of the American Museum of Natural History in New York City. Fascinated with such a find, Osborn immediately compared the specimen with "all the books, all the casts, and all the drawings" and consulted with three other scientists, two of whom were eminent specialists on fossil primates. Here, they felt, was the first proof of early man on the North American continent. They wrote an article for a scientific

---

107. Earnest Albert Hooton, *Up from the Ape,* Revised Edition (New York: The Macmillan Company, 1946), p. 329.

journal announcing the discovery, stating: "It is hard to believe that a single water-worn tooth . . . can signalize the arrival of the anthropoid primates in North America. . . . We have been eagerly anticipating some discovery of this kind, but were not prepared for **such convincing evidence** . . ."![108]
Osborn and his colleagues couldn't quite decide whether the original owner of this tooth should be classed as an apelike man or a man-like ape. He was given the important-sounding scientific name of *Hesperopithecus haroldcookii* ("Harold Cook's Western Ape") and become popularly known as Nebraska Man. The London *Daily Illustrated News* displayed a full-page spread on Nebraska Man. They reconstructed this creature from his tooth alone, exhibiting his exact shape, even to the prominent brow ridges and broad shoulders.[109] As a matter of fact, in 1925 the *Hesperopithecus* tooth was even introduced as "evidence" by the expert testimony of evolutionists in the famous Scopes "monkey trial" in Tennessee.

But two years later, Nebraska Man's career came to an abrupt halt. It turned out that he was not a man. He was not even an ape. Evolutionist Le Gros Clark explains: "As is well known, the tooth proved later to be that of a fossil peccary"[110]—a small animal resembling a pig! Dr. Duane Gish says, "This is a case in which a pig made a monkey out of an evolutionist!"[111]

Experiences like this tend to keep most scientists humble and cautious. Professor Clark goes on to say that "there

---

108.   Henry Fairfield Osborn, *"Hesperopithecus*, the First Anthropoid Primate Found in America," *American Museum Novitates*, No. 37 (April, 1922), pp. 1-5.
109.   London *Daily Illustrated News,* June 24, 1922.
110.   W. E. Le Gros Clark, *The Fossil Evidence for Human Evolution* (Chicago: The University of Chicago Press, 1955), p. 25.
111.   Duane T. Gish, *Evolution—The Fossils Say NO!* (San Diego: ICR Publishing Company, 1973), p. 91. (*Note*: This is an excellent book.)

can be few paleontologists who have not erred in this way
at some time or another!"[112]   But mistakes, of course, are
understandable. Less acceptable is outright fraud, such as
we see in the case of Charles Dawson's **PILTDOWN MAN**.

The extent to which some evolutionists have stooped to
manufacture the facts so sorely needed for their theory is
well illustrated in the case of the "earliest Englishman," as
Piltdown Man was frequently dubbed. Early in 1912, Charles
Dawson, an amateur fossil hunter, brought some specimens
to Dr. Arthur Smith Woodward, the Director of the British
Museum. Dawson said he'd found them in a gravel pit near
Piltdown, south of London.

Soon the world was informed of the discovery of most of
one side of a lower jaw, with the first and second molar teeth
still in place, and part of a skull. The skull seemed human,
but the jaw was clearly ape-like. Yet surfaces of the teeth
were flat—and only a human jaw, with its free-swinging
motion, could have worn them down to that flat-top
shape. Thus the find appeared to be a "missing link" in
human evolution. Prehistoric animal remains found in the
same gravel pit made this fossil the earliest known human.
In honor of the discoverer, Woodward named it *Eoanthropus dawsoni* ("Dawson's Dawn Man"), more commonly
called Piltdown Man.

Controversy existed among scientists, some of whom
claimed that the human cranium and ape-like jaw did not
match, but most evolutionists used Piltdown Man to their
advantage. Pictures and plaster casts of the Piltdown reconstruction were widely displayed in books and museums, and
the *Encyclopedia Britannica* called Piltdown Man the second
most important of the fossils in showing the evolution of
man, adding authoritatively: "Amongst British authorities

112.   W. E. Le Gros Clark, *The Fossil Evidence for Human Evolution*
(Chicago: The University of Chicago Press, 1955), p. 25.

there is now agreement that the skull and jaw are parts of the same individual."[113] For more than forty years Piltdown Man did his work as a cardinal member of the evolutionary Hall of Fame.

Then it was learned that Piltdown Man was **a careful, cunning forgery**—a complete FAKE! In 1953 three scientists (Dr. Kenneth Oakley, a British Museum geologist; Dr. J. S. Weiner, Oxford University anthropologist; and Dr. Le Gros Clark, professor of anatomy at Oxford University) proved that the fossils comprising Piltdown Man were a clever but shameful hoax. Using sophisticated new instruments as modern as X-ray spectrograph and Geiger counter, they subjected the hallowed Piltdown fragments to the most searching and critical examination they had ever received. Instead of being half a million years old as originally estimated, the skull was closer to several thousand—and the jawbone wasn't fossilized at all! An improved chemical dating test showed that the jaw wasn't much older than the year of its discovery.

The jaw had come from a modern ape, probably an orangutan. But the jaw and the non-human teeth had been cunningly "fossilized" by staining them with chemicals to give them the appearance of age. Moreover, telltale scratches on the molars showed beyond doubt that the teeth had been artificially filed down. In plaster casts of the Piltdown jaw studied the world over, these details were lost, but they were only too clear in the original specimens examined by these scientists in the British Museum. As stated in the *Reader's Digest* article on "The Great Piltdown Hoax": "Every important piece proved a **forgery**. Piltdown Man was a **fraud** from start to finish!"[114]

While this story shows that modern methods have improved over those of earlier years, it also shows that **scientists can be fooled** in examining and dating fossils.

---

113. *Encyclopedia Britannica* (1946 edition), Volume 14, p. 763.

114. Alden P. Armagnac, "The Great Piltdown Hoax," *Reader's Digest* (October, 1956), p. 182.

The whole fantastic story was published in *The Piltdown Forgery*, a fascinating, real-life "whodunit" by Dr. J. S. Weiner, "chief detective" in the case.[115] Although "all circumstantial evidence points to Dawson as the author of the hoax,"[116] Weiner will not flatly accuse him in the absence of absolute proof. The curious Mr. Dawson died in 1916 at the age of 52 and at the height of his fame. If his purpose in perpetrating the infamous hoax was to achieve recognition, then he died happy, for "he did win fame in his own time as the fossil was named for him —*Eoanthropus dawsoni*"![117]

Yes, Charles Dawson, like Charles Darwin, is dead—but unfortunately their legacy lives on. "Today the statues of Piltdown Man have been removed from their places in the museums and his pictures from the books, though the harm he has done in destroying people's faith in God's creation of man lives on in the lives of many. It is unfortunate that greater reserve is not used in teaching as *facts* to school children things recognized by reputable scientists as being questionable."[118]

XII. WHY IS EVOLUTION ACCEPTED?

In closing this chapter, we may well inquire, *Why do people believe in evolution?* For despite the reckless boasts about evolution made by a few over-zealous supporters, we've seen that the theory contains several FATAL FLAWS.

---

115.   J. S. Weiner, *The Piltdown Forgery* (New York: Oxford University Press, 1955. See also William L. Straus, Jr., "The Great Piltdown Hoax," *Science*, Volume 119 (February 26, 1954).

116.   Alden P. Armagnac, "The Great Piltdown Hoax," *Reader's Digest* (October, 1956), p. 182.

117.   Robert Silverberg, *Scientists and Scoundrels: A Book of Hoaxes* (New York: Thomas Y. Crowell Comapny, 1965), p. 232. See also C. L. Brace and M. F. Ashley Montagu, *Man's Evolution* (Toronto, Ontario: The Macmillan Company), p. 171.

118.   Thomas F. Heinze, *The Creation vs. Evolution Handbook* (Grand Rapids, Michigan: Baker Book House, 1970), pp. 39-40. (Excellent book.)

Evolutionary theory is not only **destitute of proof** but is positively **disproved** by every test we can presently apply to it. We seek in vain for a single SHRED of direct evidence to support it. So how can we explain the fact that millions of people today accept the evolutionary philosophy?

In the first place, Darwin presented his theory not to a hostile world but to a very receptive one, a world waiting and longing for just such a theory. True, a few ardent theologians stood up against it, but they were an exception. The world in 1859 was ready for Darwin's book, and it sold remarkably well. The first edition was **completely sold out** on the very day of publication! Historian Himmelfarb is not overstating the case when she says: "The sale of the *Origin* was beyond everyone's expectations. . . . As works of science went—and such sober works of science—the *Origin* was a popular success."[119]

You see, "up to then, those who had turned away from organized religion had done so primarily as a reaction against the corruption, intolerance, and often cruelty of the [Roman Catholic] Church, defects often equalled in the 16th through 19th centuries by the Protestants. Thus, out of **reaction against** the rigidity of the Church, and fortified by science in their doubts relating to church dogma, many were **ripe indeed** for 'the book that shook the world.' "[120]

Especially ripe were many scientists of the day who still chafed under the extreme bondage to authority in which all scientists were chained during the Dark Ages. They remembered how Galileo had been forced by the power in authority, the Roman Catholic Church, to recant his scientific opinion, an opinion now known to be the truth. The oppression of science by narrow-minded individuals led scientists to look

---

119. Gerttrude Himmelfarb, *Darwin and the Darwinian Revolution* (Garden City, New York: Doubleday & Company, 1962), pp. 253-254.

120. Marshall Hall and Sandra Hall, *The TRUTH: God or Evolution?* (The Craig Press, 1974), p. 122. (Another excellent book.)

for a way of escape, and Darwin pointed toward an attractive exit. The reaction of scientists was natural enough and quite understandable. And they, like Darwin himself, believed that the evidence needed to fill in gaps in the theory would come in the course of time.

For more than a century, biological phenomena have largely been described according to evolutionary premises. If one looks at the world through **Darwinian spectacles**, if science is viewed in an evolutionary perspective, then certain answers will automatically be ruled out.

Furthermore, evolution has become a greatly **publicized** philosophy and as such has gained adherents rapidly among both scientists and laymen. Thomas Henry Huxley, for instance, was a very good salesman! Other important spokesmen from all fields of thought have given their stamp of approval to evolution. Today we live in a society **saturated** with evolutionary dogma. Evolution is the modern, *fashionable* theory that seems to be "in" today, and many unthinking people accept it simply because it's widely accepted. They've been cowed into accepting it out of fear of being called ignorant.

Probably most educated people believe in evolution simply because they've been **told** that most educated people believe in evolution! Conformity is a powerful motivating force. Ask any teenager: If there's anything he fears, it's to be different from the crowd. But we need not be seduced by the constant refrain that "All intelligent persons agree that evolution is a fact." We should realize that **many** scientists and laymen of our day resist the regimentation attempted by evolutionists—and have the moral courage to stand by their convictions.

Perhaps others accept evolution because they **want** to believe it, they **prefer** to believe in a godless universe. For if evolution is not true, then the only alternative is divine creation—and some are very uncomfortable when made to realize that God has a direct concern with this world and with their own personal lives. So they seek by every means available, consciously or subconsciously, to relegate God to as inconspicuous a role as possible. These people eagerly embrace any philosophy that dispenses with the necessity of God. Human nature being what it is, most people believe what they **want** to believe, regardless of its truth or falsity. When people have an apparent compulsion to reject the idea of God, they welcome even unproved and unprovable "scientific" notions.

The desire to be free from one's responsibility to his Maker has turned many to evolution and atheism. For example, Aldous Huxley (Sir Julian's brother and a popular novelist) gives this frank account in a magazine article called "Confessions of a Professed Atheist: Aldous Huxley": "I had **motives** for not wanting the world to have meaning; consequently assumed that it had none, and was able without any difficulty to find satisfying reasons for this assumption. . . . For myself, as, no doubt, for most of my contemporaries, the philosophy of meaninglessness was essentially an instrument of **liberation**. The liberation we desired was . . . liberation from a certain system of morality. **We objected to the morality because it interfered with our sexual freedom.**"[121]

It's sad but true that our fallen natures resist the demands of God's Word, just as it's true that "the god of this world [Satan] hath **blinded** the minds of them which believe not."[122]

But undoubtedly the main reason most of us end up believing in evolution is that we've been TAUGHT the theory so well. For several generations now, Darwin's brainchild has been force-fed on us and our children. We've been "brainwashed" by the theory of evolution so effectively that we accept it as surely as $2 + 2 = 4$. Before graduating from

---

121. Aldous Huxley, "Confessions of a Professed Atheist: Aldous Huxley," *Report* (June, 1966), p. 19.

122. 2 Corinthians 4:4.

high school nearly all students are exposed to and indoctrinated with the current evolutionary theories on the origin
of man—but these theories are taught as *fact*.

The education of a lifetime is not without effect. Most
people **believe** what they're **taught**—whether it's true or
false. Man may pride himself on being "the thinking animal,"
but we often fail to act as rational beings. Our reluctance to
investigate may lead us to accept words of some "authority."
People believe in evolution *not* because of the **weight of
EVIDENCE**—for most have never examined that! They believe in it because of the **weight of AUTHORITY**, and we live
in an age that worships authority. Science itself has many
worshipers. It has become a virtual religion, a new faith
—scientists are its **priests** (dressed not in black robes but
in white coats), their pronouncements are its **gospel** (which
must be believed and accepted), and the laboratory is its
temple. How, then, is the average person, with little or
no special knowledge of the various sciences, to challenge
the authorities? It's natural to accept what "experts" say—
and most people do. [123]

So our minds have been **programmed**, our thinking has
been **conditioned**, our children have been **indoctrinated**
with the DOGMA of evolution. We accept in good faith the
assertions of scientists who teach the evolutionary theory.
After all, if evolution is in the textbooks and in the superbly
illustrated books published by Time-Life, it **must** be true.

Thus there are many understandable reasons why evolution has come to be so universally accepted that it per-
meates much of man's thinking today. Yet one marvels in
dismay that many intelligent people could permit themselves
to be led so far astray from the facts of science.

---

123. Unfortunately, many make the same mistake in the realm of
religion, accepting without question what some authority figure says,
instead of studying for themselves.

CONCLUSION

The general theory of evolution has been accepted without the critical analysis it must have. Too much has been taken for granted, too much has been assumed to be true. Any scientific theory must harmonize with all known FACTS. If it be negated by as much as **one** of these facts, it's a faulty theory. In this regard I like the words of Thomas Henry Huxley: "Men of science do not pledge themselves to creeds; they are bound by articles of no sort: *there is not a single belief* that it is not a bounden duty with them to **hold with a light hand** and to **part with cheerfully**, the moment it is really proved to be contrary to ANY fact, great or small."[124]

I submit not only that evolution is seen to be contrary to MANY facts, but that it is unproved, unprovable, untestable, unreasonable, and impossible! Recent research has made the evolutionary theory a **bankrupt** hypothesis. The pillars supposedly supporting the evolutionary structure are seen to be weak or nonexistent. The evolutionists' case for man's development from a nonhuman ancestor is in complete disarray, for man is more than a biological accident, more than the end product of germ, mollusk, and ape. Neither Darwin nor anyone else has PROVED the theory of evolution. The only thing Darwin proved is that it's dangerous even to THINK without God. If we leave *God* out of the picture, our speculations will ever be unwise, unfruitful, and unsafe.

---

124. Thomas Henry Huxley, *Darwiniana*, 1893 edition (printed in the U.S. by Appleton, 1901), pp. 468-469.

Chapter 5

Theistic Evolution:
Unwise Christian Compromise

Theistic evolution—as opposed to the Godless, **atheistic** variety—is an attempt to harmonize the Bible and evolutionary theory. It's a philosophy which says there IS a God and He IS the Creator—but **He uses evolution** as His tool or method. Theistic evolutionists think the Bible tells us WHO created, and evolution tells us HOW.

History does not record the name of the person who, when faced with the choice between atheistic evolution and divine Creation, first asked: "Why does it have to be *either/ or*—why can't it be **BOTH**?" Men thus try to WED the Bible doctrine of divine Creation to the godless theory of evolution in an **unholy alliance** called "theistic evolution." But the miserable marriage is doomed to fail because too many **irreconcilable differences** exist between the two!

The two concepts are *mutually exclusive*, as we'll see, and the attempt to reconcile **Scripture** with **atheistic** science is acceptable neither to Bible believers nor to mainline evolutionists. This UNWISE COMPROMISE offers no real safety and no satisfying answers as a middle ground, just as agnosticism offers no safe harbor to those adrift between belief and atheism.[1]

Unfortunately, such "harmonizing" efforts usually end up by accepting evolution lock, stock, and barrel, and relegating the Genesis story to the realm of myth.

The great tragedy is that the Christian church, in large measure, has surrendered to the doctrine of evolution! Theistic evolution is accepted today not only by the liberal Protestant churches but also by the Roman Catholic Church. Neither Darwin's *Origin of Species* nor his *Descent of Man* were ever included on the Catholic Church's INDEX of unapproved books. In fact, the *New Catholic Encyclopedia* goes so far as to state: **"The evolution of man from lower forms,** as Darwin and Wallace agreed, does not at all imply that man is a mere animal."[2]

A perfect illustration of the inroads made by theistic evolution is the fact that official Catholic doctrine, enunciated by Pope Pius XII in his 1950 encyclical *Humani Generis*, permits the belief and teaching of evolution in the church, provided that man's moral and spiritual character is still recognized as a divine creation. This is theistic evolution, pure and simple.

Some may find this alternate theory appealing because the average person hates to argue and take sides. And the theistic evolutionist, with a foot in both camps, doesn't have to argue with anyone. He can just smile and agree with both sides. But has he read the "fine print" in the Devil's contract so he's aware HOW MUCH such harmony costs? Has he compromised the Truth to such an extent that he's sold his own soul?

---

1. See Chapter 1, above.
2. *New Catholic Encyclopedia* (1967 edition), Volume 4, p. 428, article "Creation of Man."

Satan wants us to believe "we can have our cake and eat it, too." But theistic evolution is a contradiction in terms, like "wise fool."

This variant concept seeks to put a **halo** around evolutionary theory, but remember that theistic evolution is STILL evolution—cleverly camouflaged and sugar-coated, but evolution just the same.

From the scientific point of view, theistic evolution is not a satisfactory compromise. It's merely an alternate form of evolution with **no SCIENTIFIC distinction**, vulnerable to all the objections (such as GAPS in the fossil record, etc., outlined in Chapters 3 and 4) for evolution in general.

Since theistic evolution attempts to bring **God** into the picture as an evolutionary agent, let's focus on the **theological** implications of this theory, answering such questions as: *Should a CHRISTIAN believe in evolution? Can one be a true Christian and still open the door to evolutionary theory?* We'll find that just as SCIENTIFIC evidence won't support the **atheistic** version of evolution, SCRIPTURAL evidence won't support the **theistic** version. The closer we look at this theory, the more clearly we see that it's a monstrous **blasphemy** on the character of God—a **horrid libel** on the wise and loving Creator the Bible reveals.

IT ATTACKS & UNDERMINES THE SCRIPTURES

Bible scholar Louis Berkhof says this about theistic evolution: "In a word, it is a theory that is absolutely **subversive** of Scripture truth."[3]

Far from being only a slight variation on orthodox Christian belief, this theory actually calls in question the entire

---

3. Louis Berkhof, *Systematic Theology* (Grand Rapids, Michigan: Eerdmans, 1941), p. 163.

Bible account of origins. All that follows in Holy Scripture can be rightly understood only against the backdrop of Genesis. Yet evolution labels as "legends" those foundational chapters. As *Time* Magazine reports, "Evolution suggests that *Homo sapiens* is descended not from one set of parents but from many, thus making **a literal Adam and Eve** quite unlikely." [4]

Theistic evolutionists feel that Science has delivered us from having to believe the Bible story of Creation. But the rest of Scripture—especially the New Testament—frequently *quotes from* and *alludes to* the Book of Genesis, including its earliest chapters. Though many today consider the Genesis record to be only allegory, it was NOT so considered by the inspired Bible writers.

While proclaiming their belief in God, theistic evolutionists attack His Word—the only objective standard by which we may know the truth He has revealed.

ITS INFLUENCE IS OPPOSED TO CHRISTIAN SOCIETY

In His immortal Sermon on the Mount, Jesus taught that "the **meek**"—not the **aggressive**—"shall inherit the earth." [5] A follower of Christ struck on one cheek by an aggressor will "turn to him the other also." [6] But evolutionary doctrine is diametrically opposed to such noble teaching. In harmony with evolution's idea of the "survival of the fittest" in "the struggle for existence," German philosopher Friedrich Nietsche (1844-1900) directed that "Man shall be trained for war and woman for the recreation

---

4. "The Sin of Everyman," *Time*, March 21, 1969, p. 67.
5. Matthew 5:5.
6. Matthew 5:39.

of the warrior; all else is folly."[7]   According to Nietsche, the Germans were the "master race" of Supermen (*Ubermensch*) and best fitted to survive and dominate the world. Adolf Hitler was a devoted disciple of Nietsche, whose ideas were eagerly exploited by the Nazis in their ruthless rise to power. The bloody result is one of the saddest chapters in history.

The two philosophies of Christ and Nietsche can **never** be made to harmonize. For there's a **basic contradiction** between Jesus' Golden Rule of "Do unto others as you would have them do unto you"[8] and evolution's survival-of-the-fittest idea that "might makes right."

IT ATTRIBUTES TO *NATURAL* CAUSES OUR CREATOR'S *SUPERNATURAL* WORKS

It's always been Satan's plan to rob Christ of His glory as Creator.[9] The basic theory of evolution, being completely atheistic, is an outright denial of God. Theistic evolution is more subtle, more indirect in its denial, but it nevertheless places severe limitations on God's power and ability, putting Him in the position of a mere "overseer."

Yet Bible writers throughout the Scriptures accept the literal story of Creation as pure history. If Genesis is not historically true, then the other Bible writers, and Christ Himself, were guilty of either **ignorance** or **deliberate misrepresentation** when they cited the events of Creation as inspired truths. Either conclusion is unthinkable to the consistent Christian. Note the following:

---

7.   Friedrich Nietsche, *Complete Works of Nietsche*, edited by Oscar Levy (6th edition, 1930), Volume II, p. 75.

8.   See Matthew 7:12 and Luke 6:31.

9.   See the section on "Christ as Creator" in *Seven Mysteries . . . Solved!*, Volume Two, Chapter 12.

- The "wise man" SOLOMON declared: "Lo, this only have I found, that **God hath made man UPRIGHT**; but they have sought out **many inventions**."[10]

- The Apostle **PAUL** accepted the origin of man by special creation: "It is written, The first man Adam was **made a living soul**. . . . The man is not of the woman; but the woman of the man. . . . For Adam was first formed, then Eve."[11] Paul also wrote of "God, who commanded the **light** to shine out of darkness,"[12] clearly referring to Genesis 1:3.

- **JUDE**, in his New Testament letter, describes the faithful patriarch Enoch as "the seventh from Adam."[13] But *why* refer to a man as "the seventh" in ancestral line IF the starting point for that line is only a **myth**?

- If the Genesis account of Creation is a myth, we must throw out the testimony of Gospel writer **LUKE**, who traces Jesus' ancestry all the way back to "Seth, who was the son of Adam, who was the son of God."[14] Linking Adam directly to the Creator puts Luke in perfect harmony with the Genesis record and in direct opposition to ANY evolutionary theory.

- The Apostle **JAMES** also testifies on the side of divine Creation when he writes of "men, who have been **made in the likeness of God**."[15]

---

10. Ecclesiastes 7:29.
11. 1 Corinthians 15:45, 11:8, and 1 Timothy 2:13.
12. 2 Corinthians 4:6.
13. Jude 14.
14. Luke 3:38, Phillips Translation.
15. James 3:9, New American Standard Bible.

● The Apostle **PETER** supports the inspired Record of
Genesis when he writes of "Noah . . . building the ark.
Yet only eight persons were saved from drowning in
that terrible flood."[16]

● The Apostle **JOHN**, in writing the Book of Revelation,
corroborates Genesis (3:1-6) when he writes of "that **old
serpent**, called the Devil, and Satan, which deceiveth
the whole world."[17] Furthermore, John promises that
when the earth is made new, "there shall be **no more
curse**,"[18] again echoing Genesis (3:17).

● Though evolutionists scoff at the idea of God's creation
of Adam and Eve and the Flood of Noah's day, the Lord
JESUS endorsed them both. In speaking of the special
Creation of Adam and Eve as a historical fact, Christ
declared: "Have ye not read, that **He** which **made them
at the beginning** made them male and female?"[19] This
clearly refers to the account of Man's creation in Genesis 1:27—"Male and female created He them." Jesus also
put His stamp of approval on the Bible account of the
Flood in these words: "In the days that were before the
Flood they were eating and drinking, marrying and giving in marriage, until the day came that Noe [Noah]
entered into the ark."[20] Can conscientious Christians
dismiss Genesis as mere myth or legend when Christ
Himself acknowledged its accuracy?

16. 1 Peter 3:20, The Living Bible. Other support for the historicity
of the Flood is found in 2 Peter 2:5 and 3:3-7.
17. Revelation 12:9.
18. Revelation 22:3.
19. Matthew 19:4.
20. Matthew 24:38. And Hebrews 11:7 reads: "By faith Noah, being
warned by God about things not yet seen, in reverence prepared an ark
for the salvation of his household." New American Standard Bible.

The Bible states that after Adam was created, there was found **in all the animal kingdom** NO "help meet for him [that is, no companion or helper suited to his needs]."[21] This shows that Adam was **NOT related to the animals and had nothing in common with them.** That's why God specially formed Eve to be Adam's wife.

Those who believe the Bible is the Word of God can't regard the Creation record as merely **figurative** language when inspired Bible writers—and the Lord Himself— considered it literal and authoritative.

ITS BRUTAL *METHOD* IS UNWORTHY OF A GOD OF LOVE

Advocates for this theory assert that evolution is simply God's way of working. However, the question is not whether God *could* use evolutionary processes as a means of creating our world and its inhabitants but whether He *would* employ those processes in creating the earth. What about the moral aspects of this theistic theory? Would a good God use PAIN and DEATH to carry out His design for making a perfect world?

You see, the METHOD attributed to God by this theory is **unworthy** of Him and raises serious questions regarding God's character.

As two graduate students discussed theistic evolution and Creation, the more liberal fellow asked: "Why is it important to fuss over *how* it happened as long as it *did* happen and that we believe God was involved?" The other replied, "Creation, like all of God's acts, is primarily revelation—it **tells us something** about God's character. So it matters what we say about Creation because ultimately it reflects upon our understanding of God." He concluded

---

21. Genesis 2:20.

by saying, "Since the WAY a thing is made tells us something about its maker, we should be concerned about the METHODS we ascribe to our Maker."[22]

The method which theistic evolution supposes was used in Creation would be

> "As if some **lesser god** had made the world,
> But had not force to shape it as he would,"

to quote the poet Tennyson.[23]

The god postulated by theistic evolution is not the same majestic, all powerful God of the Bible. Instead, he's a bungling deity who perpetrates age upon age of bloodshed, stumbling through a slow process, making millions of mistakes in trial-and-error attempts to perfect his created organisms. "I grant that the evolution theory may indeed permit belief in a god, but *what a god!*"[24]

Evolution's bloody reign of tooth and claw for millions of years to eliminate the unfit is utterly incompatible with the Bible's portrayal of origins. The two concepts are as far from each other as the east is from the west. God's perfect work of Creation was beautiful to behold and worthy of its omnipotent Author.

"The evolutionary process depends partly on destruction of the weak by the strong. Theistic evolution makes *God* responsible for all of this, whereas the Biblical concept of a perfect creation and a subsequent fall makes *Satan* responsible for the destructive side of nature."[25]

22. Donald John, "The Creation Story," *INSIGHT* Magazine, October 11, 1977, p. 21.

23. Alfred, Lord Tennyson, *Idylls of the King: The Passing of Arthur*, Lines 14-15.

24. Francis D. Nichol, *God and Evolution* (Washington, D.C.: Review and Herald Publishing Association, 1965), p. 56.

25. Leonard Brand, "Faith and the Flood," *Ministry* Magazine (February 1980), p. 80.

Harvard's illustrious professor of zoology, Louis Agassiz, protests against the idea that God used evolution as His method of Creation in these words: "The resources of the Deity cannot be so meager, that in order to create a human being endowed with reason, He must change a monkey into a man."[26]

A *FINISHED* CREATION

Creation was not merely BEGUN at that time spoken of in the opening chapters of Genesis. The inspired Record states that it was FINISHED, and the seventh day was set apart as a special day to commemorate the COMPLETION of God's great work.

Evolution postulates an ongoing creative process continuing over millions of eons, whereas Scripture declares God's work of Creation to have been COMPLETED, at least as regards this earth: "The works were FINISHED from the foundation of the world."[27]

The Apostle Paul states the fact of a **completed** Creation when he says: "By Him were all things created."[28] Note that the verb phrase "were . . . created" is in the PAST TENSE. Therefore, Creation is not going on at present, which would be true if evolution were an ongoing creative process.

The inspired Record explicitly states that at the end of Creation week, after God had brought into being the earth with all its varied forms of plant and animal life, including Man, **God's creative work was a COMPLETED act.** Please note: "Thus the heavens and the earth **were FINISHED**, and all the host of them. And on the seventh day God **ENDED**

---

26. Louis Agassiz, *Methods of Study in Natural History* (Boston, 1863), p. iv.
27. Hebrews 4:3.
28. Colossians 1:16.

His work which He **had made**; and He **rested** on the
seventh day from all His work which He **had made**."[29]

This same thought of Creation's **completed** work is
echoed and re-echoed throughout the Bible in such passages
as the following:

Exodus 20:11 - "For in *six days* the Lord **made** heaven and
   earth, the sea, and **ALL that in them is**, and **rested** the
   seventh day: wherefore the Lord blessed the Sabbath day,
   and hallowed it."
Psalm 33:6 & 9 - "By the word of the Lord **were** the heavens
   made; and all the host of them by the breath of His
   mouth. . . . For He spake, and it **was DONE**; He commanded, and it **stood fast**."
Hebrew 4:10 - "For he that is entered into His rest, he also
   hath ceased from his own works, as **God did** from His."

DEATH CAME AT THE *WRONG* TIME

In the closing paragraphs of his book *The Origin of
Species,* Darwin wrote that "the production of the higher
animals" was brought about by "**the WAR of nature**, from
famine and **DEATH**." In the first place, ask yourself: Does
"the war of nature, from famine and death" sound like **the
means *GOD* would use** to create a world all "very good"?[30]

In the second place, recognize that evolution's claim that
death was the causative factor in producing the higher animals contradicts the Bible teaching on the cause of death.

The Scriptures plainly teach that there was no suffering
and death in the world before Adam sinned. Death entered
the world as a direct result of Man's sin:

---

29. Genesis 2:1-2.
30. See Dr. Gary Parker, "From Evolution to Creation: A Personal
Testimony," *ICR Impact Series* (San Diego: Institute for Creation Research) No. 49, July 1977, p. ii.

Color Plate #1

Adam in the Garden of Eden

Artist: Lorenzo Ghiglieri
Copyright © 1972 by Theater of the Universe

Color Plate #2

Eve in the Garden of Eden

Artist: Lorenzo Ghiglieri
Copyright © 1972 by Theater of the Universe

Romans 5:12 - "By one man [Adam] sin entered into the world, and **death by sin**; and so death passed upon all men, for that all have sinned."

1 Corinthians 15:21 - "**By man came death.**"

But if evolutionary theory were correct, there would have been BILLIONS of deaths **before** the first man ever existed! Theistic evolution asks us to believe that **suffering** and **death** existed for long ages in a SINLESS world made by a wise and holy God!

THE *FALL* OF MAN

The theme of the Bible is "the Fall of Man" into sin and his need of a Saviour. Note the sequence of Man's creation, fall, and subsequent salvation:

1. Beginning with *a PERFECT Creation*,
   there follows
2. Man's *DEgeneration* (the Fall of Adam & Eve),
   and then
3. Man's *REgeneration* (the Plan of Salvation).

But theistic evolution is totally unacceptable to all who **know** and **believe** the Bible, because it does away with our need of Jesus Christ as Saviour. The only "Fall" allowed in evolution is a **fall UPWARD**, for underlying evolutionary thought is the basic idea of PROGRESS. And if the assumption of progress is correct—if Man began from lower forms of life and is on the upgrade, constantly climbing, he's

not **a FALLEN creature** in need of a Saviour
but **a DEVELOPING organism** on the road to perfection.

Instead of being **condemned** for his mythical *"fall"* from grace, Man should be **congratulated** on the *progress* he's made! Evolutionary theory and Bible theology postulate **completely opposite trends.**

That's why it's more consistent to be an out-and-out ATHEIST than a **theistic** evolutionist! Evolution—providing for no "fall," hence needing no Saviour—is decidedly **anti-Christian.**

Ask yourself: Is the story of man's fall in Genesis **history** [31] or **myth?** Is man a **civilized ape** or a **fallen sinner?** Evolution sees man as a glorified beast, a creature who never fell but has always climbed higher and higher. Such an origin makes the death of Christ of no effect in man's behalf, as we see from the following chain of logic:

- If there was **NO FALL,** then there's **NO SIN.**

- If there's **NO SIN,** then there's **NO NEED of a Saviour** from Sin.
- Therefore, **Christ died in vain.**

So this teaching robs Christ of His divine role as Redeemer. His sacrifice redeems the fallen members of God's family—and there can be redemption only of that which was once possessed but forfeited. Man is not an upward-evolving animal but a lost sinner condemned to death. Christ gave His life to save **a fallen man,** NOT **a noble beast!**

Many who haven't really studied the subject feel they can believe in evolution and **still** believe all of the Bible except a small part at the beginning of Genesis. But God's great act of Creation is a subject not limited to one part of the Bible. Jesus said: "If ye believe not his [Moses'] writings, how shall ye believe **My** words?" [32]

---

31. The Apostle Paul obviously accepted it as literal history, writing under inspiration that **"the serpent beguiled Eve** through his subtilty." 2 Corinthians 11:3.

32. John 5:47. God's inspired penman for the Creation account in the Book of Genesis was Moses.

Evolution of ANY kind rejects the Bible account of how God directly created man. And Satan knows it's impossible to dismiss the Genesis record of Creation by calling it a "myth" or "allegory" without simultaneously undermining our faith in the rest of the Bible.

A theistic evolutionist must fight not only against **facts of science** which nullify evolutionary theory but also against **texts of Scripture** which reveal how God created the world. As Thomas F. Heinze put it, "He is following *a religion which he himself has made up.*" [33]

There's no conflict, no contradiction between God's book of nature and His written Word, for the Author of nature is the Author of the Bible. Creation and Christianity have one God.

DEISM ROBS GOD OF HIS ROLE AS *SUSTAINER*

Theistic evolution is only a step away from the unorthodox religious concept of **deism**, which teaches that God— *like an absentee landlord*—originally created Planet Earth and its primitive life forms, then concerned Himself with other business. He may occasionally stop by to see how things are going, but most of the time He lets things manage themselves in the same way we wind up a clock and leave it to run itself. In the mechanistic view of deism, our Creator is **a very impersonal God.** Theistic evolution, too, implies that God has little or no regular contact with the earth and mankind.

But God is NOT "an absentee landlord" as some suggest. In fact, He's "**not far** from every one of us: For *in Him* we **live,** and **move,** and have our **being.**" [34] It's only due to God's sustaining power that we live day by day and

---

33. Thomas F. Heinze, *The Creation vs. Evolution Handbook* (Grand Rapids, Michigan: Baker Book House, 1970), p. 51.

34. Acts 17:27-28.

moment by moment: "He giveth to all **life,** and **breath, and all things.**"[35] Every pulsing beat of the heart is an evidence of His loving care.

Deism and theistic evolution would have us believe that God created the universe but then went off and left it to evolve by itself. In contrast, the Bible teaches that God **upholds** and **sustains** every part of His creation. The pen of Inspiration writes of God's dear Son "**upholding all things** by the word of His power."[36] "Thou has **MADE** heaven, the heaven of heavens, with all their host, the earth, and all things that are therein, the seas, and all that is therein, **and Thou PRESERVEST them all.**"[37]

Paul, writing under inspiration of the Holy Spirit, declares of Christ that "all things were created by Him, and for Him: and He is before all things, and by Him all things **consist.**"[38] That word *consist* means all things "**cohere, are held together,**" as the Amplified Bible puts it. Other modern versions like the Revised Standard Version, the New English Bible, the Living Bible, the New American Standard Bible, and the New International Version make clear that Jesus "holds everything together" as the Sustainer or "upholding principle"[39] of the universe. The hand that **holds the worlds in space** is the hand that **was nailed to the cross** for us!

CONCLUSION

The divine Record is so plain, there's no excuse for wrong conclusions. "God said, Let Us make man in Our image, after Our likeness. . . . So **God created man** in His

---

35. Acts 17:25.
36. Hebrews 1:1-3.
37. Nehemiah 9:6.
38. Colossians 1:16-17.
39. Phillips translation of Colossians 1:17.

own image; . . . male and female created He them."[40] There's no ground here to suppose that man **evolved by slow degrees** from lower forms of life.

The Bible cannot be simply a "good book." It cannot be a good book if it's a book of lies. Either it's **true**— or it's not. Either it's the inspired Word of the living God— as it **claims** to be—or it's not. One or the other.

Man's hope and destiny are determined by the quality of his faith. Can we as Christians safely accept any theory which undermines our faith in the Bible? Can we accept a teaching which makes God out to be a liar? Can we afford to accept the confused theories of evolution—theistic or otherwise? If we're willing to admit into our thinking the existence of a Creator God, why should we **want** to limit His power and explain away the plain statements of His Word?

As intelligent Christians, we'll neither ignore science nor try to explain away Genesis. Those who reject the Genesis account may not realize that by so doing they reject Christianity. For evolution and Christianity are incompatible and irreconcilable. If evolution is true, then the whole fabric of Christian faith is a mass of error. Theistic evolution is a compromise theory forever opposed to the Bible.

---

40. Genesis 1:26-27.

Chapter 6

===

How Long Were
The Days of Creation?

A widespread teaching today holds that each day of
Creation Week wasn't a twenty-four-hour day but a **long**
period of time, perhaps millions of years long, covering
vast geologic ages.

This "**day-age** theory" is taught by many who profess to
believe the Bible, for they feel it solves one of the many
problems faced by advocates of theistic evolution.[1] But the
Bible resoundingly refutes the day-age concept. Let's look
at the evidence drawn not only from God's Word but also
from language, science, and logic—evidence that clearly
shows why we cannot accept this theory.

---

1. The preceding chapter discusses the compromise theory
called "theistic evolution."

CLUE #1
EACH DAY WAS A PERIOD
OF *DARKNESS* & *LIGHT*

When the Lord declares He made the world in six days and rested on the seventh, He makes it plain He means a day of twenty-four hours, for He says, "the **evening** and the **morning** were the first day . . . the **evening** and the **morning** were the second day . . . the **evening** and the **morning** were the third day," and so on. [2] No other language could have made God's thought more explicit than these words. No other terms in the Hebrew language express the idea of literal days more forcefully than the words here employed. The literal rendering of the Hebrew is, "There was **evening**, there was **morning**, day one"; "There was **evening**, there was **morning**, day two," and so on.

Thus the designation of days in Creation Week conforms exactly with the method of recording time throughout the Bible, for God taught His people that each day begins with sunset and ends with the following sunset. [3] To describe each of the six days as **an evening and a morning** certainly gives evidence that these were days just like all others that have followed since the dawn of history. As Ralph Waldo Emerson observed: "God had infinite time to give us; but how did He give it? In one immense tract of lazy millenniums? No, He cut it up into a neat succession of new mornings." A complete day of twenty-four hours is composed of a period of darkness and a period of light. Such were the original days of creation, and such are the days of earth now—darkness and light, darkness and light, as the earth

---

2. See Genesis 1, verses 5, 8, 13, 19, 23, and 31.   Lcck u/?
3. See Leviticus 23:32 and Deuteronomy 16:6.

spins on its axis. God leaves no room for philosophic speculation here: "the evening and the morning" are still the
component parts of each earthly day.

CLUE #2
HOW DID THE SEVEN-DAY
***WEEK* ORIGINATE?**

The seven-day week, an institution as old as history, has
no basis in the world of nature. Every other period of time
or grouping of days is marked by some movement of the
heavenly bodies:

- **The twenty-four-hour DAY** is determined by the
  rotation of the earth on its axis.

- **The MONTH** is marked by the revolution of the
  moon about the earth.

- **The three-hundred-sixty-five-day YEAR** is measured by the time it takes the earth to complete
  one circuit of the sun.

But from WHAT comes **the seven-day WEEK**? Nothing in
nature accounts for it. God Himself measured off the first
week as a sample for all successive weeks to the close of time.
Like every other week, it consists of seven literal days.

As the *Encyclopedia Britannica* states in its article "Calendar": "WEEK NOT ASTRONOMICAL. — The week is a
period of seven days, having no reference whatever to the
celestial motions, a circumstance to which it owes its un-
alterable uniformity. . . . It has been employed from time
immemorial in almost all Eastern countries; and as it forms
neither an aliquot [divisible] part of the year nor of the lunar

month, those who reject the Mosaic recital will be at a loss to assign to it an origin having much semblance of probability."[4]

So you see, the week, composed of seven days, is itself another proof that the days of creation were seven literal days as we have them now. It owes its origin to the creation of the world in six literal days and the Creator's rest on the seventh. If not, **how did the week ever get started?** How is that in virtually every land the week of seven days is known and recognized? The universal recognition of the week from earliest times fits perfectly with the Bible record but does **not** fit any long series of so-called geologic ages.

CLUE #3
THE *SABBATH COMMAND*
IMPLIES 24-HOURS DAYS

In the heart of the Ten Commandments is God's command to keep holy the seventh day. But the wording of the Fourth Commandment can be harmonized with the demands of logic only when the days of Creation Week are considered as solar days, for the Lord asks US to work six days and rest on the seventh day, **because He made the earth in six days and rested on the seventh.**[5] This Commandment shows that the six creation days were the same kind He allocates for our affairs each week. And remember, this parallel between the events of Creation and our present week was set up not by theologians or other well-intentioned persons but by God Himself.

---

4. *Encyclopedia Britannica* (11th edition), Volume 4, p. 988, article "Calendar."

5. Exodus 20:8-11.

The reason God gives for this command—pointing back to **His own example** of working and then resting during Creation Week—appears beautiful and forceful when we understand the days of Creation to be literal. But the unwarranted assumption that the events of the first week required thousands or millions of years strikes directly at the foundation of the Fourth Commandment and makes it something less than the reasonable requirement of a reasonable God! It represents the Creator as commanding men to observe literal days to commemorate vast, indefinite periods. It makes obscure what God has made very plain. It also implies God is a liar. The first six days of each week are given to man for labor, because God employed **the same period** of the first week in His great work of Creation; on the seventh day man is to refrain from labor, to commemorate the Creator's rest.

```
    CLUE #4
THE FIRST SABBATH WAS
NOT A GEOLOGIC PERIOD
```

The duration of the seventh day of Creation Week is determined by the length of the other six. If we assume that those days were long geologic periods, then, to be consistent, we must likewise assume that the Creator's day of rest was also a period of a million years. But in that case God is still resting, because Bible chronology indicates that only about six thousand years have elapsed since the creation of Adam. And if God is still in His seventh day, and resting, then it's difficult to explain Jesus' statement: "My Father is working still, and I am working."[6] Christians know that God has been very active in human affairs providing for man's salvation.

---

6. John 5:17, Revised Standard Version.

Another dilemma for those who wish to believe in evolution without giving up faith in the Bible is this: Adam, according to the Bible, did not die till long after the first Sabbath. But if that Sabbath is not yet ended, what about Adam? No one claims that he is still living! Furthermore, God blessed the seventh day *"because* that in it He **HAD rested** from all His work."[7] How could He bless the day **after** He **had** rested on it, if that day were a million years long and hasn't yet ended? These facts are just a few more of many that refute theistic evolution's day-age theory.

```
CLUE #5
THE AGE OF ADAM
POSES A PROBLEM
```

How anyone who accepts the Bible record as true history could think of the days of Creation as long, indefinite periods, millions of years in length, is hard to understand. For the Bible declares that Adam was created on the sixth day.[8] Thus the first two days of his life were two of the original seven days—but if we believe the day-age theory, they were millions of years in length! Even if Adam died as early as the first day of the second week, he still would have lived through one entire "period" and parts of two others. How old would that have made him, according to the theory? Well, a modest estimate would require several million years! But Genesis 5:5 states that Adam lived 930 years and died. So the day-age theory contradicts the Bible and leaves no way to compute the age of Adam. Men may choose to believe one or the other of these accounts. But there's no way to harmonize them.

---

7. Genesis 2:3.
8. Genesis 1:26-31.

> ## CLUE #6
> ## WOULD GOD CALL *SIN*
> ## "VERY GOOD"?

Suppose someone wanted to accept the Biblically-stated age of Adam as literal but still hold the day-age theory for Creation Week in general. Adam was created on the sixth day and lived 930 years. Long before those years were finished he had sinned, been driven from Eden, and in his sinful state reared a family. According to the supposition stated above, Adam must have lived his whole life—and sinned—within the span of that sixth "day," for 930 years is but a small part of a period measured in millions of years.

Now here's the point: when God finished His great work of those six days, we're told, "God saw every thing that He had made, and, behold, it was VERY GOOD."[9] But if Adam had already sinned, had already succumbed to the devil's temptations, would God say that "every thing . . . was *very good*"? No! Adam fell into sin later. And when God rested on the seventh day and looked back over Creation Week, He blessed that day as a fitting climax to a **perfect work**. Therefore, no sin had yet entered to mar the earth.

> ## CLUE #7
> ## HEBREW *LANGUAGE* SCHOLARS
> ## *REJECT* THE THEORY

We've already considered some of the **Biblical** evidence against the assumptions made by the day-age theory. Now

---

9. Genesis 1:31.

let's look at a few **linguistic** points. Actually, the idea that the Hebrew word *yom* ("day"—as in *Yom Kippur*, the Jewish "Day of Atonement") means a period of time longer than twenty-four hours finds no support in reputable Hebrew dictionaries, such as the following:

Frants Buhl – *Gesenius' Handwoerterbuch ueher das alte Testament*

Brown, Driver, & Briggs – *A Hebrew and English Lexicon of the Old Testament*

Eduard Koenig – *Woerterbuch zum Alten Testament*

Hebrew dictionaries are our primary source of reliable information concerning Hebrew words, but these standard sources know nothing of the notion that **yom** means an indefinite period millions of years long.

And Bible commentators decidedly state that **yom** when used to refer to one of the periods of creation can only mean a twenty-four-hour day. For instance, John Skinner remarks in his *International Critical Commentary (Genesis)*: "The interpretation of **yom** as *aeon*, favorite resource of harmonists of science and revelation, is opposed to the plain sense of the passage and **has no warrant in Hebrew usage**." [10]

> **CLUE #8**
> *YOM* WITH A DEFINITE NUMERAL
> *ALWAYS* MEANS 24 HOURS

The book of Genesis was written by Moses, and of course Moses did not write in English. In fact, he didn't use the word

---

10. John Skinner, *International Critical Commentary*, Volume 1, p. 21, on *Genesis*.

day at all, but the Hebrew word **yom**. This word **yom** is found 1,480 times in the Scriptures. On rare occasions it's translated by some term other than "day," but in the overwhelming number of cases its usual translated meaning is "day." Note that Genesis 1:5 uses **yom** in two different senses: "Day" (**yom**) when used with "night" (**layelah**) refers to the light part of the day, roughly twelve hours; and when the Bible says that "the first **day**" is ended, the same word (**yom**) is also used to mean a twenty-four-hour period.

Now some skeptical friend may say, "Well, since the Hebrew word **yom** doesn't always mean the same specific period, you can't be certain that **yom** in the first chapter of Genesis means a twenty-four-hour day." But there are two reasons why we can be certain.

First of all, when the Hebrew word **yom** means anything but a solar day, it's stated or plainly implied in the context. For example, Genesis 4:3 states: "And *in process of time* it came to pass, that Cain brought of the fruit of the ground an offering unto the Lord." This is clearly an indefinite period of time. Any intelligent child reading this would so understand it, for the context makes it clear. It doesn't mean an age, an eon, an era of 100 years—or 500 million years, either! It means not a specific 24-hour day, but an indefinite period after which Cain brought his offering to the Lord. This example shows how *the context makes it plain* that here **yom** doesn't refer to a solar day of twenty-four hours.

Secondly, note the following fact: In Hebrew manuscripts, in every instance where **yom** is accompanied by a definite **numeral**, it means a solar day of twenty-four hours. Without fail we have *the second* **yom** of the feast, *the third* **yom** of the journey, *the seventh* **yom** of the week, *the fifteenth* **yom** of the month, and so on—all meaning regular *days!* There's not one single exception to this rule in the whole Bible. If we apply this fact to the days of Creation Week, we note that a definite number is used with each of these periods from one to seven. This leaves only one valid conclusion: those days were 24-hour days, and the translators were *correct* in their English wording.

CLUE #9
SOUND INTERPRETATION DEMANDS
THE MOST *OBVIOUS* MEANING

A basic principle of Biblical interpretation is that students of Scripture should stick to the original and literal meaning of a word unless there's a compelling reason for adopting a derived or figurative meaning. And the whole Creation account is written as simple narrative—there's nothing in the Record to suggest that the words should not be understood in their ordinary meanings.

A good question is: If it REALLY took five billion years for God to make all things, WHY did He **tell** us it took only six days? There's every reason to believe that Moses, the inspired penman of Genesis, understood those days to mean (and intended his readers to understand them to mean) literal days. He certainly gave no hint of anything like the ideas suggested by evolutionists.

Since the Scripture Record contains no suggestion that the days of Creation were anything but literal, 24-hour days, **the burden of proof** is definitely on those who try to twist the simple, clearly-worded Genesis account to mean long ages of time!

CLUE #10
GOD *DIFFERENTIATED*
BETWEEN DAYS & YEARS

How can one seriously maintain that the days of creation were long geological ages lasting millions of years, when the Bible makes clear that **God knows the difference** between *days* and *years?* In Genesis 1:14 we read: "And God said, Let there be lights in the firmament of the heaven to divide the day from the night; and let them be for signs, and for seasons, and for *days*, and *years*." With this distinction set forth in the very Bible chapter under consideration, aren't those who contend that **seven days** means **countless years** taking undue liberties with God's Word?

Furthermore, a quick comparison of Genesis 7:11 & 24 with Genesis 8:3 & 4 shows that a record was kept of the years, months, and days in Noah's time. Each month was composed of *30 days*, and the Flood lasted *150 days* or *five months* exactly. So the Bible states that the Flood began on the seventeenth day of the **second** month and ended on the seventeenth day of the **seventh** month. The record is precise and definite, and it shows that Genesis clearly differentiates among these units of time. If God had **meant** years rather than days, He would have **said** years—for He certainly knew the difference!

CLUE #11
INSTANTANEOUS
ACCOMPLISHMENT
IS IMPLIED

Another linguistic point is this—the very wording of the Scripture narrative indicates a **short** time involved, a fact diametrically opposed to the evolutionary theory. To illustrate, in Genesis 1:3 we read that God said, "Let there be light," or, as it is in the Hebrew, *Ye-hi-or* —"Let light be!" Then follow the words, *Wa-ye-hi-or* —"And light was." The response was instantaneous. When God spoke, it was so—light existed. He didn't have to wait a million years for it to appear.

When succeeding verses record the creative words of God, in every case, without exception, the thing created was instantly there in its perfection. Other portions of Scripture bear the same consistent testimony. For instance, in Psalm 33:6 & 9 we read: "By the word of the Lord were the heavens made; and all the host of them by the breath of His mouth. . . . **For He spake, and it was done; He commanded, and it stood fast.**" Nothing in Scripture indicates that eons or long periods of time were involved. The phraseology indicates instantaneous action.

God's **new** creation will also be instantaneous, just like the **first** Creation. When Jesus returns, we'll be changed to immortality "in a *moment,* in the *twinkling* of an eye."[11] No eons of time will be required to transform these old bodies into glorious new ones!

---

11. 1 Corinthians 15:52.

CLUE #12
LONG PERIODS WERE *NOT*
NEEDED BY THE CREATOR

Aside from the clear wording of the inspired Book denoting instantaneous accomplishment, it's obvious that, if we accept God Almighty as the Creator at all, we need not insist on long, indefinite periods for the accomplishment of His creative work. If we accept the Scripture that tells us "He spake, and it was done,"[12] we needn't pretend that God had to do a **lot** of speaking over ages of time.

After all, if God is able to perform His colossal miracle of Creation in 500 million years, common-sense logic tells us He can do it in one year, one day, one second! God didn't **need** to take *even six days* to create the world, but He **chose** to do so—six *literal* days according to the Bible record, and on the seventh day He rested.

CLUE #13
IDENTICAL PHRASES SUGGEST
UNIFORM TIME PERIODS

Some proponents of the day-age theory make much of the fact that the sun and moon weren't spoken into existence till the fourth day of Creation Week, so they say no one can tell just how long the preceding "days" were. But remember, on the very first day of creation *light* had shone out of darkness. We're not told the source of this light at the beginning, except that God provided it—and in God's

---

12. Psalm 33:9.

manifestation to His people, light has always symbolized His presence. [13]   When this light appeared, the succession of night and day began, for the Bible speaks of "the evening and the morning" of even those first three days.

On the fourth day "God made two great lights; the greater light to rule the day, and the lesser light to rule the night." [14] Not only are the words **day** and **night** obviously used here as we use them today, but note also the IDENTICAL statement: "And the **evening** and the **morning** were the fourth day." [15] Hence the question that day-age theorists must answer is: IF on the fourth day and onward "the evening and the morning" means ordinary days measured by sun and moon, WHY should the identical phrase used earlier in the *same* narrative by the *same* writer mean something entirely different?

CLUE #14
CONSIDER PLANTS AND THE
***DARK* PERIOD OF EACH DAY**

We've already considered some ***Biblical*** arguments and ***linguistic*** evidence against the day-age theory. Now let's turn to the field of ***science***.

---

13. Critics of the Bible sometimes say, "**Moses made a mistake** when he wrote that God said, 'Let there be light' on the **first** day—then he turned around and wrote that God didn't create the sun till the **fourth** day! That's a direct contradiction." But almighty God is NOT dependent on the sun for light. The supposed "problem" on the Bible's *first* page disappears when we look at its *last* page, which speaks of the NEW creation of God: "And the city had **no need of the sun**, neither of the moon, to shine in it: for the glory of God did lighten it, and the Lamb [Jesus] is the light thereof. ... And there shall be **no night there**; and **they need no . . . light of the sun**; for the Lord God giveth them light." Revelation 21:23 and 22:5.

14. Genesis 1:16.

15. Genesis 1:19.

On the third day of Creation Week, God created all plant life, and on the fourth day He made the sun to shine upon the earth. Now just suppose those two days were periods of 100 million years each. How long would the dark part of each day have been? Why, 50 million years, of course. And this alternation of light and darkness took place during each of the six days. Can you imagine shrubs and flowers, grass and trees growing for 50 million years in utter **darkness**? If they did, we're confronted with a more amazing miracle than Genesis was thought to contain—the plant kingdom flourishing for ages without sunlight!

Aside from the fact that **plants need LIGHT** to survive and grow, think of the **terrible COLD** that would settle down on the earth in a month of total darkness. Temperatures fluctuate considerably even in a 12-hour period. That's why the weatherman predicts: "Low tonight, 64. High tomorrow, 82." Gradually the frozen death of the South Pole would creep over the earth, at last approaching even the terrible cold of outer space—50 million years of infernal darkness and unbroken frost, with coldness penetrating thousands of feet into the earth! All life would vanish long before the first ten years had passed—not to mention the first thousand, or hundred thousand, or million years of the 50-million years of darkness.

CLUE #15
CONSIDER PLANTS AND THE
***LIGHT* PERIOD OF EACH DAY**

Then would follow 50 million years of blazing, unceasing sunlight, with the heat rising up to unheard-of levels.[16] Plants would dry up and wither from the scorching rays of

---

16. To illustrate this with an example from the real world, consider the **moon**, which rotates *almost 30 times more slowly* than the earth,

the sun. And what we've said here about **plants** freezing to death or burning to a crisp apply just as well to **animal life** on the fifth, sixth, and seventh days of Creation Week if "the evening and the morning" were as long as the time demanded by day-age theorists. Animal life depends on plants for its existence, anyhow. How could any life— vegetable, animal, or human—exist under such conditions? It couldn't, of course. And these facts forever disprove the theory that the days of Creation were long periods of time.

CLUE #16
PLANTS *DEPEND* UPON
THE ANIMAL KINGDOM

In our ecological system, animals depend on vegetable life for nutrition and also for the oxygen released by plants during photosynthesis. But the converse is also true: Many plants are dependent on the animal kingdom. The Bible says that plants, including flowering kinds, were created on the **third** day, but no animal life was formed until the **fifth** and **sixth** days. Now, the *interdependence* of plants and animals is a very conspicuous fact in the world of living things. In the matter of pollination alone, multitudes of plants could not carry on from generation to generation without insects. For example, bees are so important as insect pollinators that the National Geographic Society estimates their agricultural value—**aside** from honey and wax production—at hundreds of millions of dollars each year.

---

making its days *that much longer* than ours. Thermal variations on the moon are consequently much greater, with the difference in temperature between the lunar night (dark side) and lunar day (bright side) being about 450° Fahrenheit.

And entomologist Ronald Ribbands states in *Scientific American* Magazine: "When we think of bees, we are apt to associate them first with honey and secondly, perhaps, with their sting. Actually it would be more appropriate to think of them first of all as the great pollinators, **without whom many of the plants upon which mankind depends would *DISAPPEAR* from the earth.**" [17]

Yet the divine Record states that seed-bearing plants flourished from the very start.[18] This would have been impossible if insects didn't appear till millions of years later, as would be the case if the days were geologic periods.

```
CLUE #17
EARTH WAS CREATED
"TO BE INHABITED"
```

Isaiah 45:18 tells us that God created the earth "not **in vain**," but "He formed it **to be inhabited**." Would God's purpose have been realized if the earth were UNinhabited by any higher beings for millions upon millions of years? "To be *inhabited*" cannot mean by *animals,* because a land in which "the beasts of the field multiply" unchecked is said to be "desolate" according to Exodus 23:29. Thus construing a "day" as untold ages rather than as twenty-four hours means the earth must be considered as created "in vain" during those supposed eons when earth was an uninhabited wasteland—for man, the crowning achievement of Creation, was formed only at the end of God's wonderful work.

---

17. Ronald Ribbands, "The Honeybee," *Scientific American* (August 1955), p. 52.
18. Genesis 1:11-12.

CLUE #18
DAY-AGE THEORY *FAILS* TO
CLOSE BIBLE-EVOLUTION GAP

Besides all the preceding arguments against the day-age theory, it's clear that interpreting **yom** as a long period of time still fails to bring about the harmony between evolution and the Bible which is so much sought by theistic evolutionists. For geology **does not teach** the evolution of the world in SIX geologic periods. In the geologic time scale, three or four **ERAS** are divided into at least eleven **PERIODS**, some of which in turn are subdivided into several **EPOCHS**. Furthermore, the ORDER of events in Genesis does not conform to those of the evolutionary scheme. So merely conceiving the six days of Creation as long periods fails to harmonize Genesis with evolutionary geology—the two systems lack important basic parallels.

CLUE #19
2 PETER 3:8 DOES *NOT*
SUPPORT THE DAY-AGE THEORY

Supporters of the day-age theory usually are content merely to assert its validity without offering much in the way of Scripture texts or other evidence as proof. However, one text they're fond of citing is 2 Peter 3:8 - "One day is with the Lord AS a thousand years, and a thousand years AS one day." In considering this text, *three things* must be borne in mind.

First of all, Peter is **not literally** equating one day and a thousand years. The text is clearly **figurative**, employing a figure of speech known as a SIMILE and using the word *AS*—the way we might say, "His heart's as big as all outdoors." A similar text is Psalm 90:4, which says: "A thousand years in Thy sight are but as yesterday when it is past, and as a watch in the night." Now are we to understand that "yesterday" and "a thousand years" are **actually** and **literally** the same? Of course not! The Psalmist is simply using a figure of speech. Taking literally a statement intended to be figurative does violence to the meaning.

Secondly, the main point Peter is trying to make here is simply this: Time means nothing to the ETERNAL God. As "the high and lofty One that inhabiteth **eternity**,"[19] God does not wear a *wristwatch*—He's not on the same *time-frame* as we are. "The **eternal** God,"[20] "the **everlasting** Father,"[21] is *above and beyond* the passage of time, and the Bible repeatedly asserts this fact. In the verse under question, Peter is explaining NOT the **duration of a DAY** but the **timelessness of GOD.**

Thirdly, let's ask: In what **setting** or context was this verse written? We must be careful not to take verses out of context,[22] lest we be among those who **twist** the Scriptures "unto their own destruction" as Peter himself puts it in the same chapter.[23] Look at the verses before and after the text in question, and you'll understand Peter's purpose in writing this verse. In this chapter Peter is discussing *Christ's Second Coming,* and in verses 3 and 4 he specifically replies to "scoffers" who walk after their own lusts, saying, "Where is the promise of His coming?" In the verse under consideration Peter answers these impatient scoffers by reminding them that God is untouched by time, yet he adds:

---

19. Isaiah 57:15.
20. Deuteronomy 33:27.
21. Isaiah 9:6.
22. It's been well said that "A **text** without a CONtext is a PREtext!"
23. 2 Peter 3:16.

"The Lord is **not slack** concerning His promise, as some men count slackness, but is longsuffering to us-ward, not willing that any should perish, but that all should come to repentance. But the day of the Lord **will come** as a thief in the night."[24] In other words, Peter's purpose in this passage is simply to show that **we should be patient** in waiting for the Lord's return, for time means nothing to our eternal God, and if Christ **seems** to be delaying His coming it's only out of mercy for those who have not yet "come to repentance."

These three reasons effectively refute the claims of those who use this verse for much-needed proof of the day-age theory.

CONCLUSION

Some would have us believe that the "days" of Creation were vast geological ages. Others contend that they were literal 24-hour periods, the same as days today. Obviously, both views can't be right. Yet Christians need not **prove** that the days of Creation were 24 hours long—that's already proven by the fact that we *HAVE* 24-hour days! The burden of proof really rests on those who contend that those "days" were long ages. To them I say, "Since all days we know about have always been 24 hours [25] long, you must **prove to ME** that the days of Creation were DIFFERENT."

We've looked at this question from several points of view:

> **Biblically,**
>
> > **linguistically,**
> >
> > > **scientifically,**
> > >
> > > > **and logically.**

---

24. 2 Peter 3:9-10.
25. Each day is 23 hours, 56 minutes, 4.09 seconds, to be exact.

The **nineteen clues** we've considered provide REASONS why we can safely conclude the days of Creation were not indefinite periods eons long but regular, literal days of 24 hours' duration. In contrast to these sound reasons which strengthen our faith in God's Word, the arguments used by day-age theorists are nothing but speculation which careful scrutiny proves false. [26]

---

26. The reader is directed to *Appendix A* at the back of this volume for a few thoughts on the harmony between "Science and the Scriptures."

? ? ? ? ? ? ? ? ? ? ? ? ? ? ? ? ? ? ? ?
?   ?
?   **MYSTERY #3**   ?
?   **DEITY OF CHRIST**   ?
?   ─────────   ?
?   ?
?   Was Jesus Christ **divine?**   ?
?   Was the humble Carpenter of Nazareth ?
?   **really** the holy Son of God?   ?
?   What can we believe about His **resurrection?** ?
?   ?
? ? ? ? ? ? ? ? ? ? ? ? ? ? ? ? ? ? ? ?

"How shall we **escape**, if we **neglect**
so great salvation?"—Hebrews 2:3

Chapter 7

Jesus Meets Every Test

The greatest ambassador for Christ the world has ever known was probably the Apostle Paul, who "preached Christ in the synagogues, that He is **the Son of God** . . . and confounded the Jews which dwelt at Damascus, **PROVING** that this is very Christ [that is, the Messiah]."[1]

Thoughtful people today may wonder how Paul was able to **prove** to skeptics the divinity of our Lord. The Book tells us how: "For he mightily convinced the Jews . . . **showing by the Scriptures** that Jesus was Christ."[2]

Yes, Paul reasoned with men from the sacred pages of God's own Word, giving **Scriptural evidence** on which to base their beliefs. "Paul, as his manner was, went in unto them, and three Sabbath days **reasoned with them out of the Scriptures . . . that this Jesus . . . is Christ.**"[3]

---

1. Acts 9:20 & 22.
2. Acts 18:28.
3. Acts 17:2-3.

ONLY JESUS FITS
ALL THE SPECIFICATIONS

Jesus' life was measured by the great PROPHETIC BLUEPRINT outlined by God in the Scriptures. Men were drawn to Christ as they compared Him with the prophetic statements of the Old Testament. His disciples unhesitatingly announced: "We have **Him of Whom Moses . . . did write**, Jesus of Nazareth."[4]

After His resurrection, Jesus reviewed with His doubting disciples the stipulations of the prophetic Word regarding Himself: "Then He said unto them, O fools, and slow of heart to believe **all that the prophets have spoken. . . .** And beginning at **Moses** and **ALL the prophets,** He expounded unto them in *ALL the Scriptures* the things *concerning Himself.*"[5]

The late Alfred E. Smith, in his 1928 Presidential campaign, was fond of saying, "Let's look at the record." That's exactly what we'll do now: take a candid look at the Bible record to see for ourselves how closely **Jesus fits the DIVINE BLUEPRINT.** Listed below are dozens of specific prophecies from the Old Testament which pointed forward to the Messiah. Each is followed by its unique fulfillment as recorded in the New Testament.

> **"These are written, that ye might BELIEVE
> that Jesus is the Christ, the Son of God;
> and that believing ye might have LIFE
> through His name."[6]**

---

4. John 1:45.
5. Luke 24:25 & 27.
6. John 20:31.

1. HIS *HUMAN* NATURE

𝔓𝔯𝔬𝔭𝔥𝔢𝔱𝔦𝔠 𝔉𝔬𝔯𝔢𝔠𝔞𝔰𝔱:

Genesis 3:15 - After the serpent tempted Eve in the Garden of Eden, the Lord God told Satan: "I will put enmity between thee and the woman, and between thy seed and **her seed** [Christ]; it shall bruise thy head, and thou shalt bruise His heel."

Satan did bruise Christ's heel when His feet were nailed to the cross. In calling Jesus "the **seed** of the **woman**," God indicated that His Promised One would come as the offspring of a HUMAN BEING, not as an angel or other creature from outer space. This verse, the first of many regarding the Messiah, teaches that while He would be truly God, He would also be *truly MAN*.

Isaiah 49:1 - "The Lord called Me from **the womb**, from the body of **My mother** He named My name." Revised Standard Version.

Historic Fulfillment:

Matthew 24:27, 30 - "The Son of **man**"

1 Timothy 2:5 - "The **man** Christ Jesus"

1 Timothy 3:16 - "God was manifest **in the flesh.**"

John 1:14 - "The Word was made **flesh.**"

Galatians 4:4 - "God sent forth His Son, **made of a woman.**"

2. TO BE A *MALE* CHILD

𝔓𝔯𝔬𝔭𝔥𝔢𝔱𝔦𝔠 𝔉𝔬𝔯𝔢𝔠𝔞𝔰𝔱:

Isaiah 9:6 - "For unto us a Child is born, unto us **a Son** is given: and the government shall be upon **His**

shoulder: and **His** name shall be called Wonderful,
Counsellor, The Mighty **God**, The Everlasting **Father**,
The **Prince** of Peace."

Historic Fulfillment:

Matthew 1:21 - "She [Mary] shall bring forth **a Son**, and
thou shalt call **His** name JESUS: for **He** shall save **His**
people from their sins."

John 3:16 - "For God so loved the world, that He gave His
only begotten **Son,** that whosoever believeth in **Him**
should not perish, but have everlasting life."

3. TO BE BORN A *JEW*

𝔓rophetic 𝔉orecast:

Genesis 22:15, 18 - "And the angel of the Lord called unto
Abraham . . . in **thy seed** shall all the nations of
the earth be blessed."[7]

> The Messiah's **race** is clearly specified. He was to
> be born a Jew—not an Egyptian nor a Chinese—
> for Abraham, "the father of the faithful," was the
> progenitor of the Jewish people.

Historic Fulfillment:

John 4:9 - The woman at the well asked Christ, "How is it
that **Thou, being a Jew**, askest drink of me, which
am a woman of Samaria? for the Jews have no deal-
ings with the Samaritans."

Matthew 1:1 - "Jesus Christ, the Son of David, the son of
Abraham."

---

7. This promise to Abraham was *repeated* for emphasis in such
verses as Genesis 12:3, 18:18, 26:4, and 28:14.

Galatians 3:14, 16 - "That the blessing of **Abraham** might come on the Gentiles **through Jesus Christ.** . . . Now to **Abraham and his Seed** were the promises made. He [God] saith not, And to *seeds*, as of many; but as of **One**, And to thy *Seed*, which is Christ."

4. FROM *DAVID'S* LINEAGE

𝔓rophetic 𝔉orecast:
Isaiah 9:6, 7 - "For unto us a child is born, unto us a Son is given: and the government shall be upon His shoulder: and His name shall be called . . . The Prince of Peace. Of the increase of His government and peace there shall be no end, upon the throne of **David.** . . ."

Jeremiah 23:5, 6 - "Behold, the days come, saith the Lord, that I will raise **unto David** a righteous Branch, and a King shall reign and prosper, and shall execute judgment and justice in the earth. . . . And this is His name whereby He shall be called, **The Lord Our Righteousness.**"

Historic Fulfillment:
Matthew 20:30 - "And, behold, two blind men sitting by the wayside, when they heard that Jesus passed by, cried out, saying, Have mercy on us, O Lord, Thou **Son of David.**"[8]

Acts 13:23 - **"Of this man's seed** ["**David**" verse 22] hath God *according to His promise* raised unto Israel a Saviour, Jesus."

---

8. See also Matthew 15:22; Luke 18:35-39; John 7:42; 2 Timothy 2:8. The genealogy of Jesus is recorded in Matthew 1:1-16 and in Luke 3:23-38—note especially Matthew 1:1 & 6 and Luke 3:31, showing the link to David.

Romans 1:3 - "His Son Jesus Christ our Lord . . . was made of **the seed of David,** according to the flesh."

Revelation 22:16 - "I Jesus...am...**the offspring of David.**"

5. *PLACE* OF BIRTH

𝔓𝔯𝔬𝔭𝔥𝔢𝔱𝔦𝔠 𝔍𝔬𝔯𝔢𝔠𝔞𝔰𝔱:

Micah 5:2 - "But thou, **BETHLEHEM** Ephratah, though thou be **little** among the thousands of Judah, yet **out of thee shall He come forth** unto Me that is to be **Ruler** in Israel; whose goings forth have been from of old, **from everlasting.**"

> Today at Christmas we sing **"O Little Town of Bethlehem"**—though perhaps we're only dimly aware of the song's full significance. This remarkable prophecy *pinpointed* the Messiah's birthplace **more than seven hundred years** before that joyous event took place!

Historic Fulfillment:

Matthew 2:1 - "Jesus was born in **BETHLEHEM** of Judea."[9]

> It's thrilling to see how *God arranged matters* to have Jesus born in **Bethlehem** even though Joseph and Mary lived in **Nazareth!** Consider the following:

Luke 2:1-6, 11 - "It came to pass in those days, that there went out a decree from Caesar Augustus, that all the world should be taxed. . . . And all went to be taxed, every one into his own city. And **Joseph** also went up from Galilee, out of the city of **Nazareth, unto** the city of David, which is called **Bethlehem;** (because he was of the house and lineage of David:)

---

9. Read Matthew 2, verses 1-6.

To be taxed with Mary his espoused wife, being great with child. And so it was, that, while they were there, the days were accomplished that she should be delivered. . . . For unto you is born this day **in the city of David** a Saviour, which is Christ the Lord."

Truly, as poet William Cowper put it, "God moves in a mysterious way, His wonders to perform."[10]

6. *TIME* OF BIRTH

Prophetic Forecast:

Daniel 9:21-26 - The angel Gabriel gave Daniel this important message from heaven: "Know therefore and understand, that **from** the going forth of the commandment to restore and to build Jerusalem **unto the Messiah the prince** shall be seven weeks, and threescore and two weeks."[11]

To explain all the ramifications of this time prophecy would be a study in itself, but suffice it to say, **it's possible to prove BY MATHEMATICS that Jesus is the Messiah** (by counting from the decree to restore and rebuild Jerusalem to His birth and anointing by the Holy Spirit at His baptism). Christ's contemporaries understood this time prophecy and were indeed looking for the Messiah in His day, even asking John the Baptist if *he* were the Promised One.[12]

---

10. From "Light Shining Out of Darkness," in Cowper's *Olney Hymns* (1779).

11. The specific verse quoted above is Daniel 9:25.

12. See Luke 3:15-16 and John 1:19-27.

Historic Fulfillment:

Mark 1:15 - When Jesus began His ministry, John the
    Baptist told the people, "**The time is fulfilled**, and
    the kingdom of God is *at hand*."

Galatians 4:4 - "When the fulness of **the time was come**,
    God sent forth His Son."

7. *VIRGIN* BIRTH

Prophetic Forecast:

Isaiah 7:14 - "The Lord Himself shall give you a sign; Be-
    hold, **a VIRGIN shall conceive** and bear a Son."

Historic Fulfillment:

Luke 1:26-35 - "The angel Gabriel was sent from God unto
    a city of Galilee, named Nazareth, To a **virgin** es-
    poused to a man whose name was Joseph, of the
    house of David; and **the virgin's name was Mary.**
    . . . And the angel said unto her . . . behold, thou
    shalt conceive in thy womb, and bring forth a Son. . . .
    Then said Mary unto the angel, How shall this be,
    seeing I know not a man? And the angel answered
    and said unto her, The Holy Ghost shall come upon
    thee, and the power of the Highest shall overshadow
    thee: therefore also that holy thing which shall be
    born of thee shall be called **the Son of God.**"

Matthew 1:18-25 - "Now the birth of Jesus Christ was on this
    wise: When as His mother was espoused to Joseph,
    before they came together, she was found with child
    of the Holy Ghost. Then Joseph her husband, being
    a just man, and not willing to make her a public
    example, was minded to put her away privately. But
    while he thought on these things, behold, the angel

Harry Anderson

Color Plate #3

**No Room at the Inn: Joseph and Mary
vainly seek a resting place in Bethlehem.**

Artist: Harry Anderson

of the Lord appeared unto him in a dream, saying,
Joseph, thou son of David, fear not to take unto thee
Mary thy wife: for that which is conceived in her is
of the Holy Ghost. . . . Then Joseph being raised from
sleep did as the angel of the Lord had bidden him,
and took unto him his wife: And **knew her not** till
she had brought forth her firstborn Son . . . JESUS."[13]

8. GIVEN ROYAL *GIFTS*

𝔓rop𝔥etic 𝔉orecast:

Psalm 72:10, 11, 15 - "The **kings** of Tarshish and of the isles
shall **bring PRESENTS**: the kings of Sheba and Seba
shall **offer GIFTS**. Yea, all kings shall **fall down
before Him**: all nations shall serve Him. . . . And
to Him shall be given of the GOLD of Sheba."

Isaiah 60:3, 6 - "And the **Gentiles** shall come to Thy light,
and **kings** to the brightness of Thy rising. . . . The
multitude of camels shall cover thee, the dromedaries
of Midian and Ephah; all they from Sheba shall
come; **they shall bring GOLD and INCENSE**."

Historic Fulfillment:

Matthew 2:1, 2, 11 - "Now when Jesus was born in Bethlehem
. . . there came Wise Men from the east to Jerusalem,
Saying, Where is He that is born King of the Jews?
for we have seen His star in the east, and are **come
to worship Him**. . . . And when they . . . saw the
young Child with Mary His mother, and fell down,

---

13. Paul was inspired to write Galatians 4:4 - "When the fulness of
the time was come, God sent forth His Son, **made of a woman**"—NOT
"a woman and a man"—because **God** was His Father through the agency
of the Holy Spirit. See Matthew 1:18-20 and Luke 1:35.

and worshipped Him: and when they had opened
their treasures, **they presented unto Him gifts;
GOLD, and FRANKINCENSE, and MYRRH.**"

9. FLIGHT INTO EGYPT

𝔓𝔯𝔬𝔭𝔥𝔢𝔱𝔦𝔠 𝔉𝔬𝔯𝔢𝔠𝔞𝔰𝔱:
Hosea 11:1 - "When Israel was a child, then I loved him,
and **called My Son out of Egypt**."[14]

Historic Fulfillment:
Matthew 2:13-21 - "Behold, the angel of the Lord appeareth
to Joseph in a dream, saying, Arise, and take the young
Child and His mother, and **flee into Egypt**, and be
thou there until I bring thee word: for Herod will seek
the young Child to destroy Him. When he arose, he
took the young Child and His mother by night, and
departed into Egypt: And was there *until* the death of
Herod: that it might be fulfilled which was spoken of
the Lord by the prophet, saying, **Out of Egypt have
I called My Son**. . . . But when Herod was dead,
behold, an angel of the Lord appeareth in a dream to
Joseph in Egypt, Saying, Arise, and take the young
Child and His mother, and go into the land of Israel:
for they are dead which sought the young Child's
life."

---

14. Interestingly enough, this verse from Hosea has a double ap-
pli-cation, as seen from the following: First, when the children of Israel
were slaves to Pharaoh, God called them out of Egypt in the great Exodus
led and recorded by Moses (Exodus 4:22-23). Secondly, Joseph and Mary
fled into Egypt with the Holy Child to escape the murderous designs of
Herod. After Herod had died, God through an angel "called His Son out of
Egypt." Under inspiration, gospel writer Matthew recognized in Jesus'
experience the historical fulfillment of this prophecy.

---
10. HEROD'S
SLAUGHTER OF CHILDREN
WAS FORESEEN

Prophetic Forecast:

Jeremiah 31:15 - "Thus saith the Lord: A voice was heard in Ramah, *lamentation*, and *bitter weeping*; **Rachel weeping for her children** refused to be comforted for her children, **because they *were not.*"**

Historic Fulfillment:

Matthew 2:1-8 - "In the days of Herod the king, behold, there came wise men from the east to Jerusalem. . . . Then Herod, when he had privately called the wise men . . . said, Go and search diligently for the young Child; and when ye have found Him, *bring me word again*, that I may come and worship Him also. When they had heard the king, they departed. . . . And *being warned of God in a dream that they should not return to Herod*, they departed into their own country another way. . . . Then Herod, when he saw that he was mocked of the wise men, was exceeding wroth, and sent forth, and **slew all the children** that were in Bethlehem, and in all the coasts thereof from **two years old and under**, according to the time which he had diligently inquired of the wise men. **Then was fulfilled that which was spoken by Jeremy the prophet,** saying, In Rama was there a voice heard, lamentation, and weeping, and great mourning, Rachel weeping for her children, and would not be comforted, because they are not."

11. *HERALDING FORERUNNER*

𝔓𝔯𝔬𝔭𝔥𝔢𝔱𝔦𝔠 𝔍𝔬𝔯𝔢𝔠𝔞𝔰𝔱:

Isaiah 40:3 - "The voice of him that crieth *in the wilderness*, Prepare ye the way of the Lord, make straight in the desert a highway for our God."

Malachi 3:1 - "Behold, I will send **My messenger**, and he **shall prepare the way before Me** . . . saith the Lord of hosts."

Luke 1:17 - Before John the Baptist was born as a miracle baby, the angel Gabriel told Zacharias, his elderly father, that "he [**John the Baptist**] **shall go before Him** [the Messiah] . . . to make ready a people prepared for the Lord."

Historic Fulfillment:

Matthew 3:1-3 - "In those days came **John the Baptist,** preaching *in the wilderness* of Judea, And saying, Repent ye: for the kingdom of God is at hand. For **this is He** that was spoken of by the prophet Esaias [that is, Isaiah], saying, The voice of one crying in the wilderness, **Prepare ye the way of the Lord,** make His paths straight."

Matthew 11:10-11 - Jesus Himself said, concerning **John the Baptist:** "This is he, of whom it is written, Behold, I send **My messenger** before Thy face, which **shall prepare Thy way before Thee.**"

John 1:19-27 - "This is the record of **John** [**the Baptist**], when the Jews sent priests and Levites from Jerusalem to ask him, Who art thou? . . . What sayest of thyself? He said, **I am the voice of one crying in the wilderness,** Make straight the ways of the Lord, as said the prophet Esaias."

12. *ANOINTED* BY *HOLY SPIRIT*

𝔓rophetic 𝔍orecast:

Isaiah 11:1, 2 - "There shall come forth a rod *out of the stem of Jesse* [the father of David], and a Branch shall grow out of his roots: **And the Spirit of the Lord shall rest upon Him.**"

Isaiah 42:1 - "Behold My Servant, whom I uphold; Mine Elect, in whom My soul delighteth; I have put **My Spirit** upon Him: He shall bring forth judgment to the Gentiles."

Isaiah 61:1, 2 - "The **Spirit of the Lord God** is upon Me; because the Lord hath anointed Me to preach good tidings unto the meek, He hath sent Me to bind up the brokenhearted, to proclaim liberty to the captives, and the opening of the prison to them that are bound; To proclaim the acceptable year of the Lord."

Historic Fulfillment:

Matthew 3:16, 17 - "And Jesus, when He was baptized, went up straightway out of the water: and, lo, the heavens were opened unto Him, and He saw **the Spirit of God** descending like a dove, and **lighting upon Him**: And lo a voice from heaven, saying, This is My beloved Son, in Whom I am well pleased."

Luke 4:14-21 - "And Jesus returned in the power of the **Spirit** into Galilee: . . . and, as His custom was, He went into the synagogue on the Sabbath day, and stood up for to read. And there was delivered unto Him the book of the prophet Esaias [Isaiah]. And when He had opened the book, He found the place where it was written, **The Spirit of the Lord is upon Me**, because **He hath anointed Me** to preach the gospel to the poor; He hath sent Me to heal the brokenhearted, to preach deliverance to the captives, and recovering of sight to the blind, to set at liberty them that are bruised, To preach the acceptable year of the Lord. And He closed the book, and He gave it again to the minister, and sat down. And the eyes of all them that were in the synagogue were fastened on Him. And He began to say unto them, **This day is this Scripture fulfilled in your ears.**"

Acts 10:38 - At His baptism,   **"God anointed Jesus of Nazareth with the Holy Ghost and with power...."**

13. TO *OPEN BLIND EYES*

𝔓rophetic 𝔉orecast:
Isaiah 42:6, 7 - "I the Lord have called Thee . . . for a Light to the Gentiles; To **open the blind eyes.** . . ."

Historic Fulfillment:
Mark 10:46-52 - "**Blind Bartimaeus** ... sat by the highway side begging. And when he heard that it was Jesus of Nazareth, he began to cry out, and say, Jesus, Thou Son of David, have mercy on me.... And Jesus answered and said unto him, What wilt thou that I should do unto thee? The blind man said unto Him, Lord, that I might receive my sight. And Jesus said unto him, Go thy way; thy faith hath made thee whole. And **immediately he received his sight,** and followed Jesus in the way."

Christ's ministry of miracles is so well known that there's danger we might take it for granted. But the Record says: **"Since the world began was it not heard that *any* man opened the eyes of one born blind."**[15]

---

15. John 9:32.

Read all the ninth chapter of John's Gospel for a dramatic account of Jesus performing that very miracle among many.

14. *REJECTED* BY MEN

Prophetic Forecast:
Isaiah 53:3 - "He is **despised and rejected** of men; a Man of sorrows, and acquainted with grief: and we hid as it were our faces from Him; He was **despised**, and **we esteemed Him not.**"

Historic Fulfillment:
John 1:10, 11 - "He was in the world, and the world was made by Him, and **the world knew Him not.** He came unto His own, and **His own received Him not.**"

John 7:5, 48 - These verses show that not only the Pharisees and rulers rejected Jesus, but even His own "brethren"—members of His own household—refused to believe in Him, at least before His resurrection.

15. *TRIUMPHAL* ENTRY

Prophetic Forecast:
Zechariah 9:9 - "**Rejoice** greatly, O daughter of Zion; **shout**, O daughter of *Jerusalem*: behold, **thy King**[16] cometh unto thee: He is just, and having salvation; lowly, and **riding upon an ass**, and upon a **colt** the foal of an ass."

16. "Pilate wrote a title, and put it on the cross. And the writing was, JESUS OF NAZARETH THE KING OF THE JEWS. . . . Then said the chief priests of the Jews to Pilate, Write not, The King of the Jews; but that He **said**, I am King of the Jews. Pilate answered, What I have written I have written." John 19:19-22.

Historic Fulfillment:

Matthew 21:1-9 - "And when they drew nigh unto *Jerusalem*
. . . then sent Jesus two disciples, saying unto them,
Go into the village . . . and . . . *ye shall find an ass tied,
and a colt with her.* loose them, and bring them unto
Me. And if any man say ought unto you, ye shall
say, The Lord hath need of them, and straightway he
will send them. . . . And the disciples went, and did
as Jesus commanded them, and brought *the ass*, and
the colt, and put on them their clothes, and they set
Him thereon. And a very great multitude spread their
garments in the way; others cut down branches from
the [palm] trees, and spread them in the way . . . saying, **Hosanna to the Son of David: Blessed is He**
that cometh in the name of the Lord."[17]

16. *BETRAYAL BY A FRIEND*

Prophetic Forecast:

Psalm 41:9 - "Yea, mine own **familiar friend** in whom I
trusted, **which did eat of My bread**, hath lifted up
his heel against Me."

Historic Fulfillment:

John 13:18-26 - "Jesus . . . was troubled in spirit . . . and said,
Verily, verily, I say unto you, that **one of you shall
betray Me.** . . . One of His disciples . . . said unto
Him, Lord, who is it? Jesus answered, He it is, to
whom I shall give a sop [of bread], when I have
dipped it. And when He had dipped the sop, He
gave it to **Judas Iscariot.**"

---

17. Compare Luke 19:29-38.

Judas was one of the trusted inner circle—the Twelve who knew Christ best. As a "familiar friend," he betrayed Jesus with a **kiss**.[18]

17. THE *TRAITOR'S FEE*

Prophetic Forecast:
Zechariah 11:12 - "I said unto them, If ye think good, **give me my price**; and if not, forbear. So they weighed for my price **thirty pieces of silver**."

Historic Fulfillment:
Matthew 26:14-16 - "Then one of the twelve, called Judas Iscariot, went unto the chief priests, and said unto them, What will ye **give me**, and I will deliver Him unto you? And they covenanted with him for **thirty pieces of silver**. And from that time he sought opportunity to betray Him."

18. PURCHASE OF *POTTER'S FIELD*

Prophetic Forecast:
Zechariah 11:13 - "I took the thirty pieces of silver, and **cast them to the potter in the house of the Lord**."

Historic Fulfillment:
Matthew 27:3-7 - "Then Judas, which had betrayed Him, when he saw that He was condemned, repented himself, and brought again the thirty pieces of silver to the chief priests and elders, saying, I have sinned in that I have betrayed the innocent blood. And they said, What is that to us? See thou to that. And he **cast**

18. See Matthew 26:21-25, 46-50 and Mark 14:10, 17-22, 44-45.

down the pieces of silver in the temple, and departed, and went and hanged himself. And the chief priests took the silver pieces, and said, It is not lawful for to put them into the treasury, because it is the price of blood ["blood money"]. And they took counsel, **and bought with them the POTTER'S FIELD, to bury strangers in.**"

Acts 1:16-19 - Judas's blood money "**purchased a field** with the reward of iniquity. . . . And it was known unto all the dwellers at Jerusalem; insomuch as that field is called in their proper tongue, Aceldama, that is to say, The field of blood."

In the last three prophecies alone, we find *the exact fulfillment* of the following **seven points**:

1. Jesus would be BETRAYED
2. By a FRIEND (not an avowed enemy)
3. For THIRTY (neither more nor fewer) pieces
4. Of SILVER (not gold)
5. Which would be THROWN DOWN (not placed)
6. In the HOUSE of the LORD (not elsewhere).
7. The MONEY would then be used to BUY the POTTER'S FIELD (not something else). [19]

In so vital a matter as Jesus' divinity, we cannot plead ignorance. God gives us the facts we need to draw intelligent conclusions. We have a **multitude** of Prophetic Forecasts with corresponding Historical Fulfillments for *both Christ **and** Antichrist* (see Chapter 18).

---

19. See Josh McDowell, *Evidence That Demands a Verdict* (San Bernardino, Calif.: Here's Life Publishers, c. 1979), Volume I, p. 159.

19. *FORSAKEN* BY DISCIPLES

𝔓𝔯𝔬𝔭𝔥𝔢𝔱𝔦𝔠 𝔍𝔬𝔯𝔢𝔠𝔞𝔰𝔱:
Zechariah 13:7 - "Awake, O sword, against My Shepherd, and against *the Man that is My Fellow*, saith the Lord of Hosts: **smite the Shepherd and the sheep shall be scattered.**"

Historic Fulfillment:
Matthew 26:31 & 56 - "Then saith Jesus unto them, All ye shall be offended because of Me this night: for it is written, I will **smite the Shepherd, and the sheep of the flock shall be scattered abroad....** But all this was done, that the Scriptures of the prophets might be fulfilled. **Then all the disciples forsook Him, and fled.**"[20]

20. ACCUSED BY *FALSE WITNESSES*

𝔓𝔯𝔬𝔭𝔥𝔢𝔱𝔦𝔠 𝔍𝔬𝔯𝔢𝔠𝔞𝔰𝔱:
Psalm 35:11 - "**False witnesses** did rise up; they laid to My charge things that I knew not."

Psalm 27:12 - "**False witnesses** are risen up against Me, and such as breathe out cruelty."

Psalm 109:2 - "The mouth of the wicked and **the mouth of the deceitful** are opened against Me: they have **spoken against Me with a lying tongue.**"

Historic Fulfillment:
Mark 14:55-59 - "The chief priests and all the council *sought for witness against Jesus* to put Him to death; *and found none.* For many bare **false witness**

---

20. Compare Mark 14:27 & 50 and John 16:32.

Seven Mysteries . . . Solved!

against Him, but their witness agreed not together. And there arose certain [men], and bare **false witness** against Him . . . but neither so did their witness agree together."

21. *SILENT* UNDER ACCUSATION

Prophetic Forecast:
Isaiah 53:7 - "He was oppressed, and He was afflicted, yet He opened not His mouth: He is brought as a lamb to the slaughter, and as a lamb before her shearers is dumb, so **He openeth not His mouth.**"

Historic Fulfillment:
Matthew 26:63 - During His trial, "Jesus held His peace."

Matthew 27:12-14 - "When He was accused of the chief priests and elders, **He answered nothing.** Then said Pilate unto Him, Hearest Thou not how many things they witness against Thee? **And He answered him to never a word**; insomuch that the governor marvelled greatly."[21]

22. *BEATEN & SPAT UPON*

Prophetic Forecast:
Isaiah 50:6 - "I gave **My back** to the **smiters**, and My cheeks to them that pluck off the hair: I hid not **My face** from shame and **spitting.**"

Isaiah 53:5 - "He was **wounded** for our transgressions, He was **bruised** for our iniquities: the chastisement of our peace was upon Him; and with **His stripes** we are healed."

---

21. Compare Acts 8:26-35.

Historic Fulfillment:
Matthew 26:67 - "They **spit in His face**, and **buffeted Him**; and others **smote Him** with the palms of their hands."

John 19:1 - "Pilate . . . took Jesus, and **scourged Him**."

Luke 22:63-64 - "The men that held Jesus mocked Him, and **smote Him**. And when they had blindfolded Him, **they struck Him on the face**, and asked Him, saying, Prophesy, who is it that smote Thee?" [22]

23. *NAILED* TO A CROSS

Prophetic Forecast:
Psalm 22:16 - "They **pierced** My **hands** and My **feet**."

Isaiah 49:16 - "Behold, I have **graven thee** upon the **palms** of My **hands**."

Zechariah 13:6 - "And one shall say unto Him, What are these **wounds** in Thine **hands**? Then He shall answer, Those with which **I was wounded in the house of My friends**."

John 3:14 - "As Moses lifted up the serpent in the wilderness, [23] even so must the Son of man be **lifted up**."

John 8:28 - "Then said Jesus unto them, When ye have **lifted up** the Son of man, then shall ye know that I am He."

John 12:32 - "And I, if I be **lifted up** from the earth, will draw all men unto Me. This He said, signifying **what death** He should die."

---

22. Compare Matthew 27:26 & 30 and Mark 14:65 & 15:19.

23. When poisonous serpents attacked God's sinful people in the wilderness, "Moses made a serpent of brass, and **put it upon a pole**, and it came to pass, that if a serpent had bitten any man, when he beheld the serpent of brass, he lived." See Numbers 21:5-9.

When Jesus repeatedly prophesied that He would be "lifted up," He was predicting His own crucifixion.

Historic Fulfillment:
Matthew 27:35, Mark 15:25, Luke 23:33, John 19:18 - "They **crucified** Him." [24]

24. NUMBERED WITH *TRANSGRESSORS*

Prophetic Forecast:
Isaiah 53:12 - "He was **numbered with** the **transgressors**."

Historic Fulfillment:
Mark 15:27-28 - "And **with Him** they crucify **two thieves**; the one on His right hand, and the other on His left. And the Scripture was **fulfilled**, which saith, And He was numbered with the transgressors." [25]

25. GARMENTS *DIVIDED*

Prophetic Forecast:
Psalm 22:18 - "They **part My garments** among them, and **cast lots upon My vesture**."

---

24. "Doubting" Thomas refused to believe eye-witness reports of Christ's resurrection, saying, "Except I shall see **in His hands the print of the nails**, and put my finger into the print of the nails, . . . I will not believe." With loving patience, the risen Lord allowed Thomas personally to examine and touch those wounds (John 20:24-27). Many victims of crucifixion were simply **tied** to crosses rather than nailed and then left to die a lingering death from hunger and thirst. But Jesus' hands and feet were indeed "pierced" when He was nailed to Calvary's cross.

25. See also Matthew 27:38 and Luke 23:33.

Historic Fulfillment:

John 19:23-24 - "Then the soldiers, when they had crucified Jesus, took His **garments, and made four parts**, to every soldier a part; and also **His coat**: now the coat was without seam, woven from the top throughout. They said therefore among themselves, Let us not rend it, but **cast lots** for it, whose it shall be: that the Scripture might be **fulfilled**, which saith, They parted My raiment among them, and for My vesture they did cast lots. These things therefore the soldiers did."

This twofold prediction was remarkably fulfilled: The heathen soldiers did just as Scripture foretold, **parting** or dividing up some of His garments and **casting lots** for the other! This proves again that **every Old Testament prophecy concerning the Messiah met its EXACT fulfillment in Jesus Christ.** You've just read the record of the Apostle John—see also Matthew 27:35, Mark 15:24, and Luke 23:34. As Paul said, "In the mouth of *two* or *three* witnesses shall every word be established." 2 Corinthians 13:1 (compare Deuteronomy 17:6).

26. MOCKED & RIDICULED

Prophetic Forecast:

Psalm 22:7-8 - "All they that see Me **laugh Me to scorn**: they shoot out the lip, they **shake the head**, saying, **He trusted on the Lord** that He would deliver Him: **let Him deliver Him**, seeing He delighted in Him."

Historic Fulfillment:

Matthew 27:39-43 - "They that passed by **reviled Him, wagging their heads**, and saying, ... He saved others, Himself He cannot save. If He be the King of Israel, let Him now come down from the cross, and we will believe Him. **He trusted in God; let Him deliver Him** now, if He will have Him."

27. *PRAYED FOR* PERSECUTORS

𝔓𝔯𝔬𝔭𝔥𝔢𝔱𝔦𝔠 𝔉𝔬𝔯𝔢𝔠𝔞𝔰𝔱:
Isaiah 53:12 - "He . . . **made intercession** for the transgressors."

Historic Fulfillment:
Luke 23:34 - "Then said Jesus, **Father, forgive them**; for they know not what they do."

Here Jesus practiced what He preached in His Sermon on the Mount: "Pray for them which despitefully use you, and persecute you." [26]

28. OFFERED *GALL & VINEGAR*

𝔓𝔯𝔬𝔭𝔥𝔢𝔱𝔦𝔠 𝔉𝔬𝔯𝔢𝔠𝔞𝔰𝔱:
Psalm 69:21 - "They gave Me also **gall** for My meat; and in My thirst they gave Me **vinegar** to drink."

Historic Fulfillment:
Matthew 27:34 - "They gave Him **vinegar** to drink mingled with **gall**: and when He had tasted thereof, He would not drink." [27]

---

26. Matthew 5:44 & Luke 6:28.
27. See also Matthew 27:48 and John 19:28-29.

29. *LONELY & FORSAKEN*

Prophetic Forecast:

Psalm 22:1 - "My God, My God, why hast Thou forsaken Me?"

Historic Fulfillment:

Mark 15:34 - "At the ninth hour Jesus cried with a loud voice, saying, *Eloi, Eloi, lama sabachtani?* which is, being interpreted, My God, My God, why has Thou forsaken Me?"

30. *EARTHQUAKE* FOLLOWED ANGUISHED CRY

Prophetic Forecast:

Psalm 18:6-7 - "In My distress I called upon the Lord, and **cried unto My God**: He heard My voice out of His temple, and My cry came before Him, even into His ears. **Then the earth shook and trembled**; the foundations also of **the hills moved and were shaken**, because He was wroth."

Historic Fulfillment:

Matthew 27:46, 50-54 - "Jesus, **when He had cried again with a loud voice,** yielded up the ghost [and died] . . . and **the earth did quake, and the rocks rent.** . . . Now when the centurion, and they that were with him, watching Jesus, saw **the earthquake,** and those things that were done, they feared greatly, saying, **Truly this was the Son of God.**"

31. *DARKNESS* COVERED LAND

𝕻𝖗𝖔𝖕𝖍𝖊𝖙𝖎𝖈 𝕱𝖔𝖗𝖊𝖈𝖆𝖘𝖙:

Amos 8:9-10 - "And it shall come to pass in that day, saith the Lord God, that **I will cause the sun to go down AT NOON, and I will darken the earth** in the clear day... and I will make it **as the mourning of an only Son.**"

Historic Fulfillment:

Matthew 27:45 - "**From the sixth hour there was darkness** over all the land unto the ninth hour."

"The sixth hour" by Jewish reckoning was **NOON.** Jesus hung upon the cross for three hours—from noon till 3 p.m. on the day we call "Good Friday"—but the sun itself refused to look upon the awful scene.

32. SIDE *PIERCED*

𝕻𝖗𝖔𝖕𝖍𝖊𝖙𝖎𝖈 𝕱𝖔𝖗𝖊𝖈𝖆𝖘𝖙:

Zechariah 12:10 - "They shall look upon Me Whom **they have pierced**, and they shall mourn for Him, as one mourneth for **His only Son.**"

Historic Fulfillment:

John 19:34-37 - "One of the soldiers with a spear **pierced His side,** and forthwith came there out blood and water. . . . These things were done, that the Scripture should be **fulfilled, . . . They shall look on Him whom they pierced.**"

John 20:24-27 - "But Thomas, one of the twelve, . . . said unto them, Except I shall see in His hands the print of the nails, and put my finger into the print of the nails, and **thrust my hand into His side,** I will

not believe. . . . Then saith He [Jesus] to Thomas,
Reach hither thy finger, and behold My hands; and
reach hither thy hand, and thrust it into My side:
and be not faithless, but believing."

33. *"CUT OFF"* FROM LIFE

Prophetic Forecast:

Daniel 9:26 - "After threescore and two weeks **shall Messiah be cut off. . . .**"

Isaiah 53:8 & 12 - "He was **cut off out of the land of the
living.** . . . He hath poured out His soul unto **death.**"

Historic Fulfillment:

Matthew 27:50 - "Jesus . . . **breathed His last.**" Today's
English Version.

Acts 2:22-23 - "Jesus of Nazareth . . . ye have . . . crucified
and **slain.**"

34. DIED TO SAVE *OTHERS*

Prophetic Forecast:

Daniel 9:26 - "Messiah [shall] be cut off, but **not for Himself.**"

Isaiah 53:4-12 - "Surely He hath borne **OUR** griefs, and
carried **OUR** sorrows. . . . He was wounded for **OUR**
transgressions, He was bruised for **OUR** iniquities:
the chastisement of **OUR** peace was upon **Him**; and
with His stripes **WE** are healed. All **WE** like sheep
have gone astray; **WE** have turned every one to his
own way; and **the Lord hath laid on HIM the
iniquity of US ALL.** . . . For the transgression of my
people was He stricken. . . . My righteous Servant

[shall] justify **MANY**; for He shall bear **THEIR** iniquities. . . . He bare the sin of **MANY**."

Historic Fulfillment:

Matthew 20:28 - "The Son of man came . . . **to give His life a ransom for MANY**."

Romans 5:6-8 - "Christ died **for the ungodly**. . . . While we were yet sinners, Christ died **for US**."

1 Peter 2:21 & 24; 3:18 - "Christ also **suffered for US**. . . . Who His own self **bare OUR sins** in His own body on the tree . . . the Just **for the unjust**, that He might bring us to God."

1 John 2:2 - "He is the propitiation **for OUR sins**: and not for ours only, but also **for the sins of the WHOLE WORLD**."

A beautiful statement on this subject is from *The Desire of Ages*, an inspiring biography of our Saviour by E. G. White: "Christ was treated as **we** deserve, that we might be treated as **He** deserves. He was condemned for **our sins**, in which He had no share, that we might be justified by **His righteousness**, in which we had no share. He suffered the **death** which was ours, that we might receive the **life** which was His."[28]

35. NO BONE BROKEN

Prophetic Forecast:

Psalm 34:20 - "He keepeth all His bones: **not one** of them is **broken**."

28. Ellen G. White, *The Desire of Ages* (Boise, Idaho: Pacific Press Publishing Association, c. 1940), p. 25.

Historic Fulfillment:

John 19:31-36 - "The Jews, therefore, because it was the preparation,[29] that the bodies should not remain upon the cross on the Sabbath day, (for that Sabbath day was an high day,) besought Pilate that their **legs** might be **broken**, and that they might be taken away. Then came the soldiers, and **brake the legs** of the first, and of the other which was crucified with Him. **But when they came to Jesus, and saw that He was dead already, THEY BRAKE NOT HIS LEGS. . . .** And he that saw it bare record, and his record is true: and he knoweth that he saith true, *that ye might believe.* For these things were done, that the Scripture should be **fulfilled**, A bone of Him shall not be broken."

The import of this prophecy and fulfillment may not be apparent at first, but in His great sacrifice **Jesus was a type of Passover lamb**. That's why John the Baptist pointed to Jesus and proclaimed, "Behold the Lamb of God, which taketh away the sin of the world."[30] And Paul says: "**Christ our Passover** is sacrificed for us."[31] God had clearly told His people in regard to the Passover lamb: "neither shall ye break a bone thereof."[32] Thus it was important that the soldiers did not break Jesus' legs—He is our Passover offered "once for all."[33] In every detail, **Christ FITS the Divine Blueprint!**

---

29. "The preparation" means Friday, the sixth day of the week, used by God's faithful people to prepare for the Sabbath by finishing all work, cleaning up, etc. Mark 15:42 defines it as "the preparation, that is, the day before the Sabbath."

30. John 1:29.
31. 1 Corinthians 5:7.
32. Exodus 12:43 & 46 and Numbers 9:12.
33. Hebrews 10:10.

36. BURIED IN *RICH MAN'S TOMB*

𝔓𝔯𝔬𝔭𝔥𝔢𝔱𝔦𝔠 𝔉𝔬𝔯𝔢𝔠𝔞𝔰𝔱:
Isaiah 53:9 - "He made **His grave** . . . **with the rich** in His death."

Historic Fulfillment:
Matthew 27:57-60 - "When the even was come, there came **a rich man** of Arimathea, named Joseph, who also himself was Jesus' disciple: He went to Pilate, and begged the body of Jesus. Then Pilate commanded the body to be delivered. And when Joseph had taken the body, he wrapped it in a clean linen cloth, and **laid it in his own new tomb.**" [34]

37. COULDN'T BE *HELD* IN TOMB

𝔓𝔯𝔬𝔭𝔥𝔢𝔱𝔦𝔠 𝔉𝔬𝔯𝔢𝔠𝔞𝔰𝔱:
Psalm 16:10 - "Thou wilt **not** leave My soul in **hell**; neither wilt Thou suffer **Thine Holy One** to see **corruption**."

"*Hell*" here is from the Hebrew *Sheol* and simply means **the grave**—see any Bible dictionary. "Corruption" refers to the *rotting decomposition* of a dead body in the grave over the course of time.

Historic Fulfillment:
Acts 2:31-32 - "He [God] seeing this before spake of the resurrection of Christ, that His soul was **not left in hell**, neither His flesh did see **corruption**. This Jesus hath God **raised up** whereof we all are witnesses."

---

34. Compare Mark 15:43-46, Luke 23:50-53, and John 19:38-42.

38. AROSE ON *THIRD DAY*

𝔓rophetic 𝔉orecast:

Matthew 17:22-23 - "Jesus said unto them, "The Son of man shall be betrayed into the hands of men: And they shall kill Him, and **the third day He shall be raised again.**"[35]

John 2:18-21 - "The Jews . . . said unto Him, What sign shewest Thou unto us . . .? Jesus answered and said unto them, Destroy this temple, and **in three days I will raise it up.** Then said the Jews, Forty and six years was this temple in building, and wilt Thou rear it up **in three days?** But He spake of the temple of **His body.**"[36]

Historic Fulfillment:

Luke 24:6, 34, 46 - "He is not here, but is **risen.** . . . **The Lord is risen indeed.** . . . Thus it behoved Christ to suffer, **and to rise from the dead the third day.**"

Christ not only foretold the *fact* of His resurrection but also specified the *length of time* He would be in the grave! His enemies, remembering His prediction, even took precautions against it[37]—but their efforts proved futile. Our next chapter will be devoted entirely to Christ's marvelous *resurrection.*

---

35. See also Matthew 16:21.
36. The apostle Paul makes clear in such verses as 1 Corinthians 5:16-17 and 6:19 and 2 Corinthians 6:16 that our body is "the temple of God."
37. Matthew 27:62-66.

39. *ASCENDED* TO HIS FATHER

𝔓𝔯𝔬𝔭𝔥𝔢𝔱𝔦𝔠 𝔉𝔬𝔯𝔢𝔠𝔞𝔰𝔱:

Psalm 68:18 - "Thou has **ascended on high**, Thou has led captivity captive: Thou hast received gifts for men."

Psalm 110:1 - "**The Lord** said unto **my Lord**, Sit Thou at **My right hand**, until I make Thine enemies Thy footstool." (The two divine Beings here designated "Lord" are God the Father and God the Son.)

Psalm 24:7-10 - These verses describe **Christ's triumphant re-entry into heaven:**

"Lift up your heads, O you gates!
And be lifted up, you everlasting doors!
And the King of glory shall come in.
Who is this King of glory?
The Lord strong and mighty,
The Lord mighty in battle.
Lift up your heads, O you gates!
And lift them up, you everlasting doors!
And the King of glory shall come in.
Who is this King of glory?
The Lord of hosts,
He is the King of glory."[38]

Historic Fulfillment:

Luke 24:51 - "And it came to pass, while He blessed them [the disciples], He was parted from them, and **carried up into heaven.**"

---

38. Quoted from the New King James Version.

Acts 1:9 - "And when He had spoken these things, while they [the disciples] beheld, **He was taken up**; and a cloud received Him out of their sight."

Mark 16:19 - "After the Lord had spoken unto them, **He was received up into heaven**, and sat on **the right hand of God**."

Acts 2:32-35 - "This Jesus hath God raised up . . . being **by the right hand of God** exalted. . . . For David is not ascended into the heavens: but he saith himself, **The Lord** said unto **my Lord**, Sit Thou on **My right hand**, until I make Thy foes Thy footstool."

Acts 7:55-56 - Stephen, the first Christian martyr, gave this testimony just before he died: "But he, being full of the Holy Ghost, looked up steadfastly into heaven, and saw the glory of God, and Jesus standing on **the right hand of God**, and said, Behold, I see the heavens opened, and the Son of man standing on **the right hand of God**."

Romans 8:34 - "It is Jesus that died, yea rather, that is risen again, who is even at **the right hand of God**, who also maketh intercession for us."

Ephesians 1:20 - God "wrought in Christ, when He raised Him from the dead, and **set Him at His own right hand** in the heavenly places."

Ephesians 4:8-10 - "**He ascended up on high**."

Hebrews 1:3 - Jesus, after He had "purged our sins, **sat down on the right hand of the Majesty on high**."

1 Peter 3:22 - Jesus Christ "is **gone into heaven**, and is **on the right hand of God**."

Revelation 12:5 - The promised "Man child . . . was **caught up unto God**, and to His throne."

THE CREDENTIALS OF
CHRIST ARE CONVINCING

Jesus tells us: **"Search the Scriptures**; for in them ye think ye have eternal life: and **they are they which testify of Me.**"[39] The "Scriptures" He refers to are the Old Testament—the only part of the Bible written at that time.

The prophecies pointing to the Messiah are all A MATTER OF RECORD. They were published to the world long ago in the Old Testament. And when we read about the life and experience of Jesus Christ in the New Testament, we find that **He fits those divine prophecies precisely.** Either Jesus *is* the Son of God, or there's **no such thing** as Messianic prophecy!

Those who reject Jesus as the Son of God may claim He **deliberately set out** to fulfill prophecy—for example, He rode the donkey into Jerusalem on purpose because the Scripture predicted that. But this objection seems plausible only until we realize that **most prophecies concerning the Messiah were TOTALLY BEYOND HUMAN CONTROL,** such as His *place* of birth, His *time* of birth, His *race* and *family heritage*, details of His *betrayal*, the manner of His *death* and burial, and so on. Remember also that **more than FOUR HUNDRED YEARS** elapsed between the last book of the Old Testament and the first book of the New Testament, so no collusion between writers was possible.

Jesus warned that many impostors would come, saying, "I am Christ."[40] And some have come claiming to be the Messiah. But the true Christ, or Messiah, had to be born in Bethlehem, had to begin His earthly ministry in A.D. 27, and had to be crucified in A.D. 31. We've seen that Jesus'

---

39. John 5:39.
40. Matthew 24:5.

birth in Bethlehem was a miracle in itself, since His family lived in Nazareth. And both sacred and secular history record that He appeared on the scene at the **exact time** predicted. We could possibly find **one** or **two** of these prophecies fulfilled someone else's life—but *not ALL of them!* One or two prophecies fulfilled in a person's life would hardly convince anyone to accept that individual as the divine Son of God, the Saviour of mankind. But the CUMULATIVE EFFECT of fulfilling **all** of them in specific detail is over-whelmingly persuasive! These multiple strands of fulfilled prophecy, bound together **like the wires of a great cable,** make a bond of evidence no power on earth can break.

CONCLUSION

I trust this study has strengthened your faith. You've been exposed to dozens of Bible facts about the Son of God. You've been brought **face to face with Truth**—an encounter that could be your own "rendezvous with destiny."

Intelligent people are willing to believe in God and His Son, but they demand credible reasons for their faith. Fortunately, the abundant evidence for Christ's divinity makes our decision to accept Him as Lord and Saviour an easy one. These prophecies gave much information about Jesus in advance of His coming so we might not only recognize **HIM** as the Messiah but also have increased faith in the **BIBLE** as the inspired Word of God. Christianity's documented credibility proves that **the believer has made no mistake—**
Jesus truly IS the Son of God.

In closing this chapter, remember Jesus' experience when He confronted a man possessed by demons who "cried out with a loud voice, saying, Let us alone; what have we to do with Thee, Thou Jesus of Nazareth? Art Thou come to destroy us? **I know Thee who Thou art; the Holy One of God.**"[41] "Unclean spirits, when they saw Him, fell down before Him, and cried, saying, **Thou art the Son of God**"![42] And greedy exorcists, trying to profit by casting out demons in the name of Jesus and Paul, were confronted by a demon who said, "Jesus I know, and Paul I know; but who are you?"[43]

Did you get that? Even evil spirits recognize our Lord as "the Holy One of God"! One went on record as saying, "Jesus I know." Friend, do YOU know Him?

---

41. Luke 4:33-34 (and Mark 1:23-24).
42. Mark 3:11. See also Mark 5:1-9 and Luke 4:41.
43. Acts 19:13-15, the New King James Version.

Chapter 8

The Resurrection of Christ: Myth or Miracle?

The credibility of Christianity stands or falls with the resurrection of Jesus Christ. For the resurrection is not merely one Christian doctrine among many—it's the great funda mental which is absolutely vital and essential. Faith in the resurrection is the very keystone in the arch of Christian faith, and when it's removed, all the rest inevitably crumbles into ruin. [1] Had there been no **resurrection**, there would have been no **Christian Church!** The movement Jesus started would have come to a *literal dead end* with the execution of the carpenter-teacher.

So through the centuries the resurrection has been the storm center of the attack upon the Christian faith: **disprove** the resurrection, and you **dispose** of Christianity. As Paul put it, "If Christ be not risen, then is our preaching vain, and your faith is also vain." [2] And Christ Himself deliberately staked His whole claim to men's belief upon His

---

1. Paraphrased from Henry P. Liddon, *Sermons* (New York: The Contemporary Pulpit Library, 1888), p. 73.
2. 1 Corinthians 15:14.

resurrection: When asked for a sign of His divinity, He pointed to His resurrection as His single and sufficient credential.[3]

HOAX or HISTORY?

The resurrection of Jesus Christ is either the greatest *miracle* or the greatest *delusion* history records. If it's true, then it's the Supreme Fact of history, and failure to adjust one's life to its implications means irreparable loss. If it's not true, if Christ has not risen, then Christianity is all a fraud—a heartless hoax foisted on the minds of men.

The **meaning** of the resurrection may be a theological matter, but the **fact** of the resurrection is a historical one.[4] For "Christianity is a historical religion. It claims that God has taken the risk of involving Himself in human history, and the facts are there for you to examine with the utmost rigour. They'll withstand any amount of critical investigation."[5]

The witness of history gives clear, abundant evidence in this case. William Lyon Phelps, distinguished professor at Yale for more than forty years and author of some twenty volumes, asserted that "The historical evidence for the resurrection is **stronger** than for any other miracle anywhere narrated."[6] And the evidence is conclusive.

Professor Thomas Arnold, for fourteen years headmaster of Rugby School in England, author of the three-volume

---

3. Matthew 12:38-40 & John 2:18-21. B. B. Warfield's statement along these lines is quoted in J. N. D. Anderson, *Christianity: The Witness of History* (Tyndale Press, 1970), p. 103.

4. This thought was first expressed by Wilbur M. Smith in his excellent book *Therefore, Stand* (Boston: W. A. Wilde Co., 1945), p. 386.

5. Michael Green, *Man Alive!* (Downers Grove, Illinois: Inter-Varsity Press, 1968), p. 61.

6. William Lyon Phelps, *Human Nature and the Gospel*, pp. 131-132.

History of Rome, appointed to the chair of Modern History at Oxford, was certainly well acquainted with the value of evidence in determining historical facts. This great scholar declared: "The evidence for our Lord's life and death and resurrection may be, and often has been, shown to be satisfactory; it is good according to the common rules for distinguishing good evidence from bad. Thousands and tens of thousands of persons have gone through it piece by piece. . . . I myself have done it many times over, . . . and I know of no one fact in the history of mankind which is proved by **better and fuller evidence** of every sort, to the understanding of a fair inquirer, than the great sign which God hath given us that Christ died and rose again from the dead."[7]

And John Singleton Copley, better known as Lord Lyndhurst and recognized as one of the great legal minds in British history, was Solicitor-General of the British government in 1819, attorney-general of Great Britain in 1824, three times Lord Chancellor of England, and elected in 1846 High Steward of Cambridge University, thus holding in one lifetime the highest offices possible for a judge in Great Britain. When Lord Lyndhurst died, a document found in his desk, in his own handwriting, gave an account of his Christian faith, in which he wrote: "I know pretty well what evidence is; and I tell you, **such evidence as that for the Resurrection has never broken down yet.**"[8]

Let's examine and thoroughly sift this evidence by considering the arguments critics put forth as theoretical alternatives to the fact of Christ's resurrection. The subject is one that will repay very careful study.

---

7. Thomas Arnold, *Sermons on the Christian Life—Its Hopes, Its Fears, and Its Close*, 6th edition (London, 1859), p. 324.

8. John Singleton Copley (Lord Lyndhust), quoted in Wilbur M. Smith, *Therefore, Stand* (Boston: W. A. Wilde Co., 1945), pp. 425 & 584.

I. THE FABRICATION THEORY

Some unbelievers try to dismiss the whole story of the resurrection by branding it all a fabrication, a deliberate lie concocted by the disciples. But few intelligent critics go that far—for good reason. Consider the following:

Does a LIE have power to **transform lives**? If not, how can we account for the **remarkable change** that took place in the disciples? In the first place, they were SAD. "Almost every home has mourned the loss of some dear one in death. Where real love exists, the weary hours, days, and weeks drag by slowly, with the wound seemingly not healing. Here was One, dearly loved, deeply mourned over, and greatly missed. Yet only three days after His death (some 36 hours), His closest friends had cast off all sorrow and were greatly rejoicing. A broken heart is not that easily cheered, unless there has been a resurrection."[9]

In the second place, the disciples were FEARFUL of their personal safety. The authorities were so violently hostile that anyone connected with Jesus was very apprehensive. The disciples fled in obvious panic and for the most part hid behind locked doors. Yet they soon preached so boldly that neither prison, persecution, nor the threat of death could silence them.

- What changed the cowardice of *Peter*, "cringing under the taunt of a maid in the court of the high priests and denying with a curse that he knew 'this man of

---

9. Leslie G. Storz, "Many Infallible Proofs," *Review and Herald* Magazine (April 4, 1968), p. 6.

whom ye speak'"?[10] What changed his crippling fear into missionary zeal almost overnight?

- Consider *James*, the brother of Jesus. He was outside the original circle of apostles and their friends. He had few, if any, illusions concerning his own brother. During Christ's life, the attitude of James was cold and even hostile—the record says plainly that he did **not** believe in Jesus.[11] Yet he became a dominant figure in the Christian movement at Jerusalem, and Paul calls him one of the "pillars" of the church.[12] How do we account for the amazing change that took place in James? The simple answer is that the living Lord had appeared to him.[13]

- Take *Thomas*, the doubter whose name has become a byword for skepticism. Till he saw Jesus with his own eyes after the resurrection, he refused to believe even the testimony of his friends, the other disciples.[14] But Thomas, too, made a complete about-face after seeing his Lord risen from the grave.

- *Paul*, also, was miraculously changed. At first he had no intention of ever believing in the resurrection and eagerly persecuted the "fanatics" who did. But Saul, the proud, aggressive persecutor was suddenly changed into Paul, the apostle of the Lord. On the road to Damascus he had the shock of his life. He started for Damascus determined to stamp out Christianity—he arrived there an utterly shaken and repentant man. He began by being the outstanding figure on **one** side of the controversy and ended by becoming the outstanding figure on the **other**. Why

---

10. Albert Roper, *Did Jesus Rise from the Dead?* (Grand Rapids: Zondervan Publishing House, 1965), p. 50. See Matthew 26:69-75, Mark 14:66-72, Luke 22:54-62, and John 18:25-27.
11. Matthew 13:55-58, Mark 6:3-6, and John 7:5.
12. Galatians 1:19 and 2:9.
13. 1 Corinthians 15:7.
14. John 20:24-29.

should a man of this tough breed be **uprooted** in an **instant** from his most cherished beliefs and swept into the camp of his most hated enemies?[15] What *was* the discovery that so staggered Paul on the road to Damascus? The only adequate cause for such a total reversal was that he had *seen* the resurrected Lord.[16]

The remarkable transformation of the disciples is perhaps the greatest evidence of all for the resurrection. Not only were all the disciples **changed** in a very short time from utter dejection to triumphant joy, but their faith was *sustained throughout a life of devotion that ended in a martyr's death.*

The first law of human nature is self-preservation. Yet this theory asks us to believe that the disciples would **give their lives** for what they KNEW to be false! If these men consciously told falsehoods, they must have had some motive for doing so. What was the motive? It was not to gain popularity, for their message was supremely displeasing to many. It was not to make money, for the disciples were practically penniless till the day they died. These people all had little to gain and much to lose by talking, but talk they did.

The most convincing testimony anyone can give for the truth of a statement is to suffer rather than deny it. The disciples didn't need to suffer—they could have escaped persecution simply by abstaining from preaching Christ and His resurrection. But prison, torture, and death couldn't alter their conviction that Jesus was alive. To their last breath they continued to teach the resurrection of Christ.

---

15. Paraphrased from Frank Morison, *Who Moved the Stone?* (Downers Grove, Illinois: Inter-Varsity Press, 1967), pp. 142-143.
16. Acts 7:58 – 8:4 and 9:1-31.

They could do **no more** than SEAL their testimony with their BLOOD. This the disciples did: Within three decades most of them perished violently for their adherence to the resurrection story. They suffered the supreme penalty for their convictions in the manner of that barbaric age—James in Jerusalem itself, Peter and Paul in Rome. If the resurrection had been a lie, surely one of the conspirators, in disillusionment or agony, would have divulged the secret. The fact that **they remained steadfast even in the face of execution** stamps the fabrication theory itself a falsehood.

Not only would men not die to uphold a mere lie, but the **character** of the *converted* disciples was such that they would not lie under any circumstances. "They gave the world the highest moral and ethical teaching it has ever known; *and* they lived it—as even their opponents were forced to admit."[17]

Is it credible that men could concoct such a fraud as the resurrection story and then continually lie while teaching converts to *"lie not* one to another,"[18] warning that liars will find their place at last in the lake of fire? Is it credible that these men made it their lifework to propagate a LIE and then succeeded in turning multitudes of wicked people to lives of virtue and honesty?

"To have persisted in so gross a falsehood, after it was known to them, was not only to encounter, for life, all the evils man could inflict from **without**, but to endure also the pangs of **inward** and conscious guilt; with no hope of future peace, no testimony of a good conscience, . . . no hope of happiness in this life or in the world to

---

17. J. N. D. Anderson, *The Evidence for the Resurrection* (Downers Grove, Illinois: Inter-Varsity Press, c. 1966), p. 8.

18. Colossians 3:9.

come. . . . If then their testimony was **not TRUE**, there was **no possible motive** for its fabrication."[19]

Some critics try to make a case for the fabrication theory by pointing to slight discrepancies in certain details of the gospel story. It's true that there are a few minor differences among the four accounts written by the gospel writers, such as the fact that Matthew says the women who came back to the tomb to anoint Jesus' body encountered an angel who told them that Christ has risen, whereas Mark says it was a young man, Luke says two men, and John says two angels. It's reasonable to assume that the angels took human form so these friends of Jesus wouldn't be frightened. That's why Luke reported two "men" and John reported two "angels." Slight discrepancies on minor points constitute a strong argument for the VALIDITY of the Scripture accounts. Eyewitnesses may be suspected of **collaboration** and **collusion** if their accounts are identical in every detail because *no two people see the same thing in exactly the same way.*

For instance, the assassination of John F. Kennedy has been treated differently by every author who has dealt with the subject. Some see a conspiracy while others see a lone

---

19. This statement comes from the pen of Simon Greenleaf (1783-1853), famous Royall Professor of Law at Harvard University who succeeded Justice Joseph Story as the Dane Professor of Law in the same University upon Story's death in 1846. The *Dictionary of American Biography* states that "To the efforts of Story and Greenleaf is to be ascribed the rise of the Harvard Law School to its eminent position among the legal schools in the United States." Greenleaf produced a famous work entitled *A Treatise on the Law of Evidence* (1842), still considered the greatest single authority on evidence in the entire literature of legal procedure. In 1846, while Professor of Law at Harvard, this brilliant jurist wrote a volume entitled *Testimony of the Evangelists, Examined by the Rules of Evidence Administered in Courts of Justice.* Our quotation was taken from pages 29-30 of that book, a reprint of which was published in 1965 by Baker Book House, Grand Rapids, Michigan.

fanatic causing the death of the President, and so on. All these reports leave some question as to the precise way in which the President was shot, but they don't leave a shred of doubt about the historical fact that the President was indeed shot. Future archaeologists finding a shelf of twentieth-century books on JFK's death will be all the more convinced that it really occurred by the very fact that people with *different* points of view *all agreed* that he had been shot.

The Gospels may be compared to four windows through which we look into a room from four different angles. The four views of Christ's life may appear contradictory on the surface, but really these brief records complement and supplement each other in a most harmonious way. If all the writers gave identical word-for-word reports, critics could say we don't have **four** reports but only **one**—and then they'd ask, "How can we trust only one witness?" But the Gospel writers make no pretense of agreeing, even though Mark's Gospel, the earliest version of what happened, was accessible to both Matthew and Luke when they wrote, and all three of those Gospels were common property when John produced his work. If this fundamental doctrine of the church were mere fabrication, care would have been taken to have all accounts of it in strict agreement.[20]

The resurrection story rings true also because of these points:

- How can we explain that *awkward interval of seven weeks* between the resurrection and its first public proclamation? No fabricator of false evidence would so arrange the story. The only adequate explanation of this interval is provided by the records themselves: The disciples spent the first forty days in intermittent fellowship with

---

20. Compare Alfred Edersheim, *The Life and Times of Jesus the Messiah* (Grand Rapids: William B. Eerdmans Publishing Co., 1962), Volume II, p. 628.

their risen Lord. After His Ascension to heaven, they
waited the next ten days, as Christ had commanded, for
the Holy Spirit who was to fill them with power.[21]

● Also, the Gospel records *tell the unflattering truth* about
Peter's denial of Christ during the Lord's trial. Peter was
a major leader in proclaiming the resurrection story, yet
many of the facts recorded about him are the type which
conspirators would not have reported, much less invented.
(Who would have invented that story of Peter and the
other disciples falling asleep when needed in the grav-
est hour of their Master's peril?[22]) The only explanation
for such humiliating facts to appear in pro-Christian
documents, written by Peter's friends, is that they were
reporting the absolute truth.

● Another fact to remember is that the disciples proclaimed
Christ's resurrection at a time when *many people were
still alive* who KNEW about the events reported, "for this
thing was not done in a corner."[23] No one could now
publish a biography of Ronald Reagan full of anecdotes
that were quite untrue. They'd be contradicted at once.
But when Peter gave his sermon on the Day of Pentecost,
we find no refutation given by the Jewish leaders to his
bold proclamation of Christ's resurrection. Even years
later, when Paul wrote, many men were alive who knew
all the facts and who, if Paul's account were false,
could have refuted him with ease.

But "**the silence of the Jews speaks louder than the
voice of the Christians**"[24] and is as eloquent a proof of

21. Acts 1:3-9.
22. See the Bible references in footnote #10, above, and also
Matthew 26:36-46, Mark 14:32-42, and Luke 22:39-46.
23. Acts 26:26.
24. Josh McDowell, *Evidence That Demands a Verdict* (San Bernardino, Calif.: Here's Life Publishers, Inc., 1979), Volume I, p. 225.
This book is an excellent resource.

the resurrection as the apostles' witness. We must account for not only the enthusiasm of Jesus' friends but the paralysis of His foes. The best that the enemies of Christ could do in response to the preaching was to sneer or laugh it off or threaten the disciples with arrest or death if they did not remain silent. But why didn't they deny the tomb was empty? Because they knew it was empty. And why didn't they produce the body of Christ and silence the disciples once and for all? Because there no longer was a dead body to produce. Christ had risen a triumphant Conqueror over death, and the disciples were telling the truth.

One last point overlooked by the fabrication theory is the great fact of the Christian Church: To what does it owe its origin and existence? The church did not just HAPPEN but had a definite cause. If the disciples' experience with their Lord had ended with His death on the cross, the Christian Church would not have come into existence. [25]

Yet consider the success of the early church: In Jerusalem the resurrection was preached within a few minutes' walk of Jesus' empty tomb, and not only were *thousands* converted in a single day[26] but "a great company of the *priests* were obedient to the faith."[27] Peter and the others were announcing an almost incredible thing to an unbelieving crowd, but instead of being laughed into silence, they won the crowd over. These disciples were themselves Jews, with centuries of privileged pedigree behind them, yet they threw it all away and became Christians. The whole system of Judaism was rocked to its foundations by this

25. This point is made by H. D. A. Major in *The Mission and Message of Jesus* (New York: 1938), p. 213, and by Paul E. Little in *Know Why You Believe* (Wheaton, Illinois: Scripture Press Publications, Inc., 1967), p. 62.
26. Acts 2:41, 47, and 4:4.
27. Acts 6:7.

preaching.[28] And the believers did not remain in Judea—
they "turned the world upside down."[29]   They spread their
new teaching so far and wide that even some "of Caesar's
household"[30] became Christians.

Think of it: Those few despised Jews, without worldly
power or prestige, went into all provinces of the Roman
Empire, to men of other races and religions, and persuaded
them to believe—not by scores, or hundreds, or thousands,
but literally and ultimately by millions. They persuaded
Roman citizens to believe when to believe meant suffering
ridicule, persecution, and even death in the arena.[31] The
full power of the Empire was against them. Yet the Christian Church did emerge! How can anyone say that the whole
new direction given the course of history by those few men
in first-century Palestine is founded on a lie? No, my friend,
these facts prove the resurrection story to be more than the
happy ending to a fairy tale. The fabrication theory has had
to be abandoned because it cannot bear close scrutiny.

II. THE HALLUCINATION THEORY

In order to avoid some of the difficulties inherent in
the fabrication theory, a few critics have proposed the hallucination theory. This says that the disciples were perfectly
sincere in their belief that Christ had risen from the dead
because of hallucinations caused by a fervent religious experience. They weren't lying—they were simply deceived
and deluded.

---

28. Paraphrased from Michael Green, *Man Alive!* (Downers Grove,
Illinois: Inter-Varsity Press, 1968), p. 48—a very valuable book.

29. Acts 17:6.

30. Philippians 4:22.

31. See Hebrews 11:35-38 for a catalog of the hardships and trials
suffered by the early Christians.

However, modern medicine has shown that even psychological phenomena obey certain laws and may be subjected to certain tests. Let's examine the validity of the hallucination theory.[32]

In the first place, it's been found that, just as some persons make better subjects for hypnosis than others, *only certain types of persons* are likely to suffer from hallucinations.[33] Normally, psychiatrists find that persons prone to hallucinations are "high-strung," highly imaginative, and very nervous. A critic may point to Christ's reported appearance to Mary Magdalene and dismiss it as the hallucination of a distraught, hysterical woman. But remember that Christ appeared to all sorts of people! Aside from the women, there were Peter, the impetuous fisherman; Thomas, the miserable skeptic; Matthew, the hard-headed tax collector; the rest of the Twelve, who knew Him so well; James, His incredulous brother; and other disciples. It's impossible to dismiss these revelations of the Lord as mere hallucinations of deranged minds.[34]

Another well-established fact about hallucinations is that they're *highly individualistic* in nature. A drunkard may think he sees snakes, but they're all in his own mind. One individual may hallucinate and believe he's Napoleon, but it's rare to find many people from very different backgrounds all suffering from the same delusion. A whole asylum of insane patients may have hallucinations at the same time, but the hallucinations will all be different. Yet here we have the same phenomena reported by otherwise rational

---

32. For much of this material on the hallucination theory, the author is indebted to McDowell, *op. cit.*, pp. 247-255; Anderson, *Evidence ...* , pp. 20-23; and Green, *op. cit.*, pp. 46-47.

33. Paul William Peru, *Outline of Psychiatric Case-Study* (New York: Paul B. Hoeger, Inc., 1939), pp. 97-99.

34. Paraphrased from John R. W. Stott, *Basic Christianity* (Downers Grove, Illinois: Inter-Varsity Press, 1971), p. 57.

fishermen, tax collectors, close relatives, and on one occasion a crowd of over **five hundred people** at once![35] If this theory were correct, we have in this collective hallucination something new in the annals of psychiatry!

A third difficulty with this theory is that hallucinations *tend to recur* over a long period of time with some degree of regularity, either increasing or decreasing in frequency as time goes by.[36] Someone who suffers from obsessions continues to suffer from them. But the phenomena we're considering occurred during a short period of forty days and then dramatically ceased. **None** of the people involved **ever** claimed to have experienced a later repetition.[37] If the appearances of the risen Lord were hallucinations, why did they stop so abruptly? Believers know that the Lord ascended to heaven after forty days. But critics who reject Christ's *resurrection* also reject His *ascension* and thus cannot account for the abrupt ending of His appearances. The hallucination theory is inconsistent with the fact that the appearances ended so suddenly.

However, some may suggest that the appearances were not hallucinations—perhaps they were optical illusions or supernatural **visions** of some sort. The following objections preclude this possibility:

- How could a "vision" *roll away the heavy stone* from the tomb?
- Another problem with the vision hypothesis is that *it presupposes a miracle to get rid of a miracle*. For the only objection to the fact of Christ's bodily resurrection is that it's a miracle and violates natural law, which

---

35. 1 Corinthians 15:6. See *Appendix C* at the back of this volume for a chart of Christ's post-resurrection appearances.

36. Peru, *loc. cit.*

37. Christ did appear to Saul/Paul at a later date, but the circumstances on that occasion were altogether exceptional. See Acts 9:1-31.

skeptics won't accept. But a supernatural vision is a miracle, too, and also violates natural law—so what's the point? This hypothesis is **a solution which doesn't solve, an explanation which doesn't explain.**[38]

● The vision theory also fails to do justice to the *empty tomb*. Many counter-arguments studiously avoid reference to the empty tomb, but obviously if those who preached the resurrection had merely been deluded by "visions" or hallucinations, the foes of Christ would have effectively silenced them by producing Jesus' body.

● Furthermore, the vision theory overlooks some very pertinent facts of the Gospel accounts. For when Christ appeared to His disciples, they actually thought they *were* seeing a vision or that He was just a spirit. He convinced them **He had a material body** with "**flesh and bones**" by letting them touch Him and by eating in their presence.[39] So the testimony of the apostles does not depend on glimpsing a fleeting apparition. It rests instead on *firm sensory experiences* during prolonged interviews: They SAW Him, HEARD Him, TOUCHED Him. What more evidence could they want?

A final fact which lays the hallucination theory to rest is this: Most, if not all, hallucinations concern *an expected event*—meditated upon and desired by the recipient for a long time. For instance, a lonely mother may so fervently **long** for the return of her runaway son that she actually believes she sees him. In other words, hallucinations require an anticipating spirit of hopeful expectancy which makes the wish become father of the thought.[40] To have an experience like this, one first intensely **wants** to believe he

---

38. See Albert Roper, *Did Jesus Rise from the Dead?* (Grand Rapids: Zondervan Publishing House, 1965), p. 34.

39. Luke 24:36-43. See also John 20:24-29.

40. Peru, *loc cit.*

envisions something and then attaches reality to his imagination. But in the disciples' case, we find nothing of this "wish fulfillment." Overwhelming evidence shows **they were not expecting Christ to rise again.** Though Christ Himself anticipated His death and resurrection, and plainly predicted it to His disciples and others, the Gospel writers frankly admit that such predictions really didn't penetrate their minds till the resurrection was an accomplished fact.[41]

When the women trudged through dark streets that early morning to anoint Christ's body more properly than they had during His hurried burial, they weren't **expecting** Him to be alive. Instead, they were puzzling over a practical problem: "Who shall roll us away the stone from the door of the sepulchre? . . . for it was very great."[42] Even the empty tomb did not cause the women to believe, for Mary Magdalene simply thought His dead body had been stolen: "They have taken away my Lord, and I know not where they have laid Him."[43] Also, she failed to recognize Christ during the first few moments He appeared to her.[44] When these first witnesses to Christ's post-resurrection appearances ran to tell the other disciples, they couldn't believe it.[45] It seemed too good to be true.

The resurrected Lord scolded some of His followers for being "slow of heart to believe."[46] The ones to whom He spoke these words were so far from expecting Christ to be alive they didn't even recognize Him at first.[47] They didn't

---

41. When Jesus foretold His death and resurrection to His disciples, **"they understood none of these things."** Luke 18:31-34. See also Matthew 16:21 and John 20:9.
42. Mark 16:3-4.
43. John 20:13.
44. John 20:14-16.
45. Mark 16:11-14 and Luke 24:8-11.
46. Luke 24:25. See also Mark 16:14.
47. Luke 24:15-16 and 30-31.

expect to see a dead man walking around any more than we would. They were skeptical because they failed to comprehend Jesus' many promises that He would rise again.[48] No, the disciples weren't expecting the resurrection or even sentimentalizing over its possibility. Therefore, the appearances of the risen Christ were NOT hallucinations caused by wish-fulfillment regarding things the disciples were hoping for, yearning for, and expecting.

III. THE DISCIPLES STOLE THE BODY

Critics realiize that if the tomb is empty, it must be the result of either a human or divine act. Since they reject the divine in this case, some have formulated the theory that the disciples stole the body. In fact, this theory is older than any other, having been invented by the Jewish leaders early that resurrection morning. Here's the record: When the Roman soldiers guarding Jesus' tomb witnessed His miraculous resurrection, they ran "into the city, and showed the Chief Priests all the things that were done."[49]

Note that the Chief Priests "**never questioned** the report of the guards. They did not themselves go out to see if the tomb was empty, because they **knew** it was empty. The guards would never have come back with such a story as this, unless they were reporting actual, indisputable occurrences."[50] The message of Christ's resurrection was delivered to the Jewish authorities by their OWN witnesses,

---

48. For instance, when Jesus warned His disciples "that they should tell no man what things they had seen, till the Son of Man were risen from the dead . . . they kept that saying within themselves, questioning one with another what the rising of the dead should mean." Mark 9:9-10.

49. Matthew 28:11.

50. Wilbur M. Smith, *Therefore, Stand* (Boston: W. A. Wilde Co., 1945), pp. 375-376.

"the soldiers they themselves had posted, the most unimpeachable witnesses possible."[51] They accepted the soldiers' testimony because they knew *the guards had no reason to lie.* Instead of questioning the veracity of the guards, they decided to bribe them. "When they were assembled with the elders, and had taken counsel, they *gave large money* unto the soldiers, saying, **Say ye, His disciples came by night, and stole Him away while we slept.** And if this come to the governor's ears, we will persuade him, and secure you. So they took the money, and did as they were taught: and this saying is commonly reported among the Jews until this day."[52]

So the Roman soldiers sold their integrity for a bribe. They went in before the priests carrying **the greatest message ever given the world**; they went out burdened with a bag of **money**. Although those who *wished* this lie to be true accepted it,[53] we cannot—for the following reasons:

The disciples *WOULD NOT* perform this deed even if they **could**, for this theory reduces the followers of Christ to the level of common grave robbers—body snatchers— who would desecrate the grave of their beloved Master. But why would they do such a thing? What would they **want** with a dead body? What could they do with it—except perhaps destroy it or hide it so it could never be found again?

---

51. R. C. H. Lenski, *The Interpretation of St. Matthew's Gospel* (Columbus: The Wartburg Press, 1943), p. 1161.

52. Matthew 28:12-15.

53. Evidently the Jewish rulers **themselves** did not believe what they instructed and bribed the soldiers to say. If they *did,* why weren't the disciples at once ARRESTED and QUESTIONED? The act imputed to them was a serious offense against authority. Why were they never PUNISHED for their crime? Nowhere is it intimated that the rulers even **attempted** to substantiate their charge. See Richard W. Dickinson, *The Resurrection of Jesus Christ Historically and Logically Viewed* (Philadelphia: 1865), pp. 31-32.

MORALLY & ETHICALLY Impossible

But assuming that the disciples did sink so low as to snatch Christ's body from the tomb with the object of fabricating a story of His resurrection, this theory ignores the fact that the apostles *would not lie* (with the exception of Judas, who was already dead, or Peter before he was converted[54]). The moral codes of some pagan religions permitted lying. But the stern, strict virtues of Christianity demand clean hearts and pure lives. As pointed out above, it's inconceivable that these eleven apostles would *all* agree to enter into such a vile conspiracy as this. No wonder few even among skeptics hold this theory today.

PSYCHOLOGICALLY Impossible

Even if the early Christians did feel that "the end justifies the means" and compromised their consciences to such an extent that they did decide to rob the grave and lie about the pretended resurrection—they *still* wouldn't be so foolish as to *die* for a lie! Is it reasonable to suppose that *none* of them *ever* admitted the deception even under torture or at martyrdom? This point was established earlier.

Furthermore, the disciples weren't even *thinking* about any resurrection! They were in no mood to plan a commando raid such as the theft of the body would entail. Sorrow lay like a lead weight on their hearts and made them as inanimate as the corpse they were supposed to have stolen. Steal the body to promote belief in the resurrection? Why would they promote a belief they *themselves* didn't have?[55] Utterly disheartened, their hopes dashed by Christ's death, they were anxious only to run away, hide, and forget the whole affair.

---

54. See Luke 22:31-34.
55. Paraphrased from A. B. Bruce, *The Training of the Twelve* (Grand Rapids: Kregel Publications, 1971) p. 494.

And not just the *depression* of the disciples counteracts this theory but also their *timidity*—frail and fearful creatures, they fled as soon as they saw Him taken into custody.[56] For instance, Peter, seemingly the most courageous, trembled at the voice of a servant girl and three times denied that he even knew Christ. Would they have jeopardized themselves by undertaking so perilous an enterprise on behalf of a man who apparently had cruelly imposed on their trust?[57] We know these eleven men pretty well, and until they actually spent time with their resurrected Lord, there was no trace of a daring ringleader among them with the imagination to plan a *coup* like that and carry it through without detection.

PHYSICALLY Impossible

Moreover, the disciples *COULD NOT* perform this deed even if they **wanted** to. For even if we grant that these overwrought, harassed people had the originality and daring to conceive such a plan, they never could have carried it out because of the *guards* at the tomb. At least four points should be noted about these guards.

1. The guards were *trained Roman soldiers* from the legion at Jerusalem. One critic thought they were Jewish temple police because of Pilate's reply when Jewish leaders requested a guard to watch Christ's tomb: He said, "Ye have a watch: go your way, make it as sure as ye can."[58] This was construed to mean, "You have guards of your own." But most authorities make plain that what Pilate meant was "You want a guard detachment to watch the

---

56. Mark 14:50.
57. Paraphrased from Samuel Fallow, ed., *The Popular and Critical Bible Encyclopedia and Scriptural Dictionary* (Chicago: The Howard Severance Co., 1908), Volume III, p. 1452.
58. Matthew 27:65.

tomb?—you have it." His prompt consent showed no reluctance to grant their wish. Two facts—that the Chief Priests **needed Pilate's authorization**[59] and that the guards **feared his punishment**[60]—prove those guards were NOT Jewish temple police but Roman soldiers under the the Roman governor's authority. The iron discipline of trained Roman legionnaires is what enabled Imperial Rome to sweep the world with its power.

2. The guards were *heavily armed,* as were all Roman soldiers. As far as weaponry goes, the Roman soldier carried the famous Roman PIKE (a spear over 6 feet long with a sharp iron head, similar to a javelin), a large SHIELD, a SWORD (this was a thrusting rather than a slashing weapon, nearly 3 feet long), and a DAGGER (worn at the left side of his belt). In addition, he wore a breast-plate and helmet for protection in battle. In short, the Roman soldier was strictly disciplined and extremely well equipped. The picture he presented was that of a **human fighting machine**.

3. The guards at the tomb must have been *strong enough numerically* to do the job. When Pilate told the priests to "make it as sure as ye can," he was giving them carte blanche to secure the tomb against any eventuality—demonstrations, riots, vandalism, body snatching, etc. Some scholars estimate the number of guards at as high as one hundred soldiers (a squad under the command of a centurion).

4. Whatever the number of soldiers in the squad detailed to guard Jesus' tomb, we can be sure *they were awake.* "Punishment in the Roman army was severe in comparison with that in modern armies."[61] One authority

---

59. Matthew 27:62-64.   60. Matthew 28:14.

61. George Currie, *The Military Discipline of the Romans from the Founding of the City to the Close of the Republic* (Abstract of his thesis published at Indiana University, 1928), p. 33.

mentiions no less than eighteen offenses punishable by death, and declares that "fear of punishments produced faultless attention to duty."[62] It was death for a Roman sentinel to sleep at his post, so it's unthinkable that the **whole guard**, without exception, would fall asleep at once—especially with authorities so anxious that the grave remain undisturbed. **One** soldier might drop off to sleep briefly while on duty, but a whole **squad?** Never! "Soldiers cold-blooded enough to gamble over a dying victim's cloak[63] are not the kind to be hoodwinked by timid Galileans or to jeopardize their Roman necks by sleeping on their post."[64] Besides, even if the guards HAD all fallen asleep, how could a group of grave robbers roll back a huge, heavy stone so noiselessly as to **awaken** no one???

For a few fearful, defenseless disciples to overpower heavily armed, well-trained Roman soldiers, break the Roman seal affixed to the heavy stone over the door to the tomb and then escape unharmed while carrying a dead body *would indeed be a Mission Impossible!*

And two other facets of this trumped-up story don't ring true. Remember that the Jewish leaders told the guards to say they were "sleeping" while the disciples stole away the body of Christ. But *if they were asleep, how could they know* who stole the body or what had happened to it? "What judge would listen if you said that while you were asleep, your neighbor broke in and stole your TV set? Who knows what goes on while he's asleep? Testimony like this would be laughed out of any court."[65] The story is obvi-

---

62. *Ibid.*, p. 42.

63. Matthew 27:35, Mark 15:24, and John 19:23-24.

64. Albert Roper, *Did Jesus Rise from the Dead?* (Grand Rapids: Zondervan Publishing House, 1965), p. 33.

65. Paul E. Little, *Know Why You Believe* (Wheaton, Illinois: Scripture Press Publications, Inc., 1967), p. 64.

ously false in any event: If the soldiers were awake, they wouldn't allow anyone to steal the body; if they were asleep, they wouldn't know what had happened.

The final point that refutes this theory also lends great credibility to the whole resurrection story. We've already referred to the silent witness of the empty tomb. However, **the tomb wasn't really empty!** Inside was another silent but eloquent witness: *the graveclothes.* You see, God sent a dazzling, powerful angel at the proper moment to roll away the boulder from Christ's tomb.[66] He removed the enormous stone as we would a pebble. "His countenance was like lightning, and his raiment white as snow: and for fear of him the keepers [the Roman guards] did shake, and became as dead men."[67] Angelic hands unbound the wrappings from Jesus' body. But the graveclothes (the napkin which bound the head and the linen cloths which shrouded the body) were not thrown carelessly aside—they were carefully folded, each in a place by itself. This is what Peter and John noticed when they first ran to the tomb.[68]

Also, when the disciples buried Jesus, they added to the wrapped linen clothes about 100 pounds of "a mixture of myrrh and aloes ... as the manner of the Jews is to bury."[69]

---

66. Matthew 28:2.
67. Matthew 28:3-4.
68. John 20:3-7.
69. John 19:39-40. Verse 40 says, "Then took they the body of Jesus, and wound it in linen clothes *with the spices....*" But the practice of the time was also to *anoint* the body with a semiliquid unguent such as spikenard. The head and hair were also anointed with this unguent. But when our Lord's body was hurriedly prepared for burial on Friday afternoon, sunset was fast approaching and with it the sacred hours of the Sabbath. So the body was simply wrapped with the linen using the myrrh and aloes. Then on Sunday morning the women were seeking to repair this omission as far as they could by bringing spikenard or some other costly unguent to complete the anointing. See also Luke 23:53 – 24:1.

Seven Mysteries . . . Solved!

Aloes is a fragrant wood pounded to dust; myrrh is an aromatic gum. This combination made the graveclothes adhere and cling to the body, so they could not be removed quickly. Therefore, the disciples would never have stolen the body *naked*, dishonoring it and losing time stripping it, giving the terrible guards a chance to awake and seize them.[70] Robbers would never remove the graveclothes—fear of detection would make them act as quickly as possible. And they certainly wouldn't take time to arrange them neatly! Criminals don't leave looted, vandalized premises in a neat and tidy condition. On the contrary, disorder and disarray are a prowler's earmarks.[71] So the graveclothes constitute a remarkable piece of evidence. In fact, when John followed Peter into the tomb, the Record says "he saw, and believed."[72] What did he see that made him believe? It wasn't just the **absence** of the body but the **presence** of the neatly-placed graveclothes!

IV. ENEMIES OF CHRIST TOOK HIS BODY

We've just seen that the lie about the disciples stealing the body won't fool anyone. So some critics say: Suppose, then, that the chief priests or the Roman authorities moved the body to prevent possible veneration of the tomb—to keep it from becoming a shrine and place of pilgrimage. Though this may sound plausible at first, it poses too many problems to be a theory we can accept. Note the following points:

---

70. See John Chrysostom, Archbishop of Constantinople in the 4th century, *Homilies on the Gospel of Saint Matthew*, in *A Select Library of the Nicene and Post-Nicene Fathers of the Christian Church*, edited by Philip Schaff (New York: The Christian Literature Company, 1888), Volume X, p. 530.

71. Paraphrased from Albert Roper, *Did Jesus Rise from the Dead?* (Grand Rapids: Zondervan Publishing House, 1965), p. 36.

72. John 20:8.

In the first place, what we've just said about *the graveclothes* applies to this theory as well: No grave-robber would carefully remove and fold the wrappings. He'd simply take the body, graveclothes and all.

If the body really were removed by mortal hands, *quite a few people* would need to be involved: Several men would be needed to move away the stone and to carry the body, presumably a considerable distance, to a new hiding place. And the Roman guards would all have to be in collusion with this scheme. *So isn't it strange* that with the passing of time *not one* of the many persons involved *ever* "talked" and divulged the secret? In our day we've seen that John Dean told all he knew about the Watergate cover-up even though he went to jail briefly himself for his part in it. It's unbelievable that not a single witness or party to this supposed conspiracy ever told what really happened, even on his deathbed, especially in a matter of such intense interest at the time!

Thirdly, the Jewish leaders and Pilate had no real motive for such a scheme. There's no evidence that any of Christ's enemies wanted to have His body removed. At long last, they had Jesus where they wanted Him—dead and buried. They were interested only in keeping Him there, which is why they had the squad of soldiers assigned to guard His tomb. As for Pilate, it would've been to the governor's advantage to keep the body in its grave. His main interest was to keep things under control. If he **had** removed the body, it's incredible that he wouldn't have informed the chief priests so they could produce Christ's corpse when confronted with the preaching of His resurrection.

Besides all this, any claim that Jesus had on people's belief would have been forfeited after three days if He had not risen. For Christ often asserted not merely that He'd arise from the dead but that He would arise *within three days.*[73]

---

73. Matt. 16:21, 17:22-23, Mark 9:31, Luke 9:22, and John 2:19-21.

The Jewish leaders' request for the guard shows they were aware of Christ's claim—it was that claim which aroused their concern. So instead of bothering to move Jesus' body, all they had to do was guard it carefully till the three days were past. Thus this theory dies for lack of motive.

But just for the sake of argument, suppose we grant the possibility that Christ's foes moved His body for some reason we can't fathom. Remember that within seven short weeks Jerusalem was seething with the preaching of the resurrection. The Jewish leaders had reason to worry—the Scriptures say "they feared the people, lest they should have been stoned" for sentencing a righteous Man to death.[74] They arrested the apostles and told them, "Behold, ye have filled Jerusalem with your doctrine, and **intend to bring this man's blood upon us.**"[75] In this extremity, *why* didn't they simply *produce the body* of Jesus? They could have nipped in the bud any Christian movement by saying, "Wait! We moved the body—Christ didn't rise from the dead." They could have shown exactly where His body was buried and called as witnesses those who had helped move it. As a last resort, they could have recovered the corpse, put it on a cart, and triumphantly wheeled it through the streets of Jerusalem.[76] The fact that they did *none* of these things demolishes this theory.

V. JOSEPH OF ARIMATHEA REMOVED THE BODY

Another theory says Joseph of Arimathea moved the body to a more suitable resting place. In this connection

---

74. Acts 5:26.

75. Acts 5:28.

76. Paraphrased from Josh McDowell, *Evidence That Demands a Verdict* (San Bernardino, California: Here's Life Publishers, Inc., 1979), Volume I, p. 246.

we must understand that critics and believers look upon Joseph in two different ways, which we'll consider briefly:

Critics say he was a pious Jew and respected member of the Sanhedrin. But then he surely would have *produced the body* when the Jewish leaders needed it to refute the resurrection story.

Also, Joseph couldn't have undertaken the grisly task of moving the body alone, so *some of his helpers might have divulged his secret.* And it's unlikely that he'd act without prior knowledge of the authorities. Dr. Wilbur Smith makes the point that "the problem of the Roman soldiers still faces us. When they were paid to watch that tomb, they were not told to make an exception of Joseph. . . . They would no more have allowed Joseph to take out that body than they would have allowed one of the [other] disciples to do so." [77]

Finally, *what motive* could he possibly have had? If a so-called "more suitable" tomb were really available to Joseph, why hadn't he used it for Jesus' body in the first place?

Christ believers, on the other hand, accept the Bible statements that Joseph of Arimathea was a secret disciple of Jesus.[78] Neither he nor Nicodemus[79] had openly accepted the Saviour while He was living. They knew such a step would exclude them from the Sanhedrin (the "supreme court" of the Jews, of which they were members), and they hoped to protect Him by their influence in its councils.

The fact that *Joseph loved Jesus* is evident from the fact that he took His body down from the cross with his own hands[80] "and laid it in his own new tomb."[81] The impression

---

77. Wilbur M. Smith, *Therefore, Stand* (Boston: W. A. Wilde Co., 1945), p. 380.

78. Matthew 27:57, John 19:38 and 12:42.

79. John 3:1-6, 7:50, and 19:39.

80. Luke 23:50-53.

81. Matthew 27:60.

given is of a man compelled to seize the last fleeting opportunity to align himself with the cause of Jesus before it
was too late. Would he incur the contempt of his old associ-
ates, the deep hostility of the Priesthood, and the disgrace of
following a discredited, crucified prophet—only to remove
the body 36 hours later and lose the glorious consolation
of having his revered leader rest in his own tomb? He surely
had no finer tomb in which to place Jesus' body than the
one reserved for himself.

Also, if for some unknown reason he had wanted to
move Christ's remains, he chose *a strange time of day* to
perform a perfectly legitimate operation which could have
been done much more easily during daylight hours. (If this
theory is correct, he as a Jew would have had to act between
the close of the Sabbath and the first crack of dawn—when
the women arrived at the tomb to find it already empty.)

Joseph of Arimathea, an "honourable . . . good . . . just"
man, [82] certainly would have **informed** his fellow disciples
of his action in moving the body—so they could NOT have
preached that Christ rose from the dead without *deceiving
people with deliberate lies*, as discussed above.

This theory also fails to explain **Christ's appearances**
to many people. (See *Appendix C* at back of this book.)

Finally, this theory fails to account for the fact that no
tomb supposed to contain the remains of Jesus ever became
a shrine or object of veneration. This is inconceivable if Jesus
really were buried elsewhere than in the vacant tomb. Yet no
trace exists of anyone paying homage at the shrine of Jesus
Christ, as Moslems make pilgrimages to Mohammed's tomb
at Medina. Wouldn't Mary, His mother, ever wish to spend
a few moments at that site? Not only she, but also Peter and
John and many others would feel the call of a sanctuary that

---

82. Mark 15:43 & Luke 23:50.

held the remains of the Great Teacher.[83] If Christ's followers really knew their Lord were buried somewhere, isn't it
strange that His grave didn't become a place of reverence
and pilgrimage?

VI. THE WOMEN WENT TO THE WRONG TOMB

In 1907 Prof. Kirsopp Lake, D.D., a liberal New Testament
scholar and professor at the University of Chicago, wrote a
book[84] proposing the theory that the women simply made
a mistake identifying the grave in the dim light of the early
dawn. Lake doubts that the women could be certain which
grave held Jesus' body, since he says Jerusalem's neighborhood is full of rock tombs, so it wouldn't be easy to tell one
from another. He also feels that instead of being close to the
tomb at the moment of burial, the women were more likely
watching from a distance. If so, they would have had limited
power to distinguish between one rock tomb and another close
to it. Lake suggests that, on reaching an unexpectedly
open tomb, they encountered a young man—possibly the
gardener—who, recognizing their errand, tried to tell them
they'd come to the wrong place. "He is not here," he said.
"See the place where they laid Him." Then he probably
pointed to the next tomb. But the women, frightened at the
detection of their errand, fled without waiting for the young
man to finish his statement and thus explain their mistake.
Lake also asks us to believe that the women didn't tell the
apostles this stupendous news for seven weeks, whereupon
they started at once to preach it on the Day of Pentecost.

83. Attorney Frank Morison raises these points in his excellent book
Who Moved the Stone? (Downers Grove, Illinois: Inter-Varsity Press,
1967), p. 137.

84. Kirsopp Lake, *The Historical Evidence for the Resurrection of
Jesus*, pp. 250-253.

The supposition that the women went to the wrong tomb
leaves several important questions unanswered:

- Is it likely that *all three* of the women who had so
  lovingly and courageously attended to the last rites of
  Jesus on Friday afternoon would mistake the location of
  His tomb a mere 36 hours later? Would any rational person *forget so quickly* the place where a dear loved one was
  laid to rest? While it's possible for anyone to make a
  mistake, in this case it's most unlikely—for at least two
  reasons: (1) The women **knew** they had to return to finish
  the task of proper burial. Planning to return early Sunday
  morning, they'd logically seek out landmarks to remember, as we seek location markers to recall where we parked
  our car in a crowded parking lot. (2) Why should a tomb
  be so confusing and difficult to identify, since it was lo-
  cated in a **private garden**,[85] not a **public cemetery**?
- Can it be argued that *Peter and John* also went to the
  wrong tomb? It's inconceivable that both Peter and John
  would succumb to the *same* mistake. Certainly Joseph of
  Arimathea, who owned the tomb, would have solved the
  problem by correctly identifying it for them![86]
- Can we believe that neither the women nor the disciples
  ever *went back to the tomb to be sure* that the right tomb
  was really empty? Isn't it likely they would "double-
  check" on such an important matter?

Prof. Lake blames the supposed mistake on the early
morning darkness. But *if it was so dark* that the women
accidentally went to the wrong tomb, it's quite improbable
that the "gardener" would have been at work. And if it was
late enough and *light enough* for him to be at work, it's im-

---

85. John 19:41.
86. Paul E. Little, *Know Why You Believe* (Wheaton, Illinois:
Scripture Press Publications, Inc., 1967), p. 65.

probable that the women would have made a mistake. The early hour poses a problem for those who hold this theory.

Also, if this theory is true, why didn't the priests produce the young "gardener" and explode the whole delusion by securing his testimony as evidence that the women went to the wrong tomb?[87] The young man was **not** the gardener—he was an angel from heaven.

Furthermore, how does this theory account for *the many appearances* the living Christ made to others besides the women?

To make his theory more plausible, Professor Lake **deliberately misquoted** the angel's words to the women by **leaving out the key words** "He is risen" from the middle of his statement. The true quotation reads: "Fear not ye: for I know that ye seek Jesus, which was crucified. He is not here: for **He is risen**, as He said. Come, see the place where the Lord lay. And go quickly, and tell His disciples that **He is risen from the dead. . . .**"[88] The impulse to theorize may be strong, but arbitrarily ignoring part of the evidence is a questionable practice for scholars or anyone else seeking truth.

One further point is all we need to dispose of this theory completely: IF the resurrection story arose because the women went to the wrong tomb, **why didn't the priests go to the RIGHT tomb and produce the body?**

VII. THE SWOON THEORY

Stated as fairly as possible, this final theory asserts that Christ did not actually die on the cross but simply swooned—fainted away—from pain, shock, and loss of blood.

---

87.   See Frank Morison, *Who Moved the Stone?*   (Downers Grove, Illinois: Inter-Varsity Press, 1967), pp. 97-102.

88.   Matthew 28:5-7. See also Mark 16:6-7 and Luke 24:5-7.

He was believed to be dead by all, since medical knowledge was limited at that time. Taken down from the cross in a state of swoon, He was placed in the tomb by those who mistakenly believed Him to be dead. The cool temperature of the grave revived Him enough so that eventually He was able to come forth from the tomb. His ignorant disciples couldn't believe this was a mere resuscitation—they insisted it was a miraculous resurrection from the dead.[89]

This theory ignores several vital facts. First of all, it wasn't until the end of the seventeenth century that a skeptic named Venturini first propounded this theory, and he overlooks the fact that **all early historical accounts are emphatic about the fact that Christ died.** There's clear evidence that **even the Jewish leaders, the ENEMIES of Jesus, believed He was dead.** For we read that they went to Pilate, saying, "Sir, we remember that that deceiver said, **while He was YET ALIVE,** After three days I will rise again"[90]—and they asked to have guards placed at the tomb.

Among all the insinuations levelled against Christianity since the beginning, no whisper has ever been heard that Jesus didn't die.[91] Testimony is positive and unanimous that He died a martyr's death.

----

89. Paraphrased from J. N. D. Anderson, *Christianity: The Witness of History* (Tyndale Press, c. 1970), p. 7.

90. Matthew 27:63.

91. Basic to Christian thought is the doctrine that Christ, the Son of God, died on the Cross to pay the penalty for our sins. His death, as a divine sacrifice, provides the basis of our salvation when we accept Jesus as our Saviour. Groups or individuals who deny this Bible teaching cannot be considered Christian. Yet Mary Baker Eddy, the woman who founded the religion called "Christian Science," wrote this about Christ's condition between His crucifixion and resurrection: "His disciples **believed** Jesus to be **dead** while He was hidden in the sepulchre, whereas **He was ALIVE.**" —*Science and Health with Key to the Scriptures* (Boston: Trustees under the Will of Mary Baker G. Eddy, 1875 & 1934), p. 44. She makes this

Furthermore, Roman soldiers were familiar with evidences of death and with the sight of death following crucifixion. **They knew a dead man when they saw one.** Their commanding officer certified Jesus' death to the governor, Pontius Pilate, [92] who seemed surprised at the report that Christ was dead already. [93] Pilate verified this point by direct questioning of the centurion before giving permission for the disposal of the body. [94] If Pilate himself was sufficiently convinced by the centurion's assurance of Christ's death, perhaps we can accept his certification also.

The record is clear that "when they [the soldiers] came to Jesus, [they] saw that **He was dead already.** . . . But one of the soldiers with a spear pierced His side, and forthwith came there out *blood and water.*" [95] In other words, they knew He was dead, but just to make doubly sure they pierced His heart with a spear. There's no indication the body made any movement when the lance penetrated. But the point I wish to make is well expressed by British writer Michael Green:

> Had Jesus been alive when the spear pierced His side, strong *spurts* of blood would have emerged with every heartbeat. Instead, the observer noticed semi-

---

amazing statement on her own authority alone, giving no sources, ancient or modern, nor offering any Scriptural evidence. (Again with no evidence to support her statement, Mrs. Eddy also denies the doctrine of the Holy Trinity—Father, Son, and Holy Spirit as three Persons in one: p. 515 of her book.) Professor Smith is bold to say: "Let us remember that the one who, herself, said that death was something **unreal**, in fact, that there **was** no death, is held in the chains of death in a burial plot outside of Boston, where her grave is visited by many of her deceived followers each year. I refer to Mrs. Mary Baker Eddy."—Wilbur M. Smith, *Therefore, Stand* (Boston: W. A. Wilde Co., 1945), p. 385.

92. Paraphrased from Michael Green, *Man Alive!* (Downers Grove, Illinois: Inter-Varsity Press, 1968), pp. 32-33.

93. Mark 15:44.

94. Mark 15:43-45.

95. John 19:33-34.

solid dark red clot seeping out, distinct and separate
from the accompanying watery serum. This is evidence of massive clotting of the blood in the main
arteries, and is exceptionally strong medical proof of
death. It is all the more impressive because the evan-
gelist [the apostle John] could not possibly have realized its significance to a pathologist. The "blood and
water" from the spear-thrust is **proof positive** that
Jesus was already dead.[96]

Samuel Houghton, M.D., the great physiologist from the
University of Dublin, comments on this very point: "The
importance of this is obvious. It shows that the narrative in
St. John XIX could never have been invented; that the facts
recorded must have been seen by an eye-witness; and that
the **eye-witness** was so astonished that he apparently thought
the phenomenon miraculous."[97]

PHYSICALLY Impossible

The swoon theory also completely ignores the *deadly
character of the wounds* inflicted upon Jesus. First of all, He
was beaten with a brutal instrument called a *flagrum* which

---

96. Michael Green. *Man Alive!* (Downers Grove, Illinois: Inter-
Varsity Press, 1968), p. 33.

97. Samuel Houghton, quoted in Frederick Charles Cook. *Commentary on the Holy Bible* (London: John Murray, 1878), p. 350. The
Apostle testified: "He who has **seen** has borne witness, and his witness is
true; and he **knows** that he is telling the truth, so that you also may believe."
John 19:35, New American Standard Bible. A major medical publication
recently addressed the issue of Christ's death when three experts conducted
a post-mortem review and concluded that "interpretations based on the
assumption that Jesus did not die on the cross appear to be at odds with
modern medical knowledge." See William D. Edwards (pathologist from
the Mayo Clinic), *et al.*, "On the Physical Death of Jesus Christ," *Journal
of the American Medical Association* (March 21, 1986), Volume 255,
pp. 1455-1463.

uses sharp pieces of bone and metal to lacerate human flesh as it lashes the victim. The Hebrews limited by law the number of strokes to forty, but the Romans set no such limitation, so the victim was at the mercy of his scourgers. Early historians describe the horrible nature of the Roman scourging as **almost equivalent to capital punishment,** for the sufferer's veins were laid bare and sometimes the very muscles, sinews, and bowels of the victim were open to exposure.[98] It's been conjectured that Christ's scourging even surpassed the severity of the normal one, judging by the vile mood of the soldiers who beat Jesus with their fists as they mocked and spat upon Him.[99]

Furthermore, crucifixion was an excruciatingly painful death, in which every nerve throbbed with incessant anguish. The lacerated veins and tendons, the loss of strength from the ebbing away of blood, the hopelessness of human aid when it was most needed—all these took their toll on the victim's utterly collapsed constitution. If Jesus **were** still alive when placed in the tomb, He would have been bleeding from FIVE gaping wounds, one caused by the spear which formed a hole large enough for a hand to enter.[100] Then He was placed on the cold slab of a tomb in April without food or water or medical attention or human help of any kind. To think that this would **revive** Him instead of **finishing** His flickering life is to believe the impossible.[101]

Then, too, there's *the problem of the stone* which sealed the mouth of the tomb. Matthew speaks of this rock as "a

---

98. John P. Mattingly, *Crucifixion: Its Origin and Application to Christ* (unpublished Th.M. thesis, Dallas Theological Seminary, May 1961), pp. 21, 33, and 73.

99. Matthew 26:67-68, Mark 14:65, and Luke 22:63-65.

100. John 20:27.

101. See J. N. D. Anderson, "The Resurrection of Jesus Christ," *Christianity Today* (March 29, 1968), p. 7.

great stone."[102] Mark says, "It was **very great.**"[103] No doubt
such stones were so large and consequently of such tremendous weight that several men were required to move
them. The three women knew their combined strength
couldn't move it.[104] Yet this theory asks us to believe
that Jesus, greatly weakened by loss of blood and suffering
terribly from his wounds, single-handedly performed the
superhuman feat of moving that enormous stone!

Next, *what about the guards*? It's absurd to suppose
that Jesus, staggering half-dead out of the tomb, could have
fought off the Roman guards and made good His escape even
if He had somehow managed to move away the stone.

Late in the afternoon on the day of the resurrection, two
disciples were on their way to Emmaus, a small town **seven
miles** from Jerusalem. They hadn't gone very far when they
were joined by Christ (whom they failed to recognize at first
because of their dejected mood). The Record tells us that
Jesus walked the distance with them.[105] Are we to believe that
Jesus, on feet which had been **pierced through and through**
only two days before, walked without difficulty those miles
between Emmaus and Jerusalem?? Are these the actions of a
man who had just been taken down half-dead from the cross
and laid in a grave in a state of complete exhaustion?

The swoon theory would have us believe that simply
the cool restfulness of the tomb revived and invigorated the
unconscious Lord. Yet one who has fainted away is ordinar-
ily revived NOT by being *shut up in a cave* but by being
brought out into the fresh air.

Even if Jesus were not dead and happened to regain consciousness in the sealed tomb, how could He manage—alone

102. Matthew 27:60.
103. Mark 16:4.
104. Mark 16:3.
105. Luke 24:13-35 and Mark 16:12.

—to free Himself from *the constricting graveclothes* wrapped over His hands and arms as well as the rest of His body? This would be an *escape act worthy of Houdini himself!* Yet suppose we grant that it were accomplished:

> If a merely **human** Jesus had recovered from a swoon, he would NOT have left the tomb without the graveclothes, for modesty would have prevented him from going forth *naked.* But if the **Son of God** rose in an immortal body, clothed with power from on high, clothes were superfluous, and the stately majesty of deity could have taken the time to fold the napkin which loving hands had wrapped around His head.[106]

PSYCHOLOGICALLY Impossible

We've just seen that removal of the heavy stone and other considerations make the swoon theory **a PHYSICAL impossibility.** Be aware also of **the PSYCHOLOGICAL impossibility** inherent in this hypothesis. How could someone who crept half-dead out of a tomb, needing bandaging, strengthening, and tender care, give the disciples the impression that he was the Lord and Conqueror over death and the grave? The pitiful picture given couldn't possibly change their sorrow into enthusiasm or elevate their reverence into worship.[107]

A further psychological impossibility in the swoon theory, since it eliminates the whole Ascension narrative, is that it must "account for the sudden cessation of Christ's appearances by supposing that He withdrew Himself completely,

---

106. Floyd E. Hamilton, *The Basis of Christian Faith*, p. 304.
107. These thoughts are paraphrased from a skeptic who didn't believe at all in Christ's resurrection but who nonetheless **repudiates** the fanciful idea of the swoon theory, David Friedrich Strauss, in his book *The Life of Jesus for the People*, English translation, 2nd edition (London: Williams and Norgate, 1879), Volume I, p. 412.

to live and die in absolute seclusion."[108] He must have retired to some solitary retreat unknown even to closest friends. At the very time His church was rising around Him—while it was torn by controversies, exposed to trials, and placed in circumstances making it most dependent on His aid— He was **absent** from it to spend the rest of His days in solitude. And then at last He must have died—no one can say where, when, or how![109]

MORALLY & ETHICALLY Impossible

Finally, we must face **the MORAL and ETHICAL impossibility** that Christ would be party to a colossal lie. For "IF Jesus had only swooned, He could not, without injury to His character, allow anyone to believe He'd been dead."[110] Remaining silent, He would have been a liar and deceiver of the worst sort. The swoon theory would make the Lord of truth the author of error.

CONCLUSION

We've analyzed the seven major theories offered as alternatives to the fact of Christ's resurrection.

1. The **FABRICATION** Theory
2. The **HALLUCINATION** Theory
3. The **DISCIPLES** Stole the Body
4. **ENEMIES** of Christ Took His Body
5. **JOSEPH of ARIMATHEA** Removed the Body
6. The Women Went to the **WRONG TOMB**
7. The **SWOON** Theory

108. E. H. Day, *On the Evidence for the Resurrection* (London: Society for Promoting Christian Knowledge, 1906), p. 50.

109. Paraphrased from William Milligan, *The Resurrection of Our Lord* (New York: The Macmillan Company, 1927), p. 79.

110. E. Le Camus, *The Life of Christ* (New York: The Cathedral Li-brary Association, 1908), Volume III, p. 485.

We've seen that these theories lack credibility. A point that needs stressing is that **evidence must be considered as a WHOLE.** It's comparatively easy to find an alternate explanation for one or another of the different strands of testimony. But such explanations are worthless unless they fit the other facts as well. A number of different theories, each of which might conceivably fit **part** of the evidence, can provide no alternative to the **ONE** explanation which fits the whole. [111]

We've seen that in an age which calls for evidence, the Christian can intellectually defend his belief. The critic, on the other hand, must abandon these theories when shown that they're impossible. As the great detective Sherlock Holmes wisely told Dr. Watson, "When you have eliminated the impossible, whatever remains, however improbable, MUST be the truth." [112]

Yes, the resurrection is the truth—the very stubbornness of the facts themselves force us to that conclusion. Both the MISSION and MESSAGE of Christ would have counted for nothing had He not risen from the dead. The grave in the garden is empty—we've seen the irresistible logic of that fact. But the resurrection never becomes *a fact of experience* **till the risen Christ lives in the heart of the believer.** The most important thing about the resurrection is not an empty tomb in Palestine two thousand years ago, but the risen Lord today, whom we can meet and know for ourselves. Belief in Christ takes *more* than a mere acknowledgment of evidence. Pilate heard that Jesus arose—it troubled him till the day he died, but it didn't save him. You see, *conviction* is not the same as *COMMITMENT!*

---

111. Paraphrased from British attorney J. N. D. Anderson in "A Dialogue on Christ's Resurrection," *Christianity Today* (April 12, 1968), p. 105.

112. Sherlock Holmes, in Arthur Conan Doyle, *The Sign of Four.*

The resurrection of Christ is not a myth but a miracle. Confucius's tomb is occupied. Buddha's tomb is occupied. Mohammed's tomb is occupied. But Jesus' tomb is EMPTY! Mountains piled upon mountains over His grave could not have prevented His coming forth. And this fact **matters to US**, for it seals the certainty of **our own** future resurrection. Christ triumphantly declares: "I am the Resurrection, and the Life: he that believeth in Me, though he were dead, yet shall he live."[113] To every faithful follower, Jesus says: "Because **I** live, **ye** shall live also. . . . I am He that liveth, and was dead; and, behold, I am alive for evermore, Amen."[114]

---

113. John 11:25.
114. John 14:19 and Revelation 1:18.
       Don't be caught DEAD——without Jesus.

Chapter 9

Life's Greatest Question

One summer, a little girl who never went to church attended vacation Bible school in her neighborhood. She rushed home the first day and breathlessly told her mother: "Know what, Mom? Jesus is a **real Person**, not just a **swear word!**"

To many, Jesus Christ is nothing but a convenient cussword, yet He was a real Person. But **what else** was He? Was He really the divine Son of God? That's the crucial question.

Sometimes Jesus asked embarrassing questions. Once He asked the Pharisees, "**What think ye of Christ? Whose Son is He?**"[1] And he asked His disciples, "**Whom do men say that I the Son of man am?**"[2] Hearing that some thought He was simply one of the prophets, Jesus pressed His followers for a more **personal** answer to *THE GREATEST QUESTION EVER ASKED:* "But **whom say YE that I am?**"[3]

---

1. Matthew 22:42.
2. Matthew 16:13.
3. Matthew 16:15.

Thoughtful people today puzzle over this same vital question. They ponder the matter and still ask: "Wasn't Jesus just a very good man and a great teacher—a 'son of God' in the same sense that we're ALL children of God?"

This chapter will give reasons why Christians believe Jesus was much more than human—much more, even, than the greatest MAN who ever lived. Jesus *was* and *is* GOD in the fullest sense of that term, the **divine Son of God** who "thought it not robbery to be EQUAL with God,"[4] and the Second Member of the Holy Trinity. First, let's examine some Scripture statements which are quite clear and consistent:

Testimony of God the Father:
"This is **My beloved Son,** in whom I am well pleased."[5]

Testimony of the Angel Gabriel:
"He shall be . . . called the **Son of the Highest.**"[6]
"He shall **save** His people from their **sins.**"[7]

Testimony of John the Baptist:
"Behold the **Lamb of God,** which **taketh away the sin** of the world. . . . This is the **Son of God.**"[8]

Testimony of Judas, His Betrayer:
"I have sinned in that I have betrayed **the innocent blood.**"[9]

---

4. Philippians 2:6.
5. A Voice from heaven proclaimed these words on **two** occasions, recorded in Matthew 3:17 & 17:5. Compare Isaiah 42:1, Matthew 12:18, Mark 1:11 & 9:7, Luke 3:22 & 9:35, and 2 Peter 1:16-18.
6. Luke 1:32.
7. Matthew 1:21.
8. John 1:29 & 3.
9. Matthew 27:4.

*Testimony of the **Roman Commander** at the Crucifixion:*
"Truly this Man was the **Son of God**."[10]

*Testimony of the **Apostle Peter**:*
"Salvation is found in **no one else**, for there is **no other name**
under heaven given to men, by which we **must** be saved."[11]

*Testimony of the **Apostle Paul**:*
"We have a great High Priest, that is passed into the heavens,
Jesus the Son of God."[12]

*Testimony of the **Apostle John**:*
"These are written, that ye might believe that
Jesus is the Christ, the **Son of God**; and that believing
ye might have **life** through His name."[13]

*Testimony of **Christ Himself**:*
"I am the **Way,** the **Truth,** and the **Life**:
no man cometh unto the Father, but by Me."[14]

"I am the **Door**: by Me if any man enter in,
he shall be saved."[15]

"I am the **Resurrection**, and the **Life**: he that believeth
in Me, though he were dead, yet shall he live."[16]

"I am the **Light of the world**."[17]

---

10.   Mark 15:39 (and Matthew 27:54).
11.   Acts 4:12, New International Version.
12.   Hebrews 4:14.
13.   John 20:31.
14.   John 14:6.
15.   John 10:9.
16.   John 11:25.
17.   John 8:12 & 9:5.

"I am the **living Bread** which **cometh down from heaven:**
If any man eat of this bread, he shall live forever."[18]

"**I came down from heaven**, not to do mine own will,
but the the will of Him that sent Me."[19]

"**I am from above. . . . I am not of this world. . . .** If ye
believe NOT that **I am He, ye shall DIE in your sins.**"[20]

"For God so loved the world, that He gave His **only begotten
Son**, that whosoever believeth in Him should not perish,
but have **everlasting life.**"[21]

"The High Priest questioned Him, 'Are you the Christ,
the **Son of the Blessed One?**' Jesus said, '**I am.**'"[22]

"The woman said, 'I know that **Messiah** . . . is coming.
When He comes, He will explain everything to us.'
Then Jesus declared, '**I** who speak to you **am He.**'"[23]

After healing the man born blind, Jesus asked him,
"'Do you believe in the **Son of God?**' He answered and said,
'Who is He, Lord, that I may believe in Him?'
And Jesus said to him, 'You have both seen Him and **it is He
who is talking with you.**' Then he said, 'Lord I believe!'
And he worshiped Him."[24]

---

18. John 6:51.
19. John 6:38.
20. John 8:23-24.
21. John 3:16.
22. Mark 14:61-62, New English Bible.
23. John 4:25-26, New International Version.
24. John 9:35-38, New King James Version.

THE STUPENDOUS CLAIMS OF CHRIST

Christ did make astonishing claims about Himself. No wonder the Pharisees were incensed to hear such enormous claims coming from the lips of this humble carpenter of Nazareth! But the claims of Jesus weren't those of a mere human teacher.

No other religious teacher made such claims about himself. For example, consider **Gautama Buddha** (563-483 B.C.), the founder of Buddhism, a religion which has influenced perhaps half the human race. Men called him Buddha, "the enlightened one." He believed that he had a marvelous doctrine to offer men, but he never sanctioned or encouraged anyone to worship him. He urged his followers not to think of him but rather to concentrate on his teaching.

Confucius (551-479 B.C.), the first and greatest of Chinese philosophers, with charming humility declared: "How dare I lay claim to holiness or love? A man of endless craving, who never tires of teaching, I might be called, but nothing more."[25]

Finally, **Mohammed** (A.D. 570-632), the Arabian prophet of the sixth century A.D. and the founder of Islam, laid claim to no special significance for himself. He said he was just a man like other men. An old tradition has him say: "Praise me not as Jesus the son of Mary is praised."

In sharp contrast to the attitude of these great religious leaders, however, stand the astounding claims of Christ, who declared with supreme confidence: "**All power** is given unto Me in heaven and in earth."[26] Yet many today ignore those claims and prefer to think of Him simply as a dedicated, serious young man with a great concern for people. In some cases those who consider Jesus as nothing more than "a good man, a great teacher" pride themselves on their

25. *The Sayings of Confucius*, translated by Leonard Lyall, p. 35.
26. Matthew 28:18.

reasoning ability and the cool logic of their intellects, and
they sometimes look down upon the believer in Christ as
being emotional rather than coolly logical. But let's scruti-
nize their position and see how logical it really is.

Remember that **in no uncertain terms**, Jesus CLAIMED
to be the Son of God. But if He was NOT what He claimed to
be, He was a blasphemous LIAR—the greatest hypocrite the
world has ever seen and worthy of no honor whatsoever.
Consider the strong statements of Christ quoted above in
relation to the words of a modern writer, C. S. Lewis. In his
stimulating little book *Mere Christianity,* the late Mr. Lewis
examines Christ's claim to divinity:

> One part of the claim tends to slip past us unnoticed
> because we've heard it so often that we no longer see
> what it amounts to. I mean the claim to forgive sins:
> any sins. Now **unless** the speaker is God, this is really
> so **preposterous** as to be comic. We can all under-
> stand how a man forgives offenses against himself.
> You tread on my toe and I forgive you, you steal my
> money and I forgive you. But what should we make
> of a man, **himself** unrobbed and untrodden on, who
> announces that he forgave you for treading on **other**
> men's toes and stealing **other** men's money? Asi-
> nine fatuity is the kindest description we should give
> of his conduct. Yet this is what Jesus did. He told
> people that their sins were forgiven,[27] and never
> waited to consult all the other people whom their sins
> had undoubtedly injured. He unhesitatingly behaved
> as if **He** was the party chiefly concerned, the person
> chiefly offended in all offenses. This makes sense
> **only** if He really was the God whose laws are bro-
> ken and whose love is wounded in every sin. In the

---

27. Matthew 9:2, Luke 7:48-50, etc.

mouth of any speaker who is not God, these words imply a **silliness** and **conceit** unrivalled by any other character in history.

Yet (and this is the **strange, significant** thing) even His **enemies**, when they read the Gospels, do not usually get the impression of silliness and conceit. Still less do **unprejudiced** readers. Christ says that He is "humble and meek"[28] and we believe Him; not noticing that, if He **were** merely a man, humility and meekness are the very **last** characteristics we could attribute to some of His sayings.

I am trying here to prevent anyone saying the **really foolish** thing that people often say about Him: "I'm ready to accept Jesus as a great moral teacher, but I don't accept His claim to be God." That is the one thing we must **not** say. A man who was merely a man and said the sort of things Jesus said would **NOT** be a great moral teacher. He would either be a lunatic—on a level with the man who says he is a poached egg—or else he would be the Devil of Hell. You *must* make you choice. Either this man was, and is, the Son of God: or else a madman or something worse. You can shut Him up for a fool, you can spit at Him and kill Him as a demon; or you can fall at His feet and call Him Lord and God. But let's not come with any patronizing nonsense about His being a great human teacher. He has not left that open to us. He did not intend to.[29]

Yet a friend of mine, a very successful dentist, once argued: "Jesus was simply an effective leader who realized that no one would follow him unless he appeared strong, confi-

---

28. See Matthew 11:29.

29. C. S. Lewis, *Mere Christianity*, Revised Edition (New York, The Macmillan Company, 1960), pp. 55-56.

dent, and extraordinarily resourceful. So when he made
those extravagant claims, he knowingly and deliberately
stretched the truth—but he did it for a good **cause.**"

In other words, my friend felt that Jesus believed the
END justifies the MEANS. **Hitler** was that kind of leader,
and we give him the respect that kind of leadership deserves.
And if Christ were the same kind of leader—a "great moral
teacher" who **departed** from strict adherence to truth if
and when it suited His purpose—then He would deserve no
more respect than unscrupulous men like Hitler.

In thinking of Jesus as a leader, bear in mind what His
mission, His purpose was. Christ was not concerned about
breaking the yoke of Roman bondage. If that were His objective, He was singularly UNsuccessful, for all His disciples lived and died under Roman rule. He was NOT a pol-
itical reformer—as He Himself put it: "My kingdom is not
of this world."[30]

No, Christ's mission clearly was a *spiritual* one—
His goal: to teach men the truth about God and to **save** men
from their **SINS.** Is it reasonable, then, to think He'd resort
to the **SIN** of **lying** to accomplish His purpose? Those who
believe this theory about Christ are willing enough to impute
good motives to His telling lies but unwilling to accept Him
as the divine Son of God.

If the whole fabric of Christ's ministry was merely a web
of *well-intentioned falsehood*, this theory still places Him in
the class of LIAR, for **a lie is a lie** regardless of motive.

JESUS CHRIST: DECEIVER or DIVINE?

Taking into account the lofty claims of Christ, certain
implications become clear. To say that "Jesus was **a good
man** but not the divine Son of God" is not open to us as a

---

30. John 18:36.

valid option—simply because **good men don't lie!** Let's cross this option off our list, as I have below:

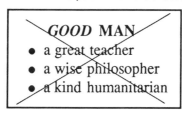

We're left, then, with *only three possibilities* when we consider Christ. He was either:

(1) A **madman**—a lunatic babbling insane claims born of delusions of grandeur, who unintentionally deceived people, *or*

(2) A **bad man**—a charlatan and impostor who deliberately tried to deceive people, *or*

(3) A **God-man**—the divine Son who honestly was what He demonstrated Himself to be, bringing eternal salvation to all who accept and follow Him.

We can graphically show these three options below: [31]

*MAD*MAN	*BAD* MAN	*GOD*-MAN
• demented	• a charlatan	• the Lord
• deluded	• a phony	• the Saviour
• deranged	• an impostor	• the Son of God

---

31. Further discussion of this "trilemma" may be found in Josh McDowell, *Evidence That Demands a Verdict* (San Bernardino, Calif.: Here's Life Publishers, 1979), Volume I, pp. 103-107.

So make your choice—LUNATIC, LIAR, or LORD—what think **ye** of Christ? It's difficult to judge Him insane, for His teachings have the authentic ring of truth and rank among the most noble utterances in history. And it would be strange indeed if He were simply a bad man telling lies—He'd certainly be a **fool** to **die** for His claims to divinity if they were only fabrications, for they were what led to His crucifixion. The only alternative left for us to accept is that **Jesus Christ is exactly what he claimed to be**—the divine Son of the living God!

You see, Jesus didn't leave an equivocal middle road open to us. On the contrary, He declared: "He that is not **with** Me is **against** Me."[32] And "I know your works: you are neither cold nor hot. Would that you were cold or hot! So, because you are lukewarm, and neither cold nor hot, I will spew you out of My mouth."[33]

But he did leave us an open invitation to receive Him: "Behold, I stand at the door, and knock: if **any man** hear My voice, and open the door, I will come in to him, and will sup with him, and he with Me."[34]

At this point some may respond by saying, "Suppose that you've overcome my reluctance to accept Jesus—to regard Him as something **more** than just a **good man**. Suppose I accept the logic of what you've said thus far. I still don't see why this is such a *vital* question for anyone."

The vital nature of your decision for Christ is easily seen by examining three Scriptural facts:

---

32. Matthew 12:30.
33. Revelation 3:15-16, Revised Standard Version.
34. Revelation 3:20.

A. The PENALTY - *"The wages of sin is DEATH."* [35] *"The soul that sinneth, it shall DIE."* [36] Just as God warned **Adam and Eve** very clearly what the penalty for disobedience would be,[37] He wants **us also** to understand the fatal consequences of sin.

B. The PEOPLE INVOLVED - *"ALL have sinned, and come short of the glory of God."* [38] *"There is NONE righteous, no, not one."* [39] This universal truth includes **me**—and **you**—and **everyone else** in this world of sin. And in consequence of *A*, above, it means that we're all condemned to death.

C. The REMEDY - *"He was wounded for OUR transgressions . . . and the Lord hath laid on HIM the iniquity of us all."* [40] *"Christ also hath once suffered for sins, the JUST for the UNJUST, that He might bring us to God."* [41] God's problem was to show mercy while still maintaining justice. He couldn't **excuse man** without condoning sin. And He couldn't **abolish His Law** without undermining the very foundation of Heaven's government. But He **could** *die in man's place*, and this He did. He showed His love for man and met the demands of a broken law in one majestic Sacrifice to pay the penalty of sin.

These texts are just a "mini-course" in the science of salvation, but—like it or not—they certainly affect our eternal destiny.

---

35. Romans 6:23.
36. Ezekiel 18:4 & 20.
37. Genesis 2:16-17 & 3:3 – "Thou shalt surely DIE."
38. Romans 3:23.
39. Romans 3:10.
40. Isaiah 53:5-6.
41. 1 Peter 3:18.

CONSIDER CALVARY

When Jesus died, "PARDON" was written across the sins of the whole human family—though we must **individually accept** the pardon God so graciously provides. When Jesus died, the basis of our salvation became clear—what had been *the SIN issue* became *the SON issue*, for He signed the emancipation papers of the race with His own blood.

While this is not the place to go into a detailed analysis of God's great plan of salvation, we should understand that since "The wages of sin is death," **Jesus died in our place** as the sacrificial Lamb of God, the divine Substitute. We must individually come to the point where we can say, *"I* caused the death of Christ. He climbed the hill called Calvary for *me.* Those nails were *mine.* Because of my sins, *my* hand held that hammer. *I* pierced His sinless flesh and caused His blessed blood to flow. Christ died the death that was *mine."*

God's invitation still remains open: "whosoever" *will* receive Him may do so. Said Jesus: *"Whosoever* therefore shall confess Me before men, him will I confess also before My Father which is in heaven. BUT whosoever shall deny Me before men, him will I also deny before My Father which is in heaven."[42]

The Apostle Paul warns of that future day when even the **wicked** will acknowledge Christ as Lord and Master—though such an act will then be too late to save them: "For we shall ALL stand before the judgment seat of Christ. . . . That at the name of Jesus **every** knee should bow . . . and **every** tongue confess that Jesus Christ is Lord, to the glory of God the Father."[43]

---

42. Matthew 10:32-33.
43. Romans 14:10, and Revised Standard Version of Philippians 2:10-11.

Color Plate #4

Christ hangs upon the cross in painful anguish.

Artist: John Steel

How is it with you, my friend? "What think **ye** of Christ?" Don't wait until it's too late and then acknowledge Christ as Lord. Prepare now to **respond as Peter did** when Jesus asked him *LIFE'S GREATEST QUESTION:* "Simon Peter answered and said, **Thou art the Christ, the Son of the living God.** And Jesus answered and said unto him, Blessed art thou, Simon Barjona: for flesh and blood hath not revealed it unto thee, but My Father which is in heaven."[44]

---

44. Matthew 16:16-17.

? ? ? ? ? ? ? ? ? ? ? ? ? ? ? ?
?   ?

MYSTERY #4
STATE OF THE DEAD

What happens when a man **dies?**
Are the dead really **dead?**—or **alive**
somewhere else? Will the wicked
be punished by burning **forever?**

? ? ? ? ? ? ? ? ? ? ? ? ? ? ? ?

"**I will show thee** that which is noted in
the Scripture of Truth."—Daniel 10:21

Chapter 10

Solving the Mystery of Death

Benjamin Franklin said it: "In this world nothing is certain but *death* and *taxes*." How true that is! Every last one of us has "a rendezvous with Death"[1] because death is life's common denominator. It doesn't matter who we are—rich or poor, black or white, male or female—as far as this world goes, the Road of Life we travel has a **dead end.**

But though death is *the one universal experience shared by all*, we know very little about it. Perhaps that's why it holds great fascination. No one who's walked this earth can deny wondering what awaits him in "the great beyond." Even Henry Ward Beecher, perhaps the most famous American clergyman of the nineteenth century, said in his last, dying words: "Now comes the mystery." Let's face it: Death is **the ULTIMATE mystery**, the final question mark. No one really knows what happens when we die.

---

1. Poet Alan Seeger (1888-1916) was killed in World War I after writing:
"I have a rendezvous with Death
At some disputed barricade. . . .
I shall not fail that rendezvous."

Many opinions are voiced. Much speculation is heard. Stop a dozen people on the street and you'll hear many different ideas expressed on the mystery we call death. One will say: "When a man dies, that's it—there's no hereafter, no **nothin'**. Death is *The End.* Period."

Another, who doesn't feel that death puts a period to life, says: "No! You're wrong. You NEVER really die. Death is like a **door** we pass through to a whole new existence.[2] After you die, you're more alive than you've ever been before!"

A third will say: "Well, I think it's true that you're still alive, still conscious, after you die. But **where you go** depends on **how you've lived**. Good people go straight to heaven—bad ones go straight to hell—for all eternity."

Someone else may say: "I think death is just a sleep, so it's nothing to fear. We take **a deep, dreamless sleep** in the grave until the resurrection."

Other opinions are usually variations on the thoughts expressed above. But that's all they are—mere opinions—for no one really knows, and death remains the GREAT UNKNOWABLE, **life's most perplexing puzzle**.

For any human without divine help to philosophize and theorize about death's enigma is to be

like a **blind man** . . .

in a **pitch-dark room** . . .

looking for a **black cat** . . .

that **isn't there**!

But note that I said "without divine help." Some people seek help from spirit mediums, seances, and the like. Others accept the "pop" theology offered by Broadway and Hollywood, whose characters in *Our Town* and *Heaven Can Wait* are perfectly conscious and very much alive after death.

---

2.   The famous prayer of Saint Francis of Assisi, so often quoted for the inspiration it contains, closes with the words:

"It is in **DYING** that we are **BORN** to eternal **LIFE**."

So where can we get the real help we need? Where can we turn for answers to this final riddle? Well, the only Source that even pretends to give an authoritative answer is God's Book, which was written not by men but by the supernatural power of the Holy Spirit.[3] So let's not waste time on man's idle speculation and guesswork—let's solve the mystery of death by consulting Him who has **CONQUERED** death. By using *inspired information* from the Word of God, we can **fit the puzzle pieces together.**

PUZZLE PIECE #1:
GOD ALONE IS IMMORTAL

We'd best begin by defining our terms: *MORTAL* means "subject to death" or "destined to die." *IMMORTAL* means "exempt from liability to die" or "imperishable."

It's *fashionable* today, in many popular churches, to speak of "the immortal soul." Fashionable, yes—but Scriptural? No. So much pulpit pounding is done in the attempt to impress congregations that they're "immortal" and possess "immortal souls"—that it may surprise many to learn that, according to the Bible, **only God** is immortal or has immortality.

Strong's Exhaustive Concordance is perhaps THE standard reference used for word study in the Holy Scriptures, since it systematically lists every single word used in the Authorized King James Version of the Bible. But *Strong's* knows nothing of the phrase "immortal soul." Instead, it shows us that the word *immortal* is used ONLY **ONCE** in

---

3. "All Scripture is given **by inspiration of God.** . . . Holy men of God spake as they were **moved by the Holy Ghost.**" 2 Timothy 3:16 and 2 Peter 1:21.

the entire Bible. And in the one place this word occurs it applies *not to man* but to *"the only wise GOD."*[4]

Furthermore, in the same epistle, the inspired theologian Paul explicitly declares that "the King of kings, and Lord of lords . . . **ONLY hath immortality.**"[5]

Not everything in life—or even in the Bible—is as plain as that. The primary fact we must nail down on the authority of the Word of God is that the Lord alone is immortal. Turn to those texts and read them with your own eyes in your own Bible! When the Bible plainly declares that God alone is immortal, that "[He] **ONLY** hath immortality," we needn't waste our time trying to find Scripture verses that say MAN is immortal or has an immortal soul—for *we won't find them.* The Holy Spirit does not contradict Himself.

PUZZLE PIECE #2:
MAN IS "MORTAL"—SUBJECT TO DEATH

Instead of finding contradictory statements attributing immortality to man, we find clear evidence from God's Word that our Creator MADE us as **mortal** creatures subject to **death**. Note the following Scriptures:

● "The Lord God commanded the man [Adam], saying, Of every tree of the garden thou mayest freely eat: But the tree of the knowledge of good and evil, thou shalt *not* eat of it: for in the day that thou eatest thereof **thou shalt surely DIE.**"[6]

---

4. 1 Timothy 1:17. Despite the strong current of popular theology and the official stance of his own church, one Roman Catholic at St. Ambrose College observed: "There is **no such phrase in Scripture** as 'immortal soul' or 'immortality of the soul' or its equivalent; there is only the **promise** of immortality."—Father Joseph E. Kokjohn, "A HELL of a Question," *Commonweal* (January 15, 1971), p. 368.

5. 1 Timothy 6:15-16.

6. Genesis 2:16-17.

- And Eve knew that "God hath said, Ye shall *not* eat of it, neither shall ye touch it, **lest ye DIE.**"[7]

- "Shall **MORTAL man** be more just than God?"[8]

- The Bible does say that man can *become* immortal, and God encourages us to "**SEEK for** glory and honour and **IMMORTALITY, eternal life.**"[9] If we're *ALREADY immortal* by nature, why would God tell us to "seek" it? We don't have to *seek* something we already *have.*

- Paul urges us to "**Fight** the good fight of faith, **lay hold on eternal life,** whereunto thou art called."[10] Again, why "fight" to "lay hold" on something IF we already *possess* it?

- With perfect consistency, Paul explains that we mortals are NOT immortal NOW but will be changed to that status when Jesus comes: "For this corruptible must *put on* incorruption, and **this MORTAL must *put on* IMMORTALITY.**"[11] We wouldn't need to "put on" immortality if we already had it.

- "The wages of sin is **DEATH,** but the **GIFT of God** is eternal life through Jesus Christ our Lord."[12]

----

7. Genesis 3:3.
8. Job 4:17. Man's BODY is neither just nor unjust, so this text speaks of the MAN himself, the whole man, who is said to be "mortal."
9. Romans 2:7. Dr. William Temple, late Archbishop of Canterbury, wrote: "Man is **not immortal** by NATURE or by RIGHT, but he is *capable* of immortality and there is offered to him resurrection from the dead and life eternal IF he will receive it from God and on God's terms." Again, "Eternal life is always the gift of God," and *not* the "natural property of human nature."—*Nature, Man and God* (London: Macmillan Co., Limited, 1953), pp. 472 & 464.
10. 1 Timothy 6:12.
11. 1 Corinthians 15:53.
12. Romans 6:23.

- Jesus says: "Behold, I come quickly; and **My reward is with Me**, to give every man according as his work shall be." [13]

The Bible, therefore, is clear. The second fact we can nail down with certainty is that **man is mortal** by nature but may conditionally, if faithful, attain immortality as a gift when Jesus returns with His rewards.

Before proceeding any further, however, let's establish one important fact at the very outset: *ALL* Christians believe in a life after death. There's no argument on this point. [14] The Bible question, "If a man die, shall he live again?" [15] is answered in ringing tones of affirmation by all who believe in Jesus. The difference of opinion arises on *when* the dead will live again and on the very *nature* of man himself. The issue is between a belief in **CONDITIONAL immortality** versus a belief in **INNATE immortality**.

Believers in CONDITIONAL immortality assert that man is a mortal creature but can attain immortality *on condition of faith in Christ* and that he receives it only at the resurrection when Christ returns. Believers in INNATE immortality hold that man has an imperishable soul and therefore *already does* possess immortality which is inherently his, a part of his very nature.

Obviously, these two philosophies are mutually exclusive and cannot both be true: Either immortality is the gift of God, a gift reserved for believers and conferred when Christ returns, *OR* man is innately immortal. One of these teachings is in accord with Bible truth, and one is in harmony with the devil's first lie to mankind. Let's see which is which.

---

13. Revelation 22:12.
14. A sign on an office wall says: "Those who believe the dead never come to life should be here at quitting time."
15. Job 14:14.

PUZZLE PIECE #3:
SATAN'S MOST SUCCESSFUL LIE

Long before the rise of Christianity, ancient pagan religions taught that the soul is immortal. This is one of the basic tenets of Hinduism with its teaching of reincarnation. It's also written in Egypt's *Book of the Dead* and carved on statuary in that land. The Greeks built a whole philosophy on the age-old belief that the soul does not die but lives on independent of the body. Plato was their leading philosophic writer, and basic in both his and Socrates' teachings was this belief that the soul of man can never die. [16]

But the *origin* of today's misunderstanding about death goes back beyond the heathen philosophies of Egypt or Greece. It started in the Garden of Eden, when Satan preached the first sermon on the immortality of the soul—a sermon only five words long. God had warned Adam and Eve that if they ate of the forbidden fruit they would "surely die." [17] Satan, speaking through the serpent to Eve, directly contradicted God by saying: **"Ye shall *NOT* surely die."** [18] But people have been dying ever since that statement was made. It was a lie, the first lie ever told in this world, by the one Jesus called "the father of [lies]." [19]

Satan's first sermon succeeded so well, he's been preaching it ever since. And he still succeeds—his ancient lie in various forms has been handed down from one era

---

16. Later, those pagan ideas infiltrated Christian thinking as a result of attempting "to interpret and explain **Scripture** in terms derived primarily from **Plato**" and were "inherited from **Athens,** not **Jerusalem.**" —Father Joseph E. Kokjohn, "A HELL of a Question," *Commonweal* (January 15, 1971), p. 368.
17. Genesis 2:15-17 and 3:1-3.
18. Genesis 3:4.
19. John 8:44.

to another—so that today **"that old serpent, called the Devil, and Satan . . . deceiveth the WHOLE WORLD"!**[20]

Sometimes when people hear a discussion of this whole subject of death—the nature of man and the state of the dead—they impatiently ask: "Well, what *difference* does it make, anyway, what we believe about death?" **The difference lies in whether we believe *GOD* or the *DEVIL*.** Adam and Eve believed the Devil, and they brought death upon themselves and all their posterity. *Ideas have consequences*: Because our first parents bought the Devil's lie that "Ye shall NOT surely die"—**this planet became the CEMETERY of the Universe** where EVERYONE dies!

So far, *three* of our puzzle pieces have snapped neatly together:

1. God—and God **only**—is immortal.
2. Man is **mortal** but may attain immortality as a gift.
3. The idea of innate immortality originated with **Satan** himself.

PUZZLE PIECE #4:
DEATH IS A "SLEEP"

God, the only One who really knows what death is like, tells us over and over again in both Old and New Testament Scriptures that death is a "sleep." For instance:

• Writing under inspiration, the Psalmist David prayed to God lest He **"SLEEP the SLEEP of death."**[21]

• "Now shall I **SLEEP in the dust**; and thou shalt seek me in the morning, but I shall *not be*."[22]

---

20. Revelation 12:9.
21. Psalm 13:3.
22. Job 7:21.

- "Them that **SLEEP** **in** **the** **dust** **of** **the** **earth** **shall** **AWAKE**, some to everlasting life, and some to shame and everlasting contempt." [23]

- "Now the days of David drew nigh that he should **die**. . . . So David **SLEPT with his fathers**, and was *buried*." [24]

- Miracles occurred when Jesus died on the cross: "The earth did quake, and the rocks rent; and the graves were opened; and many bodies of the **saints** **which SLEPT arose**, and came out of the graves after His resurrection, and went into the holy city, and appeared unto many." [25]

- "**AWAKE**, thou that **SLEEPEST**, and *arise from the dead*." [26]

- When the Jews stoned Stephen to death as the first Christian martyr, the Bible says, "he **fell ASLEEP**." [27]

These are but a few of many examples from such diverse Bible writers as David and Matthew, Job and Paul, and others who consistently speak of death as a "sleep." But let's close this discussion with an example from our Lord's own lips. One day Jesus received news that His friend Lazarus was very sick. After waiting two days before going to Lazarus, Jesus said:

---

23. Daniel 12:2.
24. 1 Kings 2:1 & 10.
25. Matthew 27:51-53.
26. Ephesians 5:14. Interestingly enough, we call a burial ground a "cemetery"—from the Greek *koimeterion*, "**SLEEPING** place."
27. Acts 7:60.

- "Our friend Lazarus SLEEPETH; but I go, that I may AWAKE Him out of SLEEP. Then said His disciples [knowing how helpful bed-rest is to sick people], Lord, if he sleep, he shall do well. Howbeit **Jesus spake of his DEATH**: but they thought that He had spoken of taking rest in sleep. Then said Jesus unto them plainly, **Lazarus is DEAD.**"[28]

Speaking of death as a sleep is an appropriate, beautiful metaphor. But when the Word of God uses that term so consistently, it becomes more than a convenient euphemism for an unpleasant subject. For all who take the Bible seriously, it becomes FACT. And death itself becomes nothing to fear: It's comforting to realize that just as sleep comes at the end of day, so death's quiet, restful sleep comes at the end of life.[29]

PUZZLE PIECE #5:
THE DEAD SLEEP UNTIL THE RESURRECTION

The Psalmist says, "As for me, **I will behold Thy face** in righteousness: I shall be satisfied, **when I AWAKE**, with Thy likeness."[30] You see, David didn't expect to go to heaven immediately when he died. If he had, he would have seen God's face during all these intervening centuries. But a correct understanding of God's plan made him look forward to seeing His Redeemer at the still-future resurrection, when he and all other saints will "awake" at the same time.

None of the other Bible writers believed that *death* is the time of reward, either. We've already noted that Jesus said: "Behold, I **COME** quickly; and **My reward is WITH Me,**

---

28. John 11:11-14.
29. Psychiatrists know that death holds a terror for many people. But "men fear death as children fear the dark"—because it is unknown. Once we know the truth about death, that it's simply a sleep, its horror is dispelled.
30. Psalm 17:15.

to give every man according as his work shall be."[31] "For the Son of man shall COME . . . ; and THEN He shall reward every man according to his works."[32]

Peter reinforces the fact that *David did not go to heaven when he died*: "Men and brethren, let me speak freely unto you of the patriarch David, that he is both DEAD and BURIED, and his sepulchre is with us unto this day. . . . For David is not ascended into the heavens"![33] Could language be clearer than that? These lines are from Peter's Pentecost sermon, but clergymen intent on teaching man's innate immortality seldom quote them. Instead, such preachers argue: "Of course David's body is dead and buried—we never said his body is ascended into heaven, but his soul IS." However, this explanation is less than convincing to all who note that Peter spoke not of "David's body" but of "David," the man himself. Christ resurrects the WHOLE person.

All dead believers from all time shall awake and arise at the same fateful moment—when Jesus returns: "Thy dead men shall live, TOGETHER WITH my dead body shall they arise. AWAKE and sing, ye that dwell in dust: . . . and the earth shall cast out the dead. . . . For, behold, the Lord cometh out of His place to punish the inhabitants of the earth for their iniquity."[34]

Though God gives us the *promise* of eternal life, we don't receive that wonderful gift at the moment we die. I repeat: God does not receive us into His presence ONE BY ONE as we individually die. No, we're all going to be resurrected and taken to heaven TOGETHER—Peter and Paul and John, David and Daniel and Job, and you and I—together! God

---

31. Revelation 22:12. And Isaiah 40:10 says, "Behold, the Lord God will come. . . . Behold, His reward is with Him."
32. Matthew 16:27.
33. Acts 2:29 & 34.
34. Isaiah 26:19-21.

calls this a "better" plan: "These all [the faithful dead], having obtained a good report through faith, **received NOT the promise** [eternal life]: God having provided some **better** thing for us, that **they WITHOUT US should NOT be made perfect.**"[35]

"Man lieth down, and riseth not: **TILL the heavens be no more,**[36] **they shall not AWAKE, nor be raised out of their SLEEP.**"[37]

"As in Adam **all die,** even so in Christ shall all be **made ALIVE.** But every man in his own order: Christ the first-fruits; afterward they that are Christ's **at His COMING.**"[38]

Paul says plainly: "**If the dead RISE NOT, . . . then they which are fallen asleep in Christ ARE PERISHED.**"[39] Now ask yourself, WHY would dead Christians be "perished" if they're already consciously enjoying heaven's bliss? Why do we need the resurrection if DEAD believers are already ALIVE up in heaven?[40] Those who answer, "We need the resurrection because our *bodies* are dead in the grave but our *souls* are alive in heaven" **must supply the much-needed PROOF** that souls are alive after death. "Perished" sounds as if the opposite is true: Without resurrection there'd be NO future life of any kind for the believer.

---

35. Hebrews 11:39-40. See also verse 13.

36. A reference to the fact that, when Jesus returns, great upheavals of nature will occur. Not only will there be a tremendous earthquake and devastating hail (Revelation 16:18-21) but also we'll see "**heaven departed** as a scroll when it is rolled together" (Revelation 6:14), as if God's hand pulls aside the curtain and **the sky opens up!**

37. Job 14:10-12.

38. 1 Corinthians 15:22-23.

39. 1 Corinthians 15:16-18.

40. In the same chapter, Paul again emphasizes the **absolute necessity** of the resurrection, asking what advantage is anything in life, even heroic efforts, "IF the dead RISE NOT?" 1 Corinthians 15:32. But who would *need* the resurrection IF the dead were already praising God up in heaven?

"If a man die, shall he live again? all the days of my appointed time will I wait,⁴¹ **till my CHANGE come. Thou shalt CALL**, and I will answer Thee."⁴² Job's "CHANGE" from mortal to immortal will take place "at the last trump" when Jesus returns in glory. Paul says: "Behold, I show you a mystery; **we shall not all SLEEP, but we shall all be CHANGED**, in a moment, in the twinkling of an eye, at the last trump: for the trumpet shall sound, and the dead shall be raised incorruptible, and we shall be CHANGED."⁴³

In the passage quoted above, Job's inspired pen wrote that God will "CALL" His sleeping saints back to life. Note how Paul describes the same event: "This we say unto you by the Word of the Lord, that we which are **alive** and remain unto the coming of the Lord shall not prevent [precede] them which are **asleep** [or dead]. For the Lord Himself shall descend from heaven **with a SHOUT**, with the voice of the archangel, and with the trump of God: and **the DEAD in Christ shall rise first**: Then we which are ALIVE and remain shall be caught up together with them in the clouds, to meet the Lord in the air: and so shall we ever be with the Lord. Wherefore **comfort one another** with these words."⁴⁴ Here Paul comforts them with the doctrine of the resurrection. He didn't comfort them with the notion that the dead are already in heaven because they have immortal souls, for he didn't believe that.

Job mentioned the Lord's "call," and Paul mentions His lifegiving "shout." Jesus Himself explains further when He

41. "Wait" **WHERE?** Job himself answers: "If I wait, the **GRAVE** is mine house: I have made my bed in the darkness." Job 17:13.
42. Job 14:14-15.
43. 1 Corinthians 15:51-55. Paul means "We shall not all sleep" the sleep of death before Jesus returns—some will be alive to see that dazzling sight. But *ALL* the saints, those who have died and those who remain alive, "shall all be **changed**" into immortal, incorruptible beings.
44. 1 Thessalonians 4:15-18.

says, "Marvel not at this: for the hour is coming, in the which all that are in the graves shall hear His voice, and shall come forth; they that have done good, unto the resurrection of life; and they that have done evil, unto the resurrection of damnation."[45] Please note that when the dead "hear His voice, and . . . come forth," they do NOT come *down from heaven* or *up from hell*—for that's not where they are! Where are they? Jesus says they're "**in the GRAVES.**"

Can you recall when you were little and your family went to spend the day over at Grandma's or some other relative's house? You'd burn up so much energy running around, as kids do, that you soon grew tired and maybe a little cranky. So Mom put you to sleep on Grandma's bed while the grown-ups continued to chat and visit. Then, when it was time to leave, Dad would gently shake you and say, "Wake up, Sleepy-head, it's time to go home." That's how it'll be when Jesus comes, only much more thrilling—like a father calling, "**Wake up—it's time to go HOME!**"

Condemned to death in a Roman prison, Paul stated in the last letter he ever wrote: "I am now ready to be offered, and the time of my departure is at hand. I have fought a good fight, I have finished my course, I have kept the faith: **HENCEFORTH there is LAID UP for me a crown of righteousness, which the Lord, the righteous Judge, shall give me AT THAT DAY: and NOT to ME ONLY, but unto ALL THEM ALSO that love His appearing.**"[46] No one needs an advanced degree in theology to understand what Paul is saying here. He knew he'd receive his "crown" NOT when he died a martyr's death but in the future—"at that day" of the Lord's "**appearing.**" And he knew, too, that "ALL" the redeemed will receive theirs on the **same** glorious day. We DON'T go to heaven when we die but sleep in the grave till Jesus comes to resurrect us.

45. John 5:28-29.
46. 2 Timothy 4:6-8.

PUZZLE PIECE #6:
THE DEAD ARE NOT CONSCIOUS

We know already that the Bible calls death a sleep. But what kind of sleep is it? A sleep plagued by nightmares—or filled with pleasant dreams? Or maybe a deep, dreamless sleep, oblivious to the passing of time, so morning seems to come the moment after we place our head on the pillow?

The Bible clearly teaches that the latter is true, for God's Word declares that the dead are not conscious. Here are verses unequivocal in their meaning:

- "The living know that they shall die: but **the dead KNOW NOT ANYTHING**. . . . Also their **love**, and their **hatred**, and their **envy**, is now **PERISHED**."[47] Advocates for innate immortality admit that the body dies but argue that the real man, his mind and personality—his soul—can never die. Yet this verse speaks of a man's MIND, not his body. A man's BRAIN dies with the rest of his body. **Intellectually**, "the dead *know not anything*." **Emotionally**, their love, hatred, and envy are *"perished."* [48]

- When a man dies, "his breath goeth forth, he returneth to his earth; **in that very day HIS THOUGHTS PERISH**."[49] No one can misinterpret that verse without being guilty of *theological vandalism*. Obviously God is using strong language to indicate **absolutely NO MENTAL ACTIVITY**. If the dead man's "thoughts perish," then he's not conscious of any thoughts and is therefore **not conscious**, period.

---

47. Ecclesiastes 9:5-6.
48. Today's English Version, published by the American Bible Society, says: "Their loves, their hates, their passions, all died with them."
49. Psalm 146:4.

- "Whatsoever, thy hand findeth to do, do it with thy might; for **there is no . . . KNOWLEDGE, nor WISDOM, in the grave, whither** *thou* **goest.**"[50] Those who contend that only one's *body* goes into the grave will find no comfort in this verse, for it does not say "in the grave, whither thy *body* goest" but "whither *THOU* goest." Again, no mental activity or consciousness is ascribed to the dead.

- "**The dead PRAISE NOT the Lord,** neither any that go down into silence."[51] But they *would* praise God devoutly and fervently—IF they were conscious!

- "O Lord, . . . **in death there is NO REMEMBRANCE of Thee:** in the grave who shall give Thee thanks?"[52] If the righteous dead were really conscious and taken to heaven at death, they wouldn't need to remember God —they'd see Him face to face. But that's not true. The dead are not conscious: "there is **no remembrance**" *even of God!*

- "**The grave cannot praise Thee, death can not celebrate Thee:** they that go down into the pit cannot hope for Thy truth. **The LIVING, the living, HE shall praise Thee**, as I do this day."[53]

- "**While I live** will I praise the Lord: I will sing praises unto my God **while I have any being.**"[54] The idea here is that after we die, we not only cannot praise the Lord, but we don't even have "any BEING."

---

50. Ecclesiastes 9:10.
51. Psalm 115:17.
52. Psalm 6:5.
53. Isaiah 38:18-19.
54. Psalm 146:2.

- The Bible calls the grave, where the dead abide, *"the land of forgetfulness,"* [55] a very appropriate name for the place where inhabitants "**know not anything**," where one's "**thoughts perish**," where "there's NO **remembrance**" and NO "**praise**" and NO "**thanks**" even of God. Forgetfulness, indeed!

The false teaching that man is conscious after death has become so widespread that some men's thinking has become twisted. They know that if they fall down and hit their head they may become unconscious and not know anything. But they think that if they hit their head a little **harder**, they'd DIE and then know **everything**!

Preachers who spread the popular but unscriptural teaching that the dead are alive and conscious in "the great beyond," lead their listeners to believe that dead persons "are looking down on us right now! They can see us. Why, they know what we're doing every day of our lives."

But if the dead are still consciously awake and aware of what's going on in this world and can WATCH us, it poses a problem: A young lady said that after her cousin was killed in the war, she was nervous and embarrassed about undressing or bathing. People whose opinion she respected told her that the dead are still perfectly conscious and looking down on us. Her cousin had been only a few years older than she, and the thought that he could WATCH her even though he was dead made her uncomfortable!

However, that's not the way things are. The Bible soundly refutes the idea that the dead are not really dead but are simply alive somewhere else. And it refutes the idea that the dead are conscious and watching what happens in this world. Your Bible says that when a man dies, even "his SONS come to *honour*, and **he knoweth it NOT**; and they are brought *low*,

55. Psalm 88:12 (read verses 10-12).

but **he perceiveth it NOT** of them."⁵⁶ Obviously, if a dead
man were conscious of what's going on here on Planet Earth
and able to watch from the vantage point of heaven, he'd be
most interested in and concerned about those he loves—his
own flesh and blood. But God's Word says he doesn't know
what happens even to "his SONS"! Their successes and
failures alike are not perceived by him.

God's way is the best way, and that's certainly the case
here. If our beloved dead could look down from heaven and
watch the world going from bad to worse, watch our trials and
tragedies, perhaps with sickness and suffering—with no opportunity to intervene—it could be mental torture worse than
the torments of hell. But that's not God's plan. The dead
simply rest in deep, dreamless sleep until the resurrection,
and the passage of time—be it centuries or seconds—seems
but a moment to them. "The dead know not anything" of
what happens to us or others alive today.

Further proof that death is **a state of oblivion and total
unconsciousness** is seen in the fact that the Bible records
cases of dead people who DID come back to life. What did
they know, what could they tell us of that unique and wonderful experience? Nothing—absolutely not one thing! When
Jesus' friend Lazarus died, the Master miraculously resurrected him. "When Jesus came, He found that [Lazarus] had
lain in the grave **four days** already."⁵⁷ His body had begun to
decompose: when Jesus ordered the stone to be taken away
from the grave, Lazarus' sister cautioned, "Lord, by this time
he stinketh: for he hath been dead four days."⁵⁸

Think of it! Four glorious days to spend amidst the beau-
ties of heaven! Surely Lazarus would have much to tell about
the dazzling experience IF he had really gone to heaven and IF

56. Job 14:21.
57. John 11:17.
58. John 11:39.

he had even been conscious. If that miracle happened today, Lazarus would be overwhelmed by reporters, hounded by talk-show hosts to describe his experience in great depth, and his book would be an instant best-seller. Instead, Lazarus was strangely silent. He had no message from beyond the grave. Not a single word is recorded in Scripture about even one thing he'd seen or heard during those four days. His reaction is incredible if he were conscious and aware of his after-death experience, but it's exactly what we'd expect from one who had slept an unconscious, dreamless sleep.[59]

The silent reaction of Lazarus is not unique. Your Bible records SEVEN instances of dead people brought back to life—besides Jesus' own resurrection. Those seven miracles of triumph over death are as follows:

DEAD PERSON	RAISED BY	REFERENCE
The widow's son	Elijah	1 Kings 17:17-24
The Shunammite's son	Elisha	2 Kings 4:18-37
The widow's son at Nain	Jesus	Luke 7:11-17
The daughter of Jairus	Jesus	Luke 8:41-42, 49-56
Lazarus	Jesus	John 11:1-45, 12:1, 9
Tabitha / Dorcas	Peter	Acts 9:36-42
Eutychus	Paul	Acts 20:9-12

Check out these Scriptures for yourself. You'll find that NONE of those favored individuals said as much as **a single syllable** about their remarkable experience! But this is what I love about Bible truth: How consistent it is! Advocates for man's natural immortality must wish desperately for proof

---

59. Something else to consider is this: If Lazarus had **really** been in heaven amid the indescribable glories of Paradise, would Jesus be doing His friend **a favor** to bring him back to this wretched, sin-cursed planet?

on their side of the case. Instead, **the puzzle pieces keep fitting together** to form the picture presented here.

PUZZLE PIECE #7:
"SOUL" IS A KEY WORD

Paul said, "I pray God your whole spirit and soul and body be preserved blameless unto the coming of our Lord Jesus Christ."[60] Three components are mentioned here: spirit, soul, and body. We all know what the body is, since it's visible and tangible. But what can we learn about those two mysterious entities, the soul and spirit?

BIRD'S-EYE VIEW
of the BIBLE WORD SOUL

OLD TESTAMENT HEBREW WORD	NEW TESTAMENT GREEK WORD	BASIC MEANING
nephesh	*psuche*	person
		being
"NEFF-esh"	"psoo-KAY"	life
		creature

Let's consider the Bible word *soul*. How was Adam created? "The Lord God formed man of the dust of the ground, and breathed into his nostrils the breath of life; and **man BECAME a living soul**."[61] Carefully note what the Bible says—and what it does **NOT** say. It says, "Man BECAME a living soul." It does not say, "Man HAS a soul," as if the man is one thing and the soul is a separate something he possesses. **Man does not *HAVE* a soul. Man *IS* a soul**, a living creature, a person.

---

60.   1 Thessalonians 5:23.
61.   Genesis 2:7.

In fact, the most accurate definition of the word *soul* is "person, being, life, or creature." Modern versions of the Bible recognize this and translate "**a living soul**" of Genesis 2:7 more clearly for us. Note the following examples:

"a living BEING"   - New King James Version
"a living BEING"   - New American Standard Bible
"a living BEING"   - New American Catholic Edition
"a living BEING"   - New International Version
"a living BEING"   - Revised Standard Version
"a living PERSON" - The Living Bible

Once again, observe that **Man does not HAVE a person** or a soul. **Man IS a person** or a being or a soul. So it's theologically correct to say: "That poor *soul* is struggling along on a fixed income," meaning "That unfortunate person." A person is a soul. You are a soul.[62]

But someone may say: "Wait a minute—I don't want to get caught up in WORDS. Just answer me one thing: Our physical **bodies** die, but our **souls** can never, ever die, can they?"

Well, God says that they can and do: "**The SOUL that sinneth, it shall DIE.**"[63] *WHY* did the Holy Spirit inspire Ezekiel to write those words (twice in one chapter!) if the pagan Greeks were right in asserting that the soul of man

---

62. PEOPLE can *touch* things or *eat* things, but a non-material "essence"—as some people describe a soul—cannot perform those actions. Yet God says: "If a **soul** *TOUCH* any unclean thing, . . . he also shall be unclean, and guilty. . . . The **soul** which hath *TOUCHED* any such shall be unclean . . . unless **he** wash **his flesh** with water." And "The **soul** that *EATETH* it shall be cut off from **his** people. . . . Every **soul** that *EATETH* that which died of itself . . . **he** shall both wash **his clothes**, and bathe **himself** in water." Leviticus 5:2, 22:6, 7:18-25, 17:12 & 15. **Souls are people** who not only "touch" and "eat" things, they also have "flesh" and "clothes" which must be washed!

63. Ezekiel 18:4—*repeated* for emphasis in verse 20.

Seven Mysteries . . . Solved!

is "imperishable"? You can understand why preachers who
insist that "we HAVE an IMMORTAL soul" don't like to
quote this verse.

But God simply uses the word "soul" in the way we've
just learned: A soul is a person, and if a person sins, he or
she will die. Note some modern translations of Ezekiel 18:4:

- **"The PERSON** who sins is the one who **will die."**
  —Today's English Version
- "It is for a man's own sins that **HE will die."**
  —The Living Bible
- **"The SOUL** who sins **will die."**
  —New American Standard Bible (a footnote
  on *soul* says "**PERSON**").

The Bible word *soul* may also mean "life."[64] For instance,
Jesus taught that "whosoever will save his **LIFE** shall lose it:
and whosoever will lose his **LIFE** for My sake shall find it.
For what is a man profited, if he shall gain the whole world,
and lose his own **SOUL**? or what shall a man give in exchange
for his **SOUL**?"[65] In recording this passage, Matthew wrote
the Greek word *psuche* four times, but the King James translators twice rendered it "life" and twice "soul." You can see
for yourself that the two words are interchangeable. And you
can see, further, that "life" is not something naturally and
irrevocably ours—we CAN lose it, for we're NOT inherently
immortal.

---

64. Psalm 22:20 says, "Deliver my soul [*nephesh*, life] from the
sword." (If a soul were our non-material "essence," a sword couldn't hurt
it.) Ezekiel 22:27 speaks of the wicked who "destroy **souls** [*nephesh*, lives],
to get dishonest gain." In Psalm 31:13 David says: "They took counsel
together against me, they devised to take away my **life** [*nephesh*, soul]."
In Jeremiah 38:16 the words "soul" and "life" are BOTH translated from
the SAME Hebrew word, *nephesh*. The meanings are interchangeable.
65. Matthew 16:25-26. Similarly translated in Mark 8:35-37.

When Peter says Noah's Ark saved "eight souls,"[66] he means eight **persons** or eight **lives**, and modern translations render it so.

Did you know that the Bible word "soul" applies not only to men but also to animals? The **very same** Hebrew words translated "living soul" (*nephesh chayyah: nephesh* meaning "soul" or "creature" and *chayyah* meaning "living") and applied to MAN in Genesis 2:7 are translated "living creature" and applied to ANIMALS in many instances, such as the following:

- "God created great whales, and every **living creature** [**living soul**]."[67]

- "God said, Let the earth bring forth the **living creature** [**living soul**] after his kind, cattle," etc.[68]

- "And out of the ground the Lord God formed **every beast of the field**, and **every fowl of the air**; and brought them unto Adam to see what he would call them: and whatsoever Adam called **every living creature** [**living soul**], that was the name thereof."[69]

In the New Testament, the Greek word *psuche* is used the same way: John saw one of the Seven Last Plagues poured out "upon the SEA; and it became as the blood of

66. 1 Peter 3:20.
67. Genesis 1:21.
68. Genesis 1:24.
69. Genesis 2:19.

a dead man: and every **living soul** [the fish and other sea creatures] **died** in the sea."[70]

These Bible facts show that while man IS elevated above the beasts, it's *not* on the basis of any unscriptural fictions regarding the SOUL, for animals are "souls" or "creatures," too. The thing that elevates man above the level of beasts is that he alone in all Creation was made in the "image" or "likeness" of God.[71] What does this mean? It means that between man and beast at least **FIVE distinctions** can be made, as follows:

1. Man was created with an INTELLECT, with powers of REASON far above those of the beast.
2. Man was created with the capacity to WORSHIP, which none of the lower animals possess.
3. Man was created with the ability to use LANGUAGE far above the simple growls and grunts, the whines and whimpers of mere beasts.
4. Man was created with a MORAL NATURE, a CONSCIENCE sensitive to right and wrong, which is something completely foreign to beasts of the field. This last distinction gives rise to a fifth:
5. Man will answer at a FINAL JUDGMENT day for all his deeds. The beasts will not.

We could mention other distinctions, such as the RESURRECTION which man alone is promised. But the point is:

---

70. Revelation 16:3. This verse shows (a) that the word "soul" may apply to sea creatures we call marine life as well as to man, and (b) that a "living soul" may **DIE**—an inconceivable concept IF the soul were immortal. Furthermore, note the repeated statements as to a "living" creature or soul: The adjective *living* would be superfluous and redundant if *nephesh* or *psuche* meant by itself an immortal, never-dying entity. But inspired Bible writers deliberately added the adjective "living."

71. This fact is repeated several times in Scripture. See Genesis 1:26, 1:27 (twice in this one verse), 5:1, 9:6, 1 Corinthians 11:7.

the Bible makes NO distinction between man and beast on the basis of what some call "man's immortal **soul**." No one dares to say *animals* have immortal souls! The Bible tries to correct misconceptions and misunderstandings on this point as follows:

- "That which befalleth the sons of men befalleth beasts; even one thing [death] befalleth them: **as the one dieth, so dieth the other**; yea, **they have all one breath**; so that **a man hath no pre-eminence above a beast**: for all is vanity. **All go unto one place;**[72] all are of the dust, and all turn to dust again. Who knoweth the spirit of man that goeth upward, and the spirit of the beast that goeth downward to the earth?"[73]

That last sentence is an unfortunate translation which sometimes misleads people. Modern versions make Solomon's thought more clear:

- "**WHO KNOWS** whether the spirit of man goes upward and the spirit of the beast goes down to the earth?"—Revised Standard Bible
- "**WHO KNOWS** if the spirit of man rises upward and if the spirit of the animal goes down into the earth?"—New International Version
- "**WHO CAN PROVE** that the spirit of man goes upward and the spirit of animals goes downward into dust?"—The Living Bible
- "**HOW CAN ANYONE BE SURE** that a man's spirit goes upward while an animal's spirit goes down into the ground?"—Today's English Version

---

72. "All" creatures—men and animals, good and bad—"go unto ONE place": the **GRAVE**. At the time of death, man goes NOT to *heaven* or *hell* or *purgatory* or *limbo* or some unknown *"spirit world."* He goes into the **GRAVE**, like the animals, where he awaits the Judgment and the call of the Lifegiver.

73. Ecclesiastes 3:19-21.

The passage quoted above says that animals and man
"have **all one BREATH**" and translates "breath" from the
Hebrew word *ruach* which is often translated "spirit"—for
spirit and *breath* are synonymous. In fact, the New American Standard Bible renders that final line as follows:
"WHO KNOWS that the **BREATH** of man ascends upward
and the **BREATH** of the beast descends downward to the
earth?" So let's turn to the word *spirit*.

PUZZLE PIECE #8:
"SPIRIT" IS A KEY WORD

Let's consider the word *spirit* as used in the Bible. Its
basic root meaning is "breath," seen in such words as "re-
SPIRation." "Spirit" is an English translation of the Latin
spiritus, which of course is not found in the original Bible
manuscripts at all. Instead, the New Testament used the
Greek word *pneuma*, which gives us words like **pneumonia**,
a disease that obstructs *breath* and re*spir*ation. **Pneumatic**
balloon tires are blown up with "breath" or compressed *air*.

BIRD'S-EYE VIEW
of the BIBLE WORD **SPIRIT**

OLD TESTAMENT HEBREW WORD	NEW TESTAMENT GREEK WORD	BASIC MEANING
ruach	*pneuma*	breath ghost[74]
"ROO-akh"	"pNOO-mah"	wind

---

74. "Ghost" and "spirit" are equivalent terms, the only difference
being that "spirit" comes from the Latin "*spiritus* while "ghost" comes
from the German *geist*. (A *poltergeist* is a noisy spirit or mischievous ghost,
and *zeitgeist* means the spirit of the age or times.) When we die, we

Remember that when God first made Adam, He used **two components**: "the DUST of the ground" and "the BREATH of life." When our Creator combined those two elements, "man became a living **soul**"—a living, breathing **person**. The miraculous process just described is called creation; the opposite process is called death. Note how the Bible describes these two processes and also how the parallel structure shows the terms "spirit" and "breath" to be synonymous, equivalent terms:

- "Thou sendest forth Thy **SPIRIT**, they are **created**. . . .
  Thou taketh away their **BREATH**, they **die**,
  and return to their dust."[75]

- "The **SPIRIT** of God hath made me, and
  the **BREATH** of the Almighty hath given me life."[76]

- "If he gather unto Himself **His SPIRIT and
  His BREATH**; all flesh shall perish together,
  and man shall turn again unto dust."[77]

Let's remind ourselves of *two obvious facts* about our breath or spirit:

First, our breath / spirit **does not EXIST apart from our body**—take away our body and lungs, and we stop breathing.

Second, our breath/spirit **is not the CONSCIOUS part of us that THINKS**—our brain does that. Advocates for natural immortality reluctant to accept these basic facts

"give up the **ghost**" or "**breathe** our last." See Matthew 27:50, Mark 15:37, Luke 23:46, and John 19:30 in different versions.

75. Psalm 104:30 & 29.
76. Job 33:4.
77. Job 34:14-15. Note the **equivalence** of "spirit" and "breath." For instance, Isaiah 42:5 says God "giveth BREATH unto the people . . . and SPIRIT to them that walk" the earth.

need to remember *WHERE* God's spirit *IS* in each of us. I am alive "all the while my **BREATH** is in me, and **the SPIRIT of God is *in my NOSTRILS*.**"[78] That's where our Creator placed it in the beginning: "The Lord God formed man . . . and breathed *into his NOSTRILS* **the BREATH of life.**"[79]

What happens when a man dies? Read the wise man Solomon's inspired description: "Man goeth to his *long home* [the grave], and the mourners go about the streets. . . . Then shall the **DUST** return to the earth as it was: and the **SPIRIT [BREATH]** shall return unto God who gave it."[80]

At least three points should be observed about this verse:

1. There's no implication that man's BREATH or SPIRIT is man's personality or "essence"—"the man himself." On the contrary, Solomon here uses the *neuter* pronoun "IT." Remember that when Jesus died, He committed His spirit (*pneuma*) into His Father's hands.[81] IF the body were a mere shell and the spirit "the real man," how strange that "three days" later Christ explicitly declared: "**I am *not yet* ascended to My Father.**"[82] Those who teach that the spirit is a person's "very essence" contradict Christ and claim He had ascended to His Father on Friday afternoon! However, we must conclude that the spirit (*pneuma*) which leaves the body at death is NOT "the real man."[83]

2. Also, there's no implication that man's BREATH or SPIRIT is a *conscious* entity. Since Solomon says the

---

78. Job 27:3.

79. Genesis 2:7. This breath/spirit from God is our source of life. James 2:26 says, "The body without the spirit [breath] is dead."

80. Ecclesiastes 12:7.

81. Luke 23:46.

82. John 20:17.

83. See D. E. Mansell, "The Nature of Man," in *Doctrinal Discussions* (Washington, D.C.: Review and Herald Pub. Assn., 1962), pp. 195-196.

DUST returns to earth "as it WAS," we can assume that the BREATH or SPIRIT returns to God the same "as it was" before, also. Adam's breath was not conscious *before* God created him by breathing into his nostrils, so why should we assume that it's conscious after death? No *Bible student* believes in **pre-existence** of the human soul or person **before** life on earth—that concept was voiced by Plato and accepted by pagan religions of the East.[84]

3. Finally, this Biblical description of death provides no comfort to those holding the traditional view of conscious, immortal souls. For it makes **no distinction between GOOD and BAD men.** It says the spirits of ALL the dead go back to God at the moment of death—everyone from the Apostle Paul to Adolf Hitler. If the traditional view were true, then this verse would put **even Judas himself** consciously, joyously, actually in the presence of God! But Universalism is a heresy few Christians can accept.

To close this discussion of man's spirit/breath, let's look at the opposite, complementary processes of *creation* and *death* as if they were **mathematical equations.**[85] Please note:

> **DUST** *plus* **BREATH/SPIRIT** equals **LIFE,**
> a living soul.
> **DUST** *minus* **BREATH/SPIRIT** equals **DEATH,**
> a dead creature.

The **soul,** then, is the **combination** of body and breath. It's the resultant **life,** the whole **being.** That's how the Bible teaches it. A good analogy is:

---

84. Latter-day Saints (Mormons) do teach the idea of man's existence before birth but of course make no claim to get that doctrine from the Holy Bible.

85. Based on Genesis 2:7 and Ecclesiastes 12:7.

> ## LIGHT BULB *plus*
> ## ELECTRIC CURRENT equals LIGHT.

That *combination* brings about the resultant light. *Take away* either the bulb OR the current, and the light is gone. **Where did the light go?** It didn't "go" anywhere. It simply ceased to exist. And exactly the same thing happens to the soul when a man dies. The soul or person doesn't "go" anywhere—he simply ceases to exist as a conscious personality until the resurrection.

We've examined the Bible words "soul" and "spirit" and found **no evidence** of or support for natural immortality. Two more important pieces fit into our puzzle!

PUZZLE PIECE #9:
PAUL *VERSUS* PLATO

Ralph Waldo Emerson was right when he said, "Thoughts rule the world."[86]   Always and forever, the battle is for **man's MIND.** Different schools of thought contend for supremacy: competing ideas are discussed, issues are debated, conclusions are drawn. And from the arena of ideas emerge results that change civilization and determine destinies.

Two of the foremost spokesmen for ideas were the apostle Paul and the Greek philosopher Plato. Both were brilliant thinkers. Both loved wisdom and sought Truth. Both left legacies for all future generations. But there the similarities end, for **their ideas were DIAMETRICALLY OPPOSED to each other.**

Paul was the prime spokesman of the Judæo-Christian heritage, hand-picked by God to give the world His heaven-inspired message. Plato, on the other hand, was steeped in

---

86.   Ralph Waldo Emerson, "Progress of Culture," Phi Beta Kappa Address, July 18, 1867.

the pagan traditions and heathen philosophies of Greece. But let's make one thing clear: **The Devil always MIXES good with evil.** He knows from long experience that people will swallow his half-truths and sly lies if he sugar-coats them with good, wise, worthwhile ideas. He even quotes Scripture when it suits his diabolical purpose.[87] So Greek civilization—and Plato's ideas—were NOT all bad. **Greek art and architecture** are among mankind's timeless treasures. And even today, we cherish the concept of **democracy** which Greece invented and gave to the world.

But when we come to Plato's ideas on the nature of man, on the state of the dead and immortality—when we measure those ideas against the standard of God's Word— we must conclude that **they come from ANOTHER source of inspiration.**

The ideas Plato wrote in his *Dialogues* he ascribed to his friend Socrates.[88] Socrates, who taught by the oral method of questions and answers, died leaving nothing in writing, so Plato's pen preserved the ideas of both philosophers. Socrates clearly believed that his concept of death was inspired. He spoke of "the **familiar oracle within me**" and told how he followed the promptings of this oracle in his daily decisions of life.[89] Yet God commands that "A man also or a woman that hath **a familiar spirit**, or that is a wizard, shall surely be **put to death**,"[90] for He knows the so-called "familiar spirit" is that of a demon or devil.

---

87. For instance, Satan quoted holy Scripture to Christ during the temptation in the wilderness. See Matthew 4:1-11, especially verse 6.

88. This fact makes it difficult to tell which ideas Plato presents were really those of Socrates, or Plato's own, or a combination of the two. That's why Plato's "picture has been suspected on the ground that Plato used Socrates as a 'mouthpiece' for speculations of his own." *Encyclopedia Britannica* (1967 edition), vol. 20, p. 819, article "Socrates."

89. *The Works of Plato*, translated by Benjamin Jowett (New York: Tudor Publishing Co.), *Dialogues of Plato: Apology*, section 40, p. 131.

90. Leviticus 20:27. See also 1 Chronicles 10:13, Isaiah 19:3, etc.

When the condemned Socrates said, "I may and must pray to **the gods** to prosper my journey from this to that other world,"[91] he was referring not to the one Creator God we know and worship. He meant the many pagan gods of polytheistic Greece.

Plato's errors on the subject of death and immortality fall under three headings. He thought that:

(1) Man is a **dualistic** being, comprised of body and soul.

(2) Death is a **friend** that liberates the soul.

(3) The soul is **immortal and imperishable.**

Examine these ideas yourself and make up your own mind. *Plato's first error* **divides man into a distinct dichotomy, or dualism, of BODY and SOUL.**

a. Leading his students with a series of questions, he asks: "Is not one part of us **body**, and the rest of us **soul**?"[92] (Then he elicits the response that the body is "the seen" while the soul is "not seen.")

b. Plato, whose philosophy was extremely ANTI-physical, ANTI-material, asserts that the soul "is engrossed by the **corporeal**," *burdened* by "the continual association and constant care of the **BODY**. . . . And this, my friend, may be conceived to be **that HEAVY, WEIGHTY, EARTHY element of sight** by which such **a soul is DEPRESSED and DRAGGED DOWN** again into the visible world."[93]

We've already seen how the Bible teaches the unity of man—man does not *HAVE* a soul as a separate entity he possesses—man *IS* a soul, a unified person, a living being. The soul has no existence apart from the body.   The whole

---

91. *Dialogues of Plato: Phaedo*, section 117, p. 270.
92. *Dialogues of Plato: Phaedo*, section 79, p. 217.
93. *Dialogues of Plato: Phaedo*, section 81, p. 220.

man—body and soul—dies, and the whole man—body and soul—is resurrected on the last day. The false dualism fostered by Plato led him to **depreciate the body** as of little consequence, it being simply a mortal husk or outer shell. This is in common with HEATHEN religions that **punish the body** to "earn points" in the spiritual realm. But Christian teaching does *not* assert that the material world is evil: all things, including the body, were created by God and were described as "good . . . *very* good."[94] Paul, instead of discounting and disparaging the body as Plato does, teaches us to honor and care for it as "the temple of God."[95]

Plato's second error seems to follow logically from his first, teaching that **death is a FRIEND** to be welcomed with joy, for death liberates the soul from its body prison. Consider the following:

a. "Those of us who think that death is **evil** are in **error**."[96]

b. "Will he [who is about to die] not depart with joy? Surely, he will, my friend, if he be a true philosopher. For . . . **there only, and nowhere else, he can find wisdom** in her purity. And if this be true, he would be very absurd, as I was saying, if he were to fear death."[97]

c. "True philosophers . . . have always been **enemies of the body**, and wanting to have the soul alone, . . . **rejoicing . . . to be rid of the company of their enemy**."[98]

---

94. Genesis 1:4, 10, 12, 18, 21, 25, 31—repeated throughout Creation Week!

95. See 1 Corinthians 3:16-17, 6:19-20, 2 Corinthians 6:16, & Romans 12:1. A Christian, therefore, will be *health conscious* not just for selfish **physical** reasons but for **religious** reasons.

96. *Dialogues of Plato: Apology*, section 40, p. 132.

97. *Dialogues of Plato: Phaedo*, section 68, p. 200.

98. *Dialogues of Plato: Phaedo*, section 68, p. 199.

d. Plato inquires, "[Isn't death] the **release** of the soul from the **chains** of the body? . . . And what is that which is termed death, but this very separation and **RELEASE of the soul from the body?**"[99]

e. Plato would have us believe death is an **achievement,** an accomplishment to be desired: "Being dead is the **ATTAINMENT** of this separation [of soul and body] when the soul exists in herself."[100]

f. If death is such a friend, such an attainment, one may wonder whether SUICIDE may not be a good idea—to hurry things along. Such an inquiry was expressed: "Why, when **a man is better dead,** he is not permitted to be his own benefactor, but must wait for the hand of another." The only reply given to this apparent inconsistency is: "There is a doctrine uttered in secret that a man is a prisoner who has no right to open the door of his prison and run away; this is a great mystery which I do not quite understand."[101]

These ideas crept into the Church when Greeks and Romans "converted" to Christianity but still clung to their pagan beliefs. Ignorant of the Scriptures, people eventually accepted these teachings as Biblical, and the Church carried them to all the world. The once pure Christian faith combined Scripture and man-made traditions. Satan, twisting every truth in Scripture, led men to call evil good and good evil. But God says, "**WOE** unto them that call evil good, and good evil; that put darkness for light, and light for darkness; that put bitter for sweet, and sweet for bitter!"[102]

---

99. *Dialogues of Plato: Phaedo*, section 67, p. 199.
100. *Dialogues of Plato: Phaedo*, section 64, p. 194.
101. *Dialogues of Plato: Phaedo*, section 62, p. 191.
102. Isaiah 5:20.

Perhaps Satan's most successful perversion of truth is this unscriptural doctrine of the "immortal soul" which transforms *death,* **the very CURSE God gave for sin, into a BLESSING,** a portal to paradise!

The teaching of Plato that death is a **FRIEND** *directly contradicts* the inspired testimony of Paul, who calls death our **ENEMY.** The Apostle declares that Death is a terrible Intruder: **"The last *ENEMY* that shall be destroyed is DEATH."**[103]

Plato's third error is his claim that **our soul is IMMORTAL and IMPERISHABLE**—an echo of the lie that reverberates all the way from Eden!

a. The philosopher's students are cleverly led to conclude that, independent of our bodies, **"our souls EXIST in the world below . . .** and that **the souls of the dead are in existence."**[104]

b. But the pagan philosopher goes even further when he asserts that "Our souls must have **existed BEFORE** they were in the form of man—**without bodies,** and must have had intelligence. . . . Our souls must have had a **PRIOR existence.** . . . Our souls must have **existed BEFORE we were born."**[105]

c. "The soul," says Plato, "is in the very likeness of the divine, and **IMMORTAL . . . INDISSOLUBLE."**[106] Those who agree with Plato sometimes reason thus: "I think Plato is right. We ARE 'in the very likeness of the divine,' for even the Bible says, 'God created man in His own image.'[107] And since God is immortal, if we're created

103. 1 Corinthians 15:26.
104. *Dialogues of Plato: Phaedo,* sections 71-72, pp. 205-206.
105. *Dialogues of Plato: Phaedo,* section 76, p. 213.
106. *Dialogues of Plato: Phaedo,* section 80, p. 218.
107. Genesis 1:27.

in His image, we must be immortal, too!" But the problem with this line of reasoning is that we have no valid reason to SINGLE OUT immortality as the only attribute of God. Our great Creator is *not only* immortal or never-dying. He's *also* omnipotent or almighty, omniscient or all-knowing, and omnipresent or everywhere at once! Who among us is so bold as to claim *those* attributes for puny man?

d. Plato, *on no higher authority than his own reason*, dares to say: "When the man is dead **the soul dies not with him.**"[108]

e. By using mental gymnastics involving such opposites as odd and even numbers or heat and cold—concepts **hardly analogous** to the opposites of death and immortality!—Plato leads his willing student along a chain of reasoning which concludes: "Then the soul is IMMORTAL? Yes, he said. And may we say that **this is PROVEN?** Yes, abundantly proven."[109]

f. Finally, Plato triumphantly declares: "Beyond question, **the soul is IMMORTAL and IMPERISHABLE,** and our souls will truly exist in another world!"[110]

This chapter as a whole has already refuted this unsupported Greek concept, but note the contrast: Plato argued for natural, innate immortality and knew nothing about the resurrection God has promised.[111] On the other hand, writes

---

108. *Dialogues of Plato: Phaedo,* section 88, p. 230.
109. *ialogues of Plato: Phaedo,* section 105, p. 225.
110. *Dialogues of Plato: Phaedo,* section 107, p. 257.
111. "The idea of a resurrection of the body is **contrary** to Platonic principles. The entire scheme is to **get rid** of the body and all its functions, not to save it. . . . The body [says Plato] is an impediment, a hindrance, and the prison of the soul; heaven is reached only in a **bodiless**

New Testament scholar F. F. Bruce, "Paul **could NOT contemplate** immortality **apart from resurrection**; for him a **body** of some kind was **essential** to personality. Our **traditional** thinking about the 'never-dying soul' which **owes so much to our Græco-Roman heritage,** makes it difficult to appreciate Paul's point of view."[112] That's the problem: we've been "brainwashed" by ideas that Paul and Peter—and Jesus—never taught!

Condemned to death, Socrates said, "The hour of departure has arrived, and we go our ways—I to die, and you to live. **Which is better God only knows.**"[113] Exactly! Socrates didn't know. Plato didn't know. Only God knows, and He lovingly told us about it in the sacred pages of His Book. So *think it through:* Are we actually expected to take Plato's **WORD for it** that the DEAD are ALIVE?— especially when his theories are refuted at every point by God's Word?

Socrates' question about "which is better"—life or death —ECHOES the Devil's lie in Eden and implies death is a *beneficial* experience,[114] whereas God teaches that **death was a PUNISHMENT for sin.** Paul says: "By one man [Adam] sin entered the world, and death by sin; and **so**

---

condition, in which the soul is free from every taint of the body. The doctrine of immortality reached its highest point in Plato, and all subsequent writers who dealt with the future life **followed in his footsteps.**"—Calvin Klopp Staudt, *The Idea of the Resurrection in the Ante-Nicene Period* (Chicago: 1909), pp. 66-67.

112. F. F. Bruce, *Paul—Apostle of the Heart Set Free* (Grand Rapids, Mich.: William B. Eerdmans, 1978), p. 311.

113. *Dialogues of Plato: Apology,* section 42, p. 134. Man's Maker is best able to inform us on the nature of His creation and the truth about death. On these topics, one verse of Scripture outweighs a whole book of Socrates *via* Plato.

114. Part of the Serpent's lie to Eve was that "your eyes shall be *opened,* and ye shall be as *gods,* knowing good and evil." Genesis 3:5.

death passed upon all men, for that all have sinned."[115]
Preachers who speak of "immortal souls" are ECHOING
Plato, who taught that very thing, **not Paul**, who taught
that only God has immortality. Thus they unwittingly perpetuate the Devil's legacy of lies.

PUZZLE PIECE #10:
THE WAGES OF SIN = DEATH

If we go back to the beginning of the story and the root
of the problem, we find God has a most instructive lesson to
teach us. So let's go back to Adam and Eve, when death first
entered the picture. God, who does nothing without good
reason, imposed death as a consequence of and punishment
for the sin of disobedience. Read how God dealt with the
crisis of man's fall into sin when Adam and Eve disobeyed:

> The Lord God said, "Behold, . . . lest he [Adam]
> put out his hand and **take also of the Tree of Life,
> and eat, and live forever**"—therefore the Lord God
> **sent him out** of the Garden of Eden to till the ground
> from which he was taken. **So He drove out the man**;
> and He placed **cherubim** [angels] at the east of the
> Garden of Eden, **and a flaming sword** which turned
> every way, **to guard the way** of the Tree of Life.[116]

God's deliberate act of purposely SEPARATING Adam
and Eve from the Tree of Life to insure He wouldn't have
immortal sinners on His hands *PROVES that man was not
inherently, naturally immortal BEFORE his fall into sin*—
or such action by God would have been useless.

Now ask yourself: IF man *was NOT immortal* even
before his sin, is it reasonable to assume he *IS immortal*
after sin entered his life?

---

115. Romans 5:12.
116. Genesis 3:22-24, New King James Version.

If man were inherently immortal, what NEED was there for any Tree of Life? It does no good for advocates of natural immortality to argue that "The Tree of Life served only to keep their physical BODIES alive." For it wasn't just Adam's *body* that sinned: it was more than his hand and teeth that sinned when he took the forbidden fruit and bit into it—it was also his mind and heart and will, his innermost being, that rebelled against his God and Maker. **The WHOLE MAN sinned, so the WHOLE MAN died**—not just his body.

You probably learned about this event as a little child. But Plato, living in a pagan culture and ignorant of sacred Scripture, inevitably left this vital fact out of his thinking. Sadly enough, religious teachers today who spread the myth of man's immortal soul should know better than to substitute **human reasoning for divine revelation**, which says, "The wages of sin is death."[117]

PUZZLE PIECE #11:
GOD FORBIDS SPIRITUALISM

Spiritualism is "the belief that the dead **survive** as spirits which can **communicate** with the living, especially with the help of a third party, called a **medium**."[118] The spiritualistic medium between our world of the living and the presumed world of the spirits of the dead is a **witch**. The definition of *witch* is "a woman supposedly having supernatural power by a compact with **evil spirits**."[119] The medium herself is on

---

117. Romans 6:23.

118. *Webster's New World Dictionary of the American Language*, College Edition (New York: The World Publishing Company, c. 1964), p. 1406, entry "spiritualism."

119. *Webster's New World Dictionary of the American Language*, College Edition (New York: The World Publishing Company, c. 1964), p. 1679, entry "witch."

on familiar terms with a particular spirit from the "other world." This particular spirit is called her "**familiar spirit**" and serves as her contact or link with "the great beyond." The meeting at which a group of spiritualists try to communicate with spirits of the dead is called a **seance.**

God is absolutely and unalterably OPPOSED to seances, to witches or anyone else with a familiar spirit, and to spiritualism in general. He says in no uncertain terms:

- "Thou shalt not suffer a witch to live."[120]

- "There shall not be found among you any one that . . . [is] a witch, or a charmer, or a consulter with familiar spirits, . . . for all that do these things are an abomination unto the Lord."[121]

- "The soul that turneth after such as have familiar spirits, . . . I will even set My face against that soul, and will cut him off from among his people."[122]

- "A man also or woman that hath a familiar spirit, or that is a wizard, shall surely be put to death."[123]

Now, with this background of facts established, we're ready for a BIG QUESTION. Ask yourself: **WHY** should God issue such **vehement, damning** prohibitions against those who might put us in touch with the dead and make it a *capital* offense—demanding their *death?*

WHY does God forbid us to consult with our departed loved ones, if they're alive and can talk to us? **WHY** is His prohibition in this regard so strong and absolute as to be utterly non-negotiable? God is our loving heavenly Father.

---

120. Exodus 22:18.
121. Deuteronomy 18:10-12.
122. Leviticus 20:6. Note again that "soul" means "person."
123. Leviticus 20:27.

Of Him we read: "No **good thing** will He **withhold** from them that walk uprightly."[124] **WHY**, then, does He withhold from us any contact with our beloved dead?

So much comfort and wisdom could be gained if we could talk, even briefly, with a loving parent who now dwells in the very presence of God! If the dead are conscious in the great beyond, **WHY** should we not consult

- great **intellectuals** like Edison and Einstein,
- great **statesmen** like Lincoln and Churchill,
- great **spiritual leaders** like Moses and Paul?

WHY should God mind or care?

The reason is as the Bible says: God knows that the **supposed** spirits of the DEAD are **really** spirits of the ENEMY—devils and demons. He knows our beloved dead are unconsciously sleeping and "know not anything." But Satan's legions pose very effectively, very convincingly, as our departed loved ones—if we allow ourselves to be deceived. They need not appear as spooks and specters or ghosts and ghouls. No, they can impersonate every detail of a dead person, copying the little mannerisms like the tilt of the head, and imitating the sound of the voice even better than Rich Little.

A grieving widow may be easy prey for the wiles of spirit mediums who would have her believe they really can contact her dead husband. She sees an apparition that looks just like the husband she misses so much. She hears his unique voice telling her things known only to her husband. She doesn't realize that demons, like our guardian angels, watch us as we grow up and know every intimate detail of our lives. It's childishly simple for devilish spirits to give VERY convincing evidence at a seance.

A minister I know tells of visiting just such a widow and studying with her the plain statements from God's Word

---

124. Psalm 84:11.

that her dead husband dreamlessly sleeps until the resurrection when Jesus will call him forth from the grave. But
she said that she still sees her husband, that he stands in
her bedroom and talks with her almost every night. Here's
a case in which God's Word runs counter to the evidence of
one's own senses! If she accepts what her **eyes** see, who is
it standing in her bedroom? Her husband. If she accepts what
her **ears hear**, who is it talking with her? Her husband.
BUT if she accepts the *infallible* Word of God, who is it
posing as her dear, departed husband? A demon from hell!

King David lost the first son born to Bathsheba when
it died in infancy. While the child was sick, David prayed
for him and grieved for his illness. But after the baby
died, David washed himself and ceased mourning, explaining, "While the child was yet alive, I fasted and wept. . . .
But now he is dead, wherefore should I fast? Can I bring
him back again? **I shall go to him, but he shall not return to me.**"[125]

How true that is! The dead cannot return to earth, even
to their loved ones. God wants us to know these things
so we won't be deceived by devils posing as spirits of the
dead. Deceptions of this kind are almost overpowering if
we believe the communications are coming from someone
we love and respect—coming from Paradise, in fact. Subtle
suggestions whispered in darkness may not seem to erode
our faith—at first. But once lying spirits gain our confidence, we believe them in spite of all the Bible says to
the contrary, and our faith is unknowingly transferred from
God to Satan. No wonder God is so incensed and so much
in earnest to protect us from the menace of spiritualism!

---

125. 2 Samuel 12:22-23. This Bible truth is reinforced by such
texts as Job 7:9-10, which says: "**He that goeth down to the grave**
shall come up no more. **He shall return no more to his house**, neither
shall his place know him any more."

This puzzle piece fits perfectly with all the others that show the dead are dead, unconsciously asleep, awaiting the call of the Lifegiver.

PUZZLE PIECE #12:
THE RICH MAN & LAZARUS

The picture in our puzzle is taking shape in a very definite way, but there are still a few pieces that don't seem to fit in. We need to examine them very carefully—from every angle—then perhaps we'll find that they DO fit, after all. One of these is the story of the Rich Man and Lazarus. [126] Let's read it:

There was a certain rich man, which was clothed in purple and fine linen, and fared sumptuously every day: and there was a certain beggar named Lazarus, which was laid at his gate, full of sores, and desiring to be fed with the crumbs which fell from the rich man's table: moreover the dogs came and licked his sores. And it came to pass, that the beggar died, and was carried by the angels into Abraham's bosom: the rich man also died, and was buried; and in hell he lift up his eyes, being in torments, and seeth Abraham afar off, and Lazarus in his bosom. And he cried and said, Father Abraham, have mercy on me, and send Lazarus, that he may dip the tip of his finger in water, and cool my tongue; for I am tormented in this flame. But Abraham said, Son, remember that thou in thy lifetime receivedst thy good things, and likewise Lazarus evil things: but now he is comforted, and

---

126. The "Lazarus" of this story is not the same one who was Jesus' friend, whom He raised from the dead. In those days, Lazarus happened to be a common name among the Jews—just as Tom, Dick, and Harry are common names today.

thou art tormented. And beside all this, between us and you there is a great gulf fixed: so that they which would pass from hence to you cannot; neither can they pass to us, that would come from thence. Then he said, I pray thee therefore, father, that thou wouldest send him to my father's house: for I have five brethren; that he may testify unto them, lest they also come into this place of torment. Abraham saith unto him, They have Moses and the prophets; let them hear them. And he said, Nay, father Abraham: but if one went unto them from the dead, they will repent. And he said unto him, If they hear not Moses and the prophets, neither will they be persuaded, though one rose from the dead. [127]

At first glance, this puzzle piece doesn't seem to fit in with the rest of the picture, for it has people talking after they're dead. But the Bible, as we've seen, presents a *clear* and *consistent* picture of the state of the dead. Keeping in mind the principle that **the Word of God NEVER CONTRADICTS itself**, how can we explain this apparent contradiction?

The problem resolves itself instantly when we determine one thing, and that is: What do we *have* here in the story of the Rich Man and Lazarus?

Is this story
1. A **LITERAL** account about **real** men and **actual** events?
Or is it
2. A **PARABLE**—a story told to teach a moral lesson?

A Bible parable is defined as "a *heavenly* story with an *earthly* meaning." The story may teach vitally important truths while not being literally true itself. Those who wish

---

127. Luke 16:19-31.

to defend the Bible sometimes have difficulty accepting the fact that parables may be figurative, fictional stories. Yet we can honor the Bible as the inspired Word of God without insisting on taking every word literally.

Proof of that is seen in our Lord's magnificent use of figurative language. He said, "Ye are the **SALT** of the earth" and "I am the **DOOR**"[128] without meaning actual minerals or wooden doors. And Jesus often used parables to teach great lessons. The Master Teacher would place a simple story alongside a profound truth, and the profound was illumined by the simple.

Commenting on the story in question, Bloomfield in his *Greek Testament* said: "The best Commentators, both ancient and modern, with reason consider it as **a parable.**"[129] *"With reason,"* he says. Let's examine some of those reasons.

NOT LITERAL BUT A PARABLE

1. *Jesus Used Parables in Addressing Crowds.* The Bible declares that Jesus not only used parables but that parables were in fact the ONE teaching device He used exclusively in teaching the people: **"All these things spake Jesus unto the multitude in PARABLES; and WITHOUT a parable spake He NOT unto them.**"[130] We may wonder why this is true. Even His disciples asked the reason for this, for great crowds of people would gather before Jesus as He sat by the seaside, "And He spake many things unto them in parables. . . . And the disciples came, and said unto Him, WHY speakest Thou unto them in parables? He answered and said unto them, Because it is given unto **you** to know the *mysteries* of the kingdom of heaven, but to **them**

128. See Matthew 5:13 and John 10:9.
129. Eminent scholars such as Whitby, Doddridge, Lightfoot, Bloomfield, Gill, Edersheim, John Wesley, and others considered it a parable.
130. Matthew 13:34.

it is not given. . . . Therefore speak I to them in parables: because they seeing see not; and hearing they hear not, neither do they understand."[131] You see, Jesus knew He had many enemies who would gladly **cut short** His ministry if they could. He could speak freely and openly with His disciples in private, but the crowds who thronged to hear Him contained both honest inquirers and enemy spies. So Jesus carefully veiled His meaning in parables which gave a lesson to the honest folk but allowed His enemies no opportunity to catch Him in His words. We read:

● "The chief priests and the scribes . . . watched Him, and sent forth **SPIES**, which should **feign** themselves **just** men, that they might *take hold of His words*, that so they might **deliver Him unto the power and authority of the governor.**"[132]

● "They send unto Him certain of the **Pharisees . . .** *to catch Him in His words.*"[133]

● "Then went the **Pharisees**, and took counsel how they might *entangle Him in His talk.*"[134]

If you and I were behind the Iron Curtain, with KGB secret police listening to every word we say, just waiting to arrest us, we'd quickly learn to speak in parables, too! Warfare often demands use of such devices as camouflage and codes, so *Jesus wisely encoded His messages and camouflaged His meaning in parables.* On the occasion in question, we know that **Pharisees WERE in the crowd**, for the story of the Rich Man and Lazarus is introduced with the

131. Matthew 13:3, 10-13.
132. Luke 20:20.
133. Mark 12:13.
134. Matthew 22:15.

words: "The Pharisees . . . heard all these things."[135] These Scriptural facts lead us to conclude that Jesus here was speaking a parable.

2. Bodily Parts. This story says nothing about "immortal souls" leaving the body at death. Instead, the rich man after he died had "**eyes**" and a "**tongue**," that is, very real bodily parts. He wanted dead Lazarus to "dip the tip of his **finger** in water." We wonder how much real water could a spirit finger apply to a spirit tongue. And what good are tongues, fingers, and eyes to *disembodied spirits?* *IF* this narrative is to be taken *literally*, then both good and bad men at death do not soar away as intangible spirits, but go to their respective rewards in real bodies with bodily parts. Yet HOW COULD they go there bodily, since their bodies were buried in the grave? This evidence alone leads the candid investigator to conclude that here we have a fictional parable, not a literal story. [136]

3. Hell Not a Suburb of Heaven. Again, if this were a literal account, an actual picture of the **geography** of heaven and hell, then the homes of the saved and the damned are forever SO CLOSE to each other that one can both *see* and *speak* across the gulf—an unthinkable situation, to say the least. Would **hearing** the constant cries of sufferers make heaven a pleasant place to spend eternity? And what kind of heaven would it be if the redeemed could **see** their unsaved friends and loved ones writhing in the tormenting flames of hell? No, saints and sinners will NOT eternally carry on conversations! Heaven and hell are not

135. Luke 16:14.
136. Bodily parts make it impossible to interpret this passage literally, so some say it's partly figurative and partly literal. But since the story is a **UNIT**, it should be considered *either* a literal, historical episode *or* a figurative parable. Who can decide which portions are literal without being guilty of manufacturing evidence?

side by side, nor in sight and hearing of each other. Insisting
that this story is literally true becomes absurd.

4. Abraham's Bosom. How could Abraham be LARGE
enough to carry Lazarus actually in his bosom? How could he
possibly carry all the saved? Surely we must conclude that
Abraham's "**bosom**"—another bodily part—*cannot* be taken
LITERALLY, as no human, whether saint or sinner, has a
breast large enough to contain all the saved. Also, note that
Lazarus was carried "into **ABRAHAM'S** bosom," NOT into
the presence of *God*, where dead saints are supposed to be.
This immediately gives us a clue that Christ was speaking
from the Pharisees' point of view: **ABRAHAM is the chief
character in this drama**, and that corresponds to *Jewish*
belief, not *Christian* teaching. But Jesus had just told the
parable of "The Unjust Steward" driving home his point that
"Ye cannot serve God and mammon."[137] "And the Pharisees
...**who were covetous** ... *derided* Him." [138] Then Jesus, the
Master Teacher, turned to the Pharisees and *compelled* their
attention by the story of the rich man and Lazarus, built on
their OWN belief which they could not mock. Jesus loved
even the Pharisees who derided His teaching, so **He met them
on their own ground and presented from their own standpoint** the lesson He wanted to impress on their hearts.[139]

---

137. Luke 16:1-13.
138. Luke 16:14.
139. That lesson teaches a number of things of great importance.
Jesus may have wished to teach truths like the following:

A. *Riches are no passport to heaven.* In Jesus' day riches were so
highly regarded as a sign of God's favor while poverty was considered a
sign of God's curse, that when the disciples heard Jesus say, "It is easier
for a camel to go through the eye of a needle, than for a rich man to enter
into the kingdom of God.... They were exceedingly **amazed**, saying, *WHO*
then can be saved?" Matthew 19:23-25. Even the disciples felt that if a
rich man couldn't be saved, it's useless for the rest of us to try. To correct
this widespread misconception, Jesus taught this parable to the "covetous"
Pharisees, with the rich man lost and the poor beggar **saved**. Jesus wanted

The phrase "Abraham's bosom" in this passage—found **nowhere else** in Scripture—is clearly NOT to be taken literally. Let's honestly ask ourselves: *"Can we believe* that all the saints are even now gathered in Abraham's bosom? If they are, in **whose** bosom does **Abraham** rest?"[140] And if "Abraham's bosom" is figurative, then "Abraham" cannot logically be literal, for it would be supremely incongruous to have Abraham literal but his bosom figurative!

5. *Josephus Documents Contemporary Jewish Belief.* Fortunately for our investigation, the great Jewish historian Josephus left on record a "Discourse to the Greeks Concerning Hades," which illuminates Jesus' story of "The Rich Man & Lazarus." Flavius Josephus was a contemporary but never a follower of Jesus. His writings constitute the most comprehensive Jewish history of that century. For information on the times and teachings of the Jews in the era of Christ and the apostles, Josephus is unsurpassed. A zealous and devout Pharisee himself, Josephus recorded the Pharisees' beliefs regarding the afterlife. Many of those beliefs were NOT Biblical. Pagan ideas had infiltrated their religion just as they have ours today. Though the Jews were custodians of God's Word, they had rejected much of it even as they rejected Christ when He came as their Messiah. Josephus wrote that Hades is **"a subterraneous region"** of "perpetual

to teach "the truth that no matter how rich a man might be, he could still be lost eternally, and no matter how poor a man might be, he still had a chance for the heavenly country, and so He depicted the **extreme cases** of the rich man and Lazarus."—Charles T. Everson, *The Rich Man and Lazarus* (Nashville, Tennessee: Southern Publishing Association, 1935), p. 7.

B. *We decide our eternal destiny in this life.* Our own daily decisions determine where we spend eternity. If self-indulgent choices fix "a great gulf" between us and God, that is our fate. There is no second chance, no future probation. We may accept salvation NOW, but when death comes, it's forever too late.

140. Dennis Crews, *The Rich Man and Lazarus* (Frederick, Maryland: Amazing Facts, Inc., 1986), p. 11.

darkness" where the lost are dragged "into the neighborhood of hell itself." But the saved are guided "unto a region of light" where "the countenances of the fathers . . . always smile upon them. . . . This place we call **THE BOSOM OF ABRAHAM**." Though the wicked damned can "SEE the place of [the saved] . . . **a CHAOS deep and large is FIXED between them**," so that no one can, "if he were bold enough to attempt it, pass over it."[141] Thus by consulting the writings of Josephus we find that the Pharisees believed in a condition of departed souls after death which **coincides exactly** with the condition described in the parable of the rich man and Lazarus, even to the naming of "Abraham's bosom" (mentioned in NO other place in Scripture), the torment of the wicked by the flames of hell, the great gulf fixed and impassable between the righteous and wicked, the two abodes within sight of each other, and this whole situation existing inside this earth, where the Pharisees believed souls went when people died. Jesus caught the Pharisees' attention, met them on their own ground, and then put on the lips of Abraham the message that would surely haunt them if they did not repent: "If they hear not Moses and the prophets [that is, if they don't believe the Scriptures], neither will they be persuaded, though one rose from the dead."[142] Those words proved true in the history of the Jews: Christ's crowning miracle was **raising the real Lazarus of Bethany to life** after he'd been dead four days, yet they refused to believe,[143] "though one rose from the dead." Even when Christ's **own** miraculous resurrection rocked the whole area of Jerusalem, they refused to believe, "though one rose from the dead." Jesus framed

---

141. Flavius Josephus, *The Works of Flavius Josephus*, translated by William Whiston (Auburn and Buffalo, New York: John E. Beardsley, no date), "Discourse to the Greeks Concerning Hades," Paragraphs 1, 2, 3, 4.
142. Luke 16:31.
143. Instead of believing, they wanted to KILL Lazarus, John 12:9-11.

His parable to teach important truths through people's *preconceived opinions*, but that doesn't mean He endorsed those opinions, any more than He **endorsed** the crafty, dishonest practices of "The Unjust Steward" when He told that parable.[144]

6. ***Prayer to the Human.*** The prayer, "**Father Abraham, have MERCY on me**," reflects the trust some mistakenly put in the human. Was Jesus actually teaching that we should pray to a **fellow mortal?** "Father Abraham" is addressed as if *he* were God, with Lazarus at his beck and call. But God alone can grant mercy. No other name but the precious name of Jesus can save us.[145] Abraham, Peter, and the Virgin Mary were all good people, but they cannot save us. They can't even HEAR us, for they're dead. Yet the pagan philosophy of "man's immortal soul" has led to the **worship of saints**, leading sincere believers to pray to other human beings. If this story depicts things as they truly are after death, then every other part of Scripture describing death is false.

7. ***Bible Not Always Literal.*** The written Word of God we call the Bible, like the living, incarnate Word we call Jesus, is unequivocally true and is the divine Source of all truth. But God and His inspired spokesmen do not limit themselves to a narrow, literal mode of discourse. We gain much comfort when we read that "The Lord is my **Shepherd**,"[146] for that figure of speech contains material for many a sermon. A fictitious parable may teach a vital, valuable lesson, but its details are NOT to be taken literally. For example, the Bible records a parable which says that **trees TALKED to each other!** Please note: "The **trees** went

---

144. Luke 16:1-13. Here Jesus taught that even a wicked person makes provision to assure his **earthly** future, and how much MORE important it is that a child of God should assure his **heavenly** future.

145. Acts 4:12.

146. Psalm 23:1.

forth . . . to anoint a king over them; and they said unto the *olive tree,* Reign thou over us. But the olive tree said unto them, . . . And the trees said to the *fig tree,* Come thou, and reign over us. But the fig tree said unto them, . . . Then said the trees unto the *vine,* Come thou, and reign over us. And the vine said unto them, . . . Then said the trees unto the *bramble,* Come thou, and reign over us. And the bramble said unto the trees, If in truth ye anoint me king over you, then come and put your trust in my shadow. . . ."[147] We have no difficulty recognizing this as a parable, for we know **trees cannot talk—and they don't have kings!**

Again, when the Holy Spirit revealed to the prophet Nathan King David's sin of adultery with Bathsheba and the subsequent murder of Bathsheba's husband, Nathan used an intriguing parable to lead David unwittingly to pronounce sentence on himself, saying: "There were two men in one city; the one rich, and the other poor. The one rich had exceedingly many flocks and herds: but the poor man had nothing, save one little ewe lamb, which he had bought and nourished up: and it grew up together with him, and with his children; it did eat of his own meat, and drank of his own cup, and lay in his bosom, and was unto him as a daughter. And there came a traveller unto the rich man, and he spared [refused] to take of his own flock and of his own herd, to dress for the wayfaring man that was come unto him; but took the poor man's lamb, and dressed it for the man that was come to him. And David's anger was greatly kindled against the man; and he said to Nathan, As the Lord liveth, the man that hath done this thing shall surely die: and he shall restore the lamb fourfold, because he did this thing, and because he had no pity. And Nathan said to David, **Thou art the man.**"[148]

---

147. Judges 9:7-15. A similar passage is found in 2 King 14:9 - "The *thistle* that was in Lebanon sent to the *cedar* that was in Lebanon, saying, Give thy daughter to my son to wife. . . ."
148. 2 Samuel 12:1-7.

No one insists that Nathan's parable be taken literally. But the story of "The Rich Man & Lazarus"—despite the difficulties outlined here—is clung to by those seeking support for teaching that man's soul exists apart from the body, support which cannot be found elsewhere in Scripture. Insisting that this story is literal, they set great value upon it as the chief pillar supporting the dogma of man's natural immortality. But many points of evidence show this story to be no more literal than other Bible parables.

8. *One of a Series of Parables.* The CONTEXT of this story shows Jesus presenting parable after parable to the Jewish multitude. The story of the Rich Man and Lazarus is the last in an unbroken series of parables addressed primarily to the Pharisees and recorded by Luke. Go back to the beginning of the preceding chapter —Luke 15—and we find that Christ began His discourse in response to the Pharisees' ridicule: "Then all the tax collectors and the sinners drew near to Him to hear Him. And the Pharisees and scribes murmured, saying, 'This man receives sinners, and eats with them.' So He spoke this parable unto them, saying . . ."[149] Five wonderful parables followed:

Reference	Parable
Luke 15:4-7	"The Lost Sheep"
Luke 15:8-10	"The Lost Coin"
Luke 15:11-32	"The Prodigal Son"
Luke 16:1-13	"The Unjust Steward"
Luke 16:19-31	"The Rich Man & Lazarus"

---

149. Luke 15:1-3, New King James Version. The Pharisees' words, intended as an **insult**, were really a **compliment** for our gracious Lord!

9. *Parables Not Always Labelled.* Some claim that because Jesus did not *say* this story was a parable, it should be taken literally. However, that's a weak position, because Jesus and Gospel-writer Luke did *not* always label a parable as such. Proof of this is seen in the case of *"The Prodigal Son,"* a story universally recognized and classified as a parable, though it simply begins: "A certain man had two sons." Incidentally, the story of that wasteful lad is sometimes called "The **Lost Son**" just as that of the rich man and Lazarus is sometimes called the great parable of "The **Lost Opportunity**," in line with Jesus' parables of "The **Lost Sheep**" and "The **Lost Coin**." Furthermore, other parables are not labelled as such in the Bible: *Jotham's parable of the trees talking* or *Nathan's parable to King David* are **NOT LABELLED** as parables—but that's exactly what they are. And that's exactly what the story of the rich man and Lazarus is.

10. *The Timing Is Fictitious.* Just as many details in this story are clearly fictitious, so also is the **timing** involved in the narrative. The sequence of events in "The Rich Man & Lazarus" *conflicts with the Bible truth that the Judgment is yet FUTURE.* Paul, speaking years after Jesus' ascension to heaven, says plainly that God "hath **appointed a day,** in the which He **WILL** judge the world."[150] Peter says, "The Lord knoweth how to . . . **RESERVE the unjust unto the day of Judgment TO BE punished.**"[151] How then could the rich man and Lazarus —and Abraham—already have received their rewards prior to the Judgment, which the Bible teaches was still future in Paul's and Peter's day?

---

150. Acts 17:31.
151. 2 Peter 2:9.

Now consider this Bible fact: God says Abraham, like all the patriarchs, has **not YET received the promise** of eternal life but is awaiting the resurrection at Christ's Return. Luke penned this parable as part of his Gospel, yet several decades later, when the Book of Hebrews was written, Abraham was **not alive**—and he's **still** not alive! In *Hebrew s 11*, God states plainly that Abraham and the other patriarchs "all died in faith, **NOT having received the promises**" of heaven and eternal life (verses 8 & 13). The faithful suffered persecution and even torture "that they might obtain a better **RESURRECTION**" (verse 35). The chapter concludes by repeating that NONE of the faithful had received their reward YET: "These all, having obtained a good report through faith, "**received NOT** the promise: God having provided some BETTER thing for us, that **THEY without US should NOT be made perfect**" (verses 39-40). Here we have an echo of Isaiah 26:19 - "Thy dead men shall live, **TOGETHER WITH my dead body shall they arise.**" So if Abraham "received not the promise" but awaits the "resurrection" that will "make perfect" God's sleeping saints ALL at once, who dares to say he's already alive?

Those who insist on taking this story literally are confronted by too many problems for their position to be a valid one. When taken literally, the story **collapses under the weight of its own inconsistencies.**[152] We've turned this story inside out and found at least *ten good reasons* why

---

152. The only point made by those who take this parable literally is that Jesus used a specific **name**—Lazarus—here, which is not the case in His other parables. But the weakness of this argument is immediately seen when we realize that "Lazarus" was a name as *common* as "Joe" or "Bob" in our culture today. Besides, a name is a useful label to *identify and differentiate a character* when more than one person is found in a story, as is the case here.

Jesus' account of "The Rich Man & Lazarus" is a parable, not an actual happening. After looking at these ten points, those who still insist this parable is a **literal** picture of life after death do so **not** *because* **of the evidence but** *in spite* **of it!** And those who understand the consistent Bible teaching on this subject have no trouble fitting this parable into the overall picture of our puzzle.

PUZZLE PIECE #13:
THE THIEF ON THE CROSS

Like "The Parable of the Rich Man & Lazarus," Christ's promise to the thief on the cross at first glance seems to contradict the many other clear statements of inspired Scripture on the subject of death. But whenever we encounter an apparent contradiction in the Bible, we immediately realize that **something is wrong**—wrong not with the Word of God but with our limited *understanding* or with the *translation* or something else. As we investigate the problem here to determine exactly what is wrong, you'll find a good name for this investigation is "**The CASE of the MIS-PLACED COMMA.**"

Let's go back 2000 years and get the picture in our mind's eye: Jesus was hanging on the cross between two thieves who were also crucified. One thief is unrepentant, but the other speaks a few words to our Lord:

"He said unto Jesus, Lord, remember me when Thou comest into Thy kingdom. And Jesus said unto him, **Verily I say unto thee, Today shalt thou be with Me in paradise.**"[153]

153. Luke 23:42-43.

PUNCTUATION NOT INSPIRED

The first point to be made is that **the *punctuation* of the Bible is NOT inspired**. It was not added till about the time of the Reformation—A.D. 1500 or so. Note too, that in the text as copied above, capitals were added to pronouns pertaining to Jesus so you can tell which "thou" pertains to whom, but otherwise it appears as in the King James Version—**without any QUOTATION MARKS around the words spoken by the thief or by Jesus.** Those were added in *still later* versions.

THISISWHATANCIENTGREEKLO
OKEDLIKEOFCOURSEITISNTGR
EEKITSENGLISH

You see, those who added the commas and other punctuation marks to the Scriptures had no help from the Greek manuscript Luke wrote, because Greek was written all in CAPITAL letters, *with no breaks between sentences*, with

NOBREAKSEVENBETWEENWORDS

—to save on costly parchments. Naturally, when punctuation marks were added, they were placed so as to **conform to the theology** of the one who put them in. Translators used their best judgment in inserting punctuation, but they were certainly not inspired. Therefore we needn't be governed by marks translators added only *four* hundred years ago when we try to find the intent of inspired writers *nineteen* hundred years ago.

Changing a comma often makes a great difference in meaning. For example, Hebrews 10:12 says, "But this Man [Jesus], after He had offered one sacrifice for sins for ever, sat down on the right hand of God." If the comma were *wrongly* placed after "sins," the passage would say Jesus

"for ever sat down on the right hand of God" and thus will NEVER return to this world. But when we rightly place the comma after "for ever," the passage says Christ sat down after offering Himself as the final, once-for-all-time Sacrifice. This is a completely different meaning, just as we'd have a completely different meaning if translators—who in general did such excellent work—had placed the comma in Luke 23:43 after "today" instead of after "thee." The two choices look like this:

King James Version

"Verily I say unto thee,
Today shalt thou be with Me in paradise."

Correct Punctuation

"Verily I say unto thee today,
Thou shalt be with Me in paradise."[154]

"Today" is **an adverb of TIME,** telling *when* something happens. It may modify the verb "say" and emphasize *when* Jesus spoke those words to the thief, **or** it may modify the verb "be" and tell *when* the thief would be with Jesus in paradise.

There are TWO very clear, very Biblical reasons why we know beyond any doubt that "today" must modify "say" and that therefore the comma was misplaced by the translators. Let's look at those two reasons.

---

154. Lest any complain that I took undue liberty in reversing the order of the pronoun in "shalt thou be," I should point out that Greek, like the Latin languages, has the pronouns (I, you/thou, he/she/it, we, they) *COMBINED in the one-word verb form.* English separates the pronoun from the verb. In Greek, therefore, "thou shalt be" is **identical** to "shalt thou be," being synthesized in the very same word.

Reason #1: JESUS DID NOT GO TO HEAVEN THAT DAY

Christ did not go to Paradise that crucifixion Friday. How do we know for sure? Well, the term "Paradise" in the Bible means "heaven," where God is, as shown by such verses as the following:

1. "A man . . . was caught up to the third **HEAVEN**. . . . This man was caught up to **PARADISE**."[155]
   (The **first** heaven is the *atmospheric heaven*, where we breathe the air and the birds fly. The **second** heaven is the *starry heaven*, where the planets orbit and the stars shine. The **third** heaven is the *divine heaven*, where angels dwell and our Lord abides.) Paul shows here that "the third heaven" where God lives is synonymous with "Paradise."

2. "The **Tree of Life** . . . is in the midst of the **PARADISE** of God." "He showed me a pure river . . . proceeding from the **throne of God**. . . . On either side of the river, was the **Tree of Life**."[156]
   These verses also show that "**Paradise**" is "**heaven**," for it is where "**the throne of God**" is.

IF Christ had gone to Paradise that Friday afternoon, He would have gone into the very presence of God. **BUT** three days later on resurrection morning, Christ Himself declared to Mary, "Touch Me not; for **I am NOT YET ASCENDED to My Father**."[157]

Are we therefore placed in *the unenviable position* of trying to decide whether to believe *either*

(1) Christ's statement to Mary on Sunday morning *OR*

(2) His promise to the thief on Friday afternoon?

155. 2 Corinthians 12:2-4, New International Version.
156. Revelation 2:7 and 22:1-2, New King James Version.
157. John 20:17.

No! Christ did NOT contradict Himself. The fault lies in the misplaced comma.

Reason #2: THE THIEF DID NOT DIE THAT DAY

Unquestionably, the thief did not die on the day Jesus gave him the promise. The thief didn't *expect* to die that day. He didn't expect *Jesus* to die that day, either. He knew crucifixion was a long, slow process that often took several days. You'll recall the astonishment of Pilate, later that afternoon, when he learned that Jesus was already dead —the Bible says, "Pilate **marvelled.**"[158]

The Jews did not want the men to hang on the crosses on that particular Sabbath, for it was the Passover weekend and a "high day."[159] Therefore, soldiers **broke the legs** of the thieves so they could not escape after they were taken down from the cross—but they did NOT break the legs of Jesus, because "He was dead already."[160]

Preachers who teach the immortal soul theory are aware of the problems posed by these facts, yet they WANT to believe that the thief died that day. So they tell their congregation that the thieves *did* die that day—from having their legs broken! Skiers or victims of car accidents have had both legs broken, but does this injury prove fatal? Criminals are *executed* by such means as beheading, hanging, electrocution, firing squad, gas chamber—but WHO has *ever* been condemned to death by leg breaking?!?

A broken leg wouldn't *kill* the thieves. It would merely render them *immobile* so they couldn't escape. You see, the Jews didn't want the men to remain on their crosses during that high holy day, but they let them lie on the ground until that day was past and then tied them on their crosses

---

158. Mark 15:44.
159. John 19:31.
160. John 19:31-33.

again till death came from lack of water and food. The Jews didn't want the thieves to escape, but **they couldn't throw them back in prison** because these condemned men had hung on a cross and were considered "cursed." We read: "CURSED is every one that hangeth on a tree," or a cross.[161] Criminals were always crucified **outside** the city.[162] Since bringing a cursed individual within their city gates would **defile** Jerusalem, and since their only prison was inside the city, the Jews had to take other measures to make sure the thieves could not escape.

Realizing that it's ridiculous to claim that breaking leg bones would kill the thieves, the preachers simply say that their legs were broken "to hasten their death." (This contention may have some validity, since victims nailed or tied to a cross found their lungs constricted unless they supported themselves with their legs, so breaking their legs made breathing more difficult. But we already know that Jesus did not meet the thief in heaven that Friday, for He did not ascend to His Father till **some time after** encountering Mary Magdalene on Sunday.) It's true that the Jews had to work fast to remove the thieves from the crosses, just as Jesus' followers had to give their Lord a hurried burial, for *the Bible day ENDED at sundown.* Listen: IF those Roman soldiers really **wanted** to **hasten** a condemned person's DEATH, they knew from training and experience how to do it. They could have **PIERCED the SIDE** of the thieves the way they did Christ's.[163] Jabbing the same spear into the thieves' hearts certainly would've "hastened their deaths." But they did not.

161. Galatians 3:13.

162. For instance, "Jesus . . . suffered **outside** the gate." Hebrews 13:12, New King James Version. And Stephen, the first Christian martyr, was stoned to death outside the city. Acts 7:58.

163. John 19:33-34. Jesus "was dead already," but the spear thrust made the soldiers doubly sure of that fact.

Seven Mysteries . . . Solved!

So the thieves were left outside the city at sundown that day miserably alive with broken legs.

Now—with these two reasons in mind—we must answer this question:

How could a *DEAD* Christ meet a *LIVING* thief
in heaven
when *NEITHER* of them went there
that day???

The answer, of course, is that He didn't. He had no intention of doing so when He made His promise. And the thief didn't even *ask* Jesus to take him to glory *that* day. The same Holy Spirit who revealed Christ's divinity to the thief also gave him the right question to ask. He asked to be a part of Christ's kingdom **when He COMES**—when He *comes* in His kingdom, not when He *goes* to the grave in His death or even when He *goes* back to heaven in His ascension. This was the same hope that Paul had,[164] and Job,[165] and all the Bible writers. The thief KNEW it wouldn't happen on that same day—that's why he said, "**REMEMBER** me."

And Jesus' response met the thief's request EXACTLY. The thief was concerned not so much with **when** he would reach Paradise, but with **whether** he'd have a place in Christ's kingdom. Jesus' majestic answer assured him that however undeserving he might feel, or however impossible it might *appear* for the dying Jesus to bring His promise to pass, he **WOULD assuredly BE there!**

Think of the circumstances under which Jesus spoke those words. Think of the significance of that word "today." Jesus boldly made this promise:

---

164. 2 Timothy 4:8. Paul knew his "crown" was "laid up" for him, to be bestowed by the Lord "**at that day** . . . [of] His **appearing.**"

165. Job 19:25-27. Job knew he would see his Redeemer when the resurrection restores his decomposed body "**at the latter day.**"

today, as His ministry was ending in agony and shame,
today, as His claim to be the Son of God appeared false,
today, as His own disciples had forsaken Him,
today, in His darkest hour, before that mocking mob,
today, amid all these forlorn prospects and blasted hopes.

The crucified Christ calmly turned to the repentant thief and majestically declared: "Verily I say unto thee **today**, thou SHALT be with Me in Paradise."

Christ *still* hasn't come in His kingdom. That's why Christians everywhere are still praying "Thy kingdom come," as He taught us. But the promise to the thief on the cross is sure and certain—he *shall* be with Christ and all the redeemed in Paradise. Moving the comma to its proper place makes the whole passage harmonious not only with itself—but with **all the rest** of Scripture teaching on the state of the dead.

Another puzzle piece fits neatly into place as we close our investigation of "The Case of the Misplaced Comma." Case dismissed!

PUZZLE PIECE #14:
"THE SPIRITS IN PRISON"

Let's read this passage from the Bible: "For Christ also hath once suffered for sins, the Just for the unjust, that He might bring us to God, being put to death in the flesh, but quickened by the Spirit: By which also He went and preached unto the spirits in prison; which sometime were disobedient, when once the longsuffering of God waited in the days of Noah, while the Ark was a preparing, wherein few, that is, eight souls were saved by water."[166] (Note that eight "souls" means eight *persons* or *lives*.)

---

166.   1 Peter 3:18-20.

Some claim that this text must refer to disembodied spirits of people who lived before the Flood, the antediluvians, and these must have been conscious or else Christ would not have gone to preach to them. Therefore, they say, here is Scriptural proof that the dead are conscious. The time when Christ supposedly carried out this preaching mission was during the three days His body was in the tomb.

But suppositions such as these can *never* be made to *harmonize* with the clear, consistent teaching of **the *rest* of Scripture** on the state of the dead. Any confusion caused by this text can be cleared up by answering a few basic questions:

A. WHEN *was this preaching done?* The Scripture itself tells us that it was "in the days of Noah, while the Ark was a preparing." It was "*WHEN* once the long-suffering of God waited in the days of Noah," *not* thousands of years later in hell.

B. HOW *was this preaching done?* Again quite plainly we read, "by the Spirit." The passage says that Christ was "put to death in the flesh, but quickened [made alive] *by the Spirit:* **BY WHICH also He went and preached** unto the spirits in prison." That is, by the ministry of Noah, who preached for one hundred and twenty years while he worked on the Ark. Noah was Christ's representative. Christ, by His Spirit, preached through Noah.[167] Noah, filled with the Holy Spirit, was Christ's spokesman preaching to the doomed antediluvians.[168]

---

167. In the very same letter Peter wrote of "the prophets" like Noah and states that "**the Spirit of Christ . . . was in them.**" 1 Peter 1:10-11. And Peter himself calls Noah "a **preacher** of righteousness." 2 Peter 2:5.

168. Another text that's similarly misconstrued is 1 Peter 4:6 - "For this cause was the gospel preached also to them that are dead, that they might be judged. . . ." This doesn't mean dead people do have the gospel preached to them. Read it carefully: "For this cause **WAS** [past tense] the gospel preached to them that **ARE** [present tense] dead." The gospel

C. *WHY was this preaching done?* There are MANY implications to such an astonishing theory that has our Lord preaching to disembodied spirits in Hell or Hades or some other intermediate place. *What message could He bring them?* Would he offer them **a second chance** even after death? If so, **WHY** single out that particular generation— why not give a second chance to **ALL** the many millions of dead? Is Peter teaching that **God plays favorites?** Is he teaching the doctrine of **purgatory?** No, Scripture makes plain that *death seals our fate* and *there is no second chance*: "It is appointed unto men ONCE to die, and *after this* the JUDGMENT."[169] Most Christians rightly reject the unscriptural teachings of purgatory and a supposed "second chance."

The **purpose** of this preaching was NOT to offer a second chance to disembodied spirits of dead sinners but **to warn the wicked living in Noah's day to repent.** The very chapter telling of God's plan to destroy the earth with a flood says: "**My Spirit** shall not always strive [or plead] with man, . . . yet his days shall be an hundred and twenty years."[170] In other words, God's Spirit patiently preached through Noah, "a preacher of righteousness," waiting a hundred and twenty years before finally destroying those who would not listen.

D. *Must "SPIRITS" mean disembodied spirits of the DEAD?* By no means. When Moses called God "the God of the *spirits* of all *flesh*," he certainly referred to men in the FLESH, **NOT men in a disembodied state,** for Moses was praying for a leader among the **living** to take his

---

was preached to them while they were alive, but after hearing the gospel, they died. Death eternally closes each case.

169. Hebrews 9:27.
170. Genesis 6:3.

place![171] Peter's word translated "spirits" is from the Greek *pneumata* plural of *pneuma,* meaning "wind," "breath," or "spirit." Breath is a conspicuous characteristic of living beings, and by the figure of speech called synecdoche, a characteristic *part* of something stands for the *whole.*[172] Thus **pneuma** (breath or spirit) stands for the whole "person."[173] Accordingly, these *"spirits"* can be considered living **human beings** which were certainly as real as the "eight *souls"* in verse 20 of the same passage.

    E. WHAT *does the "PRISON HOUSE" refer to?* Those who teach the unscriptural doctrines of purgatory, or a second chance, or the immortal soul tell us that the term "prison" refers to the **prison house of DEATH.** But several Scripture verses lead us to conclude *it is the **prison house of SIN.*** For instance, in Luke 4:17-21 Jesus read to the congregation from Isaiah 61:1-2, proclaiming **"liberty to the *captives,* the opening of the PRISON to them that are *bound.*"** Then Jesus told His listeners: **"This day** is this scripture FULFILLED **in YOUR ears."** He was addressing sinners, *not* dead people! When Jesus preached that "the truth shall make you **FREE,"**[174] He was addressing living sinners, not dead people or disembodied spirits.

---

    171. Numbers 27:15-17. "Moses spake unto the Lord, saying, Let the Lord, **the God of the spirits of all flesh,** set a **MAN** over the congregation . . . which may **lead** them."

    172. We use synecdoche ("sin-EK-duh-key") in everyday expressions: Seeing a friend in a new suit, we say, "Nice **threads!**" using the principle of PART for the WHOLE. Or meeting an old acquaintance, we say, "Five long **winters** have past since I've seen you!" using *winters* for *years* under the PART-for-WHOLE principle of synecdoche. Jesus used the same figure of speech in "the Lord's Prayer" when He asked God to "Give us this day our daily **bread**," meaning *food* in general.

    173. Paul's pen gives us similar Bible examples of synecdoche. For instance, if we compare Galatians 6:18 and 2 Timothy 4:22 with Philippians 4:23, it's clear that **"your spirit"** means *"you."*

    174. John 8:32.

God called Jesus to be "a *light* of the Gentiles; To open the *blind* eyes, **to bring out the PRISONERS from the PRISON**, and them that sit in *darkness* out of the *prison house*."[175] Now Gentiles may be sinners, with eyes spiritually blinded by the darkness of disbelief. They may be held by evil habits in sin's prison house, but they're *not DEAD*. *If they WERE dead* prisoners of sin, there'd be no hope for them and no need of preaching.

When Christ quoted Isaiah as mentioned earlier, He said, "The **Spirit** of the Lord is upon Me." Evidently the Spirit's work in Noah's day was the same as in Christ's—preaching to prisoners of sin, offering them *a way of ESCAPE.* How securely the prison house of sin held those who "were DISOBEDIENT . . . in the days of Noah" is evident from the fact that only eight persons escaped from it and survived the Flood. [176]

That Peter himself intended "prison" to mean the prison house of SIN, not DEATH, is seen from his own statement about those "who LIVE in error" and contrasts "liberty" with the "bondage" of those who "are slaves of corruption."[177] No one but Christ can set men free from the evil habits and desires with which Satan shackles them.

F. *Was Jesus ALIVE or DEAD?* The Bible itself has cleared up any misconceptions caused by this verse, but one last question should be answered: That Sabbath day after the Crucifixion, while Jesus lay quietly resting in the tomb, was He **alive** or **dead?** Obviously, He was *dead*—since He was *not resurrected* till the first day of the week. Some try to sidestep this problem by assuming that Christ's spirit remained alive even though His body died. But Christ

---

175. Isaiah 42:1, 6-7.
176. See Genesis 6:5-13, 7:13, and 1 Peter 3:20.
177. 2 Peter 2:18-19, Revised Standard Version. See Proverbs 5:22.

Himself said: "I am He that liveth, and **was DEAD**; and, behold, I am alive for evermore."[178]   He didn't say, "My *body* was dead"—He said, "*I* was dead."

Our whole chance for salvation depends on whether or not Christ actually died. IF Christ did **not die**, body and soul, then you and I must still pay the penalty for our sins, and He's not our Saviour. But we must *never* get the idea that Jesus Christ is not our Saviour or that He did not pay the full penalty for our sins by dying on the cross.[179] Christians who accept Jesus' atoning death have **grave doubts** about interpretations which have Christ prematurely alive and preaching to disembodied spirits in hell-fire while He was in the tomb.

Rightly understood, this puzzle piece from Peter is in full accord with all other Scripture teaching and fits very nicely into the overall picture.

PUZZLE PIECE #15:
SAUL & THE WITCH OF ENDOR

Although the Israelites were a theocracy, a favored nation led by God Himself who fought their battles for them, the time came when they felt this wasn't good enough for them. Rejecting God, they asked to have a regular king so they could be "like all the nations."[180] Saul, a handsome young man who stood head and shoulders taller than other people, was chosen to be king.[181] God knew Israel's desire

---

178. Revelation 1:18.
179. The only Christian denomination that openly denies the atoning death of Christ is Christian Science. Consistency forces such a position, however, since Christian Science denies death in general as well as other negative "thoughts" such as sin, sickness, etc. (See Chapter 8, above, on "The Resurrection of Christ," footnote #91.)
180. 1 Samuel 8:4-22.
181. 1 Samuel 9:2 and 10:23-24.

for a human king was unwise and would cause them to trust more in human strength and less in divine power, but He let the people have their own way and poured out His blessings upon the new king. However, Saul's presumptuous disregard of God's will proved he could not be trusted with royal power.[182]

Those who accept the theory of "man's immortal soul" point with pride to the account of King Saul's visit to the witch of Endor.[183] For after all, the passage begins by saying that the prophet "Samuel was dead . . . and buried," yet the wicked king had a witch conjure up Samuel's spirit who gave him supernatural insight into the future. Champions of the conscious state of the dead feel that here we have a puzzle piece that could never fit in with the plain Bible statement that "The dead know not anything."[184]

Here is an apparent contradiction, yet God's Word never contradicts itself. So let's ask: Is this passage REALLY Bible proof that spirits of the dead are *conscious* beings and that it's possible to *communicate* with those spirits?

Though answers to those questions may differ, one thing we can *all* agree on is that here we have the record of a **SUPERNATURAL** occurrence. However, God is not the only source of supernatural phenomena. Satan and his demons are supernatural beings who also succeed in "working **miracles**,"[185] "with all power and signs and **lying wonders**."[186] But "we are not ignorant of his devices," for God warns us that "Satan himself is transformed into an angel of light."[187] If our Archenemy can disguise himself as a friendly, dazzling angel, it's no trick at all for him or his cohorts to

---

182. For instance, note Saul's self-justifying lies in 1 Samuel 15:2-28.
183. Recorded in 1 Samuel 28:3-25.
184. Ecclesiastes 9:5.
185. Revelation 16:14.
186. 2 Thessalonians 2:9.
187. 2 Corinthians 2:11 and 11:14.

impersonate Samuel. The manifestation of Samuel's spirit
was either *real* or *apparent*, so on the basis of the evidence
all we need to determine is,

- Was it **genuine**—that is, produced by *God?*

  or

- Was it a clever **counterfeit** staged by *Satan?*

Since this passage is the *one solitary instance* in the Bible
of the supposed communication with the dead, or necro-
mancy,[188] it's worthy of close attention. As we examine
the whole account, **SEVEN FACTS stand out:**

1 - GOD Would No Longer Communicate with Saul

As Israel's first king, Saul led a nation favored by direct
communication with God. But Saul grew so disobedient that
he rarely sought advice from the Lord and refused to follow it
when it was given. Now Saul's fortunes had fallen so low
that he desperately wanted God to tell him what to do,
because "the Philistines gathered their armies together for
warfare, to fight with Israel."[189]

However, the Record clearly states that King Saul had
departed so far from God that *the Lord would not answer
him*: "When Saul inquired of the Lord, **the Lord answered
him NOT**, neither by dreams, nor by Urim, nor by prophets."[190] The Lord never turns away a soul who comes to
Him humbly and sincerely. Why, then, did He turn Saul
away unanswered? By his own acts the king had **rejected**

---

188. Interestingly enough, the unabridged dictionary defines *necro-
mancy* as "revealing the future by PRETENDED communication with
the spirits of the dead." *Webster's New International Dictionary*, Second
Edition Unabridged (Springfield, Mass.: G. & C. Merriam Company,
Publishers, c. 1950), p. 1635.
189. 1 Samuel 28:1.
190. 1 Samuel 28:6.

the methods of inquiring of God: He **despised** the counsel of God's prophet Samuel; he **exiled** God's chosen one, David; he **killed** God's priests.[191] Even now, Saul did not turn to God with humility and repentance. He wanted deliverance from his foes, not pardon for his sins. Having forsaken God, Saul's heart trembled with fear[192] when he saw the mighty Philistine armies. Earlier, God had told him by the prophet Samuel that the kingdom would be *taken away* from him as punishment for his failure to obey.[193] But Saul made no serious attempts to seek God's counsel—the Record says he "inquired *not* of the Lord."[194] Instead, the proud monarch cut himself off from God and determined to seek help from *another* source.

2 - SAMUEL Would No Longer Communicate with Saul

King Saul pursued such a disobedient course that not only God but even Samuel, God's prophet, would have nothing further to do with him. The Divine Record states that "Samuel came no more to see Saul until the day of his [Samuel's] death."[195] So Saul could not inquire of **Samuel**, who, even *before* his death, had stopped counseling Saul. Greatly irritated by heaven's silence, Saul tried to FORCE a reply.

3 - Saul Was on **Forbidden Ground**

Saul ordered his servants to find a witch who could contact the **spirit** world,[196] so he might *obtain the information which God withheld!* This was his LAST STEP in disobedience to God. Saul knew he was stepping over the line onto Satan's territory. He KNEW that God *prohibited* consulting with

---

191. See 1 Samuel 22:17-19.
192. 1 Samuel 28:5.
193. 1 Samuel 15:28.
194. See 1 Chronicles 10:13-14.
195. 1 Samuel 15:35.
196. 1 Samuel 28:7.

familiar spirits, witchcraft, sorcery, and spiritism.[197]   Saul
himself had even "**put away** those that had familiar spirits,
and the wizards, out of the land."[198]   Yet despite that prohibition he sought to *practice* what God *forbids*.

In order to practice her unholy arts, the woman of Endor
had made a pact with Satan. As a witch, she agreed to follow Satan in all things, and Satan agreed to perform wonders and miracles for her, revealing the most secret things,
if she would yield herself unreservedly to be controlled by
his Satanic majesty. This she had done.

King Saul made his visit to the witch "**by night**" to be
under cover of darkness. Furthermore, "**Saul *DISGUISED*
himself**, and put on *other raiment*,"[199] because he knew the
witch would never practice her forbidden art before the very
king who outlawed it. The picture is one of people who both
know they're doing something wrong!

Would God honor the request for information from one
engaged in the very occult practices He had forbidden? Such
a view is not only incredible but inconsistent with the entire
body of Scripture on this subject. So it's absurd to suppose
that God, having *refused* to answer Saul personally, would
then send Samuel from the so-called world of spirits, in response to the devilish incantations of a WITCH!

4 - *Saul Saw Nothing But Was Deceived*

Furthermore, **Saul was DECEIVED**: The "spirit" was not
the good man of God we call Samuel—it was a demon from

197. See Exodus 22:18, Leviticus 19:31 & 20:27, Deuteronomy
18:9-12, etc.

198. 1 Samuel 28:3. Stern measures had to be taken to stamp out
the bewitching influence of the occult. People were so deluded "they
sacrificed their sons and their daughters unto **devils**"! Psalm 106:37. The
"familiar spirits" contacted are NOT spirits of the dead but are in reality
demons, the messengers of Satan.

199. 1 Samuel 28:8.

Satan's legions. **Saul himself SAW NOTHING.** He had to ask the witch, " 'What did *YOU see?*' And the *woman* said to Saul, *'I* saw a spirit ascending out of the earth.' So he said to her, *'What* is his *form?*' And *she* said, 'an old man is coming up, and he is covered with a mantle.' And Saul PERCEIVED that it was Samuel." [200]

Having told the witch to "Bring me up Samuel," Saul naturally *jumped to the conclusion* that the spirit she claimed to see was that of Samuel. *Saul saw nothing* but had to content himself with asking what the witch saw.

5 - The Pretended Prophet ACCEPTED WORSHIP!

Saul *"stooped with his face to the ground, and bowed himself"* before the spirit. [201] If it really had been Samuel's spirit, it would NOT have received Saul's *worship.* Neither Samuel nor an ANGEL from God would have consented to receive such worship. [202] But EVIL angels—devilish spirits—would eagerly welcome it. [203]

Though the Bible states that "Samuel said," [204] when we know the prophet was already dead, we must not interpret this to mean it was actually Samuel who spoke. The writer simply describes events as they appeared, which normal narrative technique. The Bible also speaks of the sun rising and setting, [205] and so do we. Yet no one is deceived or confused by the fact that we speak simply of appearances.

---

200. 1 Samuel 28:13-14, New King James Version.

201. 1 Samuel 28:14.

202. See Revelation 19:10 and 22:8-9 for Bible proof.

203. Worship was the main thing Satan sought in tempting Christ: "All the kingdoms of the world, and the glory of them . . . will I give Thee, if Thou wilt **fall down and worship me.**" Matthew 4:8-9.

204. 1 Samuel 28:15 & 16.

205. "The sun also RISES, and the sun GOES DOWN, and hastens to the place where it AROSE." Ecclesiastes 1:5, New King James Version. Many similar texts may be cited, such as Psalm 50:1 & 113:3, Malachi 1:11, Matthew 5:45, *etc.*

Actually the sun does not rise or set; the earth simply revolves. And actually it was not God's holy prophet who came forth at the witch's incantation. Satan couldn't present the real Samuel, but he did present a counterfeit that served his deceptive purpose. If Satan can impersonate "an angel of light,"[206] he could easily imitate Samuel's voice.

Note that the spirit dared to tell Saul: "The Lord . . . is become **THINE ENEMY**."[207] Those words identify their author as Satan, who always depicts God as man's enemy. No true believer would say such a thing about God, whose very **essence** is LOVE.[208] God had not become Saul's enemy. Even though Saul had sinned, God still loved him and wanted to save him. But the lying spirit, posing as a voice from heaven, impersonated the dead Samuel and *taunted* Saul with God's decision to *"rent [rip* or *tear]* the kingdom out of thine hand,"[209] which is simply a direct quotation from 1 Samuel 15:28. Satan succeeded in completely discouraging Saul, leading him on to ruin. Several days later Saul—like Judas—took his own life.[210]

The message which the spirit impostor gave Saul contained **nothing new**, with the exception of predicting Israel's deliverance into Philistine hands, and "**tomorrow** shalt thou and **thy sons** be with me [that is, dead]."[211] The first part of this prediction was only what Satan might safely judge would happen with a strong enemy facing a

206. 2 Corinthians 11:14.
207. 1 Samuel 28:16.
208. "God IS love." 1 John 4:8 & 16.
209. 1 Samuel 28:17.
210. 1 Samuel 31:4. Oppressed by the horror of *despair*, it was impossible for Saul to inspire his army with *courage*. Having *separated himself* from the Lord, he could not lead Israel to *look to God* as their Helper. The words of doom from hell's messenger crushed all physical and moral hope from Saul.
211. 1 Samuel 28:19.

demoralized king, and the latter part was a *falsehood*. In the first place, there's no proof at all that Saul died the **next day**. On the contrary, the Record shows his death was *several* days later.[212] In the second place, *only three* of Saul's sons died in that battle against the Philistines.[213] Those three do NOT include **other** sons of Saul, such as *Ishui*,[214] *Ishbosheth*,[215] and *two others* who **lived for long years after this** till they were hanged by the Gibeonites.[216] Far from bringing Saul heavenly insight, the spirit's demoralizing message was filled with falsehood.

6 - *"Samuel" Came from the* **Wrong Direction**

Those who believe in man's "immortal soul" claim that at the moment of death good people go up to heaven and bad people go down to hell. Samuel was definitely in the "good" class: He was faithful his entire life, serving the Lord ever since his mother took him to the Temple as a small lad.[217] Therefore, advocates of natural immortality assume that he immediately **went to HEAVEN** when he died.

Many Christians believe that redeemed souls are up in heaven, in the presence of the Lord. But the apparition seen by the witch **came UP out of the EARTH**. Could that have been Samuel's immortal soul or conscious spirit? Are redeemed souls **in the earth?** Note the Bible expressions used in Saul's meeting with the witch:

---

212. 1 Samuel 29:10-11, 30:1 & 17, 31:1-6 show that *at least THREE DAYS intervened*, and probably more.
213. 1 Samuel 31:2 & 6.
214. 1 Samuel 14:49.
215. 2 Samuel 2:8-12.
216. 2 Samuel 21:8-9.
217. The story of Hannah, the barren wife who became Samuel's mother and who gave her son to the Lord's service, is full of human interest. You'll find it in the first chapter of the First Book of Samuel.

"Bring him **UP**, whom I shall name unto thee."
"Whom shall I bring **UP** unto thee?"
"Bring me **UP** Samuel."
"**ascending** out of the **EARTH**"
"An old man cometh **UP**."
"to bring me **UP**"[218]

Those expressions are **exactly** how the Bible describes
a witch's familiar spirit: "Thou shalt be brought **DOWN**,
and shalt speak **out of the GROUND**, and thy speech shall
be **LOW out of the DUST**, and thy voice shall be, as of
one that hath a familiar spirit, out of the GROUND,
and thy speech shall **WHISPER out of the GROUND**."[219]
This evidence shows that "Samuel's ghost" was not a *saint*
from heaven's glory but a *demon* from Satan's legions.

The demonic spirit impersonating Samuel pretended to be
"disquieted"[220] by Saul. This seems to teach that redeemed
saints, after departing this world, are still under the control
of sinful mortals on this earth and are compelled to obey
them. IF this spirit medium had power to **force** Samuel to
come back to earth and talk to Saul after Samuel had refused
to have anything more to do with him while he was alive,
IF every witch has the dead so completely in her power that
he can **compel** them to give information to whoever may
pay her for it, then the dead are truly to be pitied! Death
must be miserable if even the saints are liable at any time to
be called from glory at the bidding of any witch or wizard
who chooses to hold a seance.[221]

218. 1 Samuel 28:8, 11, 13, 14, 15.
219. Isaiah 29:4.
220. Or "disturbed" in most modern versions. 1 Samuel 28:15.
221. For many of the ideas expressed here, the writer is greatly indebted to the late Carlyle B. Haynes and his book *Life, Death, and
Immortality* (Nashville, Tenn.: Southern Publishing Association, c. 1952),
pp. 195-201.

7 - The Reason for Saul's Death

Finally, any who believe

(a) it really WAS Samuel and not a demon who was "brought up" and

(b) communicating with spirits of the dead is all right

will be *quickly UNdeceived* if they'll **consider the reasons for Saul's DEATH.** God sets forth those reasons quite clearly:

Saul died for his transgression which he committed against the Lord, even against the word of the Lord, which he kept not, and also **for asking counsel of one that had a familiar spirit, to enquire of it.**[222]

Saul was cut off from life for attending a seance and **inquiring of the spirits.** So here's another reason why it could NOT have been the spirit of Samuel sent by the Lord, for this would **charge God with approving and even taking part in the wickedness** which cost Saul his life!

The seven foregoing facts show that Saul's forbidden visit to the witch of Endor does not prove Samuel to be alive and conscious. It proves only that God means what He says when he warns us against dabbling in the occult.[223] The

---

222. 1 Chronicles 10:13.

223. Those who lose a loved one in death may be tempted to try to contact the dead. British writer Rudyard Kipling knew this, and his poem "En-Dor" opens with these lines:

"The road to En-dor is easy to tread
For Mother or yearning Wife."

However, the poem ends like this:

"Oh, the road to En-dor is the oldest road
And the craziest road of all!
Straight it runs to the Witch's abode,
As it did in the days of Saul,
And nothing has changed of the **sorrow** in store
For such as go down on the road to En-dor!"

We can't gain happiness by indulging in what God forbids.
Poem quoted from *Rudyard Kipling's VERSE*, Definitive Edition (Garden City, New York: Doubleday and Company, Inc., c. 1940), pp. 363-364.

prophet Samuel was—and still is—*asleep* in his grave. The "spirit" was a demon.

CONCLUSION

This last piece of the puzzle fits in perfectly, completing the picture. That picture clears up the mystery of death.

- It shows God alone to be immortal, while mortal man may be given immortality on condition of faith in his Redeemer.

- It shows that death is a deep, dreamless sleep from which we'll awaken at the resurrection.

- Man is not conscious in death, for the Bible words *soul* and *spirit* give no support to the concept of a never-dying entity existing apart from the body.

- Plato's idea of a naturally immortal soul is foreign to God's Word and irreconcilable to its plainest pronouncements, originating with the Archenemy of God.

Though the devil's doctrine[224] of natural immortality has become quite widespread, many other thinking people through the ages have protested against it. One such was William E. Gladstone, four-time Prime Minister of Great Britain, who wrote:

> The doctrine of *natural*, as distinguished from **Christian**, immortality . . . **crept into the Church, by a BACK DOOR**. . . . When arguments are offered for the purely natural immortality of the soul, they are rarely, if ever, derived from Scripture. . . . **The natural immortality of the soul is a doctrine wholly**

---

224. "The Spirit speaketh expressly, that **in the latter times** some shall depart from the faith, giving heed to **seducing spirits, and doctrines of devils**." 1 Timothy 4:1. Surely one of those doctrines is the one that came from the serpent's mouth in Eden.

unknown to the Holy Scriptures, and standing on no higher plane than that of . . . **philosophical opinion** . . . of philosophical speculations *disguised* as truths of Divine Revelation. [225]

The Bible was written not for theological scholars but for ordinary folks like you and me. Usually we don't need to analyze obscure texts to find hidden meanings in cryptic messages. All we need is common sense. For instance, Jesus spoke plainly about His return to heaven: "I go to prepare a place for you. And if I go and prepare a place for you, **I will come again, and RECEIVE you unto Myself;** that where I am, there ye may be also." [226] Let's examine the "immortal soul" theory in the light of Christ's words:

- IF we believers went to heaven at the moment of death, **WE** would be *going to HIM.* Yet Jesus' clear declaration proves that **we** won't *go to Him*—**HE** will *come to US* to achieve that grand reunion!

- There's something terribly wrong with a theory that puts each believer in heaven when he dies—with Jesus receiving *each one individually* at that time—because the Lord says He'll "receive" us *all at once* when He comes again!

---

225. William Ewart Gladstone, educated at Eton College and Oxford University, served as Member of Parliament, Master of the Mint, President of the Board of Trade, Chancellor of the Exchequer, and Prime Minister during most of the reign of Queen Victoria. Despite devoting himself chiefly to the affairs of state, Gladstone was also a theologian in his own right. The above quotations are from his significant, 370-page treatise, *Studies Subsidiary to the Works of Bishop Butler* (Oxford: The Clarendon Press, 1896), pp. 195-198.

226. John 14:2-3.

- This theory also makes a mockery of Christ's
  promise to **return** to this earth to take us home
  with Him: Who needs to *make a return TRIP* to
  get his loved ones if they're *already with* him?

Besides all this, the idea of "man's immortal soul,"
originating with Satan and perpetuated by pagan philosophy, DOES AWAY with *three* of the most fundamental
Christian doctrines:

             1. The Second Coming of Jesus
             2. The Resurrection of the Dead
             3. The Final Judgment

WHAT NEED would there be of those divine events IF
people, both wicked and righteous, go to their reward at the
moment of death? How ridiculous to go through the mockery
of a "judgment" of those already judged! Imagine calling
each sinner up from the flaming pit of hell or a believer
down from the glories of heaven to check the records to see
if he'd been sent to the right place! Such a judgment would
be an empty charade.

    WHY believe in CONDITIONAL immortality rather than
INNATE, UNconditional immortality? Because every true
Bible doctrine has **CHRIST** as its **center**. And conditional
immortality puts Christ in His proper place in the scheme of
things. For example:

- The doctrine of the *Second Coming* puts Christ
  at the center in His role as **Rescuer** from this lost
  and dying planet.

- The doctrine of the *Final Judgment* puts Christ
  at the center in His dual role as both **Judge and
  Advocate.**[227]

---

227. John 5:22 & 27, Acts 10:42, 1 John 2:1.

- And the doctrine of the *Resurrection* puts Christ at the center in His role as **Lifegiver**.

Conditional immortality keeps Christ in the center of *all three* of these vital doctrines, whereas innate, unconditional immortality nullifies any need for those events, causing them to lose their significance.

The Bible of Christianity teaches one thing about death—every pagan religion teaches quite another. Heathenism consistently teaches man's *natural* immortality. The Hindu idea of **REINCARNATION** is based upon the false doctrine of the immortal soul which has also given birth to such unscriptural concepts as **PURGATORY** and **LIMBO**.

Each of us must CHOOSE what he believes
about the state of the dead.
We can choose to believe either

Christianity or **paganism**,
Paul or **Plato**,
God or the **Devil**.

On the weight of evidence presented here,
which do YOU choose?

Chapter 11

ETERNAL TORMENT:
A Burning Issue

A **burning question** in many minds is that of the *NATURE* and *DEGREE* of the **punishment of the wicked.** People wonder about these because a popular teaching in the world today says that those who die unsaved will burn in the flames of hell through all eternity—yet our own innate sense of mercy and justice recoils at such a prospect. Perhaps we should begin by defining our terms.

WHAT "ETERNAL TORMENT" *MEANS*

The Roman Catholic Church teaches this about hell: "Hell is the place and state of **eternal punishment.** . . ."[1] Again, "Hell may be defined as the place and state in which the devils and such human beings as die in enmity with God suffer **eternal torments.**"[2]

But the Catholic Church is not alone in teaching this dreaded doctrine—this teaching is heard from many Protestant pulpits as well. Listen to Puritan preacher Jonathan Edwards:

---

1. Donald Attwater, editor, *A Catholic Dictionary,* 3rd edition (New York: The Macmillan Company, 1962), p. 226, article "Hell."

2. William E. Addis and Thomas Arnold, *A Catholic Dictionary*, second edition (London: Kegan Paul, Trench and Company, 1884), p. 395, article "Hell."

The God that holds you over the pit of hell, much as one holds a spider or some loathsome insect over the fire, abhors you, and is dreadfully provoked: His wrath towards you burns like fire; He looks upon you as worthy of nothing else, but to be cast into the fire; He is of purer eyes than to bear to have you in His sight; you are ten thousand times more abominable in His eyes than the most hateful venomous serpent is in ours. . . . O sinner! Consider the fearful danger you are in: 'tis a great furnace of wrath, a wide and bottomless pit, full of the fire of wrath. . . . 'Tis **everlasting** wrath. It would be dreadful to suffer this fierceness and wrath of Almighty God one moment; but you must suffer it through **all eternity**: there will be **no end** to this exquisite horrible misery. . . . You must wear out long ages, millions and millions of ages, in wrestling with this almighty merciless vengeance; and then when you have done so, you will know that all is but a *point* to what remains. So that your punishment will indeed be **infinite**. [3]

Talk about a **horror** story! Edwards loved to dwell upon the ghastly suffering of an endless hell. Note these terrifying words in another of his sermons describing the wicked in the roaring flames of hell:

. . . vast waves or billows of fire continually rolling over their heads, of which they shall **forever** be full of quick sense within and without: their heads, their eyes, their tongues, their hands, their feet, their loins, and their vitals shall forever be full of a glowing,

3. Jonathan Edwards, "Sinners in the Hands of an Angry God," in Bradley, Beatty, and Long, eds., *The American Tradition in Literature*, Revised (New York: W.W. Norton & Company, Inc., c. 1962), Volume II, pp. 115-119. Edwards delivered this infamous sermon on July 8, 1741, at Enfield, Connecticut.

melting fire, fierce enough to melt the very rocks
and elements; and they shall also **eternally** be full of
the most quick and lively sense to feel the torments;
not for two ages, nor for a hundred years, nor **for
ten thousand of MILLIONS of ages, one after
another, but forever and ever, without ANY end
at all, and never, NEVER to be delivered.**[4]

Sad to say, many others besides Jonathan Edwards preached
this appalling doctrine. Baptist preacher Charles Spurgeon,
master of language that he was, put it this way: "In fire exactly like that which we have on earth, thy body will lie,
ASBESTOS-like, forever unconsumed . . . all thy veins
roads for the hot feet of pain to travel on, every nerve a
string on which the devil shall ever play his diabolical tune
of Hell's Unutterable Lament."[5]

But the limits of blasphemy are not yet reached. The
following quotation turns the God of love into a monster
who *takes delight* in the woes of the lost:

God, who is of purer eyes than to behold iniquity,
cannot look [upon sinners] but with utter detesta-
tion. **His face shall be red in His anger, His eyes
shall not pity, nor His soul spare for their crying.
The day of vengeance is in His heart. It is what
His heart is set upon. He will DELIGHT in it.**
He will tread that rebel crew in His anger, and trample
them in His fury.[6]

---

4. Jonathan Edwards, *Sermons*, Volume VII, p. 166.
5. C. H. Spurgeon, Sermon preached on February 17, 1856, "The
Resurrection of the Dead," in *The New Park Street Pulpit* ([repub-
lished] Grand Rapids: Zondervan Publishing House, 1964), Volume II,
pp. 104-105.
6. Sermon by Reverend William Davidson, quoted in Carlyle B.
Haynes, *Life Death, and Immortality* (Nashville: Southern Publishing
Association, 1952), p. 340.

And the *Works of Samuel Hopkins, D.D.*, pages 457-458, declare that the burning of the wicked throughout eternity will constitute the **light** of heaven; and if hell is brought to an end, heaven would be in darkness! Men go to such lengths when lost in the mazes of their own speculation. But **thank God, this dreaded doctrine of eternal torment is not a BIBLE concept!** Revelation 21:23 says the heavenly city will have "no need of the sun, neither of the moon, to shine in it: for the glory of God did lighten it, and the Lamb is the light thereof."

An ASSAULT on the *CHARACTER* of GOD

This false teaching of endless suffering in perpetual pain, is so fiendish that most of us cannot believe it. Hideous cruelty beyond that of any earthly tyrant is ascribed to God by such a doctrine. Our minds **revolt** against such a caricature of God in His alleged fiendishness.

If the devil wanted to blacken God's character and destroy belief in His love and justice, he'd want a doctrine like this to give children nightmares and drive adults to unbelief. And if they still believed, they'd serve God out of fear. Even Satanic acts would look good in comparison.

No feat of mental gymnastics can reconcile the picture of a God of love, mercy, holiness, and justice with a theory that attacks all those divine attributes. Henry Constable, canon of the cathedral at Cork, Ireland, shows how this doctrine contradicts every attribute of God, when he asks:

> Is it the part of **love** to inflict eternal pain if it can be helped? . . . Is it the part of **mercy** never to be satisfied with the misery of others? . . . Is it essential to **holiness** to keep evil forever in existence? . . . Can **justice** be satisfied only with everlasting agonies?[7]

---

7. Henry Constable, *Duration and Nature of Future Punishment*, 6th edition (London: Edward Hobbs, 1886), p. 166, quoted in Edward Fudge, *The Fire That Consumes* (Houston: Providential Press, 1982), p. 431.

Probably no other doctrine in the Christian faith has produced more atheists than this one. You may have heard of Robert Ingersoll, perhaps the most famous (or infamous!) agnostic ever seen in America. Did you know Ingersoll's father was a Christian minister? Young Bob, who would have made a tremendous speaker and minister for God himself, heard the doctrine of eternal torment being preached and said, "If God is like that, I hate Him." Ingersoll became an infidel and a leading spokesman against God in America. And English poet Percy Shelley wrote: "God is a vengeful, pitiless, and almighty fiend." These are just two examples showing the effects of this **slanderous** teaching.

Such a grotesque doctrine is another phase of the Devil's **war** against God, the war that broke out in heaven and was transferred to this earth, as we're told in Revelation 12:7-9. Throughout this great controversy, Satan has attacked the character of God. He not only led *many angels* to join his diabolical rebellion by causing them to doubt God's wisdom and the justice of His divine government, but he also caused *our first parents* to fall by leading them to doubt God's truthfulness, contradicting the Creator with the lie that "Ye shall *not* surely die."[8]

Satan wants to paint God as a sadistic monster who plunges his victims into endless, agonizing misery. *But the facts are:*

- "God is **love**." 1 John 4:8 & 16.

- "The Lord [is] **merciful** and **gracious** . . . **forgiving**." Exodus 34:5-7.

- "The Lord God [solemnly swears], **I have NO PLEASURE in the death of the wicked**." Ezekiel 33:11.

---

8. Genesis 3:4.

That's the kind of God we worship. But in studying this whole question, I learned a new word, the word "indefeasible." Advocates of the immortal soul claim man has "*indefeasible* immortality." What does that mean? Well, "indefeasible" means "That which CANNOT be **undone** or **made void**." In other words, they believe not only that God *made* man with a so-called immortal soul[9] but that, having made him so, God *cannot* undo this act or change man back to a mortal creature. Like the mad scientist who created a Frankenstein monster, God is left with a creature He *cannot* destroy. They feel this is true because BY DEFINITION our soul is: *inherently* immortal, *innately* immortal, *indefeasibly* immortal. Consequently, they teach that man's soul by its very **nature** is imperishable and indestructible.

This theory made the corollary doctrine of eternal torment **necessary**, for if God can create life but cannot destroy it, His only recourse is to cast rebellious creatures into a lake of fire where, because they're immortal, they must burn forever. Yet reason tells us: if God created all things out of nothing, then He can reduce all things **back** to nothing—or Omnipotence has ceased to be omnipotent.

But let's examine this theory and the dilemma it poses. This doctrine drives us to one of two alternatives, and neither is acceptable.[10]

(1) If we say that the wicked **must** live forever because man has an immortal soul that God Himself is **powerless to destroy**, then we have an extremely **LIMITED** God, a God not worthy of worship, for He created us, bungled the job, and lost control.

---

9. If man really *were* inherently immortal, it would have been pointless for God to WARN Adam and Eve about death, as he did in Genesis 2:16-17 & 3:3. God's warning would have been **an empty threat!**

10. See Elizabeth Cooper, "Clearing God's Name," *Review & Herald* Magazine (December 5, 1974), p. 5.

(2) The other alternative is even more objectionable in misrepresenting God's character. It is this: If we admit that God **IS** all powerful, that He **CAN** destroy those He's created but **CHOOSES to** keep them miraculously alive, then it follows that He **WILLFULLY** will burn, scorch, and sizzle His disobedient creatures **FOREVER** as punishment for the crimes of **one short lifetime**. Talk about "cruel and unusual punishment"! It's doubtful that even the most vindictive man would wish such cruelty on his worst enemy. The God of this second alternative inspires only fear and hate, not love, for He's a sadist of the first magnitude.

It's time we cleared the good name of God of these false charges by examining what the Bible teaches about the destiny of the wicked. A theory so appalling needs to be sustained by evidence proportionately strong, yet the Bible does not corroborate it. In the first place,

HELL IS NOT BURNING *NOW.*

As we learned in Chapter 10, the Bible clearly teaches that at death man goes to neither heaven nor hell, but into the grave, to await the resurrection at Jesus' coming. In harmony with this are Peter's words: "The Lord knoweth how to deliver the godly out of temptations, and to **reserve** the unjust unto the **day of judgment to be** punished."[11] Note the expressions "reserve," "the day of judgment," and "to *be* punished," for they prove no punishment is going on **now** in some place of torment.

The prophet Job taught the same truth: "Do ye not know . . . that the wicked is **reserved** to the day of destruction? They shall be **brought forth** [resurrected] to the day of wrath."[12] The fact is, *hell hasn't happened yet.* Just as the

---

11. 2 Peter 2:9.
12. Job 21:29-30.

wicked are not burning now, being "reserved to the day of destruction," so the **righteous** are not in heaven now, their "inheritance incorruptible" being **"reserved** in heaven."[13]

Not even the devils are burning now. Jude 6 declares: "The angels which kept not their first estate, but left their own habitation, He hath **reserved** in everlasting chains under darkness, **unto the judgment of the great day.**" And Peter says: "God spared not the angels that sinned, but cast them down to hell,[14] and delivered them into chains of darkness, to be **reserved unto judgment.**"[15]

So the punishment of Satan and his demons is "reserved" till some **future** time. Evidently the devils themselves understand this, for when Jesus met two demon-possessed men, the devils "cried out, saying, What have we to do with Thee, Jesus, Thou Son of God? Art Thou come hither to torment us BEFORE THE TIME?"[16] **IF** Satan and his devils **were** confined to a place of burning now, who'd carry on their evil work? Satan's punishment is "reserved . . . unto the judgment of the great day," for he's **not yet** judged. Redeemed saints will even take part in his trial: "Know ye not that **we** shall *judge angels* [fallen angels like Lucifer]?"[17]

JUSTICE DEMANDS
THAT HELL IS NOT BURNING NOW

Not only does *Scripture* prove that punishment is yet future, as we've just seen, but *justice* also demands that it be so.

---

13. 1 Peter 1:4.

14. The word **hell** here is translated from the Greek word "Tartaros" which means simply "a dark abyss." This is the only use of *Tartaros* in the entire Bible, and nothing in this Greek word even implies a place of fire or burning. Like Jude 6, quoted above, this verse speaks not of fire but of "chains of darkness" and says judgment is "reserved" or **future.**

15. 2 Peter 2:4.

16. Matthew 8:29.

17. 1 Corinthians 6:3.

For the false theory of eternal torment, teaching that the wicked go immediately to a burning hell at the moment of death, charges God with infinitely more UNFAIRNESS than is within the power of mankind to practice. How? Because a sinner of the first century—like Cain, who killed his brother Abel—would already be burning for SIX THOUSAND YEARS. Therefore a twentieth-century sinner—like Hitler, who was responsible for slaying millions—would have a six-thousand-year lighter sentence! Where's the justice in that?

GOD'S "*STRANGE* ACT"

I'm glad we can clear away the many misconceptions about hell. But make no mistake: Hell and hell-fire are **real**, literal and hot! There IS a heaven to win and a hell to shun. There WILL be excruciating physical pain as well as unbearable mental anguish from realizing what one has lost. (Spanish writer Calderón de la Barca said, "The loss of heaven is the greatest pain in hell.") But though there's an act of final destruction, **even that destruction** is an act of LOVE, like shooting a horse that has a broken leg. Lives of rebellion have unfitted the wicked for heaven. Its purity and peace would be torture for them, and they'd long to flee from that holy place. They'll welcome destruction itself in order to be hidden from the face of Him who died to redeem them.[18] The destiny of the wicked is fixed by their own choice.

It's in mercy to the universe that God destroys sin and sinner. God will destroy Satan and his followers to make the universe safe for those wise enough to trust and follow their Creator. Sinners *will* die, but *not* at the hands of an angry God. Rather, it's more like seriously ill patients who **refuse** life-saving help from a kindly physician.

---

18. At Christ's Second Coming the wicked will call "to the mountains and rocks, **Fall** on us, and **hide** us from the face of Him that sitteth on the throne." See Revelation 6:15-17.

God's done all He could to save each rebellious individual, but in the end He respects each one's own freedom of choice. Reluctantly, like a parent who hates to punish a beloved child, God goes about His strange work of destruction—strange because for Him it's completely out of character. Note how our loving heavenly Father describes it: "The Lord shall rise up . . . He shall be wroth . . . that He may do His work, **His strange work**; and bring to pass His act, **His strange act**."[19]

Opposed to the theology of men who teach endless torment is another extreme—some believe that God is too good to punish the wicked at all. But between these two extremes is the Bible picture of a God of both **mercy** and **justice**. The word *gospel* means "good news"—and God's just and merciful punishment is part of His **good news**.

THERE WILL BE *DEGREES* OF PUNISHMENT

God is a God of infinite justice. Paul speaks of "the righteous judgment of God, who will render to every man **according to his deeds**."[20] God keeps careful record books: "And I saw the dead, small and great, stand before God; and the books were opened . . . and the dead were judged out of those things which were written in the books, **according to their works.** . . . They were judged every man **according to their works**."[21] The word "according" implies varying degrees of punishment.

Jesus Himself explicitly teaches that there will be individual degrees of punishment. He says: "And that servant, which **knew** his Lord's will, and prepared not himself, neither did according to His will, shall be beaten with **MANY stripes**.

---

19. Isaiah 28:21.
20. Romans 2:6.
21. Revelation 20:12 & 13.

But he that **knew not**, and did commit things worthy of stripes, shall be beaten with **FEW stripes**."[22]

So it's clear that some will burn briefly before dying, while others will burn longer. Probably Satan will burn longest of all, for he not only committed the most evil but also had the best opportunity in heaven to *know* "his Lord's will."

Our loving God is so fair, so just, that in the judgment He even takes into account **our place of BIRTH** and the attendant opportunities that involves. He declares: "I will make mention of Rahab and Babylon to them that know Me: behold, Philistia, and Tyre, with Ethiopia; **this** man was born **THERE**. And of ZION it shall be said, **This man was born in her**. . . . The Lord shall COUNT, when He writeth up the people, that **this man was born THERE**."[23]

Justice demands different degrees of punishment, but this would hardly be possible if all sinners were thrown into the same lake of fire and burned *throughout eternity*.

THE WICKED WILL FINALLY BE *DESTROYED*

Even though the unsaved will be punished in varying degrees, apparently for different lengths of time before dying, all will finally be destroyed—utterly, completely annihilated. The Bible is **extremely explicit** on this. Paul, for instance, gives positive testimony when he says: "The wages of sin is **DEATH**"[24]—*not* eternal LIFE in unending torture! And James says plainly, "Sin, when it is finished, bringeth forth **DEATH**."[25]

---

22. Luke 12:47-48. Other statements of Jesus, such as those found in Matthew 11:20-24 and Luke 20:45-47, prove that there will be degrees of punishment, asserting that especially wicked sinners "shall receive **greater** damnation."
23. Psalm 87:4-6.
24. Romans 6:23.
25. James 1:15.

But someone may ask, "Maybe these texts simply refer to the death of the *body*. The *soul* of man could never be destroyed, could it?" That's a good question which Christ Himself answered when He warned us to "Fear him which is able to *destroy* both soul and body in hell."[26] So obviously the soul can be destroyed.

Contrary to popular belief, the soul is neither immortal nor a conscious entity that can exist apart from the body. The word "soul" in the New Testament comes from the Greek word *psuche* (pronounced "psoo-KAY"), which simply means "life" or " living being" or " living creature." For instance, in Matthew 16:25-26 the Greek word *psuche* appears four times, but it's translated twice as "life" and twice as "soul," showing that the two terms are interchangeable. Here's how that text reads: "For whosoever will save his **life** [*psuche*] shall lose it: and whosoever will lose his **life** [*psuche*] for My sake shall find it. For what is a man profited, if he shall gain the whole world, and lose his own **soul** [*psuche*]? or what shall a man give in exchange for his **soul** [*psuche*]?"[27]

The whole man sins, so the whole man dies. His entire being, his life, his body, are **all DESTROYED.** "The candle of the wicked shall be **put out**," says the wise man Solomon.[28]

Ezekiel plainly declares: "The **soul** that sinneth, it shall *DIE.*"[29] Then a few verses later the prophet *repeats* this, for good emphasis: "The **soul** that sinneth, it shall *DIE.*"[30] The infallible Word of God ought to settle the matter. No support can be found there for the immortal-soul theory.

Furthermore, everlasting hell-fire punishment is inconsistent with the teaching of Jesus. In the most *familiar* verse

26. Matthew 10:28.
27. Chapter 10 of this present volume clarifies the Bible terms "soul" and "spirit."
28. Proverbs 24:20.
29. Ezekiel 18:4.
30. Ezekiel 18:20.

in all the Bible, John 3:16, Jesus said that whoever believed
in Him would "have everlasting life" and whoever did not
would "perish." The word *perish*—a correct translation of
the Greek—means to *cease to exist* and describes an **END**
to the punishment rather than eternal torment.

Dr. Richard Weymouth, the first to translate the New Testament into modern English and esteemed the most accomplished Greek scholar of his day, strikingly declared:

> My mind fails to conceive a *grosser misrepresenta-
> tion of language* than when five or six of the *strongest*
> words which the Greek tongue possesses, signifying
> to **destroy** or **destruction**, are translated to mean
> "maintaining an everlasting but wretched existence."
> To translate *black* as *white* is *nothing* compared to
> this. [31]

Note how clearly the Bible describes the utter destruction of the wicked, specifically how all the wicked will be
"destroyed **together**"—not burning one by one as they happen to die: "And the *destruction* of the transgressors and of
the sinners shall be **together**, and they that forsake the Lord
shall be *consumed*. . . . The strong shall be as *tow*,[32] and the
maker of it as a spark, and they shall both burn **together**,
and none shall quench them. . . . The transgressors shall be
destroyed TOGETHER." [33]

The psalmist David uses unmistakable language: "For
yet a little while, and the wicked shall **not BE**: yea, thou
shalt diligently consider his place, and it shall **not BE**. . . .

31. Richard Francis Weymouth, quoted in Edward White, *Life in Christ*
3rd ed., rev. and enlarged (London: Elliot, 1878), p. 365. Dr. Weymouth
was headmaster of Mill Hill School and the translator of *New Testament
in Modern Speech* (Boston: The Pilgrim Press, 1902).
32. "Tow" is the coarse, broken fibers of hemp or flax, before
spinning, which burns *very quickly*.
33. Isaiah 1:28 & 31; Psalm 37:38.

But the wicked shall **perish**, and the enemies of the Lord shall be as the *fat* of lambs:[34] they shall **consume**; into smole shall they *consume away."* [35]

The final chapter of the Old Testament vividly describes the sinner's fate: "For, behold, the day cometh, that **shall BURN as an OVEN:** and all the proud, yea, all that do wickedly, shall be *stubble*;[36] and the day that cometh shall **burn them UP,** saith the Lord of hosts, that it shall leave them neither root nor branch. . . . And ye shall *tread down* the wicked; for they shall be **ashes** under the soles of your feet in the day that I shall do this, saith the Lord of hosts."[37]

When the pen of Inspiration says that the day of God's judgment will not just "burn them" but will "burn them **UP,**" it means total destruction by flames, as does the plain word "ashes."

FEAR IS AN UNWORTHY MOTIVE

Believers in eternal torment object to the teaching that the Bible says complete destruction awaits the sinner. They believe mere **annihilation** isn't scary enough to be a deterrent to sin. They think sinners won't repent of wrong-doing if convinced they won't burn eternally in flames of hell.

But fear is a poor motive for intelligent beings. A wife threatened by her bullying husband may yield to his wishes. But threats won't make her love him more than she did before. Instead, she'll tend to hate him. Those who become "religious" because they **fear** hell and **fear** God are actually FARTHER from salvation than they were before.

Our loving Saviour never intended to **scare** people into heaven. True religion is more than a mere "fire escape."

---

34. Like a *grease* fire on the stove, nothing burns as readily as "fat," which water cannot extinguish—it keeps burning till it's "consumed."

35. Psalm 37:10 & 20.

36. "Stubble" is short stubs or stumps of grain, left after the harvest, which burns very fast.

37. Malachi 4:1-3.

Besides, we know that most men have remained impenitent even under the preaching of eternal torment. The natural tendency of that theory is to make men infidels instead of Christians. Most people, if made to believe that *that* is what Scripture teaches, will reject the Bible altogether.

It's love, not fear, that converts a soul. It's love, caught in one glimpse of the Saviour dying on the cross, that melts the hard heart. Understanding God's love leads to genuine conversion and saves more people in the eternal kingdom than believing the doctrine of eternal torture. In heaven the redeemed won't slink around like cowed beasts, afraid of their master's lash, but will **praise** and love God, "saying with a loud voice, WORTHY is the Lamb that was slain to receive POWER, and RICHES, and WISDOM, and STRENGTH, and HONOR, and GLORY, and BLESSING."[38] **"There is no fear in love;** but perfect love casteth out fear: because fear hath torment. He that feareth is not made perfect in love."[39]

"EVERLASTING *DESTRUCTION*"

Because the sinner's destruction is so complete—God says the wicked "shall be as though they *had not been*"[40]— the Bible uses such words as "eternal," "everlasting," and "forever and ever" in connection with the fate of the wicked. These expressions show that the overthrow of the wicked is a complete overthrow, that there'll **never** be **any** hope of recovery from their fate, for it is eternal. Their *torment* is not eternal. Their *grief* and *anguish* are not eternal. But their *destruction* IS eternal.

The apostle Paul explicitly stated this thought of the complete destruction of the wicked: "Who shall be punished with **everlasting destruction** from the presence of the Lord,

38. Revelation 5:12.
39. 1 John 4:18.
40. Obadiah 16.

and from the glory of his power."[41] And Jesus said: "These shall go away into *everlasting* **punishment**."[42] However, note carefully that "everlasting punish**MENT**" is NOT *endless punishING*. This isn't "playing with words"—the very same principle applies to such vital Bible subjects as the following:

Hebrews 5:9 teaches
not an ongoing PROCESS of **endless saving**
but a final RESULT of **"eternal salvation."**

Hebrews 6:2 teaches
not an ongoing PROCESS of **endless judging**
but a final RESULT of **"eternal judgment."**

2 Thessalonians 1:9 teaches
not an ongoing PROCESS of **endless destroying**
but a final RESULT of **"everlasting destruction."**

And Matthew 25:46 teaches
not an ongoing PROCESS of **endless punishING**
but a final RESULT of **"everlasting punishMENT."**

The "eternal" or "everlasting" pertains to the **RESULT**, not the **PROCESS**.

Furthermore, there's no dispute at all concerning the *length* or *duration* of the "punishment"—we've just read Jesus' words that it will be "everlasting." The only question is, What will that punishment BE? *If* the punishment for sin is *torment*, then there's no question but that the torment will be eternal. *If*, however, the punishment for sin is *death*,

---

41. 2 Thessalonians 1:9. In Philippians 3:18-19, Paul speaks of "the enemies of the cross of Christ, whose END is DESTRUCTION"— *not* **eternal burning**. Likewise, in Matthew 7:13-14, Jesus speaks of the "broad" and "narrow" ways and contrasts "life" with "DESTRUCTION" —*not* with **eternal burning**.
42. Matthew 25:46.

then the death will be "everlasting." And no Bible reader
disputes the fact that **"the wages of sin is DEATH."**[43]

"ETERNAL FIRE"

But what about the "everlasting fire" spoken of by Jesus
in Matthew 25:41? The words "everlasting" and "eternal"
are synonymous, and in the New Testament *both* come from
the same Greek word. In fact, verse 46 contains both words
each translated from the same original Greek word, *aionios.*
Remember, the Bible explains itself, if we only let it. We
can understand what Jesus meant here if we compare Scripture with Scripture. Jude 7 says that "Sodom and Gomorrah
. . . are set forth for an *example,* **suffering the vengeance
of ETERNAL fire."** Here's a Biblical "example" of what
hell's everlasting fire will be. God says Sodom and Gomorrah were destroyed by **"eternal fire"**—but are those cities
burning today, burning forever? Of course not! The fire did
its destructive work and then **WENT OUT** thousands of years
ago—2000 years, even, before Jude was inspired to write
his letter in the First Century A.D.!

The Apostle Peter corroborates this when he speaks of
God "turning the cities of Sodom and Gomorrah into ASHES,
condemned them to destruction, making them an example to
those who afterward would live ungodly."[44] And evidently it
does not take long for "eternal fire" to reduce whatever it
attacks to mere "ashes," for Jesus said that "the SAME DAY
that Lot went out of Sodom it rained fire and brimstone from
heaven, and DESTROYED them all."[45] Then Jeremiah tells
us that "Sodom . . . was overthrown as in a MOMENT."[46]
Here again, "eternal" means an everlasting RESULT, not
an endless PROCESS.

---

43. Romans 6:23.
44. 2 Peter 2:6, New King James Version.
45. Luke 17:29.
46. Lamentations 4:6.

Note what Dr. William Temple, late Archbishop of Canterbury, Primate of Great Britain, says about this "everlasting [*aeonian*] fire": "One thing we can say with confidence: everlasting torment is to be ruled out. If men had not **imported** the Greek and unbiblical notion [from Plato], of the natural indestruction of the individual soul, and then read the New Testament with that already in their minds, they would have drawn from it a belief, not in everlasting torment, but in ANNIHILATION. It is the FIRE that is called *aeonian*, not the LIFE cast into it."[47]

Dr. Temple adds: "Are there not, however, many passages which speak of the endless torment of the lost? No; as far as my knowledge goes there is none at all. . . . After all, annihilation IS an everlasting punishment though it is *not* unending torment."[48]

"UNQUENCHABLE FIRE"

Another adjective the Bible uses to describe hell-fire is "unquenchable." Jesus warns that the fire which punishes the wicked "never shall be quenched."[49] Is that true? Will hell-fire never be quenched? You'd better believe it! But let's understand what that means: to **quench** a fire means to **put it out**. A fire that shall never be quenched is not one that shall **never GO out** but one that *cannot be PUT out*. In 1871 the great Chicago fire destroyed that city. If we describe that fire by saying the flames could not be quenched, would you conclude that Chicago was **still burning**? No, you'd simply understand that the fire raged till it devoured everything within reach and then died down.

47. William Temple, *Christian Faith and Life* (London: SCM Press Ltd., 1954), p. 81 (from a 1931 address at Oxford's University Church.)
48. William Temple, *Nature, Man and God* (London: Macmillan Co., Limited, 1953), p. 464 (from his lectures at Glasgow University, 1932-34).
49. Mark 9:43-45.

The Bible says even **Jerusalem** was burned with a fire that could "not be quenched." God warned the ancient Jews: "But if ye will not hearken unto Me . . . then I will kindle a fire in the gates thereof, and it shall devour the palaces of Jerusalem, and **it shall NOT be QUENCHED**."[50] The literal fulfillment of this prophecy came when the Babylonians put the torch to Jerusalem.[51] But is that fire still burning? Are those Jewish "palaces" **ever consuming, yet never quite consumed?** No, but this unquenchable fire brought the city to destruction and ashes, just as hell-fire will bring the wicked to destruction and ashes. The fire which destroys the wicked MUST of necessity be UNQUENCHABLE, for if it were not, the wicked would put it out.

WORM DIETH NOT?

Some believe that Mark 9:43-48 proves the truth of the doctrine of eternal torment, for there Jesus warns the wicked against being cast into hell, "Where their worm dieth not, and the fire is not quenched." The last part of this text poses no problem, since we've just seen what "unquenchable fire" means. Let's focus, therefore, on the first part which says, "their worm dieth not."

Understand first of all that "their worm" is not a soul but only a MAGGOT, **feeding upon** a *dead* body and **not inhabiting** a *living* one. Jesus' words echo those of the prophet Isaiah, who says the redeemed "shall go forth, and look upon the **carcases [dead bodies]** of the men that have transgressed against Me: for **their worm shall not die**, neither shall their fire be quenched."[52] The picture is again that of maggots preying on dead bodies.

---

50. Jeremiah 17:27. See also Jeremiah 7:20.
51. 2 Chronicles 36:19-21.
52. Isaiah 66:24. See also verses 15-17 and 22-23.

The worm—a gnawing, carrion-eating destroyer—causes no suffering to the insensible carcass but simply hastens the disappearance of dead bodies. The worm and fire together, as agents of destruction, actually indicate the utter impossibility of eternal life in torment. This awesome warning stands for dissolution, disintegration, and final disappearance. So this text does NOT support the theory of eternal conscious suffering of the living damned. The work of the "worm" and "fire" is eternal in **results** but not in **process or duration.**

Jesus is unmistakably alluding to the ghastly scenes of the ancient Valley of Hinnom, a ravine south of Jerusalem, just outside the city wall. It was a place of fire and destruction used as a vast refuse pit. All that was worthless was cast into the Gehenna fires: refuse, animal carcasses, even corpses of criminals so wicked as to be judged unworthy of burial. Here fires were kept burning to consume the corruption, and worms preyed upon the putrefying flesh. Whatever the fire failed to consume along the outer edges of the pit, the worm would devour.

The Valley of Hinnom in Hebrew is *Ge Hinnom*, which Greek transliterates into *Gehenna*, the term for hell Christ used here. Jesus, the Master Teacher, knew His listeners were familiar with this place where refuse was burned up, having seen it with their own eyes. So in using *Gehenna* to designate the final fires of God's destructive judgments, He achieved instant communication.

But in so doing He offered no support to the doctrine of eternal torment. For the ancient fire of Gehenna was **not** a fire into which **living** persons were cast, to be **kept alive under torture,** but one into which **corpses** were cast to be **consumed.** Any part remaining unburned was devoured by worms, so nothing was left. Greek scholar Dr. R. F. Weymouth tells us:

"Gehenna of Fire Or 'Hell.' The severest punishment inflicted by the Jews upon any criminal. The corpse (after

the man had been stoned to death) was thrown out into the Valley of Hinnom (*Ge Hinnom)* and was devoured by the worm or the flame."[53]

As a place of burning, especially for the punishment of the wicked, *Gehenna* fits the modern concept of Hell—except that *Gehenna* is not presently burning but simply symbolizes the coming "lake of fire" mentioned in Revelation.

Instead of supporting the theory of "eternal torment of the damned," Christ again portrayed the doom of the wicked as destruction. The "worm," like the "unquenchable fire," is a symbol of **DEATH** and **DESTRUCTION**.

HOW LONG IS "FOREVER"?

Now let's consider the word "forever." The pen of Inspiration says the wicked will be "cast into the lake of fire . . . and shall be tormented day and night for ever and ever."[54] What's the explanation? How do we know from that very chapter of Revelation 20 that "for ever and ever" in verse 10 does **not** mean "without end"? Because verse 9 says, "And fire . . . **DEVOURED** them," and because verse 14 says, "The lake of fire . . . is the second **DEATH**." The Bible never contradicts itself. It consistently describes the end of the wicked as ultimate destruction. But English readers must remember that the Hebrew and Greek words (*olam* and *aionios*) translated "forever" in the Bible are *idioms* which don't always mean what we think they mean.

Let's ask the **Bible** what it means by "forever"—let's apply *the acid test of usage* to find the Bible meaning of this word. Exodus 21:6 describes the custom followed if a man was willing to be the slave of another man for the rest of his life: "His master shall bore his ear through with an awl;

---

53. Richard Francis Weymouth, *New Testament in Modern Speech*, 3rd edition (Boston: The Pilgrim Press, 1902), Matthew 5:22, note 12.
54. Revelation 20:10 (see also verse 15).

and **he shall serve him FOR EVER**." But how long is "for ever" in this case? Another translation says: "for the rest of his life." That's as long as he **could** serve him, of course. But it SAYS "for ever"! "For ever" in this case just means **as long as he lives.**

And what about Samuel? His mother dedicated him to the Lord. She was barren of children, so she promised that if the Lord would give her a son, she'd let him serve God all his life. As soon as the boy was weaned, she brought him to the Temple, "that he may . . . **there abide FOREVER.**"[55] How could that be? The context explains: "As **long** as he **liveth**, he shall be lent to the Lord."[56] After all, Samuel could serve the Lord only as long as he lived. Here again, the word "forever" means **for the rest of a man's life.**

Paul, writing to Philemon regarding the return of his runaway servant Onesimus, said: "Thou shouldest receive him *forever*."[57] What does that mean? Obviously, Philemon could receive Onesimus back only as long as either one of them lived. So "forever" here means **as long as life lasts.**

Commenting on this verse of Philemon 15, that scholarly reference, *The Cambridge Bible for Schools and Colleges*, says that *forever* in Biblical usage "tends to mark duration **as long as the NATURE of the SUBJECT allows.**"

Thus the time involved depends upon the **subject** to which the word *forever* or *everlasting* is applied. When used to describe God or the gift of life that God gives, it naturally means **without an end, eternal.** Applied to something transitory, such as mortal man, it means a relatively short period of time—the lifetime of that person. Please remember these simple words of Scripture: "He that hath the Son hath life; and he that hath **not** the Son of God

55. 1 Samuel 1:22.
56. 1 Samuel 1:28.
57. Philemon 15.

hath NOT life."[58] For example, "No **murderer** hath eternal life abiding in him."[59] Could God make it plainer than that?

We often use the word *forever* in the same way ourselves. For instance, when we receive a gift or award, we often say: "I'll treasure it forever." What does this really mean? As long as I live. And the idea of "forever" meaning *duration limited by the SUBJECT to which it applies* is reflected in some of our other English usage. For example, we speak of

- a "tall" MAN and think of **six** feet,
- a "tall" TREE and think of **sixty** feet,
- a "tall" MOUNTAIN and think of **six thousand** feet!

But we use the same word "tall" in each case.

The Bible applies the *same* principle to its use of the word "forever." At least 56 times the Bible uses the word "forever" for things that have already come to an end.[60] The familiar expression "for ever and ever" means literally "to the ages of the ages" and is an idiomatic expression meaning "to the end of the age," "to the end of life," or "to the end of any particular experience." And that's exactly how it's used in the Bible.

SMOKE ASCENDS FOREVER?

Speaking of the fate of those who worship the Beast and receive his Mark, Revelation 14:11 says, "the smoke of their torment ascendeth up for ever and ever." It's true that no night's rest will interrupt the suffering of the wicked: it

---

58. 1 John 5:12.

59. 1 John 3:15.

60. A Catholic professor at St. Ambrose College explains, "As for the frequently used word *eternal*, its meaning is often the same as that in many secular writings—a period of long duration, NOT necessarily time without end."—Father Joseph E. Kokjohn, "A HELL of a Question," *Commonweal* (January 15, 1971), p. 368.

will continue until they're annihilated. But those who claim this passage teaches eternal torment overlook the fact that it does NOT say their **torment** will continue forever—rather, it is the "**smoke**" of their torment that drifts on endlessly.

The psalmist wrote, "The wicked . . . shall **consume; into SMOKE shall they consume away.**"[61] That this is not endless burning is evident from the fact that the same expression is used concerning mystical "Babylon," called "the great whore": "And her smoke rose up for ever and ever."[62] This means complete and total destruction, for God says: "She shall be **utterly** burned with fire ... and shall be **found no more** at all."[63]

Bible scholars know that this phrase about "smoke rising up for ever and ever" is derived from Isaiah 34:10. A look at the context in Isaiah 34 disproves any contention about endless burning. Isaiah predicted that "The sword of the Lord" would fall upon the idolatrous city of Bozrah, twenty miles southeast of the Dead Sea. God's curse on Bozrah says, "The land thereof shall become **burning pitch. It shall not be quenched** night nor day; **the SMOKE thereof SHALL GO UP FOR EVER:** from generation to generation it shall lie waste; ... the **cormorant [pelican]** and the **bittern** shall possess it. . . . And **thorns** shall come up in her palaces, **nettles** and **brambles** in the fortresses thereof. . . . The **wild beasts** of the desert shall also meet with the wild beasts of the island . . . there."[64]

Thus God's Word in Isaiah proves that fire which makes smoke ascend "for ever and ever" **does NOT burn forever.** If it did, how could thorns, nettles, and brambles grow up and wild animals take possession of Bozrah?

---

61. Psalm 37:20.
62. Revelation 17:1, 5, 18; 19:3.
63. Revelation 18:8 & 21.
64. Isaiah 34:6, 9-14.

God repeats that city's fate: "I have sworn by Myself, saith the Lord, that **Bozrah shall become a desolation,** a reproach, a waste, and a curse; and all the cities thereof **shall be perpetual wastes."**[65] This same destiny befalls the wicked: when they're burned up as Bozrah was, their complete annihilation will last through all eternity.

PLACE of PUNISHMENT WILL BE *on EARTH*

It's fitting that the sinner will be punished on this earth, for it's here that the sins were committed. Revelation 20:9 says the resurrected wicked "went up **on** the breadth of the **EARTH** . . . and fire came down . . . and **DEVOURED** them." Also, describing Satan's doom, God says, "I will bring forth a fire . . . it shall **devour** thee, and **I will bring thee to ASHES upon the EARTH** in the sight of all them that shall behold thee . . . and never shalt thou BE any more."[66]

That's why Peter describes hell-fire by saying "The **elements shall melt** with fervent heat, **the EARTH also** and the works that are therein shall be BURNED UP. . . . Nevertheless we, according to His promise, look for new heavens and a NEW EARTH, wherein dwelleth righteousness."[67]

Therefore, since the Bible teaches

    (1) that the **place** of hell-fire punishment is **this earth,**
                and
    (2) that God's people "shall **inherit** the earth"; [68]
              it follows
    (3) that **the burning MUST come to an END.**

---

65. Jeremiah 49:13.
66. Ezekiel 28:18, 19.
67. 2 Peter 3:10 & 13.
68. Psalm 37:9 and Matthew 5:5. Proverbs 11:31 states that "the righteous shall be recompensed **in the earth:** much more the wicked and the sinner."

It does come to an end—the fire does its work and then goes out so completely that there's not even a "coal" left to warm at: The wicked "shall be as stubble; the fire shall burn them; they shall not deliver themselves from the power of the flame: **there shall not be a coal to warm at,** nor fire to sit before it."[69]

GOD WILL HAVE A *CLEAN* UNIVERSE

Thus the Bible describes the utter *extinction* of *evil* from its last and only stronghold in the universe. But the theory of eternal torment would not have it so. Instead, according to that teaching, sin and sinners would be perpetuated, living forever, hating, cursing, raising rebel hands in pain against the God of everlasting love. In that scenario, Christ's victory would never be complete, for He doesn't **destroy** evil—He only **segregates** it. The continuance of such a dark spot would forever blight God's universe.

Besides, how can there be a Paradise for any while there's unending torment for some? Each damned soul was born into the world as **a mother's child**, and Paradise cannot be Paradise for her if her child is in such a hell.[70]

No, it will not be so. God has no use for sin. There won't be a place in the universe where sin and sinners survive, even in a state of torture.

The doctrine of eternal torment WEAKENS the power and glory of the gospel in two ways:

(1) by denying Christ His ultimate triumph
in finally DESTROYING **sin,** and

---

69. Isaiah 47:14.

70. Paraphrased from Dr. William Temple, Archbishop of Canterbury, in "The Idea of Immortality in Relation to Religion and Ethics," *The Congregational Quarterly* (January, 1932), Vol. X, p. 11.

(2) by denying Christ His chief glory
in BESTOWING life eternal upon the **saved**.[71]

For if man were inherently immortal by nature, what man, saint or sinner, would need God for life itself? But God alone is the Lifegiver, the Dispenser of immortality. Immortal-soulism is immortality WITHOUT a Saviour.[72]

JESUS *PAID* THE PENALTY

We've looked at Scripture evidence, examined this question from every angle, and discovered that **the Bible presents an air-tight case** refuting the false idea of eternal torment. However, there's still one last argument against that damnable doctrine, an argument which will clinch our case, and that is the substitutionary sacrifice of Christ.

Basic to Christianity is the concept of Jesus dying in the sinner's place. This teaching is at the heart of God's plan of salvation and is accepted by every Christian. The Bible is full of the idea that Christ bore our sins—both Old and New Testaments consistently teach this. For example, Isaiah 53:6 says: "The Lord hath laid on Him the iniquity of us all." And 1 Peter 2:24 states that Jesus, our divine *Substitute*, "bare our sins in His own body on the tree."

As our divine Substitute, Christ had to suffer the penalty to which fallen man was sentenced at the beginning. If that penalty is endless suffering in the flames of hell, then the Saviour must have known that and accepted it as His fate. In that case, Jesus must suffer that penalty before we can

---

71. The Bible clearly promises eternal life to one group of people and eternal death to another group. If the latter suffered **endless** torture, then both groups would have eternal life, though one wouldn't enjoy it.

72. Any doctrine which teaches that unrepentant sinners are immortal clearly contradicts such New Testament texts as John 3:16; 1 John 3:15; 1 John 5:11-12, and many others. Such a teaching, therefore, must originate from some source other than the Author of the Bible.

go free. But in fact, the Lord would be **forever** paying that penalty and **never** satisfying its claims. Either Christ took the full punishment for sin, or even forgiven sinners will have to take it themselves.

But **thank God** that the wages of sin is DEATH. Jesus paid those wages in full. He suffered our punishment and paid our penalty—but He did NOT "burn forever." Calvary forever settles the question. The death of Christ on the cross is all-sufficient for our deliverance—we are truly redeemed! Christ did **not** taste eternal torment, but the Scriptures declare He that did "taste **death** for every man."[73] What a wonderful Saviour! Let's praise Him for paying the full penalty for our sins by His atoning death on the cross.

CONCLUSION

Friends, hell was never intended for you and me. Jesus says it will be "prepared for the Devil and his angels."[74] If we go there it won't be God's fault—rather it will be in spite of God's love and Calvary's cross. Only one thing can cause us to go to hell, and that is unforgiven sin.

No one will be lost just because he fell into the trap of sin. No one will go to hell because he stole, killed, or committed adultery. He'll go to hell because he **refused** to turn to Christ for deliverance from those sins. The greatest sin of all is to spurn salvation, and the most unanswerable question of all is: "How shall we escape if we neglect so great salvation?"[75] Let's NOT neglect salvation by refusing the way of escape God so lovingly provides!

---

73. Hebrews 2:9.
74. Matthew 25:41.
75. Hebrews 2:3.

APPENDIX A

SCIENCE and the SCRIPTURES

Today's *explosion* of knowledge [1] renders many a textbook on science out of date within a decade. The Bible is NOT a textbook on science, but it always tells the truth. And even though its pages were written many centuries ago, it contains remarkable insights into scientific principles which are as valid as tomorrow's research reports. God's written Word and the Creator's book of Nature are in perfect harmony, for they have the same Author. A few examples may serve to illustrate that harmony.

SCIENTIFIC PRINCIPLE

SCRIPTURE STATEMENT

Roundness of the earth, or the circuit of its orbit

Isaiah 40:22 - **"He sits enthroned above the CIRCLE of the earth."** New International Version. Many still thought the world to be *flat* as late as the time of Christopher Columbus (around A.D. 1500). Since Isaiah's book dates from 740 B.C., it's clear that God's inspiration put the prophet centuries ahead of his time.

---

1. Daniel 12:4 tells us that in "the *time* of the *end* . . . KNOWLEDGE shall be INCREASED."

Roundness of the earth

Psalm 103:12 - **"As far as the EAST is from the WEST, so far hath He removed our transgressions from us."** The North and South Poles are a fixed distance apart, so a traveler going northward eventually reaches the North Pole. If he then continues in the same direction, he'll be traveling southward. But this limitation is not true for one traveling eastward or westward. A person traveling eastward will *always* travel eastward, no matter how often he goes around the globe. The God who inspired this verse also created the earth, and He knew its shape was a *sphere*.

Roundness of the earth

Luke 17:34-36 - **"That NIGHT two men will be ASLEEP in the same room, and one will be taken away, the other left. Two women will be WORKING TOGETHER at household tasks; one will be taken, the other left; and so it will be with men WORKING side by side IN THE FIELDS."** Living Bible. This passage implies a **round** earth, for the instantaneous Event of Christ's Second Coming will find some retired for the night and others engaged in their daytime duties.

Gravitation: the earth hangs on nothing

Job 26:7 - **"He . . . hangeth the earth upon NOTHING."** Today astronauts take pictures showing the earth suspended in space, but in ancient days men theorized that the earth rested on the back of a huge elephant or on the shoulders of Atlas.

SCIENTIFIC PRINCIPLE	SCRIPTURE STATEMENT
Infinite number of stars	*Jeremiah 33:22* - "**The host of heaven** [the STARS] **CANNOT be NUMBERED.**" Down through the centuries, man thought he COULD count the stars, as his naked eye gazed through smogless skies at stars gleaming like diamonds against the black velvet of night. Not until Galileo invented the telescope in 1609, opening new vistas to astronomy, did we begin to realize the truth of the prophet's apparent exaggeration. Modern telescopes have increased the star count beyond human comprehension.
The moon as a non-luminous reflective body	*Job 25:5* - "**The MOON . . . SHINETH NOT.**" *1 Corinthians 15:41* - "**There is one glory of the SUN, and another glory of the MOON.**" In other words, the moon and the sun give different kinds of light. The sun is self-luminous, as are all stars, whereas the moon lights the night-time skies with reflected light only.
Atmospheric pressure	*Job 28:25* - "**To make the WEIGHT for the WINDS.**" Barometric pressure is a measure of the "weight" of air affecting a column of mercury in a barometer.
Evaporation	*Psalm 135:7* and *Jeremiah 10:13* - "**He** [God] **causeth the VAPOURS to ASCEND from the ends of the earth.**"

2. Verses like Genesis 22:17 and Hebrews 11:12 imply that the stars in the sky are as COUNTLESS as the INNUMERABLE grains of sand on the seashore! *How* did the Bible writers know? The omniscient God told them. Inspiration says, "He [God] counts the number of the stars; He calls them all by NAME. . . . His understanding is infinite." Psalm 147:4-5, New King James Version.

Protective effect of our earth's atmosphere

Isaiah 40:22 - **"It is He** [God] . . . **that stretcheth out the** [atmospheric] **heavens as a CURTAIN."** Today we know that the ozone in our atmosphere forms a thin but vital protective layer to shield us from harmful solar rays.[3] And the wispy "curtain" of air in our atmosphere protects us from the impact of meteors by burning them up through friction. As the meteors enter the atmosphere at speeds of about 40 miles per second, they become incandescent from the heat generated by friction against the air particles. "In a 24-hour period about **1,000,000** meteors . . . may strike the earth's atmosphere,"[4] but—thank God—virtually all these "shooting stars," as we call them, *burn up* before hitting the ground!

Hydrologic cycle

Ecclesiastes 1:7 - **"All the rivers run into the sea; yet the sea is NOT FULL; unto the place from whence the rivers come, thither they RETURN again."** All rivers and streams do flow down to the sea. Then the sea water evaporates, rising to form clouds. Wind blows the clouds back over the land, where they release the water in the form of rain. Then the cycle repeats itself.

---

3. "The *total* amount of ozone in a vertical column above the earth's surface, if it were separated from the air with which it is mixed and brought to conditions of normal temperature and pressure, would form a gaseous column **only a few MILLIMETERS high**. . . . However, even this *minute* amount of ozone is sufficient to absorb all the solar energy in the ultraviolet . . . thus protecting life on the earth from a LETHAL excess of short-wave radiation." *Encyclopedia Britannica* (1967 edition), Volume 16, p. 1198, article "Ozone."

4. *Encyclopedia Britannica* (1967 edition), Volume 15, p. 270, article "Meteor."

SCIENTIFIC PRINCIPLE	SCRIPTURE STATEMENT
Uniformitarianism, a geologic principle popular among evolutionists	*2 Peter 3:3-4* - "SCOFFERS" sneeringly ask, "'Where is the promise of His [Christ's] Coming?' For ever since the fathers fell asleep, all things have continued as they were from the beginning of creation." Revised Standard Version. Uniformitarianism rejects the idea of *catastrophism* with its Biblical worldwide *Flood* as an explanation for the world as we know it. It claims that the ordinary natural forces now at work—like erosion—are sufficient to account for all geologic forms. The Bible mentions this atheistic philosophy, but it's important to note that the words come from *unbelievers*.
Rock erosion	*Job 14:19* - "The WATERS WEAR the STONES." The action of running water not only erodes tremendous amounts of soil but also etches the hardest rock.
Triangular prism	*Job 38:24* - "By what way is the LIGHT PARTED . . .?" Sir Isaac Newton's experiments with optics demonstrated that a prism can *separate* white light into its component colors.
Sterile mask, quarantine	*Leviticus 13:45-46* - "The leper. . . shall put a COVERING upon his UPPER LIP, and he shall cry, Unclean, unclean. . . . He shall dwell ALONE; [outside] the camp shall his habitation be." Many valid public health measures are found in Moses' writings.

Chemical composition of our bodies

Genesis 2:7 - "**The Lord God formed Adam of the DUST of the GROUND.**" *Genesis 3:13-19* - "**And the Lord God said . . . unto Adam . . . DUST thou art.**" We now know that our bodies are composed of the same chemical elements—carbon, iron, calcium, phosphorus, etc.—found in the earth. *Poetic imagination gives the fanciful idea that little girls originated from "Sugar and spice and all things nice" and little boys came from "Snips and snails and puppy-dog tails."*[5] But God's penman for Genesis, Moses, didn't have to rely on unaided human reason, and his record of Creation is *scientifically accurate.*

Sterilization

Numbers 31:23 - "**Everything that can endure fire, you shall PUT THROUGH THE FIRE, and it shall be CLEAN. . . . But all that CANNOT endure fire you shall put through WATER.**" New King James Version.

Vital nature of the blood

Leviticus 17:11 - "**The LIFE of the flesh IS IN THE BLOOD.**" Science today knows the truth of this Bible statement, for it's the circulation of this vital fluid that carries both life-giving *oxygen* and *nourishment* to every part of our body. Yet when George Washington became sick with a bad sore throat and laryngitis, well-intentioned but ignorant men "bled" him. However, the treatment of that day only caused the patient to grow weaker: "He was *bled four times . . .* , his strength meanwhile rapidly *sinking.*"[6]

---

5. British poet Robert Southey (1774-1843), "What All the World Is Made Of."
6. *Encyclopedia Britannica* (1967 edition), Volume 23, p. 244, article "Washington, George."

SCIENTIFIC PRINCIPLE	SCRIPTURE STATEMENT
Anesthetic during surgery	*Genesis 2:21* - **"The Lord God caused a DEEP SLEEP to fall upon Adam, and he slept: and He TOOK ONE OF HIS RIBS, and CLOSED UP THE FLESH instead thereof."** Before anesthesia was discovered about a hundred years ago, skeptics would laugh at this inspired record, saying: "How ridiculous! As if anyone would remain **asleep** while you tore out one of his ribs!" But today we accept such a procedure as routine.
Psychosomatic illness, psychosomatic medicine	*Proverbs 17:22* - **"A MERRY HEART** doeth good like a **MEDICINE: but a BROKEN SPIRIT** drieth the **BONES."** *Proverbs 16:24* - **"PLEASANT WORDS are . . . HEALTH to the BONES."** The close relationship between physical and emotional health is understood more and more today.
Vitamin "A" deficiency	*Jeremiah 14:6* - **"Their EYES** did FAIL, because there was NO GRASS."** Lack of vitamin A, which is found in carrots and other vegetables as well as fish-liver oils, results in night blindness and "eventual complete blindness."[7]
Radio-TV broadcasting	*Job 38:35* - **"Can you send forth LIGHTNINGS, that they may GO, and SAY to you, 'Here we are?'"** Revised Standard Version.

---

7. *Encyclopedia Britannica* (1967 edition), Volume 23, p. 85, article "Vitamins."

One blood for all nations

Acts 17:26 - God "hath made of **ONE BLOOD** all nations of men on all the face of the earth." The many races of men *all have the same* basic blood types.

Automobiles of today, with their headlights

Nahum 2:3-4 - "The **CHARIOTS** shall be with **FLAMING TORCHES** in the day of His preparation. . . . The **CHARIOTS** shall **RAGE** in the **STREETS**, they shall jostle one against another in the **BROADWAYS**: they shall seem like **TORCHES**, they shall **RUN** like the **LIGHTNINGS**."

Human flight

Isaiah 60:8 - "**Who are these that FLY as a CLOUD, and as the DOVES to their windows?**" The prophet tries to describe what the eye of Inspiration has seen.

Atomic theory

Hebrews 11:3 - "**Through faith we understand that the worlds were framed by the word of God, so that things which are SEEN are NOT made of things which do APPEAR.**" Man NOW knows that all matter is composed of tiny molecules made up of even tinier atomic particles, so that something we see and touch—like a table or this book—is actually made of invisible *atoms*. But the question is, WHO TOLD the prophet?

SCIENTIFIC PRINCIPLE

**Destruction by
nuclear fission**

SCRIPTURE STATEMENT

2 Peter 3:10-12 - At the end of the world, "**the heavens** [the earth's atmosphere, the atmospheric heavens] **shall pass away with a GREAT NOISE, and the ELEMENTS shall MELT with FERVENT HEAT, the EARTH also and the works that are therein shall be BURNED UP.** . . . All these things **shall be DISSOLVED,** . . . **the heavens being on fire shall be DISSOLVED, and the ELEMENTS shall MELT with FERVENT HEAT.**" For centuries, skeptics would ridicule religious persons who spoke about the final destruction of the world by fire, pointing out how difficult it usually was even to keep a good **bonfire** going, so it would be absolutely beyond the realm of possibility for the whole **earth** to be on fire or the "elements" to "melt with fervent heat"! But since the atomic age began a few decades ago, science itself is worrying about that very possibility. Today marchers in the nuclear disarmament movement fear that not only *God* but *man* could destroy the earth.

The statements on the right above were all recorded many, many centuries ago on the inspired pages of Holy Scripture. The principles listed on the left were established as scientific truths much later, in some cases rather recently. But individually and collectively, they DO confirm the Bible. As English astronomer Sir William Herschel (1738-1822) stated: "All human discoveries seem to be made only for the purpose of confirming more and more strongly, the truths contained in the Sacred Scriptures."

Nature guards her secrets well. But slowly, as man's knowledge increases, **science is catching up with the Bible.**

# # #

Appendix B

What Makes You Think Jesus Is Michael, the Archangel?

Any faithful Christian finds the idea that Jesus is a mere angel utterly unacceptable. Our reaction to any such suggestion that dethrones our Lord is "No way!"—and properly so. The Jehovah's Witnesses, who do not accept the deity of Christ, sometimes use this teaching to detract from our estimation of the Lord Jesus as a full-fledged Member of the Holy Trinity. They claim that their identification of Christ as Michael lowers Him to the level of mere angels and "shows conclusively that he [Christ] is **NOT EQUAL to Jehovah God.**" [1]

Still, there are a number of good reasons why many Bible scholars believe that the Personage known in Scripture as "Michael, the Archangel," CAN be identified as our Lord, Jesus Christ—**without** accepting the belittling conclusions of Jehovah's Witnesses, **without** making the Son of God an angel, and **without** detracting one iota from His divine deity as *God* in the fullest sense of that word. Let's examine these reasons point by point.

---

1. Official Jehovah's Witnesses publication *THE WATCHTOWER* (December 15, 1984), p. 29.

POINT #1

When Jesus became the incarnate God by being born in the flesh through the Virgin Mary, He was given many appropriate names. A few of these are "Emmanuel,"[2] "Jesus,"[3] "the Lamb of God,"[4] "Christ,"[5] etc. Since we know Jesus pre-existed throughout the ages of eternity[6] long before coming as the Babe in Bethlehem, it's only natural to assume that He had **SOME** name before that time.[7] **What WAS that name?** Before we're finished here, you'll find good reason to conclude that Christ's former name in heaven was *"Michael."*

POINT #2

In Biblical times, names were looked upon as profoundly important. Nearly every name had a **meaning** which was either immediately obvious or which became apparent upon translation. For instance, a few examples may serve to illustrate the fact that the letters "**EL**" in a name pertained to *God*:

- **ELIJAH** means "my God is Jehovah."
- **DANIEL** means "judgment of God."
- **GABRIEL** means "man of God."

And the name MICHAEL means the One "who is like God." Absolutely no one is "like God" but God Himself. We know that Lucifer, in his devilish pride, said: "I will be *like the*

---

2. *Emmanuel* means "God with us," Matthew 1:23.
3. *Jesus* means "Saviour," Matthew 1:21.
4. See John the Baptist's salutation in John 1:29.
5. *Christ* means "Messiah," "anointed One," or "King," John 1:41.
6. John 17:5 & 24, John 8:58, Micah 5:2, etc.
7. For instance, the devil had the name "Lucifer" *before* rebelling against God and the name "Satan" *afterward.* See Isaiah 14:12 & Revelation 12:9.

off thy foot; for the place whereon thou standest is holy. And Joshua did so.

Any Bible student will immediately recognize the divine Being visiting Joshua on this occasion as none other than the Lord Jesus Christ in His pre-existent state. At different times, the Lord appeared to others in the Old Testament, like Abraham[11] and Jacob.[12] On this occasion with Joshua, the Bible tells us plainly only two verses beyond the portion quoted above[13] that it's "the Lord" who speaks with Joshua and tells him how to capture the city of Jericho without even fighting because the walls would come tumbling down!

But let's analyze that quoted passage a bit further. We read that the heavenly Being assumed the form of "a man" with his "sword drawn." When Joshua inquires, he's told that the Stranger is "Captain of the host of the Lord." (The Living Bible says: "**I am Commander-in-Chief of the Lord's army.**") This is just another way of saying "Archangel" or Ruler of the angel hosts.

Even though we know that this was the Archangel or Captain of the angel armies, we *also* know that **this was NO MERE ANGEL.** Two facts make this clear.

First, we read that Joshua then fell down "and did WORSHIP." And the Stranger did not **stop him** from doing so, which certainly would have been the case IF Joshua had been worshipping an angel. We know this from Revelation 19:10, when John fell down to worship an angel, the angel stopped him and said, "See thou **do it not:** . . . worship God." This truth is repeated in Revelation 22:8 & 9 - "And I John . . . fell down to worship before the feet of the angel which showed me these things. Then saith he unto me, See thou **do it not:** . . . worship God."

---

11. See Genesis 18:1-33.
12. See Genesis 32:24-30.
13. Joshua 6:2.

Secondly, this divine Being not only **accepts** the worship of Joshua but also tells him to **take off his shoes,** *"For the place whereon thou standest is HOLY."* Moses had the same experience when he met the Lord (again, Jesus in His pre-existent state[14]) at the Burning Bush and was told: "Draw not nigh hither: **put off thy shoes** from off thy feet, *for the place whereon thou standest is HOLY ground."*[15]

We see, then, that the Leader of the heavenly hosts is **no mere angel** but the divine Lord Jesus Himself!

POINT #6

Other Scriptures which mention the name Michael lead us to understand He is a Very Special Person—He must be, in fact, a heavenly Being **of ROYAL blood.** For instance, God sent the angel Gabriel to give special messages to the prophet Daniel.[16] This angel messenger told Daniel that "Michael" is **"the GREAT PRINCE who stands watch over the sons of your people."**[17]

A PRINCE is the SON of a KING, of course, and Jesus is the Son of God, the King of Heaven. Christians would call Him "the great Prince." Gabriel, in the very same book, calls "the *Messiah,* **the PRINCE."**[18] Now please note what we've learned from the pen of the same inspired writer:

A. **"Messiah"** = "the Prince"
B. **"Michael"** = "the great Prince"
C. Therefore, since "two things equal to the same thing are equal to each other," *the Messiah* and *Michael* are the same Person, Jesus Christ.

---

14. Paul says plainly that Christ was the "Rock" that followed the Israelites in their wilderness wanderings. 1 Corinthians 10:1-4.
15. Exodus 3:1-5.
16. See Daniel 8:16 & 9:21.
17. Daniel 12:1, New King James Version.
18. Daniel 9:25.

POINT #7

God's Word gives inspired insight into Lucifer's terrible rebellion against the government of God: "There was **WAR in HEAVEN**: *Michael and his angels fought against the dragon;* and the dragon fought and his angels, and prevailed not; neither was their place found any more in heaven. And the great dragon was cast out, that old serpent, called the Devil, and Satan, which deceiveth the whole world: he was cast out into the earth, and his angels were cast out with him."[19]

Fortunately the Bible here clearly identifies "the dragon" as "that old serpent, called the Devil, and Satan," so there's no question of the adversary's identity on **that** side of the controversy. And the various points considered above (the pre-existent Christ as "Commander-in-Chief of the Lord's army,"[20] etc.) lead many to conclude that the great Leader on the **other** side was none other than Christ Himself. Thus **Michael / Christ** fought against **Lucifer / Satan**—the two opposing generals leading armies of angels and devils in cosmic conflict.

POINT #8

Practically the only Bible verse quoted by those who deny that Jesus is Michael the Archangel is Jude 9, which says:

> "**Michael the Archangel**, when contending with the devil . . . said, **The Lord rebuke thee**."

Objectors think this verse proves their point because Michael, rather than rebuking the devil Himself, says: "The **LORD** rebuke thee." They reason that the Archangel cannot be the Lord Jesus, for here he's calling someone **ELSE** "the Lord."

---

19. Revelation 12:7-9.
20. Joshua 5:14, Living Bible.

But instead of accepting any man's idea or any church's teaching, let the Bible be its OWN interpreter. We gain a clearer understanding of **JUDE 9** by comparing it with **ZECHARIAH 3:2**, where Jesus is again confronting Satan. We read:

> **"The LORD said** unto Satan, **The Lord rebuke thee,** O Satan."**

This verse is *a perfect parallel* to Jude 9—almost a carbon copy—except **the names are changed**: in one He's called **"Michael"** and in the other He's called **"the Lord."**

In Zechariah's text
Jesus, referred to as "the Lord"—God the Son,
called on "the Lord" His heavenly Father to rebuke Satan.
In Jude's text
Jesus, referred to as "Michael the Archangel,"
called on "the Lord" His heavenly Father to rebuke the devil.

On both occasions, Christ knew it was pointless to argue with a closed mind. He knew it would do no good to bring "a railing accusation"[21] against the devil. He knew also that as Lord and Judge of all the universe, He WILL "rebuke" Satan some day by condemning him to the Lake of Fire.

Another perfectly permissible interpretation of these two texts is to recognize that Christ was simply speaking of **Himself** when He said, "The Lord rebuke thee"—meaning *"I* rebuke thee." Jesus often referred to Himself in "the third person singular," saying things like: "When the **Son of man** cometh, shall **He** find faith on the earth?"[22] We all know He meant "When *I* come, shall *I* find faith?" Shall we foolishly conclude that Jesus is NOT the Son of God simply

---

21. Jude 9.
22. Luke 18:8.

because in John 3:16 He referred to Himself in the third person singular ("whosoever believeth in **Him**") rather than saying "in Me"?

The Bible itself, therefore, proves this objection groundless. But aside from providing evidence **against** the theory which says "Christ cannot be the same as Michael," Jude 9 provides strong evidence **for** the fact that He IS. Let's quote the part of the verse omitted before:

"Michael the Archangel, when contending with the devil **He disputed about the body of Moses.**"

Remember that Moses died and the Lord buried His faithful servant, but his grave was not known to men. [23] Jude now reveals that the dead body was the subject of dispute between Christ and Satan. From the fact that **Moses appeared with Elijah** on the Mount of Transfiguration, [24] we may conclude that the Lord triumphed in the contest with the devil and **raised Moses from his grave.** These two—Moses and Elijah—typify **the redeemed of all ages** when Christ returns in glory:

Elijah represents those believers *alive* when Jesus comes, who'll be **translated without seeing death,** [25] and *Moses* represents those faithful believers who have *died* but who'll then be **raised from the dead.**

When the Prince of life approached the lonely grave, Satan was alarmed, for he claimed all who were in the grave as his captives and felt threatened by this invasion of his territory. "The accuser of the brethren" [26] boasted that even

23. Deuteronomy 34:5-6.
24. Matthew 17:1-9, Mark 9:2-10, Luke 9:28-36.
25. Elijah was taken to heaven without ever dying. 2 Kings 2:9-15.
26. Revelation 12:10. Satan is our accuser, but Christ is our Advocate or Defense Attorney in the Judgment. See 1 John 2:1.

the leader of God's people, Moses, the faithful servant of
God, had sinned[27] and become his prisoner. Christ refused
to argue with Satan but then and there performed His work
of breaking the devil's power and bringing the dead to life.

But here's the point: How do we KNOW it was Christ
Himself and not a mere angel that contended with Satan
over the resurrection of Moses' body? Because angels, like
ourselves, are created beings and have no power to create
life. Satan and his fallen angels are powerful supernatural
beings who falsely APPEAR to raise the dead in spiritualistic
seances and the like,[28] but they cannot really create life.
Although God empowered faithful men to resuscitate a dead
person on a few occasions, [29] those miracles were not resur-
rections to a glorious, immortal life—the people who were
raised, later died again. They were not taken bodily to heav-
en as Moses and Elijah were. Only Christ, the Lifegiver,
can raise a dead person to eternal life. **He** is our only hope,
not some angel.

If we keep this fact in mind, we come again to the conclusion that the One who contended with Satan over Moses'
body was a heavenly Being more powerful than any angel.

---

27. Numbers 20:7-12. God told Moses merely to *speak* to the rock
in the wilderness in order to bring forth water. Instead, he lost his temper
and *struck* it, twice. Not only did he disobey, but the rock represented
Christ. See 1 Corinthians 10:4.

28. When a dead person seems to appearto his loved ones, we instinctively feel an innate, **God-given fear.** This feeling of danger would
be out of place if we really WERE in the presence of our beloved dead,
but it's God's way of warning us that **demons from Satan's legions**
impersonate those who sleep in the grave. "Spirits of devils [can work]
miracles" (Revelation 16:14), but can't raise the dead. See Mystery #4,
"Solving the Mystery of Death" for more Bible facts on this subject.

29. Elisha in 2 Kings 4:32-37, Peter in Acts 9:36-42, and Paul in
Acts 20:9-10.

POINT #9

Jesus said, "**Search the Scriptures.**"[30] And a good principle of Bible study says: "Precept must be upon precept, precept upon precept; **line upon line**, line upon line; **HERE a little, and THERE a little.**"[31] We must compare **a line here** and **a line there**, in different books of the Bible, because no single writer of Old or New Testament had ALL God's truth revealed to him.

God didn't choose to put all the information on a given subject into a single Bible chapter where we could learn all He would teach us about prayer, or baptism, or heaven, or any other subject. Each inspired writer was given a glimpse of the heavenly vision. But if we're to get the WHOLE truth, we must carefully SIFT through the Bible placing "line upon line" and "comparing spiritual things with spiritual."[32]

Let's use this heaven-approved method of study right now for this question of Michael's identity. Let's **place two passages side by side** and carefully compare them:

1. *The Apostle Paul says* dead believers are resurrected at "the voice of the **Archangel.**" Please note:
   "The Lord [Jesus] Himself shall descend from heaven with a shout, with *the voice of the Archangel* , . . . and the DEAD in Christ **shall RISE.**"[33]

2. *The Lord Jesus says* dead believers are resurrected at the sound of **His own** voice. Please note:
   "The DEAD shall hear *the voice of the Son of God:* and they that hear **shall LIVE.** . . . All that are in the GRAVES shall hear **His voice,** And shall COME FORTH . . . unto the **resurrection.**"[34]

---

30. John 5:39.
31. Isaiah 28:10.
32. 1 Corinthians 2:13.
33. 1 Thessalonians 4;16.
34. John 5:25-29.

These *parallel passages* are speaking of **the same EVENT** and **the same VOICE**. Paul in Thessalonians calls it "the voice of *the Archangel*," and John in his Gospel calls it "the voice of *the Son of God.*" When Christ returns to call His faithful ones to life, every angel in heaven will come with Him: "the Son of man shall come in His glory, and **ALL** the holy angels **with** Him"[35]—*He* is their *Commander!* There's no mystery here: Jesus, the Lifegiver, is Michael, the Archangel.

These nine points clearly show that the identification of Jesus as Michael the Archangel is a valid one. Christians who accept this Bible-based teaching are not heretics who degrade Christ but faithful believers who love and honor their Lord.

---

35. Matthew 25:31.

APPENDIX C
Post-Resurrection Appearances of the Living Christ

Scripture Text:	Christ Appeared to:	Location:
John 20:1,11-18; Mark 16:9	Mary Magdalene	At Christ's tomb
Matthew 28:1-10	The other women	Returning from the tomb
Luke 24:34; 1 Cor. 15:5	The apostle Simon Peter (Cephas)	Not specified
Luke 24:13-32; Mark 16:12	Cleopas and another disciple	On the road to Emmaus
John 20:19-25; Luke 24:36-43	The 10 apostles, Thomas absent	In the Upper Room
John 20:26-29; Mark 16:14	The 11 apostles, Thomas present	In the Upper Room
John 21:1-14 & 6:1	Seven of the disciples	At the Sea of Galilee
1 Corinthians 15:6	More than 500 brethren	Not specified
1 Corinthians 15:7	His brother James	Not specified
Matthew 28:16	The eleven apostles	On a mountain in Galilee
Acts 1:2-12; Luke 24:49-52	The eleven apostles, at the Ascension	Mount Olivet, near Bethany
Acts 9:1-6; 1 Cor. 9:1 & 15:8	Saul / The apostle Paul	On the road to Damascus
Revelation 1:9-19	John the revelator	On the Island of Patmos

After His cruel death, Jesus showed himself alive **"by many infallible PROOFS."** Acts 1:3.